PRIVATE AUTONOMY IN EU INTERNAL MARKET LAW

Ambitious and innovative, this critical study offers a fresh perspective on the normative framework of the EU's internal market.

The book explores the place of the ideals of private autonomy in the EU's legal order. Indeed, it goes further to examine the parameters of their protection within both its legal and regulatory framework. Looking at the coexistence of, and interaction between, varying expressions of private autonomy, it offers a comprehensive review of the protection of private autonomy at the normative core of the internal market. The book also explores the layers of limitations and conditions imposed on the exercise of private autonomy in the internal market that generate legal tensions and conflicting forces.

In addition to plotting a systematic approach to the question, the book introduces a new framework for better understanding the correlation between the free movement and competition law regimes and the fundamental economic rights protected in the Charter.

Volume 121 in the Series Modern Studies in European Law

Modern Studies in European Law

Recent titles in this series:

The EU and its Member States' Joint Participation in International Agreements
Edited by Nicolas Levrat, Yuliya Kaspiarovich, Christine Kaddous and Ramses A Wessel

The UN Convention on the Rights of Persons with Disabilities and the European Union: The Impact on Law and Governance
Carmine Conte

EU Criminal Law, Second Edition
Valsamis Mitsilegas

The EU as a Global Digital Actor: Institutionalising Global Data Protection, Trade, and Cybersecurity
Elaine Fahey

Exporting the European Convention on Human Rights
Maria-Louiza Deftou

Judicial Authority in EU Internal Market Law: Implications for the Balance of Competences and Powers
Vilija Velyvyte

The Changing European Union: A Critical View on the Role of Law and the Courts
Edited by Tamara Capeta, Iris Goldner Lang and Tamara Perisin

The Structural Transformation of European Private Law: A Critique of Juridical Hermeneutic
Leone Niglia

The Future of EU Constitutionalism
Edited by Matej Avbelj

The Changing Role of Citizens in EU Democratic Governance
Edited by Davor Jancic

The EU and the Baltic Sea Area
Edited by Allan Rosas and Henrik Ringbom

The Evolving Governance of EU Competition Law in a Time of Disruptions: A Constitutional Perspective
Edited by Carlo Maria Colombo, Kathryn Wright and Mariolina Eliantonio

The European Integrated Border Management: Frontex, Human Rights, and International Responsibility
Giulia Raimondo

Private Autonomy in EU Internal Market Law: Parameters of its Protection and Limitation
Rufat Babayev

For the complete list of titles in this series see www.bloomsbury.com/uk/series/modern-studies-in-european-law/

Private Autonomy in EU Internal Market Law

Parameters of its Protection and Limitation

Rufat Babayev

•HART•
OXFORD • LONDON • NEW YORK • NEW DELHI • SYDNEY

HART PUBLISHING

Bloomsbury Publishing Plc

Kemp House, Chawley Park, Cumnor Hill, Oxford, OX2 9PH, UK

1385 Broadway, New York, NY 10018, USA

29 Earlsfort Terrace, Dublin 2, Ireland

HART PUBLISHING, the Hart/Stag logo, BLOOMSBURY and the Diana logo are trademarks of Bloomsbury Publishing Plc

First published in Great Britain 2024

A catalogue record for this book is available from the British Library.

A catalogue record for this book is available from the Library of Congress.

Library of Congress Control Number: 2023950830

ISBN: HB: 978-1-50992-069-3
ePDF: 978-1-50992-071-6
ePub: 978-1-50992-070-9

Typeset by Compuscript Ltd, Shannon

To find out more about our authors and books visit www.hartpublishing.co.uk. Here you will find extracts, author information, details of forthcoming events and the option to sign up for our newsletters.

To my parents, Ramis and Melahet

ACKNOWLEDGEMENTS

In writing this monograph, I have had the support of many people to whom I owe much gratitude.

I am grateful to Professors Michael Dougan, Eleanor Spaventa, and Adam Cygan for their comments and suggestions on my previous works, which laid the foundation for this monograph and inspired me to embark on this challenging yet rewarding journey.

I am thankful to my current and former Leicester Law School colleagues, who have made working on this monograph much more enjoyable and manageable with the day-to-day demands of academic life.

My special appreciation goes to Hart's editorial team, Sinéad, Sasha, Jon and Tom, for their endless patience and assistance in getting to the finishing line.

And last (by no means not least), I am indebted to the support and encouragement of my wife, Yuliya, without whom this monograph would have been completed two years earlier.

CONTENTS

TABLE OF CASES

Court Judgments

Opinions of Advocates General

ECtHR Judgments

European Commission decisions

TABLE OF LEGISLATION

Council Directives

Commission Communication

Other acts of the European Union

Introduction

> [Freedom is a state] of how far in acting [a person] can follow his own plans and intentions, to what extent the pattern of his conduct is of his own design, directed towards ends for which he has been persistently striving rather than toward necessities created by others in order to make him do what they want.[1]

Private autonomy, understood as the individual liberty of economic action and self-determination, constitutes a fundamental principle on which the ideals of liberalism rest. It occupies a broad theoretical terrain that transcends multiple disciplines, generating a variety of theoretical frameworks and propositions. As a legal concept, private autonomy is firmly entrenched within the constitutional traditions common to Member States and the European Union's core values. Most national constitutions enshrine provisions that, either explicitly or implicitly, give effect to private autonomy, which implies deep adherence to a political economy model infused by the principles underlying the liberal free-market ideology.[2] Similarly, the ideals of private autonomy permeate and radiate throughout the Union's legal system, especially the normative structure of the internal market that is central to the European integration project. However, the Union's concept of private autonomy is a judicial construct. Whilst it is undisputed that private autonomy as a principle was innate to the national legal systems prior to the inception of the (the) European Community, the founding Treaties contained no explicit reference to it. Instead, the seeds for its inclusion in the Union's legal lexicon were sown through the (then) Court of Justice of the European Communities' highly debated, early contribution to transforming the (then) Community into a rights-based constitutional legal system. Two turning points are emblematic of this development.

In the landmark ruling of *Van Gen den Loos*,[3] the Court set forth its vision of the (then) Community as 'a new legal order' based on its supremacy over national law and its direct effect to the benefit of individuals.[4] Under these doctrines, the Court equated the Treaty's prohibitions addressed to Member States with individual rights in the form of the freedoms of movement. These freedoms are generally

[1] FA Hayek, *The Constitution of Liberty* (London, Routledge & Kegan Paul, 1963) 13.

[2] M Everson and C Gonçalez, 'Article 16' in S Peers, T Harvey, J Kenner and A Ward (eds), *The EU Charter of Fundamental Rights: A Commentary* (Oxford, Hart Publishing, 2014) 438.

[3] Case 26-62 *NV Algemene Transport- en Expeditie Onderneming van Gend & Loos v Netherlands Inland Revenue Administration* EU:C:1963:1.

[4] I Maher, 'The Legal Dimension in EU Integration' in AM El-Agraa (ed), *The European Union Economics and Policies*, 9th edn (Cambridge, Cambridge University Press, 2011) 67.

perceived to extend the ideals of private autonomy across borders of Member States as the motor of the integration process designed to fuse national markets into a single economic sphere.[5] At the same time, the ideals of private autonomy occupied the forefront of the jurisprudential genesis and evolution of the Union's fundamental rights doctrine. By mirroring the legal systems of Member States, the Court elevated individual liberties such as the right to property, the freedom of occupation and the freedom to engage in economic activity to a constitutional status at the Union level through the medium of unwritten general principles of law. These entitlements were subsequently codified in the Union's Charter of Fundamental Rights (CFR). As a result, the ideals of private autonomy permeate the normative foundation of the internal market and provide a degree of legitimacy to the authority of the Union's legal order through the constitutional safeguards added to the delegated powers of the Union's institutions.

However, the gradual evolution of the European integration project has brought much complexity and ambivalence to the place of private autonomy within the Union's legal order. As pointed out by Weatherill, 'a vision of the importance of private autonomy is elusive in EU law and in the case law of the Court in particular. Sometimes, in its own right or in the guise of concern to protect legal certainty, it is a driving concern; on other occasions it must bow to pursuit of other concerns, most prominently the "effectiveness" of EU law'.[6] Indeed, the Union's legal order represents a combination of varying forms of manifestation of private autonomy and different instances of limitations imposed on its exercise. Their coexistence and intersection shape the characteristics of private autonomy that are distinctive and peculiar to the normative foundation of the internal market. First, the norms expressing the ideals of private autonomy can be split into two categories. On the one hand, they are manifested through the Treaty's free movement and competition provisions, and on the other hand, they are encapsulated in fundamental economic rights that are recognised as general principles of law and codified in the Charter. Despite their divergent traits, the normative boundaries of these sets of norms increasingly overlap due to the Court's resort to the expansive teleological interpretation of the Treaty, which poses challenges to the division of competence between the Union and its Member States. Second, neither of these norms constitutes an unfettered prerogative but can be subject to legitimate constraints. The ideals of private autonomy expressed through the Treaty's free movement provisions are framed by the regulatory autonomy of Member States. Likewise, fundamental economic rights are conditioned by policies pursued at both national and Union-wide levels. Third, in either context, the benchmarks set

[5] P-C Müller-Graff, 'Basic Freedoms: Extending Party Autonomy across Borders' in S Grundmann, W Kerber and S Weatherill (eds), *Party Autonomy and the Role of Information in the Internal Market* (Berlin, De Gruyter, 2001) 133. See also Case 15/81 *Gaston Schul Douane Expediteur BV v Inspecteur der Invoerrechten en Accijnzen, Roosendaal* EU:C:1982:135, para 33.

[6] S Weatherill, 'The Elusive Character of Private Autonomy' in D Leczykiewicz and S Weatherill (eds), *The Involvement of EU Law in Private Law Relationships* (Oxford, Hart Publishing, 2013) 26.

out for legitimate constraints are far from clear. Given the broad scope assigned to the Treaty's free movement and competition provisions, uncertainty also exists over the extent to which the achievement of the internal market objective necessitates limitations imposed on the exercise of fundamental economic rights and, at the same time, the extent to which the full realisation of these rights warrants modulation of the enforcement of the Treaty.

Against this backdrop, this study addresses the following twofold question: *which underlying normative values permeate the protection of private autonomy in the Union's legal order and, how do their correlation and coexistence shape the economic constitution established by the Treaties?* To address this question, this study aims to map the contours of protection of private autonomy by tracing the developments in the case law. Three aspects related to this concept are worth examining closely. First, its characteristics will be inferred from the juxtaposition of norms that express the individual liberty of economic action at the Union level. A specific focus is placed on the extent to which they converge despite their different normative purposes. Second, the scope of protection of private autonomy is contingent on the limitations imposed on the exercise of the individual liberty of economic action. Such impact is produced by legitimate policies pursued at national and Union-wide levels, but more importantly, by norms, which are recognised as general principles of law, codified in the Charter and laid down in the Union's secondary law, give effect to other individual entitlements of social, civil and political nature. Finally, at a more conceptual level, the distinguishing hallmark of the Union's legal system is that norms manifesting the ideals of private autonomy reciprocally limit or condition one another. Understanding the dynamics of this interplay makes it possible to shed light on the parameters of protection of private autonomy in the Union.

The analysis of the case law is informed by several strands of legal literature. This study draws on the schools of legal theory and philosophy infused by the rights-based liberal tradition.[7] Considered through this lens, the study defines the extent to which deontological and instrumentalist considerations shape the concept of private autonomy in the Union's legal order and explores the matrix of correlations existing between them. There are three dimensions to this exercise. First, it is necessary to identify normative safeguards that denote human rights characteristics intrinsic to private autonomy. Their central premise is the concept of respect for individuals as independent agents and bearers of subjective rights pursued for their conception of the good.[8] Second, this exercise entails ascertaining the degree to which norms that embody individual rights ultimately pursue the common good instead of benefiting or serving the interests of their bearers.

[7] See, eg, Hayek (n 1); R Dworkin, *Taking Rights Seriously* (Cambridge, MA, Harvard University Press, 1977); J Habermas, *Between Facts and Norms: Contributions to a Discourse Theory of Law and Democracy* (Cambridge, MA, MIT Press, 1996).

[8] T Gutmann, 'Some Preliminary Remarks on a Liberal Theory of Contract' (2013) 76 *Law and Contemporary Problems* 39, 40.

Third, it involves setting out the parameters for resolving the tensions of individual and communitarian interests and striking an optimal constitutional balance between them. In the context of the Union, the second and third steps are intricate tasks, considering the correlation of the Union's and national conceptions of the common good and its impact on the realisation of private autonomy expressed through, on the one hand, the Treaty's free movement and competition provisions, and, on the other hand, fundamental economic rights recognised as general principles of law and codified in the Charter.

This volume also relies on doctrinal writing in EU law. Countless scholarly works explore the genesis and evolution of the Union's system of human rights protection.[9] However, the number of those dissecting fundamental economic rights safeguarded at the Union level is fragmentary and sparse. Equally, there is a vast body of critical accounts of the case law on the Treaty's free movement and competition provisions,[10] which continue to generate wide-ranging debates over 'the fundamental ambitions and the institutional dynamics of the internal market bargain'.[11] While the rights-based approaches are not new to these accounts,[12] few explore the Treaty's free movement and competition rules in tandem with fundamental economic rights protected in the Union. The present study builds on this scholarship by bringing it together and complements it by bridging the identified gaps. This is achieved by collating the abovementioned norms that express the ideals of private autonomy within the Union's legal order. This exercise provides a more contextual perspective to assess the rights-based characteristics attributed to the Treaty's free movement and competition rules. Concomitantly, it makes it possible to locate the potential role of fundamental economic rights within the process of progressive liberalisation in the internal market via the gradual harmonisation and deregulation of national practices.

[9] See, eg, GF Mancini and DT Keeling, 'Democracy and the European Court of Justice' (1994) 57 *Modern Law Review* 175; JHH Weiler and NJS Lockhardt, '"Taking Rights Seriously" Seriously: The European Court of Justice and its Fundamental Rights Jurisprudence – Part I' (1995) 32 *Common Market Law Review* 51; X Groussot, *General Principles of Community Law* (Groningen, Europa Law Publishing, 2006).

[10] See, eg, E Spaventa, *Free Movement of Persons in the European Union: Barriers to Movement in Their Constitutional Context* (Alphen aan den Rijn, Kluwer Law International, 2007); N Nic Shuibhne, *The Coherence of EU Free Movement Law: Constitutional Responsibility and the Court of Justice* (Oxford, Oxford University Press, 2013); MP Maduro, 'Reforming the Market or the State? Article 30 and the European Constitution: Economic Freedom and Political Rights' (1997) 3 *European Law Journal* 55; R Schütze, 'Of Types and Tests: Towards a Unitary Doctrinal Framework for Article 34 TFEU?' (2016) 41 *European Law Review* 826; P Behrens, 'The "Consumer Choice" Paradigm in German Ordoliberalism and its Impact upon EU Competition Law' (2014) *Europa-Kolleg Hamburg, Institute for European Integration, Discussion Paper* 1/14; VJ Vanberg, 'Consumer Welfare, Total Welfare and Economic Freedom – on the Normative Foundations of Competition Policy' in J Drexl, W Kerber and R Podszun (eds), *Competition Policy and the Economic Approach: Foundations and Limitations* (Cheltenham, Edward Elgar, 2012) 52.

[11] M Dougan, 'Legal Developments' (2010) 48 *Journal of Common Market Studies* 163, 165.

[12] See, eg, C Warin, *Individual Rights under European Union Law: A Study on the Relation between Rights, Obligations and Interests in the Case Law of the Court of Justice* (Baden-Baden, Nomos, 2019); B Thorson, *Individual Rights in EU Law* (Cham, Springer International, 2016).

This volume is organised as follows. Chapter 1 explores the place of private autonomy within the framework of general principles of Union law. There are two aspects to this. The discussion first retraces the origin of private autonomy as a value that is safeguarded by general principles of law and draws the contours of its protection. It proceeds with the analysis of the case law that gives effect to the right to property and the right to engage in economic activity, the recognition of which by the Court saw the inception of fundamental rights protection at the Union level. Second, the study examines the extent of limitations and conditions imposed by general principles of law on the realisation of individual liberty of economic action. It primarily focuses on the principle of equality and non-discrimination that has undergone a metamorphosis from a catalyst of market integration to a self-standing human right in the Union's legal system and its impact on the traditional domain of private relations.

Chapter 2 takes the same analytical approach to examine the value of private autonomy apropos of the rights and freedoms enshrined in the Charter of Fundamental Rights. It starts by exploring the scope of Articles 15–17 CFR that uphold and promote the individual liberty of economic action and self-determination. It explores their role as a new platform for private actors to assert their interests in the process of enforcement of Union and national law. It then turns to the rights and freedoms that limit or condition the exercise of private autonomy. It adopts a general approach to focus on their enforceability in private relations. The horizontal direct effect attributed to these rights and freedoms, as embodiments of 'positive' entitlements, is argued to be based on satisfying specific normative requirements that are not immune to conceptual and methodological challenges.

Chapter 3 defines the boundaries of protection afforded to the ideals of private autonomy within the framework of the Treaty's free movement and competition rules. At an individual level, the functional correlation existing between these provisions is argued to translate to the guarantee of market freedom understood as the right to initiate or take part in the interstate process of competition in the internal market, free from discriminatory and non-discriminatory national measures, and the impediments created by the conduct of certain private actors deviating from the parameters of normal market behaviour. The discussion in this chapter brings to light two challenges. On the one hand, such individualisation of the Treaty's free movement provisions, despite finding support among Advocates General, is difficult to align with the Court's expansive definition of the concept of restriction to free movement that seems to equate these provisions with the right to economic freedom at large. On the other hand, such a characterisation of the Treaty's competition rules is less problematic at the level of framing the nature of the safeguarded individual right but not so at the level of the rationalisation of its protection, given the uncertainty existing over the goal(s) of competition law.

Chapter 4 investigates the normative reach of the Union's secondary law within the realm of private relations. It starts by briefly exploring the role of the harmonisation competence under Article 114 of the Treaty on the Functioning of the

European Union (TFEU) in the realisation of private autonomy in the internal market, then turning to the limitations of this principle emanating from the Union's secondary law. It falls beyond the scope of this study to conduct a comprehensive review of the Union's secondary law on consumer, environmental or labour protection that impacts private relationships. Instead, the discussion assesses the extent to which directives, even without proper implementation, can influence disputes between private parties. It focuses on the existing judicial avenues for the enforcement of directives in a private setting, despite the Court's continuous rejection of the horizontal direct effect of directives.

Chapter 5 concludes the study by analysing the coexistence and intersection between the two forms of manifestation of the ideals of private autonomy in the Union's legal order. This study approaches this task by distinguishing between, on the one hand, their general manifestation in fundamental economic rights and, on the other hand, the specific manifestation in the Treaty's free movement and competition rules. These expressions of the ideals of private autonomy are delineated along deontological versus instrumentalist lines, the interaction of which can be viewed from two perspectives: first, the study looks at the degree of convergence between fundamental economic rights with the Treaty's free movement and competition rules for it generates the dynamics of cross-fertilisation between them; and, second, it considers the possibility of a material conflict between these sets of provisions that requires delimitation of their respective spheres of application.

1

General Principles and Private Autonomy

> [I]t lies in the nature of general principles of law, which are to be sought rather in the Platonic heaven of law than in the law books, that both their existence and their substantive content are marked by uncertainty.[1]

The ideals of private autonomy are entrenched in the system of general principles of Union law. While not formally recognised as such, they constitute the core of rights and freedoms that range from the freedom of contract,[2] the freedom of trade,[3] the right to property,[4] the freedom to engage in economic or commercial activity[5] and the freedom to pursue a profession.[6] This set of rights and freedoms, albeit in different semantic configurations, is afforded constitutional protection within the legal systems of Member States. Their recognition as general principles in the case law acted as a catalyst for the development of human rights protection in the Union.[7] The reason prompting these rights and freedoms to take the forefront in this process inherently stemmed from the economic underpinnings of the internal market project. The freedoms of movement, complemented by competition rules, undoubtedly led to the greater realisation of the individual liberty of economic action and self-determination by opening new opportunities across

[1] Opinion of AG Mazák in Case 411/05 *Félix Palacios de la Villa v Cortefiel Servicios SA* EU:C:2007:106, para 86.

[2] See, eg, Case T-128/98 *Aéroports de Paris v Commission* EU:T:2000:290, para 82; Case T-24/90 *Automec v Commission* EU:T:1992:97, para 51.

[3] See, eg, Case C-295/03 P *Alessandrini and Others v Commission* EU:C:2005:413, para 90; Case C-183/95 *Affish* EU:C:1997:373, para 42.

[4] See, eg, Joined Cases C-402/05 P and C-415/05 *Yassin Abdullah Kadi and Al Barakaat International Foundation v Council of the European Union and Commission of the European Communities* EU:C:2008:461, para 355; Case C-347/03 *Regione autonoma Friuli-Venezia Giulia and Agenzia regionale per lo sviluppo rurale (ERSA) v Ministero delle Politiche Agricole e Forestali* EU:C:2005:285, para 122.

[5] See, eg, Joined Cases C-154/04 and C-155/04 *Alliance for Natural Health v Secretary of State for Health* EU:C:2005:449, para 126; Case C-84/95 *Bosphorus Hava Yollari Turizm ve Ticaret AS v Minister for Transport, Energy and Communications and Others* EU:C:1996:312, para 19.

[6] See, eg, Joined Cases C-37/02 and C-38/02 *Di Lenardo Adriano* EU:C:2004:443, para 82.

[7] C Harding, U Kohl and N Salmon, *Human Rights in the Market Place: The Exploitation of Rights Protection by Economic Actors* (Abingdon, Routledge, 2016) 108. See also Case 4/73 *Nold, Kohlen- und Baustoffgroßhandlung v Commission* EU:C:1974:51; Case 44/79 *Liselotte Hauer v Land Rheinland-Pfalz* EU:C:1979:290.

borders of Member States. However, the goal of establishment and functioning of the internal market spawned a vast system of economic dirigisme. This posed the risk of the (then) Community's measures encroaching upon the aforementioned constitutional entitlements enshrined in the legal systems of Member States. Confronted with the increasing prospect of national constitutional scrutiny that would have risked the uniformity of (then) Community law,[8] the Court found a solution by recognising these individual entitlements as forming an integral part of general principles of law. This meant that the (then) growing Community's legislation would be subject to proper legal scrutiny by the Court itself, obviating the need for such judicial oversight at the national level.[9] This development was pivotal in addressing the deficit of fundamental rights protection that persisted at the (then) Community level.[10] Against this backdrop, this chapter explores the place of private autonomy among general principles of Union law with the central aim of understanding the extent of protection afforded to it and the parameters of limitations imposed on its exercise.

I. General Principles Manifesting Private Autonomy

The evolution of fundamental rights protection unfolded in several stages, culminating with the Charter acquiring a legally binding force. Its genesis traces its roots to *Van Gend en Loos*, which effected a constitutional breakthrough by imparting normative significance to individual rights in the Union's legal order.[11] There are two aspects to this development. First, the Court used the mechanism of direct effect to equate the obligations imposed in the Treaty with the justiciable rights of individuals.[12] This meant that the ambit of such rights was not confined to the entitlements explicitly conferred on individuals but encompassed even the normative provisions that were only binding on Member States. Through the direct effect doctrine, the mutual obligations undertaken by Member States are, therefore, construed 'as rights owed by [them] to individuals which national courts must

[8] U Scheuner, 'Fundamental Rights in European Community Law and in National Constitutional Law: Recent Decisions in Italy and in the Federal Republic of Germany' (1975) 12 *Common Market Law Review* 171, 171.

[9] P Craig, 'General Principles of Law: Treaty, Historical, and Normative Foundations' in KS Ziegler, PJ Neuvonen and V Moreno-Lax, *Research Handbook on General Principles of EU Law: Constructing Legal Orders in Europe* (Cheltenham, Edward Edgar, 2022) 37.

[10] D Schiek, *Economic and Social Integration: The Challenge for EU Constitutional Law* (Cheltenham, Edward Edgar, 2012) 99.

[11] C Warin, *Individual Rights under European Union Law: A Study on the Relation between Rights, Obligations and the Interests in the Case-Law of the Court of Justice* (Baden-Baden, Nomos, 2019) 29; Case 26/62 *Van Gend & Loos v Netherlands Inland Revenue Administration* EU:C:1963:1.

[12] D Charmers and L Barroso, 'What *Van Gend en Loos* Stands for' (2014) 12 *International Journal of Constitutional Law* 105, 106.

protect'.[13] Second, the significance of *Van Gend en Loos* is not limited to the endowment of individuals with the Treaty-based justiciable rights enforceable in national courts;[14] it also paved the way for the recognition in the (then) Community's legal order of fundamental human rights that are based on unwritten sources of law. This was vindicated by the growing incongruence between the delegated powers vested in the (then) Community's institutions and the lack of embedded constitutional guarantees on such powers.

A. The Genesis of Fundamental Economic Rights *Qua* General Principles

It is no coincidence that the development of fundamental human rights *qua* general principles of Union law is historically and substantively interwoven with the protection of rights and freedoms that manifest the ideals of private autonomy. In one respect, the Treaties, notably the European Economic Community Treaty, did not affect one's entitlement to such autonomy but enhanced its exercise across Member State borders. Individuals are intimately involved in the application of the Treaty's free movement and competition rules in the sense of being direct beneficiaries of the unhindered flow of goods, services or capital throughout the internal market.[15] These provisions give effect to the liberty of acquiring, possessing and using economic goods and services as per one's will and interests and the ability to engage in legal relations of one's own choice. At the same time, the effect of the Treaties was not all favourable from the viewpoint of one's ability to exercise private autonomy. The reasons for this were threefold. First, the pursuit of the economic objectives of the Treaties was poised to lead to growing economic decision-making of the (then) Community that was bound to limit individual economic liberties.[16] Second, the Court's purposive interpretation in light of the criteria developed in *Van Gen den Loos* widened the range of immediately applicable and directly effective rules.[17] While this expanded the domain within which (then) Community law created individual rights, it also imposed constraints on commercial or economic freedom of action. Third, these developments occurred when the Treaties did not enshrine any substantive safeguards analogous to national constitutional provisions protecting fundamental human rights. The combination of these factors

[13] JHH Weiler, '*Van Gend en Loos*: The Individual as Subject and Object and the Dilemma of European Legitimacy' (2014) 12 *International Journal of Constitutional Law* 94, 96.

[14] C Joerges, 'The Law in the Process of Constitutionalizing Europe' (2002) 4 *EUI Working Paper LAW* 1, 7.

[15] F Mancini and DT Keeting, 'Democracy and the European Court of Justice' (1994) 57 *Modern Law Review* 175, 182.

[16] Scheuner (n 8) 172.

[17] Joerges (n 14) 7.

brought about a conceptual dilemma of whether the direct effect and supremacy of (then) Community law could be asserted without any fundamental rights guarantees.[18] The Court resolved it by incorporating the protection of fundamental rights into general principles of Union law.[19]

i. Private Autonomy and the Union's Institutions

In the earliest encounters, the Court rejected the invitation to review the alleged violation of a fundamental right. In *Stork*,[20] the applicant challenged the decision of the High Authority under Article 61 of the Treaty establishing the European Coal and Steel Community (hereinafter the ECSC Treaty) by invoking the right to an occupation or profession enshrined in the German Basic Law. The Court held that it '[was] only required to ensure that in the interpretation and application of the Treaty … the law [was] observed' and hence it was not competent to 'rule on provisions of national law'.[21] This finding was confirmed in *Geitling*,[22] where the applicant made a similar claim relying on Article 14 of the German Basic Law that protects the right to property. The Court found that it was not its duty 'to ensure that rules of internal law, even constitutional rules, enforced in one or other of the Member States [were] respected'.[23] It also added that 'Community law, as it [arose] under the ECSC Treaty, [did not] contain any general principle, express or otherwise, guaranteeing the maintenance of vested rights'.[24]

Many theories have been proffered to explain the Court's initial reluctance. Two in particular stand out. On the one hand, while the Court did not mean to deny the protection of the rights under the German Basic Law, it implicitly appeared to express deference to the intention of the Treaty drafters to opt for a 'national solution' concerning fundamental rights protection.[25] This also reflected the Court's self-perception at the time as 'a [traditional] international tribunal determined to preserve the *autonomy* of the system it oversaw' rather than 'a constitutional court of a supranational order'.[26] On the other hand, the Court's

[18] JHH Weiler, 'Fundamental Rights and Fundamental Boundaries: Common Standards and Conflicting Values in the Protection of Human Rights in the European Legal Space' in R Kastoryano (ed), *An Identity for Europe: The Relevance of Multiculturalism in EU Construction* (New York, Palgrave Macmillan, 2009) 79.

[19] Scheuner (n 8) 172.

[20] Case 1/58 *Friedrich Stork & Cie v High Authority of the European Coal and Steel Community* EU:C:1959:4.

[21] ibid 27.

[22] Joined Cases 36, 37, 38–59 and 40–59 *Präsident Ruhrkolen-Verkaufsgesellschaft mbH, Geitling Ruhrkohlen-Verkaufsgesellschaft mbH, Mausegatt Ruhrkohlen-Verkaufsgesellschaft mbH and I Nold KG v High Authority of the European Coal and Steel Community* EU:C:1960:36.

[23] ibid 438.

[24] ibid 439.

[25] H Rasmussen, *On Law and Policy in the European Court of Justice: A Comparative Study in Judicial Policymaking* (Dordrecht, Martinus Nijhoff Publishers, 1986) 403–04.

[26] JHH Weiler, 'Methods of Protection of Fundamental Human Rights in the European Community: Towards a Second and Third Generation of Protection' in A Cassese, A Clapham and JHH Weiler,

refusal to carry out a fundamental rights review also reflected its reluctance to hamper the Community's 'young [and] fragile' decision-making capabilities.[27] The Court's stance shielded the activity of the High Authority from the requirement of conformity with national constitutional guarantees.[28] Paradoxically, the same protective sentiment later became the primary factor that induced the Court to embrace fundamental rights protection in the form of general principles of law.

Ten years after *Stork* and *Geitling*, the Court's uncompromising stance changed. It began with *Stauder*,[29] where, in the context of the right to dignity, it held that 'the provision at issue [contained] nothing capable of prejudicing the fundamental human rights enshrined in the general principles of Community law and protected by the Court'.[30] This ruling was brief and felt 'almost accidental'.[31] The Court did not elaborate on the methodology for formulating human rights, nor did it establish the (then) Community's standards for their protection.[32] However, it paved the way for *Internationale Handelsgesellschaft*,[33] which led to the inception of the Community/Union's system of human rights protection.[34] As is well known, this ruling was not merely motivated by the Court's solicitude for human rights but stemmed from its desire to preserve the supremacy of (then) Community law that German and Italian constitutional courts questioned.[35]

The issue in *Internationale Handelsgesellschaft* related to the validity of the (then) Community's deposit system for the issue of import and export licences for agricultural goods and their forfeiture in the event of a failure to use them. This was claimed to infringe the right to economic freedom protected by the German Basic Law. The Court's verdict consisted of two findings of 'major interpretative significance'.[36] First, the Court affirmed the supremacy of (then) Community law, according to which the validity of the (then) Community's measure could not be decided according to the fundamental rights protected in national constitutions. Otherwise, in the Court's view, this would have 'an adverse effect on the

European Union – The Human Rights Challenge, Vol II: Human Rights and the European Community: Methods of Protection (Baden-Baden, Nomos, 1991) 580.

[27] Rasmussen (n 25) 404.

[28] Weiler (n 26) 576.

[29] Case 29/69 *Erich Stauder v City of Ulm – Sozialamt* EU:C:1969:57.

[30] ibid para 7.

[31] Rasmussen (n 25) 404396; see also P Pescatore, 'Fundamental Rights and Freedoms in the System of the European Communities' (1970) 18 *American Journal of Comparative Law* 343, 351.

[32] X Groussot, *General Principles of Community Law* (Groningen, Europa Law Publishing, 2006) 34.

[33] Case 1/70 *Internationale Handelsgesellschaft mbH v Einfuhr- und Vorratsstelle für Getreide und Futtermittel* EU:C:1970:114.

[34] B Davies, '*Internationale Handelsgesellschaft* and Miscalculation at the Inception' in F Nicola and B Davies (eds), *EU Law Stories: Contextual and Critical Histories of European Jurisprudence* (Cambridge, Cambridge University Press, 2017) 157.

[35] Weiler (n 26) 581.

[36] JNC Rodrigues, 'The Incorporation of Fundamental Rights in the Community Legal Order' in L Azoulai and L Poiares Pessoa Maduro (eds), *The Past and Future of EU Law: The Classics of EU Law Revisited on the 50th Anniversary of the Rome Treaty* (Oxford, Hart Publishing, 2010) 91.

uniformity and efficacy of Community law'.[37] However, the verdict did not end there. The Court held that a review was warranted in light of the 'analogous guarantee inherent in Community law', based on the fact that 'respect for fundamental rights form[ed] an integral part of the general principles of law'.[38] According to the Court, whilst 'inspired by the constitutional traditions common to the Member States', they 'must be ensured within the framework of the structure and objectives of the Community'.[39]

While *Internationale Handelsgesellschaft* did not verbalise the (then) Community-specific contours of the right to property and the right to engage in economic activity, it provided a glimpse into the nature of the supranational guarantee of these individual entitlements and human rights as a whole. This ruling did not conform to the established tradition – forged in the existing constitutional texts and international documents – of first defining the scope of the protected right and then identifying the specific conditions under which it can be legitimately limited.[40] The Court showed no attempt to elaborate on the critical characteristics of either individual entitlement. Instead, it used proportionality as a general analytical framework to assess the impugned measure, which consisted of three parts: the requirement of effectiveness, the requirement of necessity, and the requirement of proportionality in a strict sense.[41] Proportionality was not relied upon as a mere tool of administrative nature, but as a 'device of interpretation' that morphed into 'a substitute' for the traditional rights-based assessment.[42] It served as a ground for review,[43] according to which the focus was placed on whether there were sufficient reasons to support a policy choice instead of the analysis centred on laying down the normative reach of fundamental human rights.[44] As discussed later, the difference is that the former construction equates fundamental human rights with policy goals in terms of their normative value.[45]

If *Internationale Handelsgesellschaft* introduced the (then) Community's system of human rights protection, *Nold* and *Hauer* established and elaborated the accepted standard for their protection.[46] In *Nold*, the issue related to the new terms of business authorised by the Commission in the coal sector that led to the loss by the applicant undertaking of its status as a direct wholesaler and its purchase entitlements. In *Hauer*, in turn, the issue arose from the (then) Community's measure that prohibited new wine planting for three years. In both instances, the measures

[37] *Internationale Handelsgesellschaft* (n 33) para 3.
[38] ibid para 4.
[39] ibid.
[40] M Kumm, '*Internationale Handelsgesellschaft*, *Nold* and the New Human Rights Paradigm' in Azoulai and Poiares Pessoa Maduro (n 36) 110.
[41] *Internationale Handelsgesellschaft* (n 33) paras 10–11.
[42] Groussot (n 32) 21.
[43] T Tridimas, *General Principles of EU Law* (Oxford, Oxford University Press, 2006) 142.
[44] Kumm (n 40) 110.
[45] ibid 109–10.
[46] *Nold* (n 7); *Hauer* (n 7).

at stake were claimed to infringe the right to property and the right to free pursuit of business as protected under the German Basic Law. Unlike *Internationale Handelsgesellschaft*, *Nold* and *Hauer* laid down a more specific conceptual formula for protecting both individual entitlements. While not defining their actual scope, the Court found that both types of rights, 'far from constituting unfettered prerogatives, must be viewed in the light of the social function of the property and activities protected thereunder'.[47] It continued that these rights could be subject to certain limits justified by the objectives pursued by the (then) Community, provided that their substance was left untouched.[48] The significance of this formula is twofold. First, the Court appeared to demarcate the individual and social dimensions inherent in both rights.[49] The 'substance' of a right encapsulates individual proprietary or entrepreneurial interests that, to use the Dworkian term,[50] 'trump' communitarian goals. The 'social function' of a right relates to the interests that posit the prerogatives of a proper and desirable economic order.[51] Although this formula implicitly incorporated proportionality as a method of reconciliation of opposing interests, neither *Nold* nor *Hauer* assessed the three limbs under the proportionality test. In both rulings, the Court confined its reasoning to finding the legitimate 'general interest' pursued at the (then) Community level and the temporary nature of the Community's measure at stake.

ii. Private Autonomy and Member States

The next step in the evolution was the extension to Member States of the commitment to respect fundamental rights. However, such an obligation is not all-encompassing but concerns two categories of national measures. While the first category includes national measures that implement or apply Union law,[52] the second category consists of those that derogate from free movement law.[53] Both categories have generated a plethora of comprehensive commentaries. With that in mind, this section focuses on the first category of national measures as their origin is linked to the general principles expressing the ideals of private autonomy, while the second category is discussed in Chapters 2 and 5 of this volume.

[47] *Nold* (n 7) para 14; *Hauer* (n 7) para 32.

[48] *Nold* (n 7) para 14.

[49] MR Antinori, 'Does Lochner Live in Luxembourg? An Analysis of the Property Rights Jurisprudence of the European Court of Justice' (1994) 18 *Fordham International Law Journal* 1778, 1848.

[50] R Dworkin, *Taking Rights Seriously* (Cambridge, MA, Harvard University Press, 1977).

[51] Antinori (n 49) 1848.

[52] See, eg, Case C-101/01 *Criminal Proceedings against Bodil Lindqvist* EU:C:2003:596; Case C-465/00 *Rechnungshof v Österreichischer Rundfunk and Others* EU:C:2003:294.

[53] Case C-260/89 *Elliniki Radiophonia Tiléorassi AE (ERT) and Panellinia Omospondia Syllogon Prossopikou v Dimotiki Etairia Pliroforissis and Sotirios Kouvelas and Nicolaos Avdellas and Others* EU:C:1991:254.

The first category of national measures required to respect fundamental rights emerged in *Wachauf*.[54] In this case, the issue concerned the national measure implementing the (then) Community's system of milk quotas and compensation scheme for the discontinuance of milk production. According to it, a tenant farmer's right to claim such compensation was subject to a landowner's authorisation. This was claimed to infringe on the right to property since it risked depriving a tenant farmer of the fruits of his or her labour. In his Opinion,[55] AG Jacobs concurred with this assessment. According to him, although the coordination of the respective interests of a landlord and a tenant farmer was left to Member States to decide, Community law was not extraneous in this regard. He argued that it was incumbent on Member States to respect the right to property recognised by the Court when implementing the (then) Community's measures.[56] The relevance of this right followed, in AG Jacobs' view, from the fact that a milk quota could give rise to a proprietary interest for the benefit of a tenant farmer.[57] As such, the failure by a Member State to provide compensation to a tenant farmer who, on the expiry of the lease, lost the entitlement to exploit a milk quota would amount to a breach of the general principle of the right to property.[58] Premised on the analytical formula set out in *Hauer*, the Court concurred with AG Jacobs by finding that 'Community rules which … had the effect of depriving [the tenant farmer], without compensation, of the fruits of his labour and of his investments would be incompatible with the requirements of the protection of fundamental rights in the Community legal order'.[59] However, the Court's focus was not on the validity of the Community's measure but on the effect of the impugned national implementation measure.[60] In this respect, it declared that Member States were also bound by fundamental rights when implementing the provisions of (then) Community law.[61]

Wachauf firmly established that national authorities, analogous to the Union's institutions, must respect the right to property and other fundamental human rights protected as general principles of law. However, this is not a general obligation but one that operates within the area of the Union's competence and specifically applies when Member States are implementing Union law. This is based on the premise that in the context of the implementation of Union law, Member States and the Union ought not to be seen as separate entities. On the contrary, as broadly accepted, in the Union's system of governance, Member States implementing Union law often act as 'the executive branch of the Union'.[62] As

[54] Case 5/88 *Hubert Wachauf v Bundesamt für Ernährung und Forstwirtschaft* EU:C:1989:321.
[55] Opinion of AG Jacobs in Case 5/88 *Wachauf* EU:C:1989:179.
[56] ibid para 22.
[57] ibid paras 24–25.
[58] ibid para 27.
[59] *Wachauf* (n 54) para 19.
[60] NA Neuwahl, 'The Treaty on European Union: A Step Forward for the Protection of Human Rights?' in NA Neuwahl and A Rosas (eds), *The European Union and Human Rights* (The Hague, Martinus Nijhoff, 1995) 9.
[61] *Wachauf* (n 54) para 19.
[62] NJS Lockhart and JHH Weiler, '"Taking Rights Seriously" Seriously: The European Court and its Fundamental Rights Jurisprudence – Part I' (1995) 32 *Common Market Law Review* 51, 73–74.

such, it would have been inconsistent and contradictory not to subject them to the requirement of conformity to fundamental rights recognised at the Union level.[63] The essence of *Wachauf* is that national authorities enjoy a margin of discretion over the implementation of Union law, though such discretion is framed by the parameters underlying the Union's fundamental rights conception.[64] This means that a national implementation measure would be struck down if it infringes the Union's standard of human rights protection, even if it complies with a national standard.[65] Indeed, in *Wachauf*, the Court implied that if (then) Community law had granted a tenant farmer proprietary rights over a milk quota, the national implementation measure would have violated those rights by reconciling the respective interest of a tenant and a landowner through the strict application of the authorisation requirement.[66]

B. The Contours of Private Autonomy *Qua* General Principles of Law

The trilogy of *Internationale Handelsgesellschaft*, *Nold* and *Hauer* marked the first stage in shaping the commitment to protecting the right to property and the right to pursue economic activity as general principles of Union law. Despite their early recognition, the subsequent case law has yet to provide much on the level and extent of protection afforded to both. In most instances involving either of these rights, the Court often, or nearly always, considered them in abstract and merely applied (albeit not consistently) the *Nold/Hauer* formula.[67] Only common themes recurring in the case law inform the contours of the Court's understanding of both rights. The Court usually considers the principles of the right to property and the right to pursue economic activity in conjunction with one another. This manifests the existence of a close affinity between them in terms of their normative reach and the legitimacy of constraints imposed on their exercise. A restriction of both can be justified on the same grounds reflecting legitimate objectives in the general interest that include, among others, the common organisation of the market in agricultural products,[68] the protection of human and animal health,[69] international peace and

[63] Tridimas (n 43) 321.
[64] Lockhart and Weiler (n 62) 80.
[65] Tridimas (n 43) 321.
[66] Antinori (n 49) 1846.
[67] See, eg, Case 265/87 *Hermann Schräder HS Kraftfutter GmbH & Co KG v Hauptzollamt Gronau* EU:C:1989:303, para 1; Case T-390/94 *Aloys Schröder, Jan and Karl-Julius Thamann v Commission of the European Communities* EU:T:1997:51, para 125.
[68] See, eg, *Alessandrini and Others* (n 3) para 84; Case 230/78 *SpA Eridania-Zuccherifici Nazionali and SpA Società Italiana per l'Industria degli Zuccheri* EU:C:1979:216, para 21.
[69] See, eg, Case C-210/03 *Swedish Match v Secretary of State for Health* EU:C:2004:802, para 74; Case T-13/99 *Pfizer Animal Health SA v Council of the European Union* EU:T:2002:209, para 456.

security,[70] and environmental protection.[71] The obligations imposed in pursuance of these objectives are, often concomitantly, deemed not to impose intolerable and disproportionate interference with the exercise of both rights. While inherently linked, the right to property and the right to pursue economic activity do not necessarily converge. Significant differences remain between them. From a conceptual standpoint, the case law draws a line between the right to property and the freedom to conduct business along the terms proposed by AG Villalón in *Alemo Herron*.[72] According to him, if the former individual right 'operates in the sphere of tangible and intangible assets', the latter 'protects economic initiative and the ability to participate in a market'.[73] A distinction along these lines is reflected in *Zuckerfabrik*,[74] where the issue concerned the compatibility of the (then) Community's measure that introduced a special elimination levy in the sugar sector with the right to own property and the freedom to pursue economic activity. The Court dismissed the first aspect of the claim by finding that the levy did not adversely affected sugar producers' right to own property.[75] However, the second aspect of the claim was addressed in light of the *Hauer* formula, though the Court only held that the intervention with the right to pursue economic activity was not disproportionate.[76] The difference in the Court's reasoning points to a variance in the scope of these rights. The impugned measure was only found to trigger the freedom to pursue economic activity without raising any matters related to ownership over tangible and intangible assets.

i. The Principle of the Right to Property

The case law outlining the scope of the general principle of the right to property is meagre. There is no definitive guide on the nature of proprietary interests safeguarded at the Union level. The case law reveals more about what the scope of this principle excludes than what it encompasses. On several occasions, the Court emphasised that an economic operator could not claim a proprietary right in the previously held market share since it '[constituted] only a momentary economic position exposed to the risks of changing circumstances'.[77] In *SMW Winzersekt*,[78] in turn, the Court held that a wine producer could not invoke the right to property

[70] *Bosphorus* (n 5) para 24.

[71] Joined Cases C-248/95 and C-249/95 *SAM Schiffahrt GmbH and Heinz Stapf v Bundesrepublik Deutschland* EU:C:1997:377, para 73.

[72] Opinion of AG Villalón in Case C-426/11 *Mark Alemo-Herron and Others v Parkwood Leisure Ltd* EU:C:2013:82.

[73] ibid para 51.

[74] Joined Cases C-143/88 and C-92/89 *Zuckerfabrik Süderdithmarschen AG v Hauptzollamt Itzehoe and Zuckerfabrik Soest GmbH v Hauptzollamt Paderborn* EU:C:1991:65.

[75] ibid para 75. See also Case 265/87 *Hermann Schräder HS Kraftfutter GmbH & Co KG v Hauptzollamt Gronau* EU:C:1989:303, para 17.

[76] *Zuckerfabrik* (n 74) para 76.

[77] See, eg, Case C-280/93 *Federal Republic of Germany v Council of the European Union* EU:C:1994:367, para 79; Case T-254/97 *Fruchthandelsgesellschaft mbH Chemnitz v Commission of the European Communities* EU:T:1999:17, para 74.

[78] Case C-306/93 *SMW Winzersekt GmbH v Land Rheinland-Pfalz* EU:C:1994:407.

against the prohibition imposed on the use of the 'méthode champenoise' designation since all wine producers were entitled to use it.[79] More broadly, the Court also reiterated that economic operators could not have a vested right in the maintenance of advantages obtained from the establishment of the common organisation of the market.[80] Similarly, the case law is not instructive enough on the extent of ownership rights by only implicitly acknowledging a few of its elements. In *France and Ireland*,[81] the Court found that the (then) Community's special intervention measure in the beef and veal sector did not violate the right to property as it did not prevent producers from 'disposing freely of their products'.[82] Likewise, in *Deutsche Lufthansa*,[83] a claimant's plea was dismissed on the ground that there was no loss in the ability 'to exploit property in such a way as to make a profit'.[84] However, the loss of profitability, as shown below, does not necessarily entail an infringement on the right to property.

The substantive breadth of the general principle of the right to property is shaped by the three rules enshrined in Article 1 of Protocol I to the ECHR.[85] According to it, the Court conducts, though not always, a twofold query in addressing infringement claims involving the right to property. It considers whether a measure amounts to the expropriation of possession or merely imposes a limitation on its use.[86] The essence of this enquiry was encapsulated by AG Capotorti in *Hauer*.[87] According to him, two factors separate the expropriation of property from a limitation on the use of property. First, they vary in terms of 'the scale of the economic sacrifice' required from a property owner.[88] The expropriation of property deprives an owner of possession or its appreciable economic value, while a limitation of its use only reduces the extent to which possession remains at one's disposal. The second distinguishing factor is the duration of a measure.[89] The expropriation of property, by its very nature, entails the permanent deprivation of possession.

This distinction underpins the Court's understanding of the general principle of the right to property. In most instances, it tends to find no violation of the right to property by classifying an interfering measure as a mere limitation of its use. However, this does not apply to instances involving expropriation, which is more

[79] ibid para 23.

[80] See, eg, Case 59/83 *SA Biovilac NV v European Economic Community* EU:C:1984:380, para 23; Case C-69/89 *Nakajima All Precision Co Ltd v Council of the European Communities* EU:C:1991:186, para 119; *SpA Eridania* (n 68) para 22.

[81] Joined Cases C-296/93 and C-307/93 *France and Ireland v Commission* EU:C:1995:202.

[82] ibid para 64. See also Case T-390/94 *Schröder*, para 130.

[83] Case C-363/01 *Flughafen Hannover-Langenhagen v Deutsche Lufthansa AG* EU:C:2003:548.

[84] ibid para 58.

[85] See Case T-184/95 *Dorsch Consult Ingenieurgesellschaft mbH v Council and Commission* EU:T:1998:74, para 26.

[86] Joined Cases C-20/00 and C-64/00 *Booker Aquacultur Ltd and Hydro Seafood GSP Ltd v Scottish Ministers* EU:C:2003:397, paras 80–81.

[87] Opinion of AG Capotorti in *Hauer* (n 7).

[88] ibid para 8.

[89] ibid.

likely to violate the right to property. In *Biovilac*, the Court found that a measure depriving an owner of its property or the freedom to use it would encroach upon the substance of the right to property.[90] The same also follows from the Court's approach concerning the asset-freezing measures imposed on individuals. They differ from confiscation, which, as often reiterated by the Court, 'affects the very substance of [a proprietary interest in an asset]'.[91] According to *Othman*,[92] this is manifested in the fact that the confiscation of property can leave an individual '[no] means of enjoying the normal aspects of civilised existence', '[prohibit it] from engaging in any paid employment, occupation or profession' and '[exclude it] from almost all aspects of social life'.[93] Nonetheless, the temporary nature of a freezing measure does not necessarily exempt it from scrutiny. A non-permanent but long-lasting measure can lead to the same repercussions as confiscation. In *Kadi*,[94] the Court held that a measure lasting for nearly 10 years questioned the distinction between confiscation and a temporary measure.[95] This is because, as the Court continued, 'in the scale of a human life, 10 years in fact represent[ed] a substantial period of time and the question of the classification of the measures … as preventative or punitive, protective or confiscatory, civil or criminal seem[ed] now to be an open one'.[96]

ii. The Principle of the Freedom to Pursue Economic Activity

The case law also does not comprehensively define the right to pursue economic activity. Moreover, divergent terminologies are used to express this individual right. Within the framework of the *Hauer* formula, the Court referred, among others things, to the 'freedom to pursue a commercial activity',[97] 'freedom to pursue a trade or profession',[98] 'freedom to pursue an economic activity',[99] 'commercial freedom',[100] 'freedom to pursue an occupation',[101] 'entrepreneurial freedom'[102] and 'the right to carry on a business'.[103] Although these terminologies

[90] *SA Biovilac* (n 80) para 22.

[91] Case T-253/02 *Chafiq Ayadi v Council* EU:T:2006:200; para 135; Case T-49/04 *Faraj Hassan v Council and Commission* EU:T:2006:201, para 105.

[92] Case T-318/01 *Omar Mohammed Othman v Council and Commission* EU:T:2009:187.

[93] ibid paras 63–66. These were the claimant's pleas, which the Court held to be well founded.

[94] Case T-85/09 *Yassin Abdullah Kadi v Commission* EU:T:2010:418.

[95] ibid para 150.

[96] ibid.

[97] See, eg, Case C-84/95 *Bosphorus*, para 19.

[98] See, eg, Case C-90/90 *Jean Neu and Others* EU:C:1991:303, para 13.

[99] Joined Cases C-453/03, C-11/04, C-12/04 and C-194/04 *ABNA and Others* EU:C:2005:741, para 87.

[100] Case T-30/99 *Bocchi Food Trade International v Commission* EU:T:2001:96, para 69.

[101] Joined Cases C-184/02 and C-223/02 *Spain and Finland v European Parliament and Council* EU:C:2004:497, para 51.

[102] Case C-200/96 *Metronome Musik and Music Point Hokamp* EU:C:1998:172, para 26.

[103] *SA Biovilac* (n 80) para 21.

are not conceptually identical, the Court often uses them interchangeably.[104] As such, substantive characteristics attributed, or not attributed, to one extend to the rest. However, the range of such elements provided in the case law is not extensive but is confined to very few. In *Neu and Others*,[105] the Court held that the specific expression of the freedom to pursue a trade or profession was 'the freedom to choose whom to do business with'.[106] According to this finding, a measure penalising a producer for changing its customers can infringe upon the freedom to pursue a trade or profession.[107] The protection provided by this general principle does not cover claims to specific commercial interests or opportunities.[108] It also does not guarantee a particular level of productivity. In *Finsider*,[109] the Court found that (then) Community law did not guarantee 'the minimum production which [an] undertaking [considered] necessary in accordance with its own criteria of profitability and development'.[110]

Analogous to the right to property, the normative reach of the general principle of the freedom to pursue economic activity is framed by the analytical parameters of the *Nold/Hauer* formula that involves establishing whether a limitation of this individual right is disproportionate and whether it affects its 'very substance'. However, the case law does not provide clear guidance as to what constitutes the substance of this general principle of law. Broadly considered, the Court seems to distinguish two elements: the freedom to 'access a trade or profession' and the freedom to 'exercise a trade and profession'.[111] While the former element relates to the ability to engage in economic or commercial activity, the latter concerns the ability to decide how to proceed with it. The case law suggests that the freedom to exercise a trade and profession can be subject to a broad set of limitations that would likely be exculpated under the *Nold/Hauer* formula. In *SMW Winzersekt*,[112] the Court found that the prohibition imposed on the use of a specific labelling designation '[did] not impair the very substance of the right freely to exercise a trade or profession …, since [it affected] only the arrangements governing the exercise of that right and [did] not jeopardize its very existence'.[113] In *Commission v Germany*,[114] in turn, the geographical requirement for the production of quality wines was found not to affect 'the existence of the undertakings … or the substance of the freedom to choose a trade or a profession'.[115]

[104] *Spain and Finland* (n 101) 51.
[105] *Jean Neu and Others* (n 98).
[106] ibid para 14.
[107] ibid. See also Case C-307/91 *Luxlait and Victori Hendel* EU:C:1993:940, para 14.
[108] Case C-120/06 P *FIAMM and Others v Council and Commission* EU:C:2008:476, para 185.
[109] Joined Cases 63 and 147/84 *Finsider v Commission* EU:C:1985:358.
[110] ibid para 24.
[111] Tridimas (n 43) 316.
[112] *SMW Winzersekt GmbH v Land Rheinland-Pfalz* (n 78).
[113] ibid para 24.
[114] Case C-116/82 *Commission v Germany* EU:C:1986:322.
[115] ibid para 27. See also Case T-113/96 *Edouard Dubois v Council and Commission* EU:T:1998:11, para 75.

This is because, according to the Court, it merely bore 'not directly but merely indirectly on a related right since the restrictions … [had] some effect upon the possible ways in which producers run their business and, solely to that extent, upon the pursuit of a trade or a profession'.[116] In line with the Court's reasoning in *Duff and Others*,[117] it appears that only the substantial reduction of production can affect the substance of the general principle of the right to pursue economic activity. In that case, the Court found no effect on the substance of this freedom because economic operators maintained the level of production despite being unable to increase it.[118] Similarly, in *Kühn*,[119] it was held that the method for allocation of quotas for the production of milk did not affect the substance of the freedom to pursue an occupation since it did not impact the possibility for the operators in question to specialise in products other than milk on the holding concerned.[120] In the same vein, in *Boehringer*,[121] the Court found no violation in the partial forfeiture of marketing authorisations because producers remained free to market their products outside the (then) Community.[122] This line of case law suggests that the substance of the general principle of the freedom to pursue economic activity remains intact so long as some business opportunity is available that does not need to be confined to a specific industry sector or marketing method.

iii. Freedom of Contract

Despite the subtle substantive differences separating the right to property and the freedom to pursue economic activity, they are intrinsically intertwined in terms of the expression of private autonomy. One of the factors homogenising, to a certain extent, these individual entitlements is the freedom of contract that underpins the exercise of both.[123] This freedom is recognised as a general principle of Union law.[124] Analogous to other individual rights, the case law does not comprehensively outline its nature and scope, though certain constituting elements that frame the contours of its protection at the Union level can still be discerned from it. In *Werhof*,[125] the Court characterised the freedom of contract as a principle that determined the liberty of individuals to arrange their affairs by exercising the entitlement to enter into legal relationships with each other.[126] They are free to choose

[116] *Commission v Germany* (n 114) para 27.
[117] Case C-63/93 *Duff and Others* EU:C:1996:51.
[118] ibid para 30.
[119] Case C-177/90 *Kühn v Landwirtschaftskammer Weser-Ems* EU:C:1992:2.
[120] ibid para 17.
[121] Case T-125/96 *Boehringer v Council and Commission* EU:T:1999:302.
[122] ibid para 105.
[123] See, eg, Case C-707/18 *Amărăşti Land Investment* EU:C:2019:1136, para 29; Case T-873/16 *Groupe Canal+ v Commission* EU:T:2018:904, para 86.
[124] Case T-24/90 *Automec Srl v Commission* EU:T:1992:97, para 51.
[125] Case C-499/04 *Hans Werhof v Freeway Traffic Systems* EU:C:2006:168.
[126] ibid para 23. See also Case C-61/09 *Landkreis Bad Dürkheim* EU:C:2010:606, para 55; Case C-680/15 *Asklepios Kliniken* EU:C:2017:317, para 19.

with whom to form a binding arrangement and to decide on the types of obligations they are willing to undertake.

Such contractual capacity consists of several integral components. First, the principle of the freedom of contract envisages not just the ability to conclude a contract but also the freedom to decide against entering into one.[127] As held by the Court, an obligation to contract constitutes 'a substantial interference in the freedom to contract which economic operators, in principle, enjoy'.[128] Second, contracting parties are at liberty to determine the terms of a contract and amend contracts concluded by them.[129] As confirmed in *SNUA*,[130] the exercise of this right within the limits set by law represents an integral part of the freedom of contract.[131] It applies to 'the determination of consequences of a cancellation or breach of their obligations'[132] and the costs incurred by either contracting party.[133] Third, the freedom of contract encompasses the right to choose the law governing their legal relationships.[134] Apart from the right to contractual self-determination, the freedom of contract is framed by a range of responsibilities recognised in the case law. The Court acknowledged that once a contract was agreed, 'each contracting party [was] bound to honour the term of its contract and to perform its obligations thereunder'.[135] As a result, according to the Court, the 'full performance of a contract results, as a general rule, from discharge of the mutual obligations under the contract or from termination of that contract'.[136]

C. The Parameters of the Proportionality Assessment

Under the *Nold/Hauer* formula, the legitimacy of a restriction imposed on the general principles of the freedom to pursue economic activity, the right to property or the freedom of contract is contingent on the extent to which it constitutes 'disproportionate and intolerable interference'. This is often assessed based on two benchmarks: the degree of encroachment of a right and the presence of legislative discretion. It is worth considering these in detail.

[127] Opinion of AG Kokott in Case C-441/07 P *Commission v Alrosa* EU:C:2009:555, para 227.

[128] Case C-518/06 *Commission v Italy* EU:C:2009:270, para 66; Joined Cases C-215/96 and C-216/96 *Bagnasco* EU:C:1999:12, para 45; Case T-41/96 *Bayer AG v Commission* EU:T:2000:242, para 180.

[129] Case C-240/97 *Spain v Commission* EU:C:1999:479, para 99.

[130] Case C-69/97 *Commission v SNUA* EU:C:1999:204.

[131] ibid para 23.

[132] Case C-277/05 *Société thermale d'Eugénie-Les-Bains* EU:C:2007:440, para 28.

[133] Case C-437/04 *Commission v Belgium* EU:C:2007:178, para 51; Case C-707/18 *Amărăști Land Investment*, para 29.

[134] Case C-135/15 *Republik Griechenland v Grigorios Nikiforidis* EU:C:2016:774, para 42; Case C-184/12 *Unamar* EU:C:2013:663, para 49; Case C-381/98 *Ingmar GB Ltd v Eaton Leonard Technologies Inc* EU:C:2000:605, para 15.

[135] *Société thermale d'Eugénie-Les-Bains* (n 132) para 24.

[136] Case C-412/06 *Annelore Hamilton v Volksbank Filder* EU:C:2008:215, para 42.

i. Minor Effects or Substantially Negative Consequences

The Court tends to emphasise the limited effect of a measure on the exercise of individual rights and freedoms. In *Schräder*,[137] it held that the co-responsibility levy system employed in the cereal sector caused 'minor inconveniences' for cereal producers.[138] For this reason, the Court continued that a requirement that had only 'a marginal effect' upon their freedom to pursue an occupation could not impinge upon the very substance of that right.[139] In a similar vein, in *SAM Schiffahrt*,[140] the Court found that the system of contribution to scrapping funds in the inland waterways sector was not disproportionate and did not cause intolerable interference impairing the substance of the right to property and the freedom to pursue a trade or business, for it was only appropriate and beneficial for the sector, but also 'in any event relatively modest'.[141] Such characterisation is equally evident in *Keller*,[142] where the Court ruled that the (then) Community's provision on wine labelling in no way impinged upon the substance of the freedom to pursue economic activity based on the fact that '[it only placed] certain restrictions within a clearly defined sphere on the business activity of the traders'.[143]

The Court's reasoning in this line of case law imparts significance to the degree of encroachment when assessing the compatibility of interference with an individual right. The probability of infringement increases with the rise in the intensity of interference. This reflects the essence of the proportionality requirement: the greater the interference, the higher the likelihood of a measure causing 'a disproportionate and intolerable impairment of the substance of [a right]'. Nevertheless, it appears that the degree of encroachment with the substance or the exercise of a right is not always inherently decisive in the assessment process but is contingent on the nature of the objective justification. This follows from *Metallurgiki Halyps*,[144] where the Court held that 'the fact that the restrictions on production necessitated by the economic situation might affect the profitability and *very existence* of certain undertakings [could not] be considered to be an infringement of the right to property' (emphasis added).[145] As such, these undertakings could not invoke this right against the extension of the (then) Community's quota system in the steel industry 'to evade the constraints imposed upon the entire European steel industry'.[146] Along the same lines, in *Affish*,[147] the Court stated that 'the importance

[137] *Hermann Schräder* (n 67).
[138] ibid para 18.
[139] ibid.
[140] *SAM Schiffahrt* (n 71).
[141] ibid para 74.
[142] Case C-234/85 *Keller* EU:C:1986:377.
[143] ibid para 9.
[144] Case 258/81 *Metallurgiki Halyps AE v Commission* EU:C:1982:422.
[145] ibid para 13.
[146] ibid.
[147] Case C-183/95 *Affish* EU:C:1997:373.

of the objectives pursued [might] justify restrictions which [had] adverse consequences, and even substantial adverse consequences, for certain traders'.[148]

However, neither ruling addressed the correlation between these findings and the *Nold/Hauer* formula. It remains questionable how they are intended to fit within the parameters of the proportionality assessment and, more importantly, the notion of the 'untouchable' substance of a right. The main issue lies in the expansive language used by the Court. It is true that, certain disadvantageous repercussions can indeed be aligned with the proportionality assessment depending on the nature of a measure. This finds support in *Fedesa*,[149] where having first considered the appropriateness and necessity of the (then) Community's measure prohibiting the use of certain hormonal substances in livestock farming, the Court found it to justify 'even substantial negative financial consequences for certain traders'.[150] However, unlike *Fedesa*, in *Metallurgiki Halyps* and *Affish*, the Court not only referred to the financial ramifications but also adopted a broader perspective with general references to the 'very existence' of an undertaking and 'substantial adverse consequences' incurred by it. This appears to supersede any proportionality assessment by attaching legitimacy to a measure with the implications that the *Hauer* formula is, in effect, supposed to avert.

ii. The Hauer *Formula and the Margin of Appreciation*

Another factor that qualifies the *Nold/Hauer* formula is the margin of discretion assigned to the Union's legislature. Generally, a margin of discretion refers to the authority enjoyed by decision-makers to choose the means to attain the identified ends.[151] From the outset, the Court attributed a 'broad' (also referred to as 'wide')[152] form of discretion to the Union's institutions in areas in which complex economic or socio-economic evaluations are needed.[153] This concept of discretion is prominently featured in the development of the non-contractual liability of the Union's institutions under Article 340 TFEU. In *Bayerische NHL*,[154] the Court held that in a legislative field such as the common agricultural policy that presupposed wider discretion, the (then) Community's institutions did not incur liability unless they 'manifestly and gravely disregarded the limits on the exercise of its powers'.[155] As later clarified in *Bergadorm*,[156] the notion of discretion

[148] ibid para 42. See also *Dorsch Consult Ingenieurgesellschaft* (n 85) para 87.

[149] Case C-331/88 *Fedesa* EU:C:1990:391.

[150] ibid para 17.

[151] J Mendes, 'Bounded Discretion in EU Law: A Limited Judicial Paradigm in a Changing EU' (2017) 80 *Modern Law Review* 443, 462.

[152] *Spain and Finland* (n 101) para 56; *FIAMM* (n 108) para 174.

[153] *ABNA and Others* (n 99) para 69.

[154] Joined Cases 83 and 94/76, 4, 15 and 40/77 *Bayerische HNL v Council and Commission* EU:C:1978:113.

[155] ibid para 6.

[156] Case C-352/98 P *Bergaderm and Goupil v Commission* EU:C:2000:361.

forms the integral component of the doctrines of institutional and state liability.[157] This is shown in the fact that the conditions for incurring liability vary depending on the degree of discretion: while the availability of wider discretion triggers the *Bayerische NHL* threshold, the instances of considerably reduced or no discretion only require a mere infringement of Union law.[158]

The concept of wider institutional discretion also applies in the context of general principles of law protecting fundamental rights. This stems from *Leukhardt*,[159] where the (then) Community's method of calculating milk production quotas was challenged for its alleged incompatibility with the right to property and the right to pursue an occupation. The Court rejected this claim with a brief reasoning. It only held that 'when a situation necessitate[d] the evaluation of a complex economic situation, as [was] the case concerning the common agricultural policy, the Community legislature enjoy[ed] a wide discretion as to the nature and scope of the measures to be taken'.[160] It then went on to conclude that the limits of such discretion were not exceeded.[161] This reasoning marked a departure from the *Nold/Hauer* formula,[162] for the Court only briefly focused on whether the (then) Community's legislature, in adopting the impugned measure, observed the boundaries of the margin of appreciation attributed to it. Some reconciliation of these two analytical methods was provided in *SAFA*.[163] There, the Court held that the exercise of discretion by the Council and Commission over the common organisation of the market in oils and fats placed restrictions on traders' right to carry on their economic activities freely, but it could not be regarded as disproportionate interference impinging upon its very substance.[164] Although this finding seems to integrate the concept of discretion with the prerequisites of the *Nold/Hauer* formula, such a correlation is not without its dilemmas. At first glance, this may seem to pertain to the difficulty in locating the place of the concept of discretion within the framework of proportionality inquiry. However, such an attempt risks altering the normative role played by the proportionality principle in the protection of fundamental rights. It may lead to the outcome where the proportionality consideration is submitted to the institutional discretion as opposed to it controlling the limits of such discretion in the first place.

A criticism along these lines was directed towards the Court's approach in *Germany v Council*,[165] where the issue related to the compliance with the right to property and the freedom to pursue economic activity of the (then) Community's measure that set up the common organisation of banana markets through the

[157] ibid para 43.
[158] ibid para 44.
[159] Case 113/88 *Karl Leukhardt v Hauptzollamt Reutlingen* EU:C:1989:114.
[160] ibid para 20.
[161] ibid.
[162] HK Nielsen, 'The Protection of Fundamental Rights in the Law of the European Union' (1994) 63 *Nordic Journal of International Law* 213, 236.
[163] Case C-359/89 *SAFA Srl v Amministrazione delle finanze dello Stato* EU:C:1991:145.
[164] ibid para 22.
[165] Case C-280/93 *Germany v Council (Bananas)* EU:C:1994:367.

introduction of a tariff quota. Despite the reference to the *Nold/Hauer* formula, the Court considered the principle of proportionality separately by framing it around the broad margin of discretion enjoyed by the (then) Community's legislature in the agricultural sector. It declared that 'the lawfulness of a measure adopted in that sphere [could] be affected only if the measure [was] manifestly inappropriate having regard to the objective which [was pursued]'.[166] More controversially, it also added that 'while other means for achieving the desired result were indeed conceivable, [it could not] substitute its assessment for that of the Council as to the appropriateness or otherwise of the measures adopted by the Community legislature if those measures [had] not been proved to be manifestly inappropriate for achieving the objective pursued'.[167] This finding is problematic because it implies a higher burden of proof for the constitutionality review at the Union level.[168] It becomes the duty of the right holder to demonstrate the superiority of alternative methods.[169] As the paucity of successful claims suggests, this is not an easy challenge to overcome.[170] While the underlying rationale behind this approach is to attenuate hurdles to the legislative decision-making process,[171] granting unrestricted authority to the Union's legislature is contentious from the perspective of human rights protection. Given the fundamental nature of such protection, it does not suffice to merely address the (manifest) inappropriateness of a measure. It is paramount to establish reasonable proportionality between the necessity of a measure and the enjoyment of the vested individual rights.[172] Otherwise, the manifestly inappropriate test sets a high threshold of legality,[173] which in practice translates to a limited judicial review of the Union's economic policy choices.[174] This stands at odds with the intrinsic role attached to the proportionality principle to prevent excessive intrusion into individual rights by containing the exercise of public power.[175]

[166] ibid para 90.

[167] ibid para 94.

[168] This differs, for instance, from German law, where no margin of discretion is attributed to the legislature unless it is explicitly provided by law. See in this regard G Nolte, 'General Principles of German and European Administrative Law: A Comparison in Historical Perspective' (1994) 57 *Modern Law Review* 191, 197. Furthermore, the Court tends to consider the benchmarks of the proportionality assessment *in abstracto* without applying them *in concreto*. This was the complaint raised in Case T-521/93 *Atlanta and Others v Council and Commission* EU:T:1996:184. It is also reflected in the series of preliminary references made by German courts in the aftermath of *Bananas* ruling. See Case C-68/95 *T. Port v Bundesanstalt für Landwirtschaft und Ernährung* EU:C:1996:452.

[169] C Schmid, 'Multi-level Constitutionalism and Constitutional Conflicts Interconnecting the National, European and International Economic Constitutions in the Banana Dispute' (PhD thesis, European University Institute, 2001), 126.

[170] Only on a few occasions were measures found to be 'manifestly inappropriate'. See, eg *ABNA and Others* (n 99) paras 80–84.

[171] *Bayerische HNL* (n 154) para 5.

[172] U Everling, 'Will Europe Slip on Bananas? The Bananas Judgment of the Court of Justice and National Courts' (1996) 33 *Common Market Law Review* 401, 417.

[173] W Sauter, 'Proportionality in EU Law: A Balancing Act?' (2013) 15 *Cambridge Yearbook of European Legal Studies* 439, 450.

[174] T Tridimas, 'The Principle of Proportionality in Community Law: From the Rule of Law to Market Integration' (1996) 31 *Irish Jurist* 83, 87.

[175] Schmid (n 169) 127.

II. General Principles Conditioning Private Autonomy

As liberal concepts, the rights and freedoms expressing the ideals of private autonomy encapsulate two interrelated elements. On the one hand, they are generally permeated by the respect and recognition of individuals' entitlement to determine their notion of good and to act upon it.[176] Its perimeters are framed by traditional private law categories such as contract, property and tort.[177] This encompasses the ability to own and dispose of tangible and intangible assets or voluntarily enter into legally binding arrangements and define their terms. On the other hand, this category of general principles of law symbolises individual liberty of economic action free from regulation and coercion.[178] This presupposes an effective enforcement mechanism that secures a private domain against the interference of others.[179] However, in the Union's legal system, these rights and freedoms are not unfettered; their exercise is limited or conditioned by other constitutional guarantees. Among them is the general principle of equality that underwent a metamorphosis from a catalyst of market integration to a self-standing human right.[180]

First confined to sex and nationality with the subsequent expansion to new grounds such as age, disability, race and ethnic origin, the principle of equality in EU law finds its normative purpose in facilitating equal economic and social participation.[181] It is generally construed to promote 'social justice' understood in the narrow sense of not incorporating the traditional redistributive goals. Micklitz characterises it as a model that ensures 'justice through access' or 'access justice'.[182] It is guided by the philosophy of placing individuals in a position of being equipped with the necessary set of rights 'to participate and reap the benefits of the internal market' and the most competitive economy fostered by it.[183] The 'access justice' model, according to Micklitz, contains two prongs: first, it requires all market participants to have a fair and realistic chance to enter the market, consume its products and use its services; and second, it relates to the degree of justice individuals gain after acquiring equal access.[184] This resonates with what Somek refers to as 'the principle of equality of opportunity' –

[176] T Gutmann, 'Some Preliminary Remarks on a Liberal Theory of Contract' (2013) 76 *Law and Contemporary Problems* 39, 40.

[177] FA Hayek, *The Constitution of Liberty* (London, Routledge & Kegan Paul, 1963) 216.

[178] D Leczykiewicz, 'Horizontal Effect of Fundamental Rights: In Search of Social Justice or Private Autonomy in EU Law?' in U Bernitz, X Groussot and F Schulyok (eds), *General Principles of EU Law and European Private Law* (Alphen aan den Rijn, Kluwer Law International, 2013) 172.

[179] Hayek (n 177) 19.

[180] R Xenidis, 'Transforming EU Equality Law? On Disruptive Narratives and False Dichotomies' (2019) 38 *Yearbook of European Law* 2, 4.

[181] ibid 27.

[182] HW Micklitz, 'Social Justice and Access Justice in Private Law' (2011) 2 *EUI Working Papers LAW* 1, 13.

[183] ibid para 22.

[184] ibid para 23.

a better-suited medium for reconciling the concept of solidarity and competitiveness.[185] According to him, the Union's anti-discrimination law espouses this principle to afford protection to those who suffer disadvantages inflicted by the conduct of private actors or the State for their certain socially salient characteristics.[186]

Equality is a dynamic legal phenomenon that has acquired a multifaceted character in Union law. At one end, it underpins the functioning of the Treaty's free movement provisions. As is well known, they incorporate the prohibition of discrimination on grounds of nationality (or origin) that 'serve[s] the process of economic integration through the elimination of unjustified differential treatment among the factors of production of the internal market'.[187] At the other end, the concept of equality has acquired a social dimension. It is manifested in the general principle of equal treatment on grounds of sex, age and nationality in a general sense and the Union's corpus of anti-discrimination legislation adopted under Article 19 TFEU.[188] The normative reach of this general principle of law is broadly construed in the case law. As a horizontally applicable norm, it inevitably comes into conflict with the countervailing general principles of law that express the ideals of private autonomy. While its horizontality remains fragmented and manifold, the social value inherent in the Union's concept of equality can condition the extent to which private autonomy can be exercised within the boundaries of the Union's legal order.

A. The Market-Driven Principle of Non-discrimination on Grounds of Nationality

The principle of equal treatment on grounds of nationality is one of the keystones of the European integration process.[189] It finds its broad expression in Article 18 TFEU, which prohibits 'within the scope of application of the Treaties' any discrimination on grounds of nationality.[190] It is complemented by the specific enunciation of this

[185] A Somek, *Engineering Equality: An Essay on European Anti-Discrimination Law* (Oxford, Oxford University Press, 2011) 3.

[186] ibid, 4.

[187] E Muir, 'Pursuing Equality in the EU' in D Chalmers and A Arnull (eds), *The Oxford Handbook of European Union Law* (Oxford, Oxford University Press, 2015) 6.

[188] See, eg, Council Directive 2004/113/EC of 13 December 2004 implementing the principle of equal treatment between men and women in the access to and supply of goods and services [2004] OJ L373/37; Council Directive 2000/78/EC of 27 November 2000 establishing a general framework for equal treatment in employment and occupation [2000] OJ L303/16; Council Directive 2000/ 78/EC of 27 November 2000 establishing a general framework for equal treatment in employment and occupation [2000] OJ L303/16; Council Directive 2000/43/EC of 29 June 2000 implementing the principle of equal treatment between persons irrespective of racial or ethnic origin [2000] OJ L180/22.

[189] Tridimas (n 174) 76.

[190] See, eg, Case C-247/17 *Denis Raugevicius* EU:C:2018:898, para 44; Case C-22/18 *TopFit and Daniele Biffi v Deutscher Leichtathletikverband e.V* EU:C:2019:497, para 29.

principle in the Treaty's provisions on the free movement of workers, establishment and services.[191] At the outset, a conventional view would confine the scope of this principle to the exercise of state power in line with the traditional public/private divide.[192] Unlike public law, the realm of private law is commonly associated with the positive autonomy of natural and legal persons,[193] where the reasons for their actions are free from public inquiry.[194] However, the conceptual distinction between public and private spheres became blurred with the recognition of the horizontal applicability of the Treaty's free movement provisions,[195] which developed in two strands.

i. Private Actors with a Regulatory Power

The early signs of horizontality attached to the principle of non-discrimination on grounds of nationality first appeared in *Walrave*,[196] where the issue concerned the possible invocation of Articles 18, 45 and 56 TFEU against the rules adopted by the International Cycling Union. The Court found that the prohibition of discrimination on grounds of nationality, enshrined in these provisions, not only applied to the action of public authorities 'but extend[ed] likewise to rules of any other nature aimed at regulating in a collective manner gainful employment and the provision for services'.[197] This line of reasoning was subsequently confirmed and extended to other forms of collective regulation, including international and regional sports associations,[198] professional associations,[199] private law associations,[200] trade unions[201] and educational institutions.[202] The underlying rationale is influenced by the effet utile argument. The obligation not to

[191] Case C-581/18 *TÜV Rheinland LGA Products and Allianz* EU:C:2020:453, paras 28–33.

[192] For more on this, see, eg, M Mataija, *Private Regulation and the Internal Market: Sports, Legal Services, and Standard Setting in EU Economic Law* (Oxford, Oxford University Press, 2016); JJ Kuipers, *EU Law and Private International Law: The Interrelationship in Contractual Obligations* (Leiden, Martinus Nijhoff Publishers, 2012).

[193] O Cherednychenko, 'Rediscovering the Public/Private Divide in EU Private Law' (2019) 26 *European Law Journal* 27, 27.

[194] S Walkila, *Horizontal Effect of Fundamental Rights in EU Law* (Groningen, Europa Law Publishing, 2015), 132.

[195] M Mataija, 'The Public–Private Distinction, Autonomy and Free Movement: Unpacking the Assumptions' (2013) 13 *Global Jurist* 23, 30; V Hatzopoulos, *Regulating Services in the European Union* (Oxford, Oxford University Press, 2012) 302.

[196] Case C-36/74 *Walrave and LJN Koch v Association Union cycliste internationale* EU:C:1974:140.

[197] ibid para 17. This finding was reiterated by the Court in Case 13/76 *Gaetano Donà v Mario Mantero* EU:C:1976:115, para 17; Case C-415/93 *Union royale belge des sociétés de football association ASBL v Jean-Marc Bosman* EU:C:1995:463, para 82.

[198] Case C-325/08 *Olympique Lyonnais v Olivier Bernard and Newcastle* EU:C:2010:143; Case C-176/96 *Jyri Lehtonen and Castors Canada Dry Namur-Braine ASBL* EU:C:2000:201.

[199] See, eg, Case C-309/99 *Wouters and Others* EU:C:2002:98.

[200] See, eg, Case C-171/11 *Fra.bo SpA v Deutsche Vereinigung des Gas- und Wasserfaches eV (DVGW)* EU:C:2012:453.

[201] See, eg, Case C-438/05 *International Transport Workers' Federation and Finnish Seamen's Union v Viking Line ABP and OÜ Viking Line Eesti* EU:C:2007:772; Case C-341/05 *Laval un Partneri Ltd v Svenska Byggnadsarbetareförbundet* EU:C:2007:809.

[202] See, eg, Case C-94/07 *Raccanelli* EU:C:2008:425.

discriminate on grounds of nationality applies to the conduct of private actors with regulatory powers that is not 'unlike State action'.[203] This ensures that the abolition of barriers to free movement is not '[neutralised] by obstacles resulting from the exercise of their legal autonomy by associations or organizations which do not come under public law'.[204]

ii. Purely Horizontal Situations

The horizontal effect of the principle of non-discrimination on grounds of nationality is not constricted to private actors with regulatory powers. *Angonese* broadened the extent to which individuals can be bound by Article 18 TFEU and the Treaty's free movement provisions.[205] In this case, The Court was asked to rule on the compatibility with Article 45 TFEU of the refusal by a private bank to consider an application for employment without a certificate of bilingualism issued by the local public authorities. The Court found that the prohibition of discrimination on grounds of nationality under Article 45 TFEU applied equally to 'all agreements intended to regulate paid labour collectively, as well as to contracts between individuals'.[206] According to the Court, this was not called into question by the wording of this provision being formally addressed to Member States.[207] As subsequently confirmed in *Raccanelli* and *Erny*,[208] this finding represents a critical step in shaping the scope of the general principle of non-discrimination on grounds of nationality. By adding an intersubjective dimension to this principle,[209] *Angonese* conceptually widened its reach, for it affirmed that the concept of private autonomy was not necessarily immune from Union law. In doing so, *Angonese* not only shifted the hermeneutical lens established in *Walrave* but also transcended the boundaries set over the scope of the Treaty's provisions on the free movement of goods. In *Sapod Audic*,[210] the Court held that 'a contractual provision [could not] be regarded as a barrier to trade for the purposes of [Article 34 TFEU]' since it was not imposed by a Member State but was agreed between individuals.[211] *Sapod Audic* unequivocally confirmed the previous case law that only measures taken by Member States are caught by Article 34 TFEU.[212] *Angonese* and *Sapod Audic*

[203] JB Cruz, 'Free Movement and Private Autonomy' (1999) 24 *European Law Review* 603, 618.
[204] *Walrave* (n 196) para 18.
[205] Case C-281/98 *Roman Angonese v Cassa di Risparmio di Bolzano SpA* EU:C:2000:296.
[206] ibid para 35.
[207] ibid.
[208] Case C-94/07 *Andrea Raccanelli v Max-Planck-Gesellschaft zur Förderung der Wissenschaften eV* EU:C:2008:425; Case C-172/11 *Georges Erny v Daimler AG – Werk Wörth* EU:C:2014:157.
[209] Walkila (n 194) 132.
[210] Case C-159/00 *Sapod Audic v Eco-Emballages SA* EU:C:2002:343.
[211] ibid para 74.
[212] See, eg, Case C-325/00 *Commission v Germany* EU:C:2002:174, paras 14–21; Case 311/85 *VVR v Sociale Dienst van de Plaatselijke en Gewestelijke Overheidsdiensten* EU:C:1987:418, para 30; Joined Cases 177 and 178/82 *Criminal Proceedings against Jan van de Haar and Kaveka de Meern* EU:C:1984:144, para 12.

substantively differ in terms of the delimitation of private autonomy. While private employers exercising their contractual discretion are under the obligation not to discriminate on grounds of nationality, the contractual preferences of, for instance, a seller of goods are not subject to a similar requirement. Notwithstanding this apparent dissonance, *Angonese* and *Sapod Audic* can be construed to stem from the same logic that does not discard the principle of private autonomy but is informed by the salience of individual liberty for autonomous economic action.

iii. The Factor of Independent Decision-Making

A common element that seems to weave through the case law on the horizontal application of the Union's primary law is the capacity of a private body to exert authority over others.[213] What is decisive in this context is whether a private actor, either a natural or legal person, is being forced to accept certain conditions imposed by a private body and whether there are viable ways to avoid them by exercising independent decision-making. This is evident in *Ferlini*, where the Court found that Article 18 TFEU bound a group of healthcare providers for they imposed on individuals conditions that adversely affected the exercise of the freedoms of movement.[214] The deciding factor was that the individuals would have no recourse but to accept the conditions imposed on them.[215] This is also clear from *Fra.bo*, where the Court established the applicability of Article 34 TFEU to a private standardisation body by looking at whether the certification offered by it was the only available procedure or whether there were other alternative ways to obtain confirmation of compliance with a national technical standard. As other available procedures were found to be 'of little or no practical use',[216] Article 34 TFEU was deemed applicable since manufacturers from other Member States were placed in a position in which it was impossible to enter the national market unless they complied with the conditions imposed by the private standardisation body.[217]

The logic underlying the Court's approach is encapsulated by AG Maduro in *Viking*, where he defined the scope of the Treaty's free movement provisions as extending to 'private action that, by virtue of its general effect on the holders of rights to freedom of movement, [was] capable of restricting them from exercising those rights, by raising an obstacle that they [could not] reasonably circumvent'.[218] In the absence of regulatory powers held by private actors, an impediment to free

[213] S de Vries and R van Mastrigt, 'The Horizontal Direct Effect of the Four Freedoms: From a Hodgepodge of Cases to a Seamless Web of Judicial Protection in the EU Single Market?' in U Bernitz, X Groussot and F Schulyok (eds), *General Principles of EU Law and European Private Law* (Alphen aan den Rijn, Kluwer, 2013), 264.

[214] Case C-411/98 *Angelo Ferlini v Centre hospitalier de Luxembourg* EU:C:2000:530, para 50.

[215] T Papadopoulos, *EU Law and the Harmonization of Takeovers in the Internal Market* (Alphen aan den Rijn, Kluwer Law International, 2010) 167.

[216] Case C-171/11 *Fra.bo* EU:C:2012:176, para 29.

[217] Opinion of AG Trstenjak in ibid, para 50.

[218] Opinion of AG Maduro in Case C-438/05 *Viking* EU:C:2007:29, para 48.

movement in the form of discriminatory treatment on grounds of nationality may not arise in private relationships. Those affected by unequal conditions imposed by a private actor are not obligated to accept them and can obviate them by exercising their discretion to opt for other available possibilities or opportunities in the market. The reasoning along these lines pervades *Sapod Audic* and traditionally applies to contractual relationships, the foundation of which lies in the guarantee of the freedom to decide whether and under what conditions to undertake contractual obligations. Nonetheless, this freedom is not intrinsic to all private relationships due to the non-regulatory power imbalance existing among private actors. Two instances can be distinguished from the case law.

First, there is an asymmetry when a private actor holds a dominant position in the market. Its market strategies or tactics can impair free and fair competition by excluding its direct rivals or new entrants from the market. However, this matter would not fall within the ambit of the principle of non-discrimination enshrined in the Treaty's free movement provisions; instead, it is governed by the Treaty's provisions on competition. The line drawn by the Court between the respective spheres of application of these provisions is often seen as a factor to object to the horizontality of the Treaty's free movement provisions.[219] Second, interparty imbalance that diminishes the ability to exercise independent decision-making effectively can also be attributed to employment relationships traditionally involving parties with uneven bargaining positions. This appears to be the rationale behind *Angonese*, whereby private employers, similar to public ones, are obliged when exercising contractual discretion not to discriminate on grounds of nationality in relation to access to or conditions of employment. Such an obligation does not seem unreasonable if the focus is placed on employees' ability to exercise independent decision-making. While they may be free, in theory, to decide whether or not to enter into employment relationships and what conditions of employment to undertake, the effective exercise of such discretion is often not feasible in reality.[220] Securing alternative employment or changing professional qualifications is far more complex than choosing alternative goods or services available in the market.[221] The termination of employment alone is likely to lead to more far-reaching consequences for employees than for employers. Securing a new place of employment can require full-scale relocation for an employee, which is often challenging given their individual or family circumstances.[222] This can have a dissuading effect where the exercise of contractual discretion does not suffice to circumvent disadvantageous terms imposed in an employment relationship.[223] This

[219] PC de Sousa, 'Horizontal Expressions of Vertical Desires: Horizontal Effect and the Scope of the EU Fundamental Freedoms' (2013) 2 *Cambridge Journal of International and Comparative Law* 479, 486.

[220] R Babayev, 'Contractual Discretion and the Limits of Free Movement Law' (2015) 23 *European Review Private Law* 875, 885.

[221] Opinion of AG Maduro in *Viking* (n 218) para 47.

[222] T Donaldson, *Corporations and Morality* (Englewood Cliffs, NJ, Prentice Hall, 1982) 137.

[223] This could also be relevant as regards consumers. See the analysis in D Wyatt, 'Horizontal Effect of Fundamental Freedoms and the Right to Equality after *Viking* and *Mangold*, and the Implications for

conclusion resonates with the Court's characterisation of employees as 'the weaker party in the employment relationship', which prompts the need to prevent employers from imposing restrictions on their rights.[224] Employees may be dissuaded from explicitly claiming their rights vis-a-vis employers, where doing so may expose them to measures affecting their employment relationships in a manner that is detrimental to them.[225]

B. The Socially Driven Principle of Equality

The genesis of the Union's principle of equality began with its normative basis firmly entrenched in the idea of market integration. The entry into force of the Maastricht and Amsterdam Treaties brought a new social dimension to the normative construction of this principle that transcends its market logic.[226] The concept of equality has evolved into a more overarching framework that is endowed with the 'transformative' function of pursuing 'inter-personal equality' in the Union, detached from the objective of eliminating borders and reducing regulatory friction in the internal market.[227] This novel normative framework has emerged from the expansion of the scope of the principle of non-discrimination beyond sex and nationality to new grounds such as age, disability, sexual orientation, religion and racial or ethnic origin.[228] This concept of equality driven by social ideals permeates the traditional domain of private interactions, though the parameters of its applicability in this setting are far from settled.

i. Mangold *et al.: First Steps in the Process*

The first signs of the horizontal reach of the novel concept of equality appeared in *Mangold*,[229] where a challenge was brought pursuant to the Employment Equality Framework Directive in a private employment dispute against the national law that authorised the conclusion of fixed-term contracts with employees aged over 52.[230] However, the applicability of this secondary legislation was doubtful for the horizontal nature of the dispute and the period

Community Competence' (2008) 4 *Croatian Yearbook of European Law and Policy* 1, 48. According to the author, private operators should also be under the obligation not to depart from their normal terms and conditions of sale with respect to non-nationals or non-residents, unless it is part of normal market behaviour.

[224] See, eg, Joined Cases C-397/01 to C-403/01 *Bernhard Pfeiffer and Others v Deutsches Rotes Kreuz* EU:C:2004:584, para 82; Case C-429/09 *Günter Fuß v Stadt Halle* EU:C:2010:717, para 80.

[225] See, eg, Case C-55/18 *CCOO v Deutsche Bank* EU:C:2019:402, para 45; Case C-684/16 *Max-Planck-Gesellschaft zur Förderung der Wissenschaften eV v Tetsuji Shimizu* EU:C:2018:874, para 41.

[226] Tridimas (n 174) 60.

[227] Muir (n 187) 7.

[228] Xenidis (n 180) 9.

[229] Case C-144/04 *Werner Mangold v Rüdiger Helm* EU:C:2005:709.

[230] Council Directive 2000/78/EC of 27 November 2000 establishing a general framework for equal treatment in employment and occupation [2000] OJ L303/16.

remaining for its transposition. The Court approached this by finding that the Framework Directive did not lay down the principle of equal treatment in the field of employment and occupation but merely enshrined a general framework for combating discrimination on grounds of religion or belief, disability, age and sexual orientation. The Court then held that the principle of non-discrimination on grounds of age constituted a general principle of Union law, with its sources found 'in various international instruments and in the constitutional traditions common to the Member States'.[231] This meant that the observance of this principle could not be conditional upon the expiry of the transposition period envisaged for directives. The Court concluded that it was the responsibility of the national court to ensure the full effectiveness of this principle and legal protection for individuals derived from Union law by 'setting aside any provision of [conflicting national law]'.[232] The immediate effect of this finding was that a private employer could not invoke the conflicting national law in a dispute with its employees.

Mangold received extensive criticism,[233] which the Court sought to clarify in the subsequent ruling of *Kücükdeveci*.[234] This case also related to a private employment dispute that arose over a notice period for dismissal. According to the applicable national law, this period was calculated based on the length of employment with a proviso that any period prior to the employee's twenty-fifth year of age was disregarded. This law was challenged by an employee who contested her dismissal by a private employer for setting a shorter notice period despite being employed for 10 years since the age of 18. As the time for the transposition of the Framework Directive had already expired, the referred national court queried whether this secondary legislation or the general principle of non-discrimination on grounds of age pursuant to *Mangold* was to serve as a basis for the examination of the impugned national law. The Court addressed this by finding that 'the general principle … prohibiting all discrimination on grounds of age, as given expression in Directive 2000/78' was to be the required point of reference for the assessment.[235] This principle, as clarified by the Court, applied only within the scope of Union law, which was triggered by the contested matter being governed by the Framework Directive.[236] Having established the difference in treatment on grounds of age, the Court then found that the general principle expressed in the Framework Directive must be interpreted as precluding the impugned national

[231] *Mangold* (n 229) para 74.
[232] ibid para 77.
[233] See, eg, Opinion of AG Sharpston in C-427/06 *Bartsch* EU:C:2008:297, para 31; Opinion of AG Mazák in *Félix Palacios de la Villa v Cortefiel Servicios SA* (n 1) paras 87–97; Opinion of AG Geelhoed in Case C-13/05 *Chacón Navas* EU:C:2006:184, paras 46–56. See also T Papadopoulos, 'Criticising the Horizontal Direct Effect of the EU General Principle of Equality' (2011) 4 *European Human Rights Law Review* 438; A Dashwood, 'From *Van Duyn* to *Mangold* via *Marshall*: Reducing Direct Effect to Absurdity?' (2007) 9 *Cambridge Yearbook of European Legal Studies* 81, 81.
[234] Case C-555/07 *Seda Kücükdeveci v Swedex GmbH & Co* EU:C:2010:21.
[235] ibid para 27.
[236] ibid para 25.

law. While it acknowledged the lack of horizontal applicability of directives and the limits to the duty of consistent interpretation, neither was deemed material. The Court reiterated that the full effectiveness of Union law and individuals' legal protection derived from it required the national law to be disapplied.[237] This appeared to all but confirm the horizontal direct effect of the general principle of non-discrimination on grounds of age. The Court's reference to Article 21 of the Charter, in turn, foreshadowed the attribution to it of a similar legal capacity in the subsequent case law.[238]

While *Kücükdeveci* affirmed the applicability of the general principle of non-discrimination on grounds of age to private relationships, *Dansk Industri* elucidated the extent of its normative reach in this setting.[239] There, the issue concerned a dispute that arose from an employee seeking a severance allowance, which a private employer refused to grant based on the national law that barred the entitlement to it by those eligible for an old-age pension. As this national law was already declared incompatible with the Framework Directive, the national court sought clarification over its ramifications in the context of a private dispute. Given the limits to the horizontal applicability of directives, it first queried whether the general principle of non-discrimination on grounds of age had to be interpreted as precluding a private employer from invoking the contested national law. Second, the national court asked whether this principle had to be weighed against the principles of legal certainty and legitimate expectations. The Court found that the general principle of non-discrimination on grounds of age was applicable based on the subject matter of the national law being covered by the Framework Directive.[240] The Court then held that '[this principle] confer[red] on private persons an individual right which they [might] invoke as such' and it required national courts to disapply national law if it could not be consistently interpreted in line with Union law.[241] In this respect, the Court continued that a national court could not rely on the principles of legal certainty and legal expectations to enforce the conflicting national law,[242] as this would limit the effect of its interpretation of the law and deny individuals the benefits it entailed.[243]

The doctrine introduced in *Mangold* and subsequently confirmed in *Kücükdeveci* and *Dansk Industri* substantively transformed the outer boundaries of Union law by (re)conceptualising the place and function of general principles of law. This line of case law effectively confirmed the direct horizontal effect of the general principle of equality. This is revolutionary on two accounts. On the

[237] ibid para 51.

[238] See, eg, Case C-193/17 *Cresco Investigation v Markus Achatzi* EU:C:2019:43, para 77; Case C-414/16 *Vera Egenberger v Evangelisches Werk für Diakonie und Entwicklung* EU:C:2018:257, para 81.

[239] Case C-441/14 *Dansk Industri (DI), Acting on Behalf of Ajos A/S v Estate of Karsten Eigil Rasmussen* EU:C:2016:278.

[240] ibid para 25.

[241] ibid para 36.

[242] ibid para 43.

[243] ibid para 41.

one hand, a horizontal direct effect was attributed to the unwritten expression of a norm that was not enshrined in the Treaties, unlike the principles of non-discrimination on grounds of nationality and sex. On the other hand, this form of horizontal applicability distorted the traditional understanding of general principles of law as a means to protect individuals against state actions.[244] Horizontality assigned to the principle of non-discrimination on grounds of age is likely to extend to other grounds explicitly mentioned in Article 19 TFEU. While the Court has not yet ruled on this point, it would be illogical if other grounds were treated differently, for it would lead to one aspect of the right to non-discrimination being privileged over its other aspects.[245] As such, a more substantive question concerns the extent to which the general principle of non-discrimination has a binding effect in private relationships. Setting the perimeters of its horizontal direct effect is of constitutional significance since, by its construct, it permeates the traditional divide separating the public and private spheres.[246] The unqualified extension of moral standards from the realm of the former to that of the latter defies the very notion of subjective autonomy that underpins the behaviour of private actors.[247]

ii. The Horizontality Criterion: 'Within the Scope of Union Law'

Despite the paucity of case law, it is possible to distinguish specific patterns in the judicial treatment of horizontality attributed to general principles of law. First, such normative capacity is confined to situations that fall within the scope of Union law. In *Kücükdeveci*, the Court explicitly found that 'for the principle of non-discrimination on grounds of age to apply in a case … [it] must fall within the scope of European Union law'.[248] However, it is unclear how this requirement needs to be assessed. A determinant factor appears to be some element that links a factual situation to Union law.[249] It effectively operates as a trigger for the application of general principles of law, without which they are inoperable in both vertical and horizontal settings. As norms of 'second order in nature', the capacity of general principles of law to produce a legal effect is contingent on their pre-activation by 'some first order provision of Union law'.[250] While the preceding case

[244] M de Mol, 'The Novel Approach of the CJEU on the Horizontal Direct Effect of the EU Principle of Non-Discrimination: (Unbridled) Expansionism of EU Law?' (2011) 18 *Maastricht Journal of European and Comparative Law* 109, 119.
[245] S Peers, 'Supremacy, Equality and Human Rights: Comment on *Kucukdeveci* (C-555/07)' (2010) 35 *European Law Review* 849, 856. See also, Case C-356/21 *J.K. v TP S.A.* EU:C:2023:9, para 77.
[246] Walkila (n 194) 133.
[247] G Sommeregger, 'The Horizontalization of Equality: The German Attempt to Promote Non-discrimination in the Private Sphere via Legislation' in A Sajó and R Uitz (eds), *The Constitution in Private Relations: Expanding Constitutionalism* (Utrecht, Eleven International Publishing, 2005) 48.
[248] *Kücükdeveci* (n 234) para 23; *Dansk Industri* (n 239) para 24.
[249] De Mol (n 244) 125.
[250] M Dougan, 'Judicial Review of Member State Action under the General Principles and the Charter: Defining the "Scope of Union Law"' (2015) 52 *Common Market Law Review* 1201, 1218.

law envisaged two forms of trigger for their application, the *Mangold* line of case law appears to introduce a third pathway.

a. *Wachauf* and *ERT*

For the application of general principles of law, the scope of Union law is triggered by the Union's institutions exercising powers conferred by the Treaties.[251] Individuals can invoke general principles of law as a cause of action against measures adopted by them.[252] As previously discussed, *Wachauf* confirmed that even Member States must comply with general principles while implementing Union law.[253] This obligation also extends to rights and freedoms enshrined in the Charter. In *Fransson*, the Court aligned the field of application of general principles of law and the Charter in relation to Member States' action.[254] Both sets of norms are also triggered by national measures adopted in derogation from the Treaty obligations. In *ERT*,[255] the Court held that where a Member State invoked the Treaty-based derogations to justify national rules that would likely obstruct the exercise of the freedoms of movement, such justification must conform to fundamental rights *qua* general principles of Union law.[256] National derogating measures can be subject to judicial scrutiny for their conformity with general principles of Union law. It is immaterial in that respect whether a Member State seeks to justify a national measure under the express Treaty derogations or judge-made mandatory requirements. In *Familiapress*,[257] referring to *ERT*, the Court found that a Member State relying on overriding requirements to justify a restriction of the freedoms of movement must comply with general principles of Union law.[258] The effect of *ERT* and *Familiapress* is that the invocation of express derogations or mandatory requirements against the prima facie unlawful action does not take a national measure outside the scope of Union law.[259] Member States must play by the rules of the Treaty instead of their own public law framework.[260]

[251] Editorial Comments, 'The Scope of Application of the General Principles of Union law: An Ever-Expanding Union?' (2010) 47 *Common Market Law Review* 1589, 1590.

[252] E Spaventa, 'The Horizontal Application of Fundamental Rights as General Principles of Union Law' in A Arnull, C Barnard, M Dougan and E Spaventa (eds), *A Constitutional Order of States: Essays in Honour of Alan Dashwood* (Oxford, Hart Publishing, 2011) 202.

[253] Case 5 *Wachauf* (n 54) para 19.

[254] Case C-617/10 *Åklagaren v Hans Åkerberg Fransson* EU:C:2013:105, para 18. The Court found that Article 51(1), according to which the Charter applies to Member States 'only when they are implementing Union law', confirmed the extent to which they are obliged to comply with general principles of Union law.

[255] *ERT* (n 53).

[256] ibid para 43.

[257] Case C-368/95 *Vereinigte Familiapress Zeitungsverlags- und vertriebs GmbH v Heinrich Bauer Verlag* EU:C:1997:325.

[258] ibid para 24.

[259] Tridimas (n 43) 325.

[260] Dougan (n 250) 1211. However, this is not accepted by many. See FG Jacobs, 'Human Rights in the European Union: The Role of the Court of Justice' (2001) 26 *European Law Review* 331; PM Huber,

From the perspective of private relationships, the *ERT* doctrine is significant on two levels. First, a prima facie limitation of the Treaty by a national measure effectively triggers the scope of Union law for the application of general principles of law, irrespective of the circumstances in which it occurs. As follows from *Familiapress*, a national derogating measure can be subject to scrutiny based on general principles of law, even if it impacts the positions of private parties.[261] Secondly, general principles of law are also triggered when a prima facie limitation of the freedoms of movement is inflicted by a non-public/private body. This stems from *Viking* and *Laval*, which concerned the compatibility of an industrial action with the Treaty.[262] While in *Viking*, an industrial action was aimed at preventing the reflagging of a vessel in another Member State, in *Laval*, it was directed at forcing a foreign company to consent to a local collective agreement. In both rulings, the Court recognised that the right to strike as a general principle of Union law could be invoked against the claims of violation of the Treaty's free movement provisions.[263] *Viking* and *Laval* can be construed to serve as the continuation of the *ERT* doctrine.[264] Both involved a prima facie limitation of the Treaty that triggered the scope of Union law for the applicability of the general principle of law, though one difference was that such a limitation was imposed by a non-public/private body. However, it remains to be seen whether this outcome also extends to matters merely falling within the scope of the Treaty's free movement provisions without a prima facie limitation of free movement in the internal market.[265]

b. A New Category?

The *Mangold* line of case law has spawned a plethora of scholarly accounts over its role in conceptually and substantively resetting the constitutional boundaries of Union law.[266] The aspect that has drawn particular attention concerns the extent

'The Unitary Effect of the Community's Fundamental Rights: The ERT Doctrine Needs to Be Reviewed' (2008) 14 *European Public Law* 323.

[261] Spaventa (n 252) 206.

[262] *Viking* (n 218); *Laval* (n 201).

[263] *Viking* (n 218) para 44; *Laval* (n 201) para 91.

[264] X Groussout, L Pech and GT Petursson, 'The Reach of EU Fundamental Rights on Member State Action after Lisbon' in S de Vries, U Bernitz and S Weatherill (eds), *The Protection of Fundamental Rights in the EU after Lisbon* (Oxford, Hart Publishing, 2013) 103.

[265] See also Spaventa (n 252) 205.The author questioned whether the tenuous link established between a barrier and a rule in Case C-60/00 *Mary Carpenter v Secretary of State for the Home Department* EU:C:2002:434 can be sufficient.

[266] See, eg, F Fontanelli, 'Some Reflections on the General Principles of the EU and on Solidarity in the Aftermath of *Mangold* and *Kücükdeveci*' (2011) 17 *European Public Law* 225; M Beyer-Katzenberger, 'Judicial Activism and Judicial Restraint at the Bundesverfassungsgericht: Was the *Mangold* Judgment of the European Court of Justice an Ultra Vires Act?' (2011) 11 *ERA Forum* 517; D Schiek 'Constitutional Principles and Horizontal Effects: *Kücükdeveci* Revisited' (2010) 2 *European Labour Law Journal* 368; M Dougan, 'In Defence of Mangold?' in Arnull et al (n 252); S Peers, 'Supremacy, Equality and Human Rights: Comment on *Kucukdeveci* (C-555/07)' (2010) 35 *European Law Review* 849; M Schmidt, 'The Principle of Non-discrimination in Respect of Age: Dimensions of the ECJ's *Mangold* Judgment' (2005) 7 *German Law Journal* 505; S Prechal, 'Competence Creep and General Principles of Law' (2010) 3 *Review of European Administrative Law* 5.

to which it broadened the normative reach of general principles of Union law. Juxtaposed against *Wachauf* and *ERT*, it is questionable whether the *Mangold* line of case law is to be read as falling squarely within the two categories of 'implementation' and 'derogation' or introducing a novel judicial perspective to the applicability of general principles of Union law by redefining what is deemed to come 'within the scope of Union law'. *Mangold* itself certainly aligns with the reasoning in *Wachauf*. The disputed national measure fell within the scope of Union law because it was intended to transpose Directive 1999/70.[267] This was a sufficient factor to trigger the application of the general principle of non-discrimination on grounds of age. This made it possible to avoid any need to rely on Directive 2000/78, which did not apply due to the private nature of the dispute and the non-expiry of its implementation period.[268] However, it remained unclear whether the outcome would have been any different had there been no additional secondary legislation involved and had the transposition period of Directive 2000/78 already expired.

This query was first touched upon in *Bartsch* that appeared to unequivocally confine the direct effect of the general principle of non-discrimination on grounds of age to the category of 'implementation'.[269] Unlike *Mangold*, the Court found that the matter did not fall within the scope of Union law to trigger this principle. Two aspects were of particular importance. First, the Court held that no such link could be established based on Directive 2000/78. This is because the impugned national law was not a measure implementing that directive and the period for its transposition had not expired.[270] Second, the Court distinguished *Bartsch* from *Mangold* by emphasising that the national law in the former ruling was also not a measure implementing additional secondary legislation.[271] As a result, *Bartsch* made the capacity of Directive 2000/78 to operate as a trigger for the application of the general principle of non-discrimination on grounds of age conditional on, first, the national law constituting an implementation measure in relation to Directive 2000/78 and, second, the expiration of its implementation period.[272] In line with *Wachauf*, this effectively confined the horizontal application of the general principle of non-discrimination on grounds of age to the national law that qualified as an implementation measure *stricto sensu*.

Kücükdeveci, in contrast, offered a new perspective to the determination of what falls 'within the scope of Union law'. At first, its factual circumstances did not suggest a different outcome from *Bartsch*. Like its predecessor, the disputed national law in *Kücükdeveci* did not implement additional secondary legislation. Moreover, given the two requirements introduced in *Bartsch*, it appeared

[267] Council Directive 1999/70/EC of 28 June 1999 concerning the framework agreement on fixed-term work concluded by ETUC, UNICE and CEEP [1999] OJ L175.
[268] Editorial Comments (n 251) 1591–92.
[269] Case C-427/06 *Birgit Bartsch v Bosch und Siemens* EU:C:2008:517.
[270] ibid para 17.
[271] ibid para 24.
[272] Dougan (n 266) 234.

that the situation would also be deemed to fall outside the scope of Union law. While the period for the transposition of Directive 2000/38 expired before the discriminatory conduct took place, the impugned national law did not qualify as a specific implementation measure in relation to that directive. The Court, however, signalled a shift in its approach. It found that, unlike *Bartsch*, after the passage of the deadline for its transposition, Directive 2000/38 itself had the effect of bringing the disputed national law within the scope of Union law.[273] This is because it concerned the conditions of dismissal – a matter that was governed by Directive 2000/38.[274] It was, therefore, immaterial that the disputed national law did not constitute a measure of implementation within the meaning of *Bartsch*.

Kücükdeveci has generated divergent interpretative accounts. In one respect, it is not necessarily seen as a radical departure from the reasoning provided in *Wachauf*.[275] Despite not explicitly referring to it, *Kücükdeveci* can indeed be construed to concern the implementation of Union law.[276] This finds support in the Court's broad understanding of 'implementation' that translates to all circumstances where a Member State acts in 'purposeful furtherance of Union law'.[277] In *Fransson*, the Court found the fact that the disputed national law was not adopted to implement a directive was inconsequential for determining the scope of Union law.[278] It was also not affected by the discretionary powers attributed to Member States.[279] Seen in this light, *Kücükdeveci* seems to merely adjust the prerequisites set out in *Bartsch* concerning the expiry of the deadline for the transposition of Directive 2000/38.[280] As a result, before that date, a national measure comes within the scope of Union law provided that, under the requirement in *Bartsch*, it specifically implements Directive 2000/38; after that date, it is sufficient that a national measure concerns a matter governed by the directive for it to trigger the scope of Union law.

Nonetheless, doubts exist over the categorisation of *Kücükdeveci* as a mere case of 'implementation'.[281] This ruling is also construed as the authority affirming the existence of a separate category of situations falling within the scope of Union law, distinct from those of 'implementation' and 'derogation'.[282] The disputed national legislation in *Kücükdeveci* did not qualify as a measure of implementation

[273] *Kücükdeveci* (n 234) paras 23–24.
[274] ibid para 25.
[275] See, eg, G Thüsing and S Horler, 'Annotation to Case C-555/07, *Seda Kücükdeveci v Swedex*, Judgment of the Court (Grand Chamber) of 19 January 2010' (2010) 47 *Common Market Law Review* 1161, 1168.
[276] Editorial Comments (n 251) 1593.
[277] Dougan (n 250) 1212.
[278] *Fransson* (n 254) para 28.
[279] Joined Cases C-411/10 and 493/10 *NS* EU:C:2011:865, para 68.
[280] Groussout, Pech and Petursson (n 264) 110.
[281] See, Opinion of AG Bot in Case C-108/10 *Ivana Scattolon v Ministero dell'Istruzione, dell'Università e della Ricerca* EU:C:2011:211, para 119. On the meaning of 'implementation', see also F Fontanelli, 'Hic Sunt Nationes: The Elusive Limits of the EU Charter and the German Constitutional Watchdog' (2013) 9 *European Constitutional Law Review* 315.
[282] De Mol (n 244) 126; Dougan (n 250) 1224.

with respect to Directive 2000/38 or additional secondary legislation implementing it, and even long pre-dated the adoption of that directive. However, it was found to fall within the scope of Union law solely because it concerned a matter governed by Directive 2000/38. This finding suggests that the general principle of non-discrimination on grounds of age is triggered whenever the exercise of regulatory competence by Member States touches upon matters that are covered by the Union's legislative intervention.[283] Unlike the other two categories, where national measures one way or another reflect positive obligations of Member States derived from the Treaties, the broad proposition followed from the *Kücükdeveci* methodology poses far-reaching constitutional implications.[284] The reliance on the mere coincidence of a subject matter between Union and national law as a trigger for the application of the general principle of non-discrimination risks altering the established equilibrium between the realms of Union and national competence, at the very least instilling a different legal framework that governs the ability of Member States to legislate above the minimum standards adopted at the Union level.[285] This is likely to inject new dynamics into private relationships. It would be possible to invoke the general principle of non-discrimination as soon as a matter regulated at the national level forms the subject of the Union's secondary law.[286] This finds further support in *HK Danmark v Experian*,[287] where the issue concerned the alleged discriminatory treatment on grounds of age arising from the occupational pension scheme stipulated in a private contract. Analogous to *Kücükdeveci*,[288] the Court found the matter to fall within the scope of Union law for the application of the general principles of non-discrimination on grounds of age because the matter was covered by the scope *rationae materiae* and *temporis* of Directive 2000/78.[289] The question of the horizontality of this principle was not explicitly addressed, though the Court acknowledged that the directive itself could not impose obligations on private individuals.[290]

However, the subject-matter method is not consistently followed in the case law, casting doubts over the existence of a separate category based on it.[291] *Kücükdeveci* and, to some extent, *HK Danmark* remain the only rulings to endorse this line of reasoning. First, there are instances where the Court opted not to apply

[283] Editorial Comments (n 251) 1594.

[284] De Mol (n 244) 126.

[285] Editorial Comments (n 251) 1594.

[286] M Dougan, 'The Impact of the General Principles of Union Law upon Private Relationships' in D Leczykiewicz and S Weatherill (eds), *The Involvement of EU Law in Private Law Relationships* (Oxford, Hart Publishing, 2013) 80.

[287] Case C-476/11 *HK Danmark Acting on Behalf of Glennie Kristensen v Experian A/S* EU:C:2013:590.

[288] See also N Lazzerini, '(Some of) the Fundamental Rights Granted by the Charter May Be a Source of Obligations for Private Parties: AMS' (2014) 51 *Common Market Law Review* 907, 930.

[289] *HK Danmark* (n 287) para 22.

[290] ibid para 18. The Court found the occupational pension scheme, which was not prescribed by law, but included in a private contract, to be discriminatory on grounds of age, though objectively justified.

[291] See also E Hancox, 'The Meaning of "Implementing" EU law under Article 51(1) of the Charter: *Åkerberg Fransson*' (2013) 50 *Common Market Law Review* 1411, 1422.

this method despite having a clear opportunity to do so.[292] Second, *Karner*,[293] which appeared to expand the boundaries of Union law along the same logic of subject-matter overlap,[294] is no longer a good law. There, having found that the national rule on advertising was a selling arrangement and fell outside the scope of Article 34 TFEU, the Court considered its compatibility with the general principle of the freedom of expression, for it was deemed to fall within the scope of Union law.[295] This suggested that a national measure could still be subject to a fundamental rights review based on general principles of law despite falling outside the scope of the Treaty.[296] That said, this proposition appears to be overruled by *Pelckmans*,[297] the issue in which concerned the compatibility with Article 34 TFEU of the national rule on the compulsory closure of shops. Unlike *Karner*, the Court's characterisation of the contested rule as a selling arrangement meant that it fell outside the scope of Union law to trigger the relevant provisions of the Charter, the field of application of which coincides with that of general principles of Union law.[298] Third, the proposition following from *Karner* does not align with the line of case law discussed below, which signals the need for additional factors going beyond the mere overlap of a subject matter between the Union's secondary law and national law.

iii. Source of Horizontality of General Principles of Union Law

Alongside the requirement of 'falling within the scope of Union law', another discernible pattern in the judicial approach to the horizontality of general principles of Union law is the continuous references to the principle of effectiveness. It explicitly underlies the reasoning of the Court for recognising the applicability of the general principle of non-discrimination on grounds of age regardless of factual constellations. In *Mangold*, referring to *Simmenthal*,[299] the Court established the responsibility of a national court to set aside any provision of national law conflicting with the principle of non-discrimination on grounds of age to ensure the full

[292] See, eg, Case C-333/13 *Elisabeta Dano, Florin Dano v Jobcenter Leipzig* EU:C:2014:2358, paras 85–92. As pointed out by Dougan, this method should have led the Court to affirm the applicability of the Charter to the situation in which an economically inactive Union citizen was seeking to claim special non-contributory cash benefits pursuant to Regulation 883/2004. Instead, the Court found the Charter not to be applicable due to the fact that the conditions for the award of the benefits were not laid down in Regulation 883/2004, even though they were defined and regulated therein. For more on this, see Dougan (n 250) 1225.

[293] Case C-71/02 *Herbert Karner Industrie-Auktionen GmbH v Troostwijk* EU:C:2004:181.

[294] See, eg Opinion of AG Sharpston in Case C-427/06 *Birgit Bartsch* EU:C:2008:297, para 69.

[295] *Karner* (n 293) para 49. See also Case C-299/95 *Friedrich Kremzow v Republik Österreich* EU:C:1997:254, para 15.

[296] J Snell, 'Fundamental Rights Review of National Measures: Nothing New under the Charter?' (2015) 21 *European Public Law* 285, 300.

[297] Case C-483/12 *Pelckmans Turnhout NV v Walter Van Gastel Balen NV and Others* EU:C:2014:304.

[298] *Fransson* (n 254) para 18.

[299] Case 106/77 *Amministrazione delle Finanze dello Stato v Simmenthal* EU:C:1978:49.

effectiveness of legal protection bestowed on individuals under Union law.[300] In *Kücükdeveci* and later in *Dansk Industri*, the Court added that 'the need to ensure the full effectiveness of [this] principle' created a duty for national courts to decline to apply incompatible national provisions.[301] The novelty of this line of case law is expressed in the resort to the effectiveness rationale to justify the attribution of horizontal applicability to general principles of law based on directives that give effect to them, though directives themselves lack such normative capacity. In one respect, this certainly reinforced the obligation of Member States to comply with the Union's fundamental rights standards *qua* general principles of law by eliminating the disparity of treatment of vertical and horizontal relations that resulted from the limited reach of directives. However, therein lies a constitutional dilemma prompted by the mismatch in the scope of a directive acting as a trigger and that of the triggered general principle of law.[302] What is unclear is the exact parameters according to which national law is subject to judicial scrutiny under general principles of law based on directives to eliminate a threat to the effectiveness of protecting fundamental rights at the Union level.

In *Kücükdeveci*, as previously shown, the Court followed a 'structural' approach to establish the capacity of a directive to act as a trigger for the application of the general principle of non-discrimination on grounds of age. It suggests that a mere subject-matter overlap between a directive and national law is sufficient to prompt scrutiny under general principles of law. However, this differs from the Court's analytical methodology within the framework of the Charter. Unlike *Kücükdeveci*, the review of national law in the name of effectiveness is 'contextual' in its nature. This approach provides a more nuanced formula to establish the Charter's field of application over the actions of Member States, particularly in situations where a national measure does not qualify as an implementation measure *stricto sensu*. While the origin of this approach can be traced back to *Annibaldi*,[303] it first explicitly appeared in *Iida*,[304] where the Court attempted to define the notion of 'implementation' within the meaning of Article 51 CFR. Pursuant to this provision, the Charter is addressed to Member States only when they are implementing Union law. In this regard, the Court enunciated a range of criteria to establish whether a Member State's action could constitute 'implementation of Union law' to fall within its scope. This, according to the Court, includes ascertaining

> [W]hether the national legislation at issue is intended to implement a provision of European Union law, what the character of that legislation is, and whether it pursues objectives other than those covered by European Union law, even if it is capable of

[300] *Mangold* (n 229) para 77.
[301] *Kücükdeveci* (n 234) para 53; *Dansk Industri* (n 239) para 35.
[302] See *Dansk Industri* (n 239) para 23. See also Spaventa (n 252) 210.
[303] Case C-309/96 *Daniele Annibaldi v Sindaco del Comune di Guidonia and Presidente Regione Lazio* EU:C:1997:631.
[304] Case C-40/11 *Yoshikazu Iida v Stadt Ulm* EU:C:2012:691.

indirectly affecting that law, and also whether there are specific rules of European Union law on the matter or capable of affecting it.[305]

This formula was further elaborated in *Siragusa*,[306] where the issue related to the compatibility with Union law of the national policy on landscape preservation. The Court first acknowledged the link between the national policy and the Union's environmental legislation. However, this was insufficient to bring the matter within the scope of Union law to trigger the provisions of the Charter. This is because the Court considered Article 51 CFR to require 'a certain degree of connection above and beyond the matters covered being closely related or one of those matters having an indirect impact on the other'.[307] On this basis, the Court applied the criteria formulated in *Iida*, including the additional condition of whether Union law imposed a specific obligation on Member States. This was rationalised based on the objective of protecting fundamental rights in Union law, which in the Court's view '[was] to ensure that those rights [were] not infringed in areas of EU activity, whether through action at EU level or through the implementation of [Union] law by the Member States'.[308] The Court added that the ultimate reason for pursuing such an objective lay in 'the need to avoid a situation in which the level of protection of fundamental rights varie[d] according to the national law involved in such a way as to undermine the unity, primacy and effectiveness of [Union] law'.[309]

Analogous to *Kücükdeveci*, the form of assessment elaborated in *Siragusa* is also informed by the concept of the effectiveness of Union law. However, its expression in these rulings substantially varies. The distinguishing factor lies in the extent to which national law is subject to judicial scrutiny to ensure the effectiveness of protecting fundamental rights at the Union level. In *Kücükdeveci*, the scope of such a review is broadly construed as it is triggered by the mere coincidence of a subject matter between the national law under scrutiny and the Union's secondary law. In contrast, *Siragusa* narrowly defines the parameters of judicial scrutiny by employing a more contextual than abstract assessment to establish a link between Union and national law.[310] Unlike *Kücükdeveci*, *Siragusa* offers better rationalisation for bringing national law within the scope of general principles of law. The Court has already applied the *Siragusa* criteria to define the normative reach of a general principle of law.[311] However, while the extension of these criteria undoubtedly offers a more systematic approach to delimiting the boundaries of general principles of law, the prospect of judicial scrutiny consolidating around them is not entirely clear. This stems from the uncertainty over whether the *Siragusa* criteria are confined to instances not covered by the categories of 'implementation' and

[305] ibid para 79.
[306] Case C-206/13 *Cruciano Siragusa v Regione Sicilia* EU:C:2014:126.
[307] ibid para 24.
[308] ibid para 31.
[309] ibid para 32.
[310] Snell (n 296) 209.
[311] See, eg, Case C-406/15 *Petya Milkova v Izpalnitelen direktor na Agentsiata za privatizatsia i sledprivatizatsionen control* EU:C:2017:198, para 50.

'derogation' or whether they are meant to replace them as a sole method for delimiting the boundaries of Union law.[312]

iv. The Nature of the Horizontal Reach of General Principles

Given the two reoccurring patterns discussed in previous sections, the *Mangold* line of case law may not appear to transform general principles of Union law into a new source of rights and obligations enforceable between private parties. It is often interpreted as only confirming the so-called 'exclusionary' effect of the principle of non-discrimination on grounds of age, which refers to its capacity to set aside the conflicting national law.[313] Such a characterisation follows from a range of factors. In *Mangold* and *Kücükdeveci*, the judicial review under the principle of non-discrimination on grounds of age concerned solely the national law that applied to a private dispute. Having established its discriminatory effect on grounds of age, the Court instructed the referring national courts to disapply it. While it is true that this had an impact on the legal position of the other party to the dispute, this effect only indirectly or incidentally followed from setting aside the conflicting national law. The issue at stake was, therefore, the conduct of the national legislator that breached the formal requirement imposed by the general principle of discrimination on grounds of age, which was given effect in Directive 2000/78.[314] For this reason, *Mangold* and *Kücükdeveci* are seen as merely reflecting the primacy of Union law over national law rather than granting horizontal direct effect to the principle of non-discrimination on grounds of age.[315] Indeed, in neither instance had the Court considered whether this principle satisfied the traditional thresholds of clarity, precision and unconditionality.[316] On the contrary, in *Kücükdeveci*, the Court concurred with AG Bot by explicitly referring to the principle of primacy as extending to the principle of discrimination on grounds of age.[317] From this perspective, *Mangold* and *Kücükdeveci* do not seem so controversial. After all, the compliance of national law with the general principles of Union law should not vary, regardless of whether it is raised in a vertical or horizontal setting.[318]

However, the *Mangold* line of case law also supports to the broader construction of horizontality attributed to general principles of Union law. This first follows from the specific pattern of the Court's reasoning. If setting aside the contravening national law was the only intention, this could have been achieved within the framework of Directive 2000/78 alone without referring to the general principle of

[312] See also Dougan (n 250) 1232.
[313] AS Hartkamp, 'The Effect of the EC Treaty in Private Law: On Direct and Indirect Horizontal Effects of Primary Community Law' (2010) 18 *European Review of Private Law* 527, 536.
[314] K Lenaerts, 'Of Birds and Hedges: The Role of Primacy in Invoking Norms of EU law' (2006) 31 *European Law Review* 287, 307.
[315] E Muir, 'Of Ages in – and Edges of – EU Law' (2011) 48 *Common Market Law Review* 39, 43.
[316] Case 41-74 *Yvonne van Duyn v Home Office* EU:C:1974:133, para 6.
[317] ibid para 54.
[318] Lenaerts (n 314) 307.

non-discrimination on grounds of age.[319] This solution was proposed by AG Bot, who invited the Court to accept that a directive aimed at counteracting discrimination could be relied on in private proceedings to set aside the national law contradicting it.[320] The underlying reason, here, follows a fortiori from the argument based on the uniformity of compliance with Union law. Yet, the Court did not take this route and even subsequently rejected it.[321] Instead, it invoked the general principle of non-discrimination on grounds of age by reiterating that Directive 2000/78 itself could not impose obligations on private individuals.[322] This implies, *a contrario*, that the former norm is, in fact, capable of having a horizontal direct effect.[323] It is beyond doubtful that the general principle of non-discrimination on grounds of age can be applied as an autonomous ground of review, even in the context of private disputes. That said, what remains questionable is whether the horizontal reach of this principle is confined to an 'exclusionary' effect or surpasses that by acquiring a 'substitutionary' effect, which refers to the capacity of a Union norm to create, modify or extinguish individual rights or obligations instead of the conflicting national law.[324]

Since *Mangold* and *Kücükdeveci* concerned the judicial review of the contravening national law, one may gravitate towards interpreting them as only attributing an 'exclusionary' effect to the general principle of non-discrimination on grounds of age that applies whenever Directive 2000/78 itself does not.[325] Nonetheless, the Court has never divided the concept of horizontal direct effect along the distinction of 'exclusionary' and 'substitutionary' effects.[326] The case law is underpinned by a conceptual framework whereby a Union norm can either produce a horizontal direct effect in both forms or lack it altogether without any solution that falls in between.[327] In some respect, the rationale lies in the difficulties in drawing an operationalised distinction between 'exclusionary' and 'substitutionary' effects.[328] Setting aside the contravening national law often leads to the direct and immediate application of another provision of national law, though such exclusion can equally result in the direct and immediate application of a novel provision of Union law.[329] As a result, even if the Court has not explicitly confirmed the 'substitutionary' effect of the general principle, it cannot be ruled out altogether.

[319] Muir (n 315) 55.
[320] Opinion of AG Bot in *Kücükdeveci* (n 234) para 70.
[321] Case C-351/12 *OSA* EU:C:2014:110, para 48.
[322] Case C-122/17 *David Smith v Patrick Meade* EU:C:2018:631, para 48.
[323] Muir (n 315) 55. Unlike *Mangold*, the Court in *Kücükdeveci* referred to *Defrenne*. See *Kücükdeveci* (n 234) para 21.
[324] De Mol (n 244) 111.
[325] G Zaccaroni, 'More on the Horizontal Direct Effect of the Principle of Nondiscrimination on the Ground of Age: Dansk Industries (DI)' *EU Law Analysis*, 24 July 2016, http://eulawanalysis.blogspot.com/2016/07/more-on-horizontal-direct-effect-of.html.
[326] Opinion of AG Bot in *Kücükdeveci* (n 234) para 64.
[327] De Mol (n 244) 121.
[328] Opinion of AG Szpunar in C-261/20 *Thelen Technopark Berlin GmbH v MN* EU:C:2021:620, para 56.
[329] M Dougan, 'When Worlds Collide! Competing Visions of the Relationship between Direct Effect and Supremacy' (2007) 44 *Common Market Law Review* 931, 937.

More substantially, the broad characterisation of horizontality attributed to the general principle of non-discrimination on grounds of age emerges from the conceptual uncertainty regarding its mode of application. The *Mangold* line of case law portrays this general principle as a component of the Union's primary law that is of a secondary nature, for it needs pre-activation by some first-order provision of Union law.[330] However, unlike other sources of Union law, the recourse to a directive as an intermediary to apply this general principle to a private dispute opens up the prospect for the expansive reconstruction of the horizontal reach of directives. First, this is manifested in the approach used to draw a connection between a directive and a general principle of law. In *Kücükdeveci*, as mentioned earlier, the Court relied on the subject-matter overlap between Directive 2000/78 and the disputed national law to apply the general principle of non-discrimination. In this regard, it is questionable whether this method is strictly confined to instances involving the applicable national law or equally extends even to those where there is no national law to set aside. Is the fact that the nature of a private contractual dispute concerns a matter governed by a directive sufficient to trigger the application of the general principle of non-discrimination? An affirmative answer seems to follow from *HK Danmark v Experian*, where the Court found that an occupational pension scheme stipulated in a private contract fell within the scope *rationae materiae* and *temporis* of Directive 2000/78 for the application of the general principle of non-discrimination on grounds of age.[331] As this appears to be the only authority, one must be wary of reading too much into it. However, the use of this abstract methodology risks inflicting substantive limitations on the exercise of private autonomy. There is a clear possibility for the application of the general principle of non-discrimination in conjunction with Directive 2000/78 to a private relationship that has no direct or profound link to Union law,[332] thereby operating as a separate ground for judicial scrutiny and creating rights and obligations not envisaged by the applicable national law.[333]

Second, the broad construction of the horizontal reach of the general principle of non-discrimination also follows from its application to a private relationship based on a directive in the face of substantial differences existing between their spheres of application and binding force.[334] In the *Mangold* line of case law, the Court acknowledged that Directive 2000/78 could not itself produce a horizontal direct effect, yet also found that it was still capable of activating the application of the general principle of non-discrimination that possesses such normative capacity. The peculiar element in this conceptual framework is that it is premised on the dissonance of the normative reach of a directive acting as a trigger and that of the

[330] Dougan (n 250) 1218 and 1243.

[331] *HK Danmark* (n 287) para 22.

[332] De Mol (n 244) 129.

[333] See for instance its repercussions in *HK Danmark* (n 287).

[334] Joined Cases C-397/01 to C-403/01 *Bernhard Pfeiffer and Others v Deutsches Rotes Kreuz* EU:C:2004:584, para 109; Case C-282/10 *Maribel Dominguez v Centre informatique du Centre Ouest Atlantique* EU:C:2012:33, para 42.

triggered general principle of law, whereby the contours of the latter exceed what is possible solely under the former norm.[335] At first glance, the application of a general principle of law based on a directive seems to narrowly define its scope of application by confining it to the mere exclusion of the contravening national law. This is because, initially, the parameters of the normative relationship between a directive acting as a trigger and the triggered general principle of law were determined from the standpoint of the former source of the Union's secondary law. *Mangold* and *Kücükdeveci* linked the general principle of law to a directive, which seemed to suggest that the scope of application of that principle was not broader than a directive. This view found support in *Bartsch*, where the applicability of the general principle of non-discrimination was made conditional on a directive itself being applicable.[336] However, *Dansk Industri* stands as a legal authority for the opposite construction of the normative relationship between a directive and general principles of law. This is manifested in two ways. In this ruling, the Court first held that the scope of protection conferred by Directive 2000/78 did not go beyond that afforded by the general principle prohibiting discrimination on grounds of age,[337] while it also reiterated that '[this principle conferred] on private persons an individual right which they [might] invoke as such'.[338] Such reasoning reshapes the normative relationship between a directive and the triggered general principle of law. It is no longer determined from the standpoint of the former source of the Union's secondary law but the latter norm itself. It is a directive that is linked to a general principle of law and not the reverse, since the scope of application of a directive is narrower than that of a general principle of law.[339] Therefore, *Dansk Industri* transformed the relationship between a directive acting as a trigger and the triggered general principle of law. The new dynamics added to it align with the broader construction of the horizontal reach of the latter norm. It also suggests that there is no requirement of equivalence in the scope of application between the triggered general principle of law and a provision of Union law that determines its applicability. If this is indeed the case, then it would be incongruent in hermeneutic terms to confine the horizontal reach of general principles of law to instances of mere exclusion of the contravening national law.[340]

Regardless of whether the horizontal reach of general principles of law embraces both exclusionary and substitutionary effects, the main argument raised against it is the concern raised over its incompatibility with the principle of legal certainty and the protection of legitimate expectations in the context of private relationships.[341] This was, in fact, one of the questions raised by the referring court in *Dansk Industri*. Having acknowledged that under Danish law

[335] Spaventa (n 252) 210.
[336] Zaccaroni (n 325).
[337] *Dansk Industri* (n 239) para 23.
[338] ibid para 36.
[339] Zaccaroni (n 325).
[340] Spaventa (n 252) 210.
[341] See, eg, Opinion of AG Trstenjak in *Dominguez*, para 64.

an employer was not obliged to pay the severance allowance, the referring court asked whether it would be consistent with Union law to weigh the general principle of non-discrimination on grounds of age against the principles of legal certainty and the protection of legitimate expectations.[342] The Court explicitly rejected this by making two related points. First, the application of these two principles, according to the Court, would have the effect of limiting the temporal effects of its interpretation since it would render it inapplicable to the main proceedings.[343] Second, in the Court's view, the protection of legitimate expectations could not, in any event, be invoked to deny an individual the benefit of relying on its interpretation of Union law.[344] Both findings make sense when considered in the narrow context of exclusion of the conflicting national law. It would have jeopardised the unity and effectiveness of Union law had the national court been allowed to assess whether the compliance with a provision of Union law was contrary to the principle of legal certainty and the protection of legitimate expectations as defined under national law.[345] However, against the broad definition in *Dansk Industri* of the normative reach of the general principle of non-discrimination, the Court's approach to the principle of legal certainty and the protection of legitimate expectations leaves much to be desired. The Court did not attempt to provide any guidance on balancing these principles with the general principle of non-discrimination. At the same time, its reasoning seems to place the former norms hierarchically below the latter.[346]

III. Interim Conclusion

In sum, the normative framework prescribed by general principles of Union law protects the ideals of private autonomy and simultaneously conditions their exercise. Notwithstanding the aim of the original Treaties to facilitate and accelerate private initiatives of an economic nature across Member States' borders, the (then) emerging Community's system of economic dirigisme warranted the entrenchment of constitutional guarantees separate from those enshrined in national constitutions. The Court's recognition of individual entitlements, such as the right to property, the freedom of contract and the freedom to engage in economic or commercial activity, as general principles of law firmly instilled the concept of private autonomy within the Union's legal order. These principles bind the Union's institutions and Member States acting within the scope of Union law and, as will

[342] *Dansk Industri* (n 239) para 18.
[343] ibid para 39.
[344] ibid para 41.
[345] D Elkan, R Holdgaard, and GK Schaldemose, 'From Cooperation to Collision: The ECJ's *Ajos* Ruling and the Danish Supreme Court's Refusal to Comply' (2018) 55 *Common Market Law Review* 17, 39.
[346] Xenidis (n 180) 12.

be shown in the next chapter, produce a horizontal or at least quasi-horizontal direct effect. However, they are not unfettered prerogatives but are conditioned by other constitutional safeguards, including the general principle of equality and non-discrimination that has transformed from the norm driven by the market integration logic to the norm imbued by the ideals of intersubjective equality in the Union. It is submitted that the impact exerted by this principle on the exercise of private autonomy in the Union's legal order is prompted by the demands of egalitarian justice, though its parameters remain uncertain.

2

Charter and Private Autonomy

> The Charter is a shadow of Union law. Just as an object shapes the contours of its shadow, Union law also shapes the 'contours' of the Charter.[1]

General principles of law no longer exclusively operate as the norms that ensure the protection of fundamental rights in the Union.[2] The rights and freedoms codified in the Charter have now also assumed this role.[3] Among them are provisions that manifest the ideals of private autonomy. Three particularly stand out. Article 15 CFR provides that 'everyone has the right to engage in work and to pursue a freely chosen or accepted occupation'. Article 16 CFR declares that 'the freedom to conduct business in accordance with Union law and national laws and practices is recognised'. Lastly, Article 17 CFR proclaims that 'everyone has the right to own, use, dispose of and bequeath his or her lawfully acquired possessions'. According to the Explanations to the Charter, these provisions find their roots in general principles of Union law and the normative instruments underlying them. Articles 15 and 16 CFR are based on the case law recognising the right to the free pursuit of business, economic or commercial activity, the right to freely choose and practise trade or profession, and the freedom of contract. Article 17 CFR, in turn, gives effect to the right enshrined in Article 1 of Protocol I to the ECHR. Analogous to general principles of law, these provisions are not unfettered but can be subject to legitimate constraints. Their exercise is conditioned by the array of social and workers' rights protected by the Charter, including the general prohibition of discrimination on multiple grounds enshrined therein. The salient question in this context is how the coexistence and intersection of these individual entitlements shape private relationships. This warrants a close examination of the scope of rights and freedoms that manifest the ideals of private autonomy and the extent to which other rights and freedoms impose limitations and conditions on the exercise of this principle.

[1] K Lenaerts, 'In Vielfalt geeint: Grundrechte als Basis des europäischen Integrationsprozesses' (2015) 42 *Europaische grundrechte zeitschrift* 353, 354 (author's translation).

[2] X Groussout, L Pech and GT Petursson, 'The Reach of EU Fundamental Rights on Member State Action after Lisbon' in S de Vries, U Bernitz and S Weatherill (eds), *The Protection of Fundamental Rights in the EU after Lisbon* (Oxford, Hart Publishing, 2013) 97.

[3] Case C-178/15 *Alicja Sobczyszyn v Szkoła Podstawowa w Rzeplinie* EU:C:2016:502, para 20; Case C-214/10 *KHS AG v Winfried Schulte* EU:C:2011:761, para 37.

I. Provisions Expressing Private Autonomy

As a progeny of general principles of Union law, Articles 15–17 CFR represent the commitment to the political economy model infused by the principles underlying the liberal free-market construct.[4] At an individual level, these provisions uphold and promote the values intrinsic to the personal liberty to decide and pursue a course of action as per one's interests and wishes. There are two aspects to this conceptualisation. First, Articles 15–17 CFR are central to understanding individual self-conception. An economic activity in an employed or self-employed capacity enables individuals to attain freedom, equality and security. It provides a path for individuals to perform a constructive and purposeful action,[5] thus maintaining their self-esteem and the respect of others.[6] It operates as a channel for self-realisation and self-development.[7] By engaging in economic activity, individuals discover a path to combine their 'creativity, conceptual and analytic thought and manual or physical use of aptitudes'.[8] It allows them to develop and prove themselves if their productive activity requires specialised education and mastery of complex skills.[9] It also provides the opportunity to identify oneself through the engagement in a productive activity by meeting its physical and intellectual challenges, which matters for its own sake rather than merely for the material benefits it affords.[10] Second, Articles 15–17 CFR safeguard individual self-sustenance in the sense of achieving independence and self-empowerment. These provisions allow individuals to address the essential human necessities for survival.[11] A property on its own and an economic activity in an employed or self-employed capacity are means by which individuals can provide for basic needs for themselves and their families.[12] As a source of income,[13] they are fundamental to attaining one's conception of the good life.[14] Under this construction, Articles 15–17 CFR give

[4] Case C-9/99 *Echirolles Distribution SA v Association du Dauphine* EU:C:2000:532, para 25. See also S Leible, 'Fundamental Freedoms and European Contract Law' in S Grundmann (ed), *Constitutional Values and European Contract Law* (Alphen aan den Rijn, Kluwer, 2008), 65; M Everson and C Gonçalez, 'Article 16' in S Peers, T Harvey, J Kenner and A Ward (eds), *The EU Charter of Fundamental Rights: A Commentary* (Oxford, Hart Publishing, 2014) 438.

[5] G Naraine, 'Dignity, Self-Realization and the Spirit of Service: Principles and Practices of Decent Work' in D Peccoud (ed), *Philosophical and Spiritual Perspectives on Decent Work* (Geneva, International Labour Office, 2004) 96.

[6] JW Nickel, *Making Sense of Human Rights*, 2nd edn (London, Wiley-Blackwell, 2006) 158.

[7] J Sarkin and M Koenig, 'Developing the Right to Work: Intersecting and Dialoguing Human Rights and Economic Policy' (2011) 33 *Human Rights Quarterly* 1, 3.

[8] P Harvey, 'The Right to Work and Basic Income Guarantees: Competing or Complementary Goals? (2005) 2 *Rutgers Journal of Law & Urban Policy* 8, 8.

[9] Nickel (n 6) 159.

[10] H Collins, 'Is There a Human Right to Work?' in V Mantouvalou (ed), *The Right to Work: Legal and Philosophical Perspectives* (Oxford, Hart Publishing, 2017) 35.

[11] ibid 17.

[12] Naraine (n 5) 96.

[13] AL Bogg, 'Only Fools and Horses: Some Sceptical Reflections on the Right to Work' in Mantouvalou (n 10) 152.

[14] V Schultz, 'Life is Work' (2000) 100 *Columbia Law Review* 1881, 1886.

effect to the right to dignity through the manifestation of values of self-esteem and respect from others.[15]

Much like the general principles of law manifesting the ideals of private autonomy, a clear normative correlation exists between Articles 15–17 CFR. In *Schaible*,[16] AG Wahl pointed out that the freedom to pursue an occupation and the freedom to conduct business 'largely overlap[ed] in that they both relate[d] to the right of Union citizens freely to engage in and conduct an economic activity'.[17] More broadly, AG Bobek in *Lidl* drew parallels between them, for they protect 'the realm of individual autonomy in the closely related professional and business fields'.[18] This finds support in *Spain v Commission*,[19] where the Court held that the freedom to conduct business coincided with the freedom to pursue an occupation.[20] These individual entitlements are, therefore, often invoked and interpreted together.[21] In *Deutsches Weintor*,[22] the Court scrutinised the compatibility with both Articles 15 and 16 CFR of the measure that limited the use of nutrition and health claims in the marketing of foods. A comparable normative overlap also exists between Articles 16 and 17 CFR. For AG Cruz Villalón, the freedom to conduct business constitutes a corollary of the right to property within the framework of Union law and national legal systems.[23] Similarly, for AG Bobek, the freedom to conduct business 'bears a closer connection to entrepreneurial activity, with strong links to the right to property'.[24] In his view, these individual rights converge in terms of their link with the protection of personality rights of legal persons in the sense that such protection is conducive to the enjoyment of the right to property or the freedom to conduct business.[25] This logic seems to be endorsed in *Interseroh Scrap*,[26] where the Court's reasoning suggests that the protection of commercial secrets falls within the scope of both Articles 16 and 17 CFR.[27]

Articles 15–17 CFR also converge in terms of their legal effect. They are not only explicitly addressed to the Union's institutions and Member States when acting within the scope of Union law but are equally enforceable in a private setting. While this finds endorsement in the case law,[28] the Court has yet to assign horizontality

[15] Collins (n 10) 27.
[16] Case C-101/12 *Herbert Schaible v Land Baden-Württemberg* EU:C:2013:661.
[17] ibid para 25.
[18] Opinion of AG Bobek in Case C-134/15 *Lidl v Freistaat Sachsen* EU:C:2016:169, para 25.
[19] Joined Cases C-184/02 and C-223/02 *Spain and Finland v European Parliament and Council* EU:C:2004:497.
[20] ibid para 51.
[21] Opinion of AG Bobek in *Lidl* (n 18) para 21.
[22] Case C-544/10 *Deutsches Weintor v Land Rheinland-Pfalz* EU:C:2012:526.
[23] Case C-426/11 *Mark Alemo-Herron and Others v Parkwood Leisure Ltd* EU:C:2013:521, paras 48–52.
[24] Opinion of AG Bobek in *Lidl* (n 18) para 26.
[25] Opinion of AG Bobek in Case C-194/16 *Bolagsupplysningen and Ilsjan* EU:C:2017:554, para 49.
[26] Case C-1/11 *Interseroh Scrap and Metals Trading* EU:C:2012:194.
[27] ibid para 43.
[28] See, eg, Case C-70/10 *Scarlet Extended v SABAM* EU:C:2011:771.

to these provisions. Their enforceability in private relationships seems to be taken at face value, which can be rationalised in two ways. First, the normative foundation of Articles 15–17 CFR is rooted in the domain of private law principles that traditionally frame the relationships among individuals. Second, viewed strictly in a private setting, the nature of these provisions is imbued by the concept of negative rights in the sense of subjective prerogatives not to be interfered with by others. They claim for the rights holder a personal sphere of non-interference that is conducive to self-fulfilment, self-dependence and self-sustenance. However, the cross-over between Articles 15, 16 and 17 CFR does not imply an amalgamation of these provisions. The entitlements they confer on the rights holder are not identical in nature and content, though the precise criteria delineating their scope are not set out in the case law. Partly, this stems from the Court's often-favoured methodology that prioritises the proportionality-based assessment of possible justifications instead of the classification of the actual interests protected by a fundamental right.[29] Partly, it is difficult to unequivocally outline the scope of fundamental rights norms *in abstracto*,[30] which means that judicial scrutiny is often limited to a narrow set of factual constellations. Nonetheless, the broader normative contours of Articles 15, 16 and 17 CFR can still be discerned from the case law.

A. Article 16 CFR: Freedom to Conduct Business

The textual formulation of Article 16 CFR leaves much ambiguity over the exact nature of the freedom to conduct business. It merely states that this freedom 'is recognised in accordance with Union and national laws and practices'. This distinguishes it from Articles 15 and 17 CFR, which enshrine a relatively stronger safeguard. Two elements are at play here. First, unlike Article 16 CFR, Articles 15 and 17 CFR are worded with the proclamation of 'everyone has the right to …', which can be construed as identifying the right holder and highlighting their application to every person regardless of background or status. Second, unlike Articles 15 and 17 CFR, Article 16 contains a reference to 'Union and national laws and practices'. This language seems to lessen the intensity of this provision, for it explicitly acknowledges its limitations.[31] Indeed, based on the wording of Article 16 CFR, the Court confirmed that the freedom to conduct business could be subject 'to a broad range of interventions on the part of public authorities that may

[29] M Kumm, '*Internationale Handelsgesellschaft, Nold* and the New Human Rights Paradigm' in L Azoulai and L Poiares Pessoa Maduro (eds), *The Past and Future of EU Law: The Classics of EU Law Revisited on the 50th Anniversary of the Rome Treaty* (Oxford, Hart Publishing, 2010) 109.

[30] T Tridimas and G Gentile, 'The Essence of Rights: An Unreliable Boundary?' (2019) 20 *German Law Journal* 794, 809.

[31] P Oliver, 'What Purpose Does Article 16 of the Charter Serve?' in U Bernitz, X Groussot and F Schulyok (eds), *General Principles of EU Law and European Private Law* (Alphen aan den Rijn, Kluwer Law International, 2013) 285.

limit the exercise of economic activity in the public interest'.[32] Not surprisingly, the initial academic commentaries questioned whether Article 16 CFR enshrined a fundamental right instead of a non-justiciable principle within the meaning of Article 52(5) CFR.[33] This controversy was put to rest in *Sky Österreich* and the subsequent case law,[34] where the Court characterised the freedom to conduct business as a right that is not only enforceable against the Union's institutions and Member States but is also capable of producing at least quasi-horizontal effect.[35] According to the Explanations to the Charter, the constituent parts of Article 16 CFR include the freedom to exercise economic or commercial activity, the freedom of contract, and the principle of (or the right to) free competition. Therefore, the scope *ratione materiae* of this provision rests on the delineation of the specific forms of rights already recognised in the case law and now consolidated within the framework of the Charter.

i. Scope Ratione Personae

The scope *ratione personae* of Article 16 CFR does not envisage any limitation as to its right holder. The individual safeguards protected by this provision apply to all natural and legal persons so long as they are involved in a gainful activity of an economic or commercial nature throughout the Union. The scope of Article 16 CFR is not confined to Union citizens or legal persons established in Member States. The same protection is guaranteed, in a truly universal sense, to everyone, provided that a situation is governed by Union law.[36]

ii. Scope Ratione Materiae

In *Alemo-Herron*,[37] AG Cruz Villalón asserted that the freedom to conduct business protected 'economic initiative and the ability to participate in a market, rather than the actual profit, seen in financial terms, that [was] earned in that market'.[38] This was echoed in *Azarov*,[39] where the Court characterised Article 16 CFR as a norm that conferred upon its right holder the liberty to '[pursue] industrial or commercial activities for profit within the EU'.[40] The Court's definition implies

[32] See Case C-201/15 *Anonymi Geniki Etairia Tsimenton Iraklis (AGET Iraklis)* EU:C:2016:972, para 86.

[33] On the difference of views, see Oliver (n 31) 295.

[34] Case C-283/11 *Sky Österreich GmbH v Österreichischer Rundfunk* EU:C:2013:28, para 44. See also Case C-360/10 *SABAM v Netlog* EU:C:2012:85.

[35] M Everson and S Gonçalves, 'Article 16' in Peers et al (n 4) 449.

[36] Case C-398/13 P *Inuit Tapiriit Kanatami v Commission* EU:C:2015:535, para 56; Case C-72/15 *R (on the Application of PJSC Rosneft Oil Co) v HM Treasury* EU:C:2017:236, para 148.

[37] *Mark Alemo-Herron* (n 23).

[38] ibid para 51.

[39] Case T-215/15 *Mykola Yanovych Azarov v Council* EU:T:2017:479.

[40] ibid para 44.

a broader meaning to the freedom to conduct business that envisages the right to access and maintain the engagement in any form of business allowed by law. Indeed, it can be construed to cover the whole range of life cycles that a business venture usually goes through.[41] First, this includes the launch of such a venture. In *Spika*,[42] the Court found that the method of allocation of fishing opportunities based on an operator's average catch for a set period could be detrimental to the freedom of new operators to conduct business by limiting their ability to enter and operate in the market.[43] Second, the scope of Article 16 CFR extends beyond the protection afforded to individuals to establish a business by encompassing all aspects related to its operation.[44] In *UPC Telekabel Wien*,[45] the Court defined Article 16 CFR to include 'the right for any business to be able to freely use, within the limits of its liability for its own acts, the economic, technical and financial resources available to it'.[46] Pursuant to this finding, the Court in *Lidl* found that the labelling obligation, although objectively justified, was liable to limit the freedom to conduct business, for it restricted an economic actor from freeling using its resources, given the prospect of significant costs and considerable impact on the organisation of its activities.[47] Similarly, in *BB Construct*,[48] the national law that made it necessary to furnish a tax guarantee of significant value for tax payment purposes was found to impose a constraint on the unhindered use of financial resources contrary to Article 16 CFR.[49] In *PI*,[50] a restriction of the freedom to conduct business stemmed from the administrative practice of closing a commercial establishment with an immediate effect without formal notice, for it could have negative consequences on the turnover and continuation of professional activity.[51] According to the case law, the protection bestowed by Article 16 CFR equally applies to the winding-up of a business operation. In *AGET Iraklis*,[52] the Court found that the national regime imposing a framework of collective redundancies interfered with the exercise of the freedom to conduct business because it could prevent an employer from putting redundancy plans into effect.[53]

Unlike the aspects related to setting up and winding down a business operation, a considerable body of case law relates to the performative elements intrinsic

[41] B Veneziani, 'Article 16 – Freedom to Conduct a Business' in F Dorssemont, K Lörcher, S Clauwaert and M Schmitt (eds), *The Charter of Fundamental Rights of the European Union and the Employment Relation* (Oxford, Hart Publishing, 2019) 356.

[42] Case C-540/16 *UAB 'Spika' and Others* EU:C:2018:565.

[43] ibid para 33.

[44] Everson and Gonçalves (n 35) 452.

[45] Case C-314/12 *UPC Telekabel Wien GmbH v Constantin Film Verleih* EU:C:2014:192.

[46] ibid para 48.

[47] Case C-134/15 *Lidl v Freistaat Sachsen* EU:C:2016:498, para 29.

[48] Case C-534/16 *Finančné riaditeľstvo Slovenskej republiky v BB construct* EU:C:2017:820.

[49] ibid para 38.

[50] Case C-230/18 *PI v Landespolizeidirektion Tirol* EU:C:2019:383.

[51] ibid para 60.

[52] *AGET Iraklis* (n 32).

[53] ibid para 69.

to the exercise of economic or commercial activity. In *Deutsches Weintor*,[54] the Court made it clear that the complete prohibition imposed on the marketing of legally produced goods would breach Article 16 CFR. However, this does not apply to measures that 'merely control, in a very clearly defined area, the associated labelling and advertising'.[55] Under Article 16 CFR, economic actors are also entitled, as confirmed in *Interseroh*,[56] to special safeguards against the disclosure of confidential information and business secrets.[57] The same applies to the internal policies of political, philosophical and religious neutrality. In *Achbita*,[58] the Court declared that the scope of protection under Article 16 CFR encompassed the desire of an employer to project an image of neutrality,[59] the adoption of which allowed, within certain limits, for restrictions to be imposed on the freedom of religion.[60] According to the Court, for the proper implementation of such a policy, it is appropriate that employees are prohibited 'from visibly wearing signs of political, philosophical or religious beliefs', provided that this is genuinely pursued consistently and systematically.[61] However, as subsequently clarified, the mere desire to deploy a policy of neutrality is insufficient to justify a difference of treatment indirectly based on grounds of religion.[62] In the Court's view, two conditions must be met. First, a policy of neutrality must reflect the rights and legitimate wishes of an employer's customers and users.[63] Second, there must be evidence that in the absence of such a policy, an employer would face adverse consequences, given the nature of its activities and the context in which they are carried out.[64]

Integral to the effective realisation of the freedom to engage in economic or commercial activity is contractual freedom, now protected by Article 16 CFR. In *Thelen Technopark*,[65] AG Szpunar defined this freedom to include 'the freedom to conclude a contract, to choose the counterparty and to determine the content of a contract', including the right to define the amount of mutual benefits, 'in particular the price or remuneration for the other party's services'.[66] These characteristics of the freedom of contract are reflected in the case law. The Court often repeats that contractual freedom includes 'the freedom to choose with whom to do business and the freedom to determine the price of a

[54] *Deutsches Weintor* (n 22).
[55] ibid para 57.
[56] *Interseroh Scrap and Metals Trading* (n 26).
[57] ibid para 43.
[58] Case C-157/15 *Samira Achbita and Centrum voor gelijkheid van kansen en voor racismebestrijding v G4S Secure Solutions* EU:C:2017:203.
[59] ibid para 38.
[60] ibid para 39.
[61] ibid para 40.
[62] Case C-344/20 *LF v SCRL* EU:C:2022:774, para 40.
[63] Joined Cases C-804/18 and C-341/19 *IX v WABE eV and MH Müller Handels* EU:C:2021:594, para 65.
[64] ibid para 67.
[65] Case C-261/20 *Thelen Technopark Berlin* EU:C:2022:33.
[66] Opinion of AG Spunar in Case C-261/20 *Thelen Technopark Berlin* EU:C:2021:620, para 82.

service'.[67] As confirmed by the Court, from a normative standpoint, these individual entitlements operate as a right rather than a principle within the meaning of Article 52 CFR. They encapsulate the liberty of economic actors to participate in the market without being constrained by others. These individual safeguards translate into the obligation to refrain from interfering with parties' autonomy of will by prescribing the conclusion or termination of contracts or by imposing specific terms on them.[68]

The Court upheld this obligation in *YS*,[69] where it found that a national rule limited the freedom of contract as it required undertakings to pay their former employees a pension allowance of lower value than the contractually agreed amount.[70] In *Sky Österreich*, in turn, the Court concluded that, although justified on objective grounds, the obligation imposed on the holder of exclusive broadcasting rights to provide access to short extracts interfered with the freedom to conduct business.[71] This is because the holder of exclusive rights could not freely decide who it wished to enter into an agreement or determine the price to charge for granting access to short extracts.[72] On these grounds, the freedom of contract was also upheld in *Alemo-Herron*, where the issue concerned the national law that, in the event of a transfer of an undertaking, bound a new employer to collective agreements in the negotiation of which it was not involved. The Court found that an employer in these circumstances was unable to participate in the collective bargaining process by asserting its interests effectively or negotiating the aspects related to the working conditions of its new employees.[73] In the Court's view, this seriously reduced its contractual freedom to the point of adversely affecting the very essence of the freedom to conduct business.[74] In *Deutsche Telekom*,[75] the Court confirmed that the freedom to choose a contracting party is enjoyed even by dominant undertakings. According to the Court, despite their market position, they are also entitled, in principle, to decide whether to agree or refuse to conclude binding agreements with their competitors or third parties.[76]

According to the Explanations to the Charter, the freedom to engage in economic activity and contractual freedom presuppose the adherence and preservation of a system based on free competition.[77] This aspect of Article 16 CFR remains controversial and contested. It primarily stems from the uncertainty

[67] Case C-277/16 *Polkomtel sp z oo v Prezes Urzędu Komunikacji Elektronicznej* EU:C:2017:989, para 50; Joined Cases C-798/18 and C-799/18 *Federazione nazionale delle imprese elettrotecniche ed elettroniche (Anie) and Others* EU:C:2021:280, para 57.

[68] Opinion of AG Spunar in *Thelen Technopark* (n 66) para 84.

[69] Case C-223/19 *YS (Occupational Pensions of Managerial Staff)* EU:C:2020:753.

[70] ibid para 87.

[71] *Sky Österreich* (n 34) para 44.

[72] ibid.

[73] *Mark Alemo-Herron* (n 23) para 34.

[74] ibid para 35.

[75] Case C-152/19 P *Deutsche Telekom AG v Commission* EU:C:2021:238.

[76] ibid para 46.

[77] Explanations relating to the Charter of Fundamental Rights [2007] OJ C303, 23.

surrounding the question of whether the concept of 'free competition' is to be understood as a right or a mere principle within the meaning of Article 52 CFR and, concomitantly, the extent to which it can be enforceable. The concept of 'free competition', unlike the two individual entitlements discussed above, is premised on the wording of the Treaty.[78] The Explanations to the Charter specifically refer to Article 119(1) TFEU, under which 'the activities of the Member States and the Union shall include, as provided in the Treaties, the adoption of an economic policy which is … conducted in accordance with the principle of an open market economy with free competition'. Broadly considered, the link drawn between Article 16 CFR and Article 119(1) TFEU signifies the wider commitment of the Union to the model of political economy or socio-economic organisation that is infused by free market principles.[79] The Lisbon Treaty indeed brought about a change to the place of the concept of 'free competition' within the objectives of the Treaty. It no longer expressly incorporates the adherence to the principle of undistorted competition, which only appears in Protocol 27 on the internal market and competition. Notwithstanding this, there was no 'downgrade' in its legal status.[80] In *TeliaSonera*,[81] the Court confirmed that the objective of establishing the internal market enshrined under Article 3(3) TFEU included, as per the Protocol, 'a system ensuring that competition [was] not distorted'.[82] Thus, as the individualisation of the commitment to 'the principle of an open market economy with free competition', Article 16 CFR can be construed to give effect to the subjective right to free and undistorted competition recognised in the Union's legal order.

This characterisation resonates with the Treaty's competition rules that guarantee the system of free and undistorted competition in the internal market by prohibiting certain forms of market conduct by private actors with unilateral or combined market power.[83] These provisions can produce both vertical and horizontal forms of direct effect.[84] As often reiterated by the Court, they 'create rights for the individuals concerned' to be safeguarded by national courts.[85] The existence of these rights is vindicated by the availability of adequate and effective

[78] Oliver (n 31) 286.

[79] Everson and Gonçalves (n 35) 438.

[80] JL Buendia Sierra, 'Writing Straight with Crooked Lines: Competition Policy and Services of General Economic Interest in the Treaty of Lisbon' in A Biondi, P Eeckhout and S Ripley (eds), *EU Law after Lisbon* (Oxford, Oxford University Press, 2012) 355.

[81] Case C-52/09 *TeliaSonera* EU:C:2011:83.

[82] ibid para 20. See also Case C-496/09 *Commission v Italy* EU:C:2011:740, para 60.

[83] See, eg, Opinion of AG Kokott in Case C-95/04 P *British Airways v Commission* EU:C:2006:133, para 68.

[84] See, eg, Case 127/73 *Belgische Radio en Televisie and SABAM* EU:C:1974:6, para 16; Case C-282/95 P *Guérin Automobiles v Commission* EU:C:1997:159, para 39.

[85] See, eg, Case C-557/12 *Kone AG v OBB-Infrastruktur AG* EU:C:2014:1317, para 20; Case C-724/17 *Skanska Industrial Solutions* EU:C:2019:204, para 24; Case C-637/17 *Cogeco Communications Inc v Sport Portugal SA* EU:C:2019:263, para 38.

remedies. In *Courage v Crehan*,[86] the Court found that 'the full effectiveness of [the Treaty's competition rules] … would be put at risk if it were not open to any individual to claim damages for loss caused to him by a contract or by conduct liable to restrict or distort competition'.[87] This finding was subsequently confirmed in *Manfredi*,[88] where the Court held that 'any individual [could] claim compensation for the harm suffered where there [was] a causal relationship between that harm and an agreement or practice prohibited under [the Treaty's competition rules]'.[89] The grant of remedies under these rules can, therefore, be understood to signal the existence of a material link between the subjective right to compete and the realisation of the freedom to conduct business now protected under Article 16 CFR.[90]

B. Article 15 CFR: Freedom to Choose an Occupation

Article 15 CFR does not by itself define the concept of the right to work. The textual formulation of its first paragraph is confined to the proclamation that 'everyone has the right to engage in work and to pursue a freely chosen or accepted occupation'. The only guidance is provided in the Explanations to the Charter, which refer to two sources. First, they specifically mention *Nold*, where the Court, for the first time, acknowledged 'the right freely to choose and practice … trade or profession' as an entitlement protected by national constitutions, though without it being 'an unfettered prerogative'.[91] The Explanations to the Charter also refer to *Hauer* and *Keller*,[92] in which the Court reiterated its finding in *Nold* by explicitly declaring that 'the freedom to pursue one's trade or profession [was] part of the general principles of law, the observance of which it ensure[d]'.[93] Second, the Explanations to the Charter draw upon the European Social Charter and the Community Charter of the Fundamental Social Rights of Workers, highlighting the provisions contained therein that call for the effective protection of the right to earn a living. However, the Explanations to the Charter do not refer to provisions that connote the 'positive' dimension of the right to work expressed in the state duty to ensure the realisation of this right through a coherent employment

[86] Case C-453/99 *Courage v Crehan* EU:C:2001:465.
[87] ibid para 26.
[88] Joined Cases C-295/04 to C-298/04 *Vincenzo Manfredi v Lloyd Adriatico Assicurazioni SpA* EU:C:2006:461.
[89] ibid para 61.
[90] J Drexl, 'Competition Law as Part of the European Constitution' in A von Bogdandy and J Bast (eds), *Principles of European Constitutional Law* (Oxford, Hart Publishing, 2009) 694.
[91] Case 4/73 *Nold, Kohlen- und Baustoffgroßhandlung v Commission* EU:C:1974:51, para 14.
[92] Case 44/79 *Liselotte Hauer v Land Rheinland-Pfalz* EU:C:1979:290; Case 234/85 *Staatsanwaltschaf Freiburg and Franz Keller* EU:C:2005:211.
[93] *Nold* (n 91) para 13.

policy.[94] Therefore, Article 15 CFR cannot be construed to enshrine the full guarantee of the right to employment.[95] Its textual formulation does not refer to 'the right to work' but enshrines 'the right to engage in work' and 'the freedom to choose occupation'.[96] This affirms that the achievement of full employment permeates the Union discourse at the policy-making level rather than through the language of rights.[97]

i. *Scope* Ratione Personae

The scope *ratione personae* of Article 15 CFR is expressed in three parts to its structure. The first paragraph of the Article provides that 'everyone has the right to engage in work and to pursue a freely chosen or accepted occupation'. This provision is broadly worded in terms of its addressees. The reference to 'everyone' sets out a relatively generous scope for the right to work under Article 15 CFR compared to other provisions in the Solidarity title of the Charter.[98] It applies to individuals having the status of a worker or employee but equally extends to those engaged in economic activity in a self-employed capacity, for it also protects the 'right to choose an occupation'.[99] However, its scope is limited to natural persons and does not extend to corporate entities. Although the Explanations to the Charter are silent on this very point, this follows from two interrelated premises. Unlike natural persons, corporate entities do not engage in work or pursue an occupation within the meaning of Article 15 CFR.[100] The conduct of economic activity in a corporate capacity would not trigger Article 15 CFR but would instead fall within the scope of Article 16 CFR. As pointed out by AG Bobek, despite the occasional application of Article 15 CFR in conjunction with Articles 16 and 17 CFR,[101] the claims made based on the former provision primarily concern the economic activities conducted by natural persons.[102]

The broad construction of the addressees in the first paragraph of Article 15 CFR is further reinforced by the specific categories of beneficiaries identified in the second and third paragraphs.[103] The second paragraph provides that 'every citizen of the Union has the freedom to seek employment, to work, to exercise the

[94] D Ashiagbor, 'Article 15: Freedom to Choose an Occupation and Right to Engage in Work, and Article 29: Right of Access to Placement Services' in Peers et al (n 4) 428.

[95] Employment, Vocational Guidance and Training in the European Social Charter, Human Rights Social Charter monographs NO 8 (1999), 13–14.

[96] S Deakin, 'Article 15 – Freedom to Choose an Occupation and Right to Engage in Work' in Dorssemont et al (n 41) 332.

[97] D Ashiagbor, 'The Right to Work' in G de Búrca and B de Witte (eds), *Social Rights in Europe* (Oxford, Oxford University Press, 2005) 244.

[98] See also Ashiagbor (n 94) 431.

[99] See Case T-817/14 *Zoofachhandel Züpke and Others v Commission* EU:T:2016:157, para 126.

[100] Deakin (n 96) 342.

[101] See, eg, Case C-390/12 *Robert Pfleger and Others* EU:C:2014:281.

[102] Opinion of AG Bobek in *Lidl* (n 18) para 27. See also *PI* (n 50) para 54.

[103] Ashiagbor (n 97) 431.

right of establishment and to provide services in any Member State'. It is addressed to Union citizens by granting them the right to engage in cross-border economic activity in an employed or self-employed capacity. The confinement of this right to Union citizens mirrors the approach to the personal scope of the Treaty's free movement provisions.[104] On the one hand, the Explanations to the Charter stipulate that the second paragraph of Article 15 CFR deals with the Treaty's provisions on the freedom of movement for workers, freedom of establishment and freedom to provide services. On the other hand, Article 53(2) CFR also states that 'rights recognised by this Charter for which provision is made in the Treaties shall be exercised under the conditions and within the limits defined by those Treaties'. Under this provision, the Court held that 'Article 15(2) of the Charter reiterate[d] inter alia the free movement of workers guaranteed by Article 45 TFEU'.[105]

The third paragraph of Article 15 CFR concerns the rights of third-country nationals. It stipulates that '[nationals of third countries] who are authorised to work in the territories of the Member States are entitled to working conditions equivalent to those of citizens of the Union'. Compared to the first two paragraphs under Article 15 CFR, the personal scope of the third paragraph is narrowly defined. It is confined to third-country nationals who are already authorised to work in Member States. As such, Article 15 CFR plays no role in determining the access of third-country nationals to the employment market in the Union or their entitlement to free movement in the internal market.[106] This is supported by the reference included in the Explanation to the Charter, whereby the third paragraph of Article 15 CFR is premised upon Article 153 TFEU, which sets out the boundaries of the Union's social policy. According to this provision, the Union supports and complements the activities of Member States concerning 'conditions of employment for third-country nationals legally residing in Union territory'.

ii. Scope Ratione Materiae

The scope *ratione materiae* of Article 15 CFR is also framed by its structure. The first paragraph enshrines the general right to enter and pursue the chosen trade or profession, the right to seek, accept and perform employment, and the right not to be discriminated against when seeking employment and in relation to the chosen work.[107] In *Werner Fries*,[108] the Court found that the age limitation imposed on the holder of a licence to operate a commercial aircraft restricted the freedom to choose an occupation.[109] However, the Court proceeded to note that this freedom

[104] Deakin (n 96) 340.

[105] See Case C-284/15 *Office national de l'emploi (ONEm) and M* EU:C:2016:220, para 33; Case C-233/12 *Simone Gardella v Istituto nazionale della previdenza sociale (INPS)* EU:C:2013:449, para 39.

[106] Ashiagbor (n 97) 432.

[107] Deakin (n 96) 343.

[108] Case C-190/16 *Werner Fries v Lufthansa CityLine* EU:C:2017:513.

[109] ibid para 71.

was not absolute and had to be considered in relation to its social function.[110] It can be subject to restrictions that correspond to the objectives of general interest pursued by the Union.[111] On this basis, the Court found that the age limitation was justified on grounds of aviation safety.[112] In the Court's view, not only was it not disproportionate, but it also did not affect the substance of the freedom to pursue an occupation, 'since it merely impose[d] certain restrictions on the professional activity of holders of a pilot's licence who [had] attained the age of 65'.[113] The scope of Article 15 CFR thus encompasses protective safeguards against discrimination on grounds of age, though they can be conditioned by the objectives of general interest. The same also applies to the age-related social policies of Member States. In *Fuchs*,[114] the Court held that 'keeping older workers in the labour force promote[d] diversity in the workforce' and 'contribute[d] to the realising of their potential and to the quality of life of the workers'.[115] At the same time, it also found that 'the interest represented by the continued employment of those persons must be taken into account in respecting other, potentially divergent interests'.[116] In this regard, the Court acknowledged the legitimacy of the aim of 'establishing a balanced age structure in order to encourage the recruitment and promotion of young people, to improve personnel management and thereby to prevent possible disputes concerning employees' fitness to work beyond a certain age'.[117]

The case law also confirms the qualified nature of the freedom to choose an occupation and engage in work. In *Muladi*,[118] based on a claim brought by a former accredited driving examiner, the Court was asked to consider the compatibility with Article 15 CFR of the national law that subjected the issue of a certificate of professional competence to compulsory training. It found that this requirement was justified on grounds of road safety and safety of drivers, and did not constitute intolerable and disproportionate interference with the substance of the right to engage in a profession.[119] A similar conclusion was reached in *Giordano* against the claim that the Union's secondary law restricting the fishing of bluefin tuna in the Mediterranean Sea was incompatible with the right to pursue and carry out an occupation as guaranteed by Article 15 CFR.[120] Having reiterated the non-absolute nature of this provision,[121] the Court held that the restriction was in line

[110] ibid para 73.
[111] M Ruffert, 'The Right to Pursue a Freely Chosen Occupation' in D Ehlers (ed), *European Fundamental Rights and Freedoms* (Berlin, De Gruyter, 2007) 436.
[112] *Werner Fries v Lufthansa CityLine* (n 108) para 78.
[113] ibid para 75.
[114] Joined Cases C-159/10 and C-160/10 *Fuchs and Köhler* EU:C:2011:508.
[115] ibid para 63.
[116] ibid para 64. According to the Court, for instance, 'those who have reached the age at which they are entitled to a retirement pension may wish to avail themselves of it and to leave work with the benefit of that pension, instead of continuing to work'.
[117] ibid para 68.
[118] Case C-447/15 *Ivo Muladi v Krajský úřad Moravskoslezského kraj* EU:C:2016:533.
[119] ibid para 51.
[120] Case C-611/12 P *Giordano v Commission* EU:C:2014:2282.
[121] ibid para 49. See also Case C-555/10 *Commission v Austria* EU:C:2013:115, para 38.

with the objective of avoiding a serious threat to the conservation and recovery of bluefin tuna stock in the Eastern Atlantic and the Mediterranean Sea.[122]

The case law also defines the nature of individual entitlements not falling within the scope of protection under Article 15 CFR. In *Zoofachhandel Züpke*,[123] the claim, brought by animal dealers, related to the compatibility with the Charter of the Union's secondary law that prohibited the import of wild birds. In dismissing this claim, the Court held that 'any fall in turnover or any loss of profits associated with a differential in the resale price between captive bred birds and birds captured in their natural environment [could] clearly not constitute an infringement upon the very substance of fundamental rights, which [was] far wider than commercial opportunity'.[124] In *Lidl*, in turn, the Court chose to review the compatibility of the national labelling obligation in light of Article 16 CFR instead of Article 15 CFR. According to the Court, the reason lay in the fact that the labelling obligation did not limit the option available to persons 'to pursue a freely chosen ... occupation' within the meaning of Article 15 CFR.[125] In contrast, in its view, it could restrict the freedom to conduct business enshrined in Article 16 CFR.[126]

The scope *ratione materiae* of the second and third paragraph of Article 15 CFR is even more delimited. As mentioned earlier, the former provision entitles Union citizens to the freedom to seek employment, exercise the right of establishment and provide services in other Member States. As such, it reiterates the rights enshrined under Articles 45, 49 and 56 TFEU.[127] There are two facets to the normative link between these provisions and Article 15 CFR. First, under Article 52(2) CFR, the rights enshrined in the second paragraph are subject to the conditions and limits of Articles 45, 49 and 56 TFEU. Second, any restriction of these provisions would also constitute a constraint of the second paragraph under Article 15 CFR.[128] Conversely, any Union or national provision that complies with the former set of the Treaty's provisions would also be deemed to be in line with Article 15 CFR.[129]

In contrast to Union citizens, within the framework of Article 15 CFR, the extent of protection afforded to third-country nationals is substantially narrow. As mentioned earlier, the third paragraph of this provision states that 'nationals of third countries who are authorised to work in the territories of the Member States are entitled to working conditions equivalent to those of citizens of the Union'. According to the Explanations to the Charter, the reference to 'working

[122] ibid para 50.
[123] Case T-817/14 *Zoofachhandel Züpke and Others v Commission* EU:T:2016:157.
[124] ibid para 132.
[125] Case C-134/15 *Lidl GmbH & Co KG v Freistaat Sachsen* EU:C:2016:498, para 26.
[126] ibid.
[127] See, eg, Case C-237/18 *Pauline Stiernon and Others v Etat belge* EU:C:2018:630, para 22.
[128] Opinion of AG Wahl in Case C-270/13 *Iraklis Haralambidis v Calogero Casilli* EU:C:2014:1358, para 36.
[129] Opinion of AG Hogan in Case C-465/18 *AV and BU v Comune di Bernareggio* EU:C:2019:812, para 34.

conditions' is intended to be understood within the meaning of Article 156 TFEU, which refers to, among other things, basic and advanced vocational training, social security, prevention of occupational accidents and diseases, occupational hygiene, collective bargaining and association. In this regard, Article 15 CFR only presupposes equivalence in treatment between third-country nationals and Union citizens. According to the Explanations to the Charter, this is premised on Article 19(4) of the European Social Charter, which requires the Contracting Parties that migrant workers are subject to 'treatment not less favourable than that of their own nationals in respect of', for instance, remuneration and other employment conditions or the membership of trade unions and the enjoyment of benefits of collective bargaining.

C. Article 17 CFR: Right to Property

Article 17 CFR 'constitutionalises' the personal freedom to acquire assets of value and control them without the interference of others.[130] From a conceptual standpoint, it has two aspects: first, it is grounded in the interest to exclusively deal with an asset of value in a purposeful manner;[131] second, it is supported by the power to exclude others from interfering with such use.[132] The extent of the latter aspect determines the normative protection of the former. Although academic opinion varies over the centrality of either in the construction of the right to property,[133] the right to exclude others from using a given asset of value is predominantly considered to constitute the centrepiece of this individual right.[134]

i. The Source of Article 17: Article 1 of Protocol 1 to the ECHR

According to the Explanation to the Charter, Article 17 CFR is based on Article 1 of Protocol I to the ECHR. This finds its roots in the case law, which acknowledged the significance of the Convention to the protection of the right to property even prior to the entry into force of the Lisbon Treaty. In *ERSA*,[135] the Court held that 'to determine the scope of the fundamental right to property, a general principle of Community law, account must be taken inter alia of Article 1 of Protocol I to

[130] RA Spinello and M Bottis, *A Defense of Intellectual Property Rights* (Cheltenham, Edward Elgar, 2009) 149.
[131] JE Penner, *The Idea of Property in Law* (Oxford, Oxford University Press, 1997) 69–70.
[132] WM Landes and R Posner, 'Trademark Law: An Economic Perspective' (1987) 30 *Journal of Law and Economics* 265, 266.
[133] EM Glazer, 'Rule of (Out)Law: Property's Contingent Right to Exclude' (2008) 156 *University of Pennsylvania Law Review* 331, 332.
[134] See, eg, TW Merrill, 'Property and the Right to Exclude' (1998) 77 *Nebraska Law Review* 730; JY Stern, 'What is the Right to Exclude and Why Does it Matter?' in J Penner (ed), *Property Theory: Legal and Political Perspectives* (Cambridge, Cambridge University Press, 2018).
[135] Case C-347/03 *Regione autonoma Friuli-Venezia Giulia and ERSA* EU:C:2005:285.

the ECHR establishing that right'.[136] This finding is now expressed in general terms by the Charter itself. Under Article 52(3) CFR, the rights recognised by the Charter that correspond to the rights guaranteed by the ECHR shall have the same meaning and scope as the latter, though without prejudice to more extensive protection.[137] According to the Explanation to the Charter, this clause is aimed to ensure the necessary consistency between them, whereby their 'meaning and scope', 'including authorised limitations', remain the same.[138] Such an amalgamation of the normative guarantees secures the normative coherence between the Union's legal order and the ECHR in terms of protection of the fundamental right to property.[139] The explicit acceptance of the safeguards under the ECHR as a minimum threshold maintains the so-called presumption of equivalence developed by the European Court of Human Rights (ECtHR) in *Bosphorus*.[140]

The convergence between Article 17 CFR and Article 1 of Protocol I to the ECHR is manifested in their similar structure. Much like its predecessor, Article 17 CFR also comprises three main components. Its first paragraph is of a general nature that expresses the respect for private property as an institution.[141] It only differs in its specificity of enunciating ownership attributes such as 'the right to own, use, dispose of and bequeath … lawfully acquired possessions'.[142] The second paragraph under Article 17 CFR also follows the wording of Article 1 of Protocol I to the ECHR, which provides protective safeguards against property expropriation. Both provisions do not ban expropriation but add conditionality to its legitimacy, though the wording of Article 17 CFR differs from its predecessor on two accounts. First, any form of expropriation is contingent upon the payment of fair compensation.[143] Second, Article 17 CFR does not subject the legitimacy of expropriation to meeting conditions provided 'by the general principles of international law'.[144] Lastly, like Article 1 of Protocol I to the ECHR, the third sentence of Article 17 CFR states that 'the use of property may be regulated by law in so far

[136] ibid para 120.

[137] Case C-453/05 *Volker Ludwig v Finanzamt Luckenwalde* EU:C:2007:369, paras 51–52; Case C-528/15 *Al Chodor* EU:C:2017:213, para 37.

[138] Case C-400/10 PPU *J McB v LE* EU:C:2010:582, para 53; Case C-492/18 PPU *TC* EU:C:2019:108, para 57.

[139] Case C-279/09 *DEB v Bundesrepublik Deutschland* EU:C:2010:811, para 35.

[140] *Bosphorus Hava Yollari Turizm ve Ticaret Anonim Şirketi v Ireland* App No 45036/98 (ECtHR, 30 June 2005).

[141] F Becker, 'Market Regulation and the "Right to Property" in the European Economic Constitution' (2007) 26 *Yearbook of European Law* 255, 270.

[142] Charter of Fundamental Rights of the European Union [2000] OJ C364/01.

[143] Article 1 of Protocol 1 to the ECHR does not incorporate such a requirement. However, it is recognised in the case law of the ECtHR. See, eg, *Pálka and Others v the Czech Republic* App No 30262/13 (ECtHR, 24 March 2022, paras 47–51.

[144] This could be due to the inclusion of the term 'conditions provided for by law', the broad meaning of which seems to remove the need for a specific mention of 'the general principles of international law', though it can also be rationalised to convey the unique characteristics of the Union's legal order in shaping the confines of the right to property. For the latter point, see Opinion of AG Maduro in Joined Cases C-402/05 P and C-415/05 P *Yassin Abdullah Kadi and Al Barakaat International Foundation v Council* EU:C:2008:11, para 24.

as is necessary for the general interest'. This provides a platform to reconcile the needs of the general interest and the interests of an individual proprietor.[145]

ii. Scope of Application

The right to property protected by Article 17 CFR represents a strong form of authority held by an individual or corporation over an asset.[146] It is legally enforceable against others.[147] This provision encapsulates a bundle of rights,[148] including 'the right to own, use, dispose of and bequeath … lawfully acquired possessions'. As held in *Sky Österreich*,[149] the normative guarantees under Article 17 CFR concern 'rights with an asset value creating an established legal position under the legal system, enabling the holder to exercise those rights autonomously and for his benefit'.[150] This was given effect in *Inuit*,[151] where the Court found that 'Article 17 of the Charter [did] not apply to mere commercial interests or opportunities, the uncertainties of which [were] part of the very essence of economic activity'.[152] It also added that 'future income [could not] be considered to constitute 'possessions' that [might] enjoy the protection of that article unless it [had] already been earned, it [was] definitely payable or there [were] specific circumstances that [could] cause the person concerned to entertain a legitimate expectation of obtaining an asset'. The same line of reasoning extends to the entitlement to specific profit levels. In *Zoofachhandel Züpke*,[153] as mentioned previously, the Court ruled that 'any fall in turnover or any loss of profits associated with a differential in the resale price between [two different products of the same kind could] clearly not constitute an infringement upon the very substance of fundamental rights, which [was] far wider than commercial opportunity'.[154] This also applies to forms of aid received from national governments. In *ZS 'Ezernieki'*,[155] the Court concluded that 'a beneficiary who [was] obliged to repay aid obtained unduly, simply as a consequence of a failure to satisfy the conditions of their payment at issue, [could not] rely on … Article 17 of the Charter'.[156] Under this provision, therefore, the right to property only concerns any assets of value that can be held by an individual or corporation in the sense of its control, use and transferability. Insofar as an asset is lawfully

[145] Becker (n 141) 270.
[146] P Rubin and T Klumpp, 'Property Rights and Capitalism' in DC Mueller (ed), *The Oxford Handbook of Capitalism* (Oxford, Oxford University Press, 2012) 205.
[147] JE Penner, 'The "Bundle of Rights" Picture of Property' (1996) 43 *Los Angeles Law Review* 711, 712.
[148] D Sheehan, *The Principles of Personal Property Law*, 2nd edn (Oxford, Hart Publishing, 2017) 6.
[149] *Sky Österreich* (n 34).
[150] ibid para 34.
[151] Case C-583/11 P *Inuit Tapiriit Kanatami and Others v European Parliament and Council* EU:C:2013:625.
[152] ibid para 60.
[153] Case T-817/14 *Zoofachhandel Züpke and Others v Commission* EU:T:2016:157.
[154] ibid para 132.
[155] Case C-273/15 *ZS 'Ezernieki' v Lauku atbalsta dienests* EU:C:2016:364.
[156] ibid para 49.

acquired, Article 17 CFR applies to all legal positions of value that are of a material or immaterial nature.[157]

a. Assets of Material Value

Material assets relate to the entitlements to movable and immovable types of property.[158] This includes the ownership of land and anything erected or grown on it. In *Jozef Križan*,[159] the Court agreed with AG Kokott that the permit system envisaged for constructing and operating a landfill site restricted the right to property.[160] As AG Kokott further explained, the possibility under this system to challenge the substantive and procedural legality of decisions over the landfill site risked rendering certain projects impossible to implement or subjecting them to delays and restrictions in terms of their configuration.[161] Likewise, in *Pesce and Others*,[162] the Court held that the owners of agricultural holdings, who were ordered to cut down infected olive trees, could claim compensation under Article 17 CFR, even if it was not envisaged in the Union's secondary law.[163] The right to property equally presupposes various ways of ownership of movable assets, including placing them for use by others for profit. In *Pfleger*,[164] the Court found that the prior authorisation for the operation of gaming machines was restrictive of Article 56 TFEU and Article 17 CFR.[165] A similar conclusion was also reached in *Berlington Hungary*,[166] which concerned a tax increase over the operation of gaming machines outside casinos.[167] Article 17 CFR also affords protection to methods of disposing of movable properties. In *ATC*,[168] even without the claimants' plea, the Court found that the differentiated import policy regarding wild birds and captive-bred birds was not contrary to the right to property, given that unlike the former, the importing of the latter type of birds was still allowed.[169]

Furthermore, the right to property extends to assets of a pecuniary nature. In *Ledra Advertising*,[170] the Court found that the Commission was bound by Article 17 CFR in the course of the adoption of the macro-economic adjustment programme

[157] Becker (n 141) 270.
[158] JG Sprankling, *The International Law of Property* (Oxford, Oxford University Press, 2014) 23.
[159] Case C-416/10 *Jozef Križan and Others v Slovenská inšpekcia životného prostredia* EU:C:2013:8.
[160] ibid para 112.
[161] Opinion of AG Kokott in Case C-416/10 *Jozef Križan and Others v Slovenská inšpekcia životného prostredia* EU:C:2012:218, paras 183-184.
[162] Joined Cases C-78/16 and C-79/16 *Giovanni Pesce and Others v Presidenza del Consiglio dei Ministri* EU:C:2016:428.
[163] ibid para 85.
[164] Case C-390/12 *Robert Pfleger and Others* EU:C:2014:281.
[165] ibid para 57.
[166] Case C-98/14 *Berlington Hungary Tanácsadó és Szolgáltató kft and Others v Magyar Állam* EU:C:2015:386.
[167] ibid para 90.
[168] Case T-333/10 *Animal Trading Company (ATC) BV and Others v Commission* EU:T:2013:451.
[169] ibid para 190.
[170] Joined Cases C-8/15 P to C-10/15 P *Ledra Advertising Ltd and Others v Commission and ECB* EU:C:2016:701.

concerning Cypriot banks that involved measures over insured deposits held in them.[171] However, in response to the claimant's request for compensation equivalent to the diminution in value of their respective deposits, the Court found that the measures undertaken did not constitute unjustified interference with the right to property.[172] In its view, they were aimed to '[ensure] the stability of the banking system in the euro area' without 'impairing the very substance of the appellants' right to property'.[173] The assets of a pecuniary nature falling within the scope of Article 17 CFR also include rights to a social security benefit if its beneficiary has contributed to its acquisition by exercising a professional activity.[174] In *Florescu*, referring to the case law of the European Court of Human Rights (ECtHR),[175] the Court found that 'where legislation provide[d] for the automatic payment of a social benefit, it generate[d] a proprietary interest for persons meeting the requirements thereof'.[176] For this reason, it concluded that 'the rights resulting from the payment of contributions to a social security scheme thus constitute[d] rights of property',[177] though it '[could not] be interpreted as entitling a person to a pension of a particular amount'.[178]

b. Assets of Immaterial Value

Along with the ownership of material assets, the scope of Article 17 CFR encompasses assets of an immaterial nature. While the former category is defined by the factor of physical possession, the ownership of immaterial assets is expressed in specific entitlements to use or dispose of intangible assets.[179] Immaterial assets include intellectual property rights that are the products of human intellect and creativity and assets that do not have an innovative or creative aspect to them. Concerning the latter category, in *Sky Österreich*, the Court found that 'exclusive broadcasting rights [were] granted, on a contractual basis, to broadcasters for consideration, enabling the latter to broadcast certain events on an exclusive basis, thereby precluding other broadcasters from transmitting those events in any way'.[180] In the Court's view, 'these rights must not be regarded as constituting mere commercial interests or opportunities, but as having asset value'.[181] The Court used the same line of reasoning to establish the applicability of Article 17 CFR to the

[171] ibid para 67.
[172] ibid para 74.
[173] ibid.
[174] F Wollenschläger, 'Article 17(1) – Right to Property' in Peers et al (n 4) 475.
[175] *Stummer v Austria* [GC] App No 37452/02 (ECtHR, 7 July 2011), para 82.
[176] Case C-258/14 *Eugenia Florescu and Others v Casa Județeană de Pensii Sibiu and Others* EU:C:2016:995, para 50.
[177] ibid.
[178] ibid. The Court referred to *Kjartan Ásmundssonv Iceland* App No 60669/00 (ECtHR, 12 October 2004), para 39.
[179] Wollenschläger (n 174) 494.
[180] *Sky Österreich* (n 34) para 35.
[181] ibid.

right of usufruct. In *Commission v Hungary*,[182] it held that 'inasmuch as rights of usufruct over immovable property … permit[ted] the usufructuary to use and enjoy that property, they ha[d] an asset value and confer[red] on the usufructuary an established legal position, enabling him or her to exercise those rights of use and enjoyment independently, even if the possibility of transferring such rights [was] limited or precluded under the applicable national law'.[183]

Article 17 CFR expressly provides that 'intellectual property shall be protected'. According to the Explanations to the Charter, the inclusion of this provision is aimed to reflect the 'growing importance' of the protection of intellectual property,[184] expressed by the Union's secondary law in this field.[185] However, the concept of 'intellectual property' is not clearly defined. The Explanations to the Charter only provide that '[it] covers not only literary and artistic property but also patent and trademark rights and associated rights'. At the core of these entitlements lies the act of creation and its link to the creator or author regarding the entitlements flowing from it.[186] The legal recognition of such a link underpins intellectual property rights. In *Luksan*,[187] the Court emphasised that 'the principal director of a cinematographic work must be regarded as having lawfully acquired … the right to own the intellectual property in that work'[188] and the national law denying that person the exploitation rights 'would be tantamount to depriving him of his lawfully acquired intellectual property right'.[189] Along the same lines, in *Huawei*,[190] the Court found that the 'need for a high level of protection for intellectual-property rights mean[t] that, in principle, the proprietor [might] not be deprived of the right to have recourse to legal proceedings to ensure effective enforcement of his exclusive rights and that, in principle, the user of those rights … [was] required to obtain a licence prior to any use'.[191] In *Constantin Film*,[192] in turn, the Court touched upon the proprietor's broad entitlement to information in infringement proceedings. It was held that such entitlement sought 'to ensure the effective exercise of the fundamental right to property, which include[d] the intellectual property right protected in Article 17(2) of the Charter … by enabling the holder of an intellectual property right to identify the person who [was] infringing that right and take the necessary steps in order to protect it'.[193]

[182] Case C-235/17 *Commission v Hungary (Usufruct over Agricultural Land)* EU:C:2019:432, para 72.
[183] ibid 70.
[184] Explanations relating to the Charter of Fundamental Rights [2007] OJ C303, 23.
[185] See, eg, Directive 2001/29/EC of the European Parliament and of the Council of 22 May 2001 on the harmonisation of certain aspects of copyright and related rights in the information society [2001] OJ L167.
[186] Wollenschläger (n 174) 495.
[187] Case C-277/10 *Martin Luksan v Petrus van der Let* EU:C:2012:65.
[188] ibid para 69.
[189] ibid para 70.
[190] Case C-170/13 *Huawei Technologies Co Ltd v ZTE Corp and ZTE Deutschland GmbH* EU:C:2015:477.
[191] ibid para 58.
[192] Case C-264/19 *Constantin Film Verleih GmbH v YouTube LLC and Google Inc* EU:C:2020:542.
[193] ibid para 35. See also Case C-580/13 *Coty Germany GmbH v Stadtsparkasse Magdeburg* EU:C:2015:485, para 29; Case C-427/15 *NEW WAVE CZ v ALLTOYS* EU:C:2017:18, para 25.

II. Provisions Limiting Private Autonomy

Along with fundamental rights and freedoms manifesting the ideals of private autonomy, the Charter also contains a catalogue of rights and freedoms that limit or condition the exercise of such autonomy. Initially, it was not clear whether these provisions were applicable in the context of private relationships. This followed from the traditional understanding held over fundamental rights as norms limiting state actions over individuals.[194] Such a narrow construction of the Charter found support in its wording that explicitly addresses the respect for the codified rights and freedoms to the Union's institutions and Member States when implementing Union law.[195] However, the Court has confirmed the horizontal applicability of the Charter, which saw even more aspects of private relationships being brought within the scope of Union law.

A. The Test for Horizontality of the Charter's Provisions

As discussed in Chapter 1, *Kücükdeveci* was the first ruling to make a combined reference to Article 21 CFR and the general principle on non-discrimination on grounds of age in relation to the duty of a national court to set aside the contravening national law in a private setting.[196] Although the reference to Article 21 CFR was brief and was likely made to substantiate the *Mangold* doctrine,[197] *Kücükdeveci* undoubtedly paved the way for a series of rulings that confirmed the horizontal applicability of the Charter.

i. AMS: *The 'Self-Sufficiency' Condition*

Built on *Kücükdeveci, Association de Médiation Sociale (AMS)* showed the first signs of the Court embracing the horizontal direct effect of the Charter.[198] The issue raised in this case was whether Article 27 CFR, which enshrines the right of workers to information and consultation, could be invoked, either by itself or in conjunction with the provisions of Directive 2002/14,[199] in a dispute between

[194] M Fornasier, 'The Impact of EU Fundamental Rights on Private Relationships: Direct or Indirect Effect?' (2015) 23 *European Review of Private Law* 29, 31.

[195] W Lewandowski, 'The Implications of the Recent Jurisprudence of the Court of Justice of the European Union for the Protection of the Fundamental Rights of Athletes and the Regulatory Autonomy of Sporting Federations' (2020) 25 *Tilburg Law Review* 55, 56.

[196] Case C-555/07 *Seda Kücükdeveci v Swedex GmbH & Co* EU:C:2010:21, para 22.

[197] A Eriksson, 'European Court of Justice: Broadening the Scope of European Nondiscrimination Law' (2009) 7 *International Journal of Constitutional Law* 731, 738. The inclusion of reference to Article 21 of the Charter would have averted much of the criticism aimed at the methodology used by the Court in that case.

[198] Case C-176/12 *Association de Médiation Sociale v Union Locale des Syndicats CGT and Others* EU:C:2014:2.

[199] Directive 2002/14/EC of the European Parliament and of the Council of 11 March 2002 establishing a general framework for informing and consulting employees in the European Community – Joint declaration of the European Parliament, the Council and the Commission on employee representation [2002] OJ L80.

private parties to assess the compliance with Union law of the national measure implementing that directive. Having acknowledged the lack of horizontal direct effect of directives, the Court considered whether the solution adopted in *Kücükdeveci* could be applied by analogy. However, it found that the nature of the relevant provisions of Union law triggered in *AMS* and *Kücükdeveci* differed substantially. According to the Court, while Article 21 CFR is 'sufficient in itself to confer on individuals an individual right which they may invoke as such', Article 27 CFR does not have these qualities.[200] Instead, pursuant to its wording, it must be given a more specific expression by Union or national law.[201] The distinction drawn by the Court confirmed that at least some of the rights enshrined in the Charter could impose obligations on private parties.

AMS reconfigured the normative link established in *Mangold* and *Kücükdeveci* between, on the one hand, the Charter and general principles of Union law and, on the other hand, directives. Although a directive remains a component of the Union's secondary law capable of triggering the application of the Charter and general principles of law, it does not determine whether either of these norms can impose obligations in a private setting. The Court explicitly stated that since Article 27 CFR was not sufficient by itself to confer a right to be invoked as such, the outcome would not be any different had it been considered in conjunction with a directive. The outer reach of the Charter and general principles of law is rooted in their normative characteristics. The underlying rationale here echoes the observation made by AG Trstenjak in *Dominguez*,[202] where she argued that the scope of application of general principles should be ascertained separately, as otherwise the reliance on the legislative content of a directive would lead to 'an amalgamation of sources of law with different status'.[203] *AMS*, therefore, confirmed that there is no equivalence in the scope of application between general principles of law or the Charter and the provision of Union law that triggers their applicability.[204] As part of this normative detachment, the Court, for the first time, undertook an autonomous assessment of the content of a fundamental right codified in the Charter and recognised as a general principle of Union law. The main requirement for their horizontal application is that a provision must be 'sufficient in itself to confer on individuals an individual right which they may invoke as such'. Although *AMS* does not elaborate on the criteria for establishing 'sufficiency', the relevant factors appear to be the wording of the Charter and the Explanations to the Charter.[205]

[200] *Association de Médiation Sociale* (n 198) paras 44–47.
[201] ibid para 45.
[202] Opinion of AG Trstenjak in Case C-282/10 *Maribel Dominguez v Centre informatique du Centre Ouest Atlantique and Préfet de la région Centre* EU:C:2011:559. See also N Lazzerini, '(Some of) the Fundamental Rights Granted by the Charter May Be a Source of Obligations for Private Parties: *AMS*' (2014) 51 *Common Market Law Review* 907, 923.
[203] *Maribel Dominguez* (n 202) para 157.
[204] E Spaventa, 'The Horizontal Application of Fundamental Rights as General Principles of Union Law' in A Arnull, C Barnard, M Dougan and E Spaventa (eds), *A Constitutional Order of States: essays in Honour of Alan Dashwood* (Oxford: Hart Publishing, 2011), 215.
[205] *Association de Médiation Sociale* (n 198) paras 45–46.

ii. Egenberger*: Mandatory Status*

The subsequent case law further specified the requirements for the horizontal enforceability of the Charter. In *Egenberger*,[206] the Court found that the prohibition of discrimination on grounds of religion or belief enshrined in Article 21 CFR could be invoked in a private dispute to set aside the conflicting national law. This was based on two factors. First, the applicability of Article 21 CFR followed from its 'mandatory' nature as a general principle of Union law. The Court attributed this characteristic by comparing Article 21 CFR to the Treaty's provisions prohibiting discrimination on grounds of sex and nationality, the scope of which is triggered even when the adverse treatment originates from a private contractual relationship.[207] Second, in line with *AMS*, this provision satisfied the condition of 'sufficiency', for it did not need to be made more specific by Union or national law.[208] In *Egenberger*, therefore, the test for the horizontality of the Charter became more comprehensive with an extra limb added to it. While *AMS* subjected the Charter's horizontal enforceability to the structural characteristics of its provisions, *Egenberger* linked it to their broader status within the Union's legal order.[209]

iii. Bauer*: The Two-Limb Horizontality Benchmark*

The criteria developed in *AMS* and *Egenberger* were later consolidated in *Bauer*,[210] where the Court found that the right to paid annual leave under Article 31(2) CFR could be invoked in a private dispute. This stems from the fact that this provision satisfied both limbs of the horizontality test. However, unlike *Egenberger* and in line with *AMS*, the Court established the mandatory and unconditional nature of this provision by having recourse to the textual interpretation of its wording. Article 31(2) CFR, in the Court's view, enshrines the right to paid annual leave in 'mandatory terms' since it is formulated with a reference to 'every worker'.[211] As regards the condition of 'self-sufficiency', the Court compared the wording of Article 31(2) CFR with that of Article 27 CFR. Contrasted against the latter provision, Article 31(2) CFR is unconditional. It does not subject the exercise of the right to paid annual leave to 'the cases and … conditions provided for by Union law and national laws and practices'.[212] According to the Court, Article 31(2) CFR reflects 'the essential principle of EU social law' from which derogations may only be made in compliance with the strict conditions laid down by the Charter.

[206] Case C-414/16 *Vera Egenberger v Evangelisches Werk für Diakonie und Entwicklung* EU:C:2018:257.
[207] ibid para 77. See also Case C-193/17 *Cresco Investigation v Markus Achatzi* EU:C:2019:43, para 77.
[208] ibid para 78.
[209] Case C-68/17 *IR v JQ* EU:C:2018:696, para 69.
[210] Joined Cases C-569/16 and C-570/16 *Stadt Wuppertal v Maria Elisabeth Bauer and Volker Willmeroth v Martina Broßonn* EU:C:2018:871.
[211] ibid para 84.
[212] ibid. See also Case C-684/16 *Max-Planck-Gesellschaft zur Förderung der Wissenschaften eV v Tetsuji Shimizu* EU:C:2018:874, para 73.

Viewed in tandem, the criteria of mandatory and unconditional nature reflect the traditional threshold of clarity, precision and unconditionality for determining the direct effect of a provision of Union law first developed in *Van Gen en Loos*.[213] It equally mirrors *Defrenne* and *Angonese*, where the principles of non-discrimination on grounds of nationality and sex were defined as 'mandatory in nature' and extended to 'contracts between individuals'.[214]

iv. The Conditionality Criterion as a Barrier to Horizontality

It is now beyond doubt that the Charter is a normative source of individual rights and obligations. This concerns all provisions featured therein so long as they meet the two-limb test of horizontality. However, the emphasis placed on the structural characteristics of these provisions to determine their horizontal applicability is not without its difficulties. If this deference is indeed taken as a structural barrier to horizontal direct effect, it would be problematic for several provisions of the Charter.[215] This is evident in the context of Article 16 CFR, which provides that 'the freedom to conduct a business in accordance with Union law and national laws and practices is recognised'. Subjecting this provision to the second limb of the horizontality test, introduced in *AMS* and consolidated in *Bauer*, would render it ineffective in private disputes. And yet, Article 16 CFR has already been given effect in the context of private relationships. In *Scarlet Extended*,[216] the Court found that an injunction sought by a copyright holder against an internet service provider to install a filtering system to monitor and prevent copyright infringements by its customers constituted 'a serious infringement' of the freedom to conduct business.[217] In *Sky Österreich*, in turn, the obligation imposed on a holder of exclusive broadcasting rights to allow other broadcasters to produce short news reports and not to demand compensation greater than the costs incurred in providing access to a satellite signal amounted to interference with the freedom protected by Article 16 CFR.[218] Finally, in *Alemo-Herron*, the Court concluded that passing on the obligations to the new employer as a result of the transfer of an undertaking was 'liable to adversely affect the very essence of the [latter's] freedom to conduct a business'.[219]

[213] H van Eijken and S de Vries, 'Deepening and Widening of the Protection of Fundamental Rights of European Citizens vis-à-vis Non-state, Private Actors' in R Buikema, A Buyse and ACGM Robben (eds), *Cultures, Citizenship and Human Rights* (Abingdon, Routledge, 2019) 150.

[214] Case 43-75 *Gabrielle Defrenne v Société anonyme belge de navigation aérienne Sabena* EU:C:1976:56, para 39; Case C-281/98 *Roman Angonese v Cassa di Risparmio di Bolzano SpA* EU:C:2000:296, para 34.

[215] E Franziou, '(Most of) the Charter of Fundamental Rights is Horizontally Applicable' (2019) 15 *European Constitutional Law Review* 306, 321.

[216] Case C-70/10 *Scarlet Extended v SABAM* EU:C:2011:771.

[217] ibid para 48. See also Case C-360/10 *SABAM v Netlog NV* EU:C:2012:85, para 46.

[218] *Sky Österreich* (n 34) para 44.

[219] *Mark Alemo-Herron* (n 23) para 35.

Against this line of case law, the unequivocal acceptance of the reference to 'Union law and national laws and practices' as a determinant criterion of horizontality becomes rather contentious. Although, in each instance, Article 16 CFR was invoked as a mere protective shield against a private party, this line of case law nevertheless highlights the need to distinguish the Charter's provisions based on the peculiarity of the reference to 'Union law and national laws and practices' included in them. This is best illustrated by comparing the textual formulation of Article 16 CFR and Article 27 CFR. Even though these provisions are not included under the same title in the Charter, they have comparable wording. Much like Article 27 CFR, Article 16 CFR also contains a reference to 'Union law and national laws and practices'. On this premise alone, it is certainly possible to read Article 16 CFR as not specific enough to be invoked against individuals. However, a close textual reading also reveals a significant difference in the wording of both provisions. While Article 27 CFR refers to 'conditions provided for by Union law and national laws and practices', Article 16 CFR only states that 'the freedom to conduct a business in accordance with Union law and national laws and practices is recognised' with no mention of the word 'conditions'. This textual variation reveals a lack of homogeneity in the normative characteristics of the individual entitlements safeguarded by Article 16 CFR and Article 27 CFR. Under the latter provision, the guarantee of workers' right to information and consultation within the undertaking is explicitly subject to conditionality, while no such qualification is included in Article 16 CFR. Its textual formulation does not envisage any ex-ante requirements to be met to exercise of the freedom to conduct business. The reference to 'Union law and national laws and practices' merely stipulates the possibility of limitations on its exercise.[220]

This distinction finds clear support in *Viking* and *Laval*.[221] As well as broadening the extent of the horizontal direct effect of the freedom of establishment and freedom to provide services, the Court accepted that the right to collective action, enshrined in Article 28 CFR, could be invoked against private parties to justify a barrier to free movement in the internal market.[222] This is deemed possible despite the wording of Article 28 CFR, which, identically to Article 16 CFR, contains a reference to 'Union law and national laws and practices'. It is true that the Court alluded to the wording of Article 28 CFR that the right to strike was 'to be protected in accordance with [Union] law and national law and practices'.[223] Yet, this reference was only made to dismiss the alleged unfettered nature of this right rather than its very capacity of being invoked horizontally. The Court held

[220] Opinion of AG Szpunar in C-261/20 *Thelen Technopark Berlin GmbH v MN* EU:C:2021:620, para 89.

[221] Case C-438/05 *International Transport Workers' Federation and Finnish Seamen's Union v Viking Line ABP and OÜ Viking Line Eesti* EU:C:2007:772; Case C-341/05 *Laval un Partneri Ltd v Svenska Byggnadsarbetareförbundet* EU:C:2007:809.

[222] K Lenaerts, 'Exploring the Limits of the EU Charter of Fundamental Rights' (2012) 8 *European Constitutional Law Review* 375, 400.

[223] *Viking* (n 221) para 44.

that the textual formulation reaffirmed that the right to collective action could be subject to certain restrictions.[224]

The combined reading of the case law discussed above warrants a more subtle perspective on the second limb of the horizontality test that takes account of the intrinsic nature of rights or freedoms protected in the Charter. The reference to 'Union law and national laws and practices' should not automatically bar their application to private disputes. A reference that denotes the qualified nature of a right or freedom ought to be distinguished from an analogous reference that evinces conditionality attached to their enforceability. This is pertinent to fundamental economic rights that contain, in contrast to solidarity rights, an individual dimension, the respect of which entails a 'negative' obligation of conduct.

B. Article 51(1) of the Charter and the Question of Horizontality

In respect of the horizontal applicability of the Charter, much uncertainty surrounded the implications of Article 51(1) enshrined therein. It states that 'the provisions of this Charter are addressed to the institutions, bodies, offices and agencies of the Union … and to the Member States only when they are implementing Union law'. Such pronouncement of the formal addressees of the Charter prompted opposing views over its normative capacity to bind private individuals. In *Dominguez*, AG Trstenjak observed that Article 51(1) CFR was among provisions that '[indicated] an intentional restricting of the parties to whom fundamental rights were addressed, which again [shed] light on the mode of protection of fundamental rights sought by the legislature of the European Union'.[225] In contrast, AG Cruz Villalón rejected *a contrario* argument in *AMS* by finding that the 'possibility of [the horizontal application of the Charter could not] be denied on the basis of the argument that it, as a consequence of the provisions of Article 51(1), ha[d] no relevance in relations governed by private law'.[226] These views provided two teleological alternatives that differed over the Charter's place in the hierarchy of sources of Union law. At one end, a more restrictive view would see it placed alongside directives and have no horizontal reach without national implementation measures, while at the other end, a more expansive view would consider the Charter to bind individuals, coming close to the level of the Treaties.[227]

[224] ibid.

[225] Opinion of AG Trstenjak in *Maribel Dominguez* (n 202) para 80. See also V Trstenjak and E Beysen, The Growing Overlap of Fundamental Freedoms and Fundamental Rights in the Case-Law of the CJEU' (2013) 38 *European Law Review* 293, 300.

[226] Opinion of AG Cruz Villalón in Case C-176/12 *Association de Médiation Sociale v Union Locale des Syndicats CGT and Others* EU:C:2013:491, para 41.

[227] D Leczykiewicz, 'Horizontal Application of the Charter of Fundamental Rights' (2013) 38 *European Law Review* 479, 486.

In *Kücükdeveci* and *AMS* or, even later, *Egenberger*, the Court did not consider the argument against the horizontal application of the Charter based on Article 51(1) CFR. This was perhaps not deemed necessary in either of these rulings as the issue in each, despite the private context, related to the compatibility of national law with Union law. However, the silence only lasted until *Bauer*. There, the Court clarified the uncertainty on the scope of addressees of the Charter. It unequivocally found that despite the wording of Article 51(1) CFR only specifying the Union's institutions and Member States when they are implementing Union law, this provision [did not] 'however, address the question whether … individuals [might], where appropriate, be directly required to comply with certain provisions of the Charter and [could not], accordingly, be interpreted as meaning that it would systematically preclude such a possibility'.[228] This was rationalised on three grounds. First, referring to *Defrenne* and *Angonese*, the Court stated that Member States being principal addressees of certain provisions of the Union's primary law '[did not] preclude their application to relations between individuals'.[229] Second, according to the Court, the principle of non-discrimination enshrined in Article 21 CFR was already found to be 'sufficient in itself to confer on individuals a right which they may rely on as such in a dispute with another individual without, therefore, Article 51(1) CFR preventing it'.[230] Third, in the Court's view, the right to paid annual leave under Article 31 CFR, which was at stake, entailed, by its very nature, a corresponding obligation on employers to guarantee this individual entitlement.[231] With this finding, the Court left no doubt in characterising the Charter as a constitutional source of individual rights and obligations that shares the same normative parameters with other provisions of the Union's primary law.[232]

C. Liability of Private Individuals and State Liability

The recognition of the horizontal direct effect of the Charter confirmed its normative capacity to be an independent source of obligations for private parties.[233] It is true that the Charter has not so far been relied on to sanction the conduct of a private party as such but instead applied to assess the lawfulness of national law.[234] However, as AG Cruz Villalón observed in *AMS*, invalidating or setting aside the conflicting national law pursuant to the Charter inevitably results in a private party incurring an obligation that it did not initially expect to bear.[235]

[228] *Bauer* (n 210) para 87. See also *Max-Planck-Gesellschaft* (n 212) para 76.
[229] ibid para 88.
[230] ibid para 89.
[231] ibid para 90.
[232] Franziou (n 215) 317.
[233] D Leczykiewicz, 'The Judgment in *Bauer* and the Effect of the EU Charter of Fundamental Rights in Horizontal Situations' (2020) 16 *European Review of Contract Law* 323, 332.
[234] Fornasier (n 194) 44.
[235] Opinion of AG Cruz Villalón in *Association de Médiation Sociale* (n 226) para 76.

This outcome stands even if the party does not act unlawfully but merely complies with the applicable national law.[236] In the case law discussed so far, the unforeseen assumption of a new obligation led to some form of financial or non-financial burden placed on a private party. In *Mangold*, the employer was made bound by an employment contract for an indefinite period, while in *Kücükdeveci*, a longer notice period had to be provided for dismissal.[237] Similarly, in *Bauer*, the right to paid annual leave was defined as forming part of an employee's assets and transferrable.[238] This is even more apparent in *Achatzi*,[239] where the issue concerned the compatibility of the national rule that reserved the right to a paid public holiday to employees who were members of specific churches. Having found this rule to impose unjustified discriminatory treatment on grounds of religion,[240] the Court stressed that under the horizontally applicable Article 21 CFR, employers were required, pending the adoption of the compliant national law, to authorise all employees to be on a public holiday or provide a payment if this was not approved.[241] The problematic aspect of this line of case law does not rest in the verdict reached by the Court but in the lack of consideration given to the interests of private parties adversely affected as a result of the mere compliance with the conflicting national law. Two related concerns are of particular significance here.

On the one hand, among the arguments frequently proffered against the horizontality of Union law is the reservation based on the demands of legal certainty.[242] The established view is that Union law incurring negative consequences for individuals should be clear and precise, and their application must be predictable for individuals to know what course of action to undertake.[243] As discussed in Chapter 1, this was raised in *Dansk Industri*, where the referring court enquired about the possibility of balancing the general principle of non-discrimination on grounds of age with the principles of legal certainty and legitimate expectations. The Court dismissed this suggestion by finding, among other things, that the protection of legitimate expectations could not, in any event, be relied upon to deny an individual of the protection against discrimination afforded under Union law.[244] Although the referring court's request concerned the national

[236] P Craig, 'The Legal Effect of Directives: Policy, Rules and Exceptions' (2009) 34 *European Law Review* 349, 373.
[237] Fornasier (n 194) 44.
[238] Leczykiewicz (n 233) 338.
[239] Case C-193/17 *Cresco Investigation v Markus Achatzi* EU:C:2019:43.
[240] ibid para 69.
[241] ibid paras 85–87.
[242] See, eg, Opinion of AG in Case C-427/06 *Birgit Bartsch v Bosch und Siemens Hausgeräte (BSH) Altersfürsorge GmbH* EU:C:2008:517, para 31.
[243] Opinion of AG Trstenjak in *Maribel Dominguez* (n 202) para 164, with reference to Case C-17/03 *EMW and Others* EU:C:2005:362, para 80; and Case C-226/08 *Stadt Papenburg v Bundesrepublik Deutschland* EU:C:2010:10, para 45.
[244] Case C-441/14 *Dansk Industri (DI), Acting on Behalf of Ajos A/S v Estate of Karsten Eigil Rasmussen* EU:C:2016:278, para 41.

concept of legal certainty and legitimate expectations,[245] the Court's reasoning carries broad connotations. It suggests that the principle of non-discrimination not only prevails over the principles of legal certainty and legal expectations but also occupies a privileged position in the hierarchy of norms.[246] However, ascribing an outright preponderance to the former normative provision that unequivocally imposes an obligation on individuals is contentious due to what AG Geelhoed referred to as 'potentially far-reaching consequences, economic and financial, which such prohibitions of discrimination may have in horizontal relationships among citizens'.[247] This is particularly true when a private party acts in good faith and according to the applicable national law but finds itself liable for the failure committed by national authorities.[248] Such an eventuality is not analogous to the circumstances where discriminatory treatment stems from the actions of a private party.[249] AG Bobek in *Achatzi* separated these two instances, observing that there should be no remedy against a private party in the former scenario since any obligation ought to be borne by the national authorities.[250] According to him, this was because, among other things, the discriminatory treatment in that case stemmed from the conflicting national law, leaving no discretion for the private employer to make an independent decision, for it could not legitimately be expected to ignore that national law.[251] The Court did not endorse this approach. Its finding that a private employer must authorise all its employees to be on a public holiday or make an extra payment instead, pending the adoption of the complying national law, effectively grants employees a direct remedy against that employer.[252]

The second striking aspect of the Court's approach to the horizontality of the Charter is the lack of acknowledgement of the capacity to bring a claim under the doctrine of state liability for incurring an obligation due to the failure of a Member State to comply with Union law.[253] This was supported by AG Cruz

[245] R Holdgaard, D Elkan and GK Schaldemose, 'From Cooperation to Collision: The ECJ's *Ajos* Ruling and the Danish Supreme Court's Refusal to Comply' (2018) 55 *Common Market Law Review* 17, 42.

[246] R Xenidis, 'Transforming EU Equality Law? On Disruptive Narratives and False Dichotomies' (2019) 38 *Yearbook of European Law* 2, 12.

[247] Opinion of AG Geelhoed in Case C-13/05 *Sonia Chacón Navas v Eurest Colectividades SA* EU:C:2006:456, para 50.

[248] Spaventa (n 204) 216.

[249] See, eg, Case C-281/98 *Roman Angonese v Cassa di Risparmio di Bolzano SpA* EU:C:2000:296.

[250] Opinion of AG Bobek in Case C-193/17 *Cresco Investigation v Markus Achatzi* EU:C:2018:614, paras 186–87.This was, for instance, the case in *HK Danmark*, where a discriminatory treatment stemmed from a contractual clause. See Joined Cases C-335/11 and C-337/11 *HK Danmark* EU:C:2013:222.

[251] *Cresco Investigation* (n 250) paras 179 and 186.

[252] N Lazzerini, 'The Horizontal Application of the General Principles of EU Law: Nothing Less Than Direct Effect' in K Ziegler, P Neuvonen, and V Moreno-Lax (eds), *Research Handbook on General Principles of EU Law* (Cheltenham, Edward Elgar, 2022) 188.

[253] See, eg, Joined Cases C-6/90 and C-9/90 *Andrea Francovich and Danila Bonifaci and Others v Italy* EU:C:1991:428; Joined Cases C-46/93 and C-48/93 *Brasserie du Pêcheur SA v Bundesrepublik Deutschland and The Queen v Secretary of State for Transport ex parte Factortame Ltd and Others* EU:C:1996:79; Case C-224/01 *Gerhard Köbler v Republik Österreich* EU:C:2003:513.

Villalón, who argued in *AMS* that an individual who suffered damage due to the unforeseen assumption of an obligation on account of the unlawful conduct of a Member State was entitled to claim compensation from that Member State.[254] AG Bobek reiterated this point in *Achatzi* by putting forward several arguments to demonstrate the inappropriateness of granting a remedy against a private party where effective judicial protection should take the form of an action for damages against the Member State in breach of Union law.[255] For AG Bobek, first, it would be morally wrong for a private party to bear the cost of the fault attributable to a Member State.[256] Second, holding a private party liable for the fault it is not responsible for would not act as a deterrent effect vis-a-vis the Member State that is genuinely responsible for that fault.[257] Third, a remedy granted to the harmed party must only be addressed to the Member State in breach of Union law, for it would avoid double litigation arising from the harmed party suing another party and the latter bringing a claim against that Member State.[258] According to AG Bobek, this interpretation aligns with the approach in the context of unimplemented directives where the harmed party is only entitled to a remedy in the form of an action for damages against a Member State.[259] However, the standpoint taken by the Court so far does not seem to lend support to such a proposition. The Court has only acknowledged the availability of a *Francovich*-based liability claim in relation to the harmed party. In *AMS*, the Court held that 'a party injured as a result of domestic law not being in conformity with European Union law [could] none the less … obtain … compensation for the loss sustained'.[260] In *Dansk Industri*, it merely added that the capacity for a discriminated individual to bring a liability claim against a Member State did not justify a national court giving precedence to the protection of the legitimate expectations of an employer who had complied with national law.[261]

D. The Category of Principles in the Charter

Among the questions arising from *Bauer* and the preceding case law is how the horizontality test fits into the broader dichotomy of rights and principles set out in the Charter. The distinction between these two concepts is manifested in Article 51 CFR, according to which the Union's institutions and Member States, when implementing Union law, are required to 'respect the rights, observe the principles

[254] Opinion of AG Cruz Villalón in *Association de médiation sociale* (n 226) para 79.
[255] Opinion of AG Bobek in *Cresco Investigation* (n 250) para 191.
[256] ibid para 188.
[257] ibid para 190.
[258] ibid para 191.
[259] ibid para 192. See *Francovich* (n 253) para 45.
[260] *Association de Médiation Sociale* (n 198) para 50.
[261] *Dansk Industri* (n 244) para 42.

and promote the application thereof in accordance with their respective powers'. Article 52 CFR, in turn, stipulates that principles may be implemented by legislative and executive acts of the Union's institutions and Member States; as such, they 'shall be judicially cognisable only in the interpretation of such acts and in the ruling on their legality'. The Explanations to this provision add that '[principles] do not … give rise to direct claims for positive action by the Union's institutions or Member States authorities'. Although these provisions explicitly separate 'principles' from 'rights' in terms of their normative nature and legal effects, the parameters pursuant to which the Charter's provision falls under either category remain opaque. This begs the question of whether the conceptual framework underpinning the horizontality test can be construed to define the contours of the Charter's principles and their impact on the exercise of private autonomy.

i. The Charter's Principles and General Principles of Union Law

The inclusion of the reference to 'principles' in the Charter has led to much uncertainty and confusion, considering that this type of norm is ubiquitous in the Union's legal system.[262] For a better understanding of the Charter's principles, it is first necessary to distinguish them from other similarly designated norms. Union law contains a whole range of various principles with divergent normative purposes.[263] However, it is most appropriate to contrast the nature of the Charter's principles against the general principles of Union law that protect fundamental rights. This can be approached from two interrelated angles. Notwithstanding their common designation, the Charter's principles do not necessarily correspond to this category of general principles of Union law. This stems from their distinct normative characteristics.[264] General principles of Union law are norms that have 'a constitutional status' within the Union's legal order and 'a certain degree of general validity' that is not restricted to a specific area of law.[265] Having 'the general, comprehensive character', they apply beyond a circumscribed number of situations.[266] In contrast, the Charter's provisions that contain principles are

[262] T Lock, 'Rights and Principles in the EU Charter of Fundamental Rights' (2019) 56 *Common Market Law Review* 1201, 1212.

[263] For different categories of general principles, see C Hilson, 'Rights and Principles in EU Law: A Distinction without Foundation?' (2008) 15 *Maastricht Journal of European and Comparative Law* 193.

[264] For a broader view, see T Tridimas, 'The General Principles of Law: Who Needs Them?' (2015) 52 *Les Cahiers de Droit* 419.

[265] Opinion of AG Trstenjak in Case C-101/08 *Audiolux SA et al v Groupe Bruxelles Lambert SA (GBL) and Others and Bertelsmann AG and Others* EU:C:2009:410, para 87; see also Opinion of AG Trstenjak in *Maribel Dominguez* (n 202) para 99.

[266] Case C-101/08 *Audiolux SA et al v Groupe Bruxelles Lambert SA (GBL) and Others and Bertelsmann AG and Others* EU:C:2009:626, para 42. For criticism of such a characterisation, see J Basedow, 'General Principles of European Private Law and Interest Analysis: Some Reflections in the Light of *Mangold* and *Audiolux*' (2016) 24 *European Review of Private Law* 331, 348–50.

narrower in scope. This category has its origin in the concerns raised in the drafting period by some Member States wary of the inclusion of social rights as legally enforceable claims alongside traditional civil and political rights.[267] To overcome their reluctance, a compromise was found in the inclusion of Article 52(5) CFR, which attributes limited justiciability to the Charter's principles. For this reason, social rights enshrined in Title IV of the Charter are often closely associated with the Charter's principles. However, these categories do not necessarily equate to one another.[268] Title IV of the Charter contains individually enforceable rights,[269] while according to the Explanations to the Charter, the status of a 'principle' is attributed to provisions enshrined elsewhere in the Charter.[270]

From a slightly different perspective, the Charter's principles and the general principles of Union law protecting fundamental rights can also be distinguished in terms of their link to the Union's secondary law. Article 52(5) CFR defines principles as programmatic and requiring further legislative intervention.[271] In *Glatzel*,[272] the Court confirmed that the full effectiveness of the Charter's principle is subject to more specific legislative expression.[273] The Union's secondary law concretises these provisions, making them operational.[274] At first sight, this may appear to resonate with the interplay of general principles of law and directives.[275] As previously discussed, *Mangold* and *Kücükdeveci* built on it to establish the horizontality of the principle of non-discrimination on grounds of age.[276] This interplay has two layers. First, although a directive does not govern the issue of the existence of a general principle of law,[277] it nevertheless can trigger its application.[278] Second, a directive lays down a general framework for the application of a general principle of law to the extent that it serves as a de facto standard of review.[279] Despite both factors, this interplay rests on a conceptually different normative foundation.

[267] Hilson (n 263) 197.
[268] J Krommendijk, 'Principled Silence or Mere Silence on Principles? The Role of the EU Charter's Principles in the Case Law of the Court of Justice' (2015) 11 *European Constitutional Law Review* 321, 329.
[269] See *Viking* (n 221) para 43; *Laval* (n 221) para 91.
[270] Explanations relating to the Charter of Fundamental Rights [2007] OJ C303, 35.
[271] Lenaerts (n 222) 400.
[272] Case C-356/12 *Wolfgang Glatzel v Freistaat Bayern* EU:C:2014:350.
[273] ibid para 78.
[274] S Peers and S Prechal, 'Article 52 – Scope and Interpretation of Rights and Principles' in Peers et al (n 4) 1509.
[275] L Lourenco, 'Rights and Principles in the Charter and the General Principles of EU Law: "We're One, But We're Not the Same"?' (2018) 5 *e-Pública* 72, 85.
[276] Craig (n 236) 372.
[277] *Audiolux* (n 267) para 34.
[278] *Kücükdeveci* (n 196) para 27.
[279] M de Mol, 'The Novel Approach of The CJEU on the Horizontal Direct Effect of the EU Principle of Non-discrimination: (Unbridled) Expansionism of EU Law?' (2011) 18 *Maastricht Journal of European and Comparative Law* 109, 123. An important factor here is the Court's consistent reference to 'the principle of non-discrimination on grounds of age as given expression in Directive 2000/78'. For more on this, see S Prechal, 'Competence Creep and General Principles of Law' (2010) 3 *Review of European Administrative Law* 5, 17.

Its key characteristic is that even if a directive may seem to contribute to the concretisation of a general principle of law,[280] it does not establish its justiciability nor set its boundaries.[281] However, this does not apply to the Charter's principles. Their justiciability under Article 52(5) CFR is not an autonomous matter.[282] It is subject to their prior implementation and, even then, is confined to specific instances.[283]

ii. The Charter's Principles and the Horizontality Test

Article 52(5) CFR categorises the Charter's provisions into either 'rights' or 'principles' based on their legal effects. Unlike 'rights', the Charter's principles are not automatically justiciable. They cannot be invoked before the Court, nor can the Court consider them unless they have been implemented by subsequent legislative acts. Although the Charter distinguishes the normative capacity of 'rights' and 'principles', it does not include a comprehensive list enumerating the provisions that contain either 'rights' or 'principles'. The Explanations to the Charter indeed provide some examples of provisions that are recognised as a 'principle'[284] and those that are mixed in nature by containing elements that relate to both 'rights' and 'principles'.[285] Based on them, it is possible to discern a few common characteristics that define the Charter's principles.[286] However, given that they are subject to caveats and reservations, it is questionable whether the horizontality test developed in *AMS*, *Egenberger* and *Bauer* provides a more comprehensive framework to draw their contours.

At the outset, it is necessary to point out that neither *AMS* nor *Egenberger* or *Bauer* makes an explicit reference to the categories of 'rights' and 'principles' enshrined in the Charter. For this reason, the criteria for horizontal enforceability of the Charter may seem unrelated to the difference between the two categories. It is even possible to argue that this line of case law creates a hierarchy of provisions within the Charter based on the criteria of horizontality that operates in addition to the distinction drawn between 'rights' and 'principles'.[287] Yet, the criteria underpinning the horizontality test also seem suitable for the identification of the Charter's principles. This is because, whether it is the assessment of the horizontality of the Charter's provision or its qualification as a 'principle', the main concern is the degree of justiciability of a provision that is established based on the same

[280] Opinion of AG Trstenjak in *Maribel Dominguez* (n 202) para 78.

[281] See *Dansk Industri* (n 243) para 23. See also *Association de Médiation Sociale* (n 198) para 49.

[282] Hilson (n 263) 199.

[283] Lock (n 262) 1222.

[284] This includes Article 25 on the rights of the elderly, Article 26 on the integration of persons with disabilities, and Article 37 on environmental protection.

[285] It refers to Article 23 on equality between women and men, Article 33 on family and professional life; and Article 34 on social security and social assistance.

[286] Peers and Prechal (n 274) 1507.

[287] See E Franziou, 'Case C-176/12 *Association de Médiation Sociale*: Some Reflections on the Horizontal Effect of the Charter and the Reach of Fundamental Employment Rights in the European Union' (2014) 10 *European Constitutional Law Review* 332, 344; Lazzerini (n 202) 932.

factors, including its wording, purpose and nature. In fact, the parameters often formulated by many to distinguish 'rights' and 'principles' are in congruence with the criteria applied by the Court under the horizontality test.[288]

First among the common parameters is the association of the Charter's principles with norms that belong to the realm of objective law.[289] These provisions, unlike the rights in the Charter, do not endow individuals with a subjective entitlement or claim that can be invoked before a Court.[290] They do not purport to protect individuals or clearly designate them. Instead, the Charter's principles recognise a specific value or objective that must be respected and is addressed to the Union's institutions and Member States.[291] Along similar lines, the Court in *AMS* contrasted Article 27 CFR with Article 21 CFR by finding that the former provision was not 'sufficient in itself to confer on individuals an individual right which they [might] invoke as such'.[292] The emphasis placed on individualisation in the language of the Charter's provisions is also evident in *Bauer*. There, the Court saw a difference between Article 31(2) CFR and Article 27 CFR by highlighting the wording of the former provision that grants the right to paid annual leave to 'every worker'.[293] The line drawn between Articles 21 and 32(2) CFR suggests that the former provision constitutes a 'principle', while the latter holds the status of a 'right'.[294]

In *Bauer*, the Court attributed horizontal applicability to Article 31(2) CFR by finding that its wording, particularly the reference to 'every worker has', was formulated in mandatory terms. Interestingly, this reasoning aligns with the second factor commonly identified in the Charter's principles, which is the lack of specificity or precision in their wording. The 'rights' enshrined in the Charter are usually worded with terms that denote a specific subjective entitlement or clear-cut obligation emanating from them,[295] whereas the wording of the Charter's 'principles' is devoid of any rights language.[296] This was highlighted by AG Cruz Villalón in *AMS*, who, unlike the Court, elaborated on the status of Article 27 CFR. He found this provision to constitute a 'principle' relying, among other things, on the fact that its scope was 'extremely weak' since, in his view, it '[did not] define any individual legal situations'.[297] This characterisation can be extended to the provisions that are explicitly identified as 'principles' in the

[288] For a succinct overview of these criteria, see Krommendijk (n 268) 332–34.

[289] Opinion of AG Trstenjak in *Maribel Dominguez* (n 202) para 76.

[290] See T von Danwitz, 'Questionnaire', Seminar on the Charter of Fundamental Rights of the European Union (The Hague, 2011), E3.

[291] Opinion of AG Trstenjak in *Maribel Dominguez* (n 202) para 76. See also Krommendijk (n 268) 331. The author cites former EU Commissioner Antonio Vitorino.

[292] *Bauer* (n 210) para 47.

[293] ibid para 84.

[294] Unlike the Court, AG Cruz Villalón clearly defined Article 27 as a 'principle'. See Opinion of AG Cruz Villalón in *Association de médiation sociale* (n 226) para 53.

[295] Krommendijk (n 268) 332.

[296] Lock (n 262) 1218.

[297] Opinion of AG Cruz Villalón in *Association de médiation sociale* (n 226) para 54.

Explanations to the Charter. Articles 25, 26 and 34 CFR, for instance, share the same language consisting of the proclamation that 'the Union recognises and respects'. In AG Cruz Villalón's words, the obligation enshrined in these provisions is 'much more general', as their wording determines 'general matters and ones which govern the actions of all public authorities' than 'an individual legal situation'.[298]

The lack of specificity or precision in the wording of the Charter's principles is accentuated by the conditionality of their application on further legislative concretisation by Union or national law.[299] These provisions do not provide subjective entitlements that are immediate in nature.[300] Instead, they merely enshrine broad obligations, leaving their content and contours to Union or national law to substantiate.[301] This normative characteristic forms an integral part of the Court's methodology to ascertain the horizontality of the Charter's provision and its status as a 'principle'. In fact, the conditionality criterion can be construed to operate as a bridge linking these two normative assessments. In one respect, as previously discussed, the Court applied this criterion in *Egenberger* and *Bauer* to establish the horizontal direct effect of Articles 21 and 31(2) CFR. At the same time, the Court also referred to it in *Glatzel* to emphasise that Article 26 CFR was not a 'right' but a 'principle' within the meaning of Article 52(5) CFR.[302] It held that the principle enshrined in this provision could not 'confer on individuals a subjective right which they [might] invoke as such', since its full effectiveness required more specific expression given in Union or national law.[303]

The combined reading of this line of case law nonetheless obscures the conceptual purpose behind the conditionality criteria as a threshold for the justiciability of the Charter's provisions. It is questionable as to whether the framework of the Charter is meant to separate 'principles' from 'rights' generally considered or further draw a line between, on the one hand, horizontally enforceable 'rights' and, on the other hand, 'principles' and horizontally unenforceable 'rights'. The case law does not provide clear guidance on this very point, though the Court's reasoning alludes to the divergent roles played by the conditionality criterion in the context of the Charter's rights and principles. As pointed out by AG Trstenjak in *Dominguez*, even the Charter's rights can be worded in 'a legally abstract fashion' that is 'designed to be fleshed out'.[304] Along these lines, the Court in *Bauer* alluded to the fact that the right to paid annual leave required further specification in terms of its exact duration and the conditions for its exercise despite attributing

[298] ibid para 50.
[299] Opinion of AG Trstenjak in *Maribel Dominguez* (n 202) para 77.
[300] Lock (n 262) 1219.
[301] Opinion of AG Cruz Villalón in *Association de médiation sociale* (n 226) para 62.
[302] *Wolfgang Glatzel* (n 272) para 78.
[303] ibid.
[304] Opinion of AG Trstenjak in *Maribel Dominguez* (n 202) para 78.

a horizontal direct effect to it.[305] However, this form of conditionality differs from the homonymous criterion that determines the status of the Charter's principles. The need for specification or concretisation concerns not the core of the subjective entitlement protected by the Charter's right but its practical realisation,[306] whereas the Charter's principle acquires the contours of its substance from further legislative expression. The Court stressed this nuance in *Bauer* by finding that the right to paid annual leave, as regards 'its very existence', did not need concrete expression by the provisions of Union or national law.[307]

III. Interim Conclusion

In sum, analogous to general principles of Union law, the normative framework established by the Charter concurrently safeguards private autonomy and conditions its exercise. Both facets pose far-reaching implications considering that the Charter, or at least some of the rights and freedoms contained therein, can bind individuals despite the wording of Article 51 CFR. Three trends inform the Court's approach in this regard. First, the horizontality of the Charter's provision depends on its normative characteristics. It must be mandatory and unconditional for it to be 'sufficient in itself to confer on individuals an individual right which they may invoke as such'.[308] Second, these normative characteristics belong to Articles 15–17 CFR that manifest the ideals of private autonomy. While the Court has not explicitly ruled on this point, it has acknowledged their binding effect in a private setting. Their horizontal enforceability is taken at face value. It is likely rationalised based on their root firmly entrenched in the domain of private law principles that traditionally define private relationships and imbued by the concept of 'negative' rights in the sense of subjective prerogatives not to be interfered with by others. Third, horizontality equally belongs to other provisions in the Charter that limit the exercise of private autonomy. However, their enforcement in a private setting seems to strictly depend on satisfying normative preconditions, which are not immune from conceptual and methodological challenges. This appears to stem from their embodiment of 'positive' rights in the sense of providing their beneficiaries with specific claims against others.

305 *Bauer* (n 210) para 85.
306 Opinion of AG Trstenjak in *Maribel Dominguez* (n 202) para 78. According to AG Trstenjak, this is because 'the associated costs that can ultimately make realisation of such rights contingent upon the de facto economic possibilities of the State'. This factor is reflected in the Court's approach to the horizontal direct of the Treaty's provisions. See Case 43-75 *Defrenne v Sabena* EU:C:1976:56, paras 17–24.
307 *Bauer* (n 210) para 85.
308 *Association de médiation sociale* (n 198) paras 44–47.

3

The Treaty and Private Autonomy

> [I]n a common market regime, we may say that the fundamental economic aim of the Community is to ensure the free exchange of goods and services under conditions of fair competition.[1]

In the Union's legal order, the ideals of private autonomy find expression in the free movement and competition provisions enshrined in the Treaty on the Functioning of the European Union (TFEU). While the former set of rules prohibits state barriers to the cross-border flow of goods, services, capital and the mobility of persons, the latter ensures that the removal of such barriers is not undermined by certain forms of unilateral or coordinated private conduct.[2] Both provisions impose obligations that give effect to subjective entitlements to sell goods, supply services, access employment or make investments across borders of Member States. These expressions of private initiative set the dynamics of integration of national markets into a single marketplace,[3] free from fragmentation.[4] Its realisation is deeply rooted and presupposes the very authority of individuals to pursue their conception of the good by exercising control over their labour and property and engaging in legal relations of their own choice. However, what remains questionable is the extent to which the free movement and competition law regimes champion the ideals of private autonomy. Against this backdrop, this chapter draws the contours of private autonomy within the framework of these legal regimes by exploring the jurisprudential development of their normative reach.

I. Individual Rights and EU Free Movement Law

Free movement law generally refers to the framework of substantive principles that inform the interpretation and application of the Treaty's provisions that guarantee the free movement of goods, services, persons and capital between

[1] P Pescatore, 'Public and Private Aspects of European Community Competition Law' (1986) 10 *Fordham International Law Journal* 373, 379.

[2] G Davies, *European Union Internal Market Law*, 2nd edn (Oxford, Routledge-Cavendish, 2003) 136.

[3] Case 15/81 *Gaston Schul Douane Expediteur BV v Inspecteur der Invoerrechten en Accijnzen, Roosendaal* EU:C:1982:135, para 33.

[4] S Weatherill, *The Internal Market as a Legal Concept* (Oxford, Oxford University Press, 2017) 3.

Member States.[5] The Court has gradually developed these provisions into core norms that provide individuals with subjective rights to engage in economic activity across national borders. This is manifested in their recognition as directly effective and capable of being enforced before national courts.[6] From a definitional standpoint, this is also reflected in the Court's reference to them as 'fundamental principles',[7] 'fundamental rights',[8] 'fundamental freedoms',[9] 'fundamental provisions'[10] or 'one of the fundamental rules' of the Union.[11] However, the characterisation of these provisions as norms conferring individual rights is not without uncertainty. Along with the challenges posed by their comparison to traditional human rights,[12] this stems from the conceptual perplexity surrounding the nature of subjective entitlements derived from them.[13]

A. Contours of the Freedoms of Movement

The nature of individual rights embedded in the freedoms of movement revolves around understanding the ambitions and dynamics underlying the organisation of the internal market.[14] As AG Tesauro eloquently put it in *Hünermund*,[15] the central conceptual question is whether these freedoms are a set of normative provisions that are intended to liberalise intra-Union trade or 'more generally to encourage the unhindered pursuit of commerce in individual Member States'.[16] There are no conclusive answers as the case law oscillates on a spectrum between two extremes: the prohibition of discrimination as a framework principle and the more encompassing notion of economic or commercial freedom at large.[17]

i. Right to Equal Treatment (Discriminatory Restrictions)

The principle of non-discrimination is a cornerstone of the internal market. From a conceptual standpoint, it encapsulates the sustained commitment to eradicating

[5] N Nic Shuibhne, *The Coherence of EU Free Movement Law: Constitutional Responsibility and the Court of Justice* (Oxford, Oxford University Press, 2013) 3.

[6] Case 26-62 *NV Algemene Transport- en Expeditie Onderneming van Gend & Loos v Netherlands Inland Revenue Administration* EU:C:1963:1, 13.

[7] See, eg, Case C-112/00 *Eugen Schmidberger, Internationale Transporte und Planzüge v Republik Österreich* EU:C:2003:333, para 51.

[8] See, eg, Case C-222/86 *Unectef v Heylens* EU:C:1987:442, para 14.

[9] See, eg, Case C-299/19 *Techbau SpA v Azienda Sanitaria Locale AL* EU:C:2020:937, para 50.

[10] See, eg, Case C-61/08 *Commission v Greece* EU:C:2011:340, para 43.

[11] See, eg, Case C-788/79 *Herbsnell Gilli and Paul Andres* EU:C:1980:171, para 9.

[12] See F de Cecco, 'Fundamental Freedoms, Fundamental Rights, and the Scope of Free Movement Law' (2014) 15 *German Law Journal* 383, 397–407.

[13] See also T Kingreen, 'Fundamental Freedoms' in A von Bogdandy and J Bast (eds), *Principles of European Constitutional Law* (Oxford, Hart Publishing, 2009) 532.

[14] M Dougan, 'Legal Developments' (2010) 48 *Journal of Common Market Studies* 163, 165.

[15] Opinion of AG Tesauro in Case C-292/92 *Ruth Hünermund and Others v Landesapothekerkammer Baden-Württemberg* EU:C:1993:863.

[16] ibid para 1.

[17] Weatherill (n 4) 51–52.

national frontiers and protectionist instincts of Member States as a means for establishing a unified economic sphere.[18] All four freedoms of movement contain this principle. Within its framework, they function as a set of normative provisions aimed at safeguarding the individual right to engage in economic activity on equal terms in all parts of the internal market. They prohibit national measures that disadvantage or have a greater impact on out-of-state goods or persons by treating them differently compared to their similarly placed domestic counterparts.[19] Considered within this narrative, as AG Maduro outlined in *Marks & Spencer*,[20] Member States are no longer at liberty to ignore the constraints imposed by the principle of non-discrimination on the definition and application of national policies.[21] While they retain regulatory autonomy,[22] this prerogative is conditioned by the requirement that their policy choices apply equally to out-of-state economic actors and their in-state equivalents.[23] Such conditionality applies not just to the host Member State but also extends to the home Member State, for its policies must not impair the freedoms of movement by disadvantaging those who pursue economic activities in other Member States.[24]

Within the normative framework defined by the prohibition of discrimination, the objective of free movement law is confined to the guarantee of equal opportunities to reap the full benefits of market integration.[25] The analytical focus under this model centres on the comparative assessment of the treatment of out-of-state and in-state economic actors, even if the Court does not always systematically engage with the identification of comparative situations.[26] This model exclusively defines the scope of Article 35 TFEU in comparison to other sectors of free movement law.[27] In *Groenveld*,[28] the Court defined the measures having equivalent effect to quantitative

[18] Nic Shuibhne (n 5) 193.

[19] See, eg, Case 251/78 *Firma Denkavit Futtermittel GmbH v Minister für Ernähung, Landwirtschaft und Forsten des Landes Nordrhein-Westfalen* EU:C:1979:252; Case 2-74 *Jean Reyners v Belgian State* EU:C:1974:68.

[20] Opinion of AG Maduro in Case C-446/03 *Marks & Spencer plc v David Halsey (Her Majesty's Inspector of Taxes)* EU:C:2005:201.

[21] ibid para 37.

[22] N Bernard, 'Discrimination and Free Movement in EC Law' (1996) 45 *International and Comparative Law Quarterly* 82, 103.

[23] C Barnard, *The Substantive Law of the EU: The Four Freedoms*, 5th edn (Oxford, Oxford University Press, 2016) 18.

[24] Case C-224/98 *Marie-Nathalie D'Hoop v Office national de l'emploi* EU:C:2002:432, para 30; see also Case 115/78 *J. Knoors v Secretary of State for Economic Affairs* EU:C:1979:31, para 19; Case C-19/92 *Dieter Kraus v Land Baden-Württemberg* EU:C:1993:125, para 32; Case C-370/90 *The Queen v Immigration Appeal Tribunal et Surinder Singh ex parte Secretary of State for Home Department* EU:C:1992:296, para 23.

[25] Opinion of AG Maduro in Joined Cases C-158/04 and C-159/04 *Alfa Vita Vassilopoulos and Others* EU:C:2006:212, para 37.

[26] E Spaventa, *Free Movement of Persons in the European Union: Barriers to Movement in Their Constitutional Context* (Alphen aan den Rijn, Kluwer Law International, 2007) 22.

[27] See, eg, Case C-648/18 *ANRE v Societatea de Producere a Energiei Electrice în Hidrocentrale Hidroelectrica SA* EU:C:2020:723, para 29.

[28] Case 15/79 *PB Groenveld BV v Produktschap voor Vee en Vlees* EU:C:1979:253.

restrictions as 'national measures which ha[d] as their specific object or effect the restriction of patterns of exports and thereby … provided a particular advantage for national production or for the domestic market of the State in question at the expense of the production or of the trade of other Member States'.[29] Although the Court has slightly broadened the scope of Article 35 TFEU,[30] discrimination-based reasoning remains the normative framework determining the concept of export barriers.[31] The normative reach of Article 35 TFEU does not generally extend to the regulatory competence of Member States to set out their own production and manufacturing rules so long as these rules produce an equal burden on intra-state and inter-state trade.[32]

However, in the context of other free movement provisions, the Court has embraced a broader understanding of the notion of restriction that goes beyond the mere prohibition of discrimination. The rationale for this approach generally rests in the very aim of building a single marketplace, for which the prohibition of discrimination is not seen as an all-encompassing framework principle.[33] A measure can create a barrier to free movement without being discriminatory. As AG Jacobs pointed out in *Leclerc-Siplec*,[34] 'if an obstacle to inter-State trade exists, it cannot cease to exist simply because an identical obstacle affects domestic trade'.[35] Focusing only on its possible disparate impact would effectively leave it intact. This would be at odds with the legal framework of free movement law enshrined in the Treaty, the textual formulation of which refers to 'restrictions', though without necessarily qualifying them with the language of discrimination.[36] At the same time, this begs the question of how far the construction of the notion of restriction beyond discrimination stretches the normative boundaries of free movement law.

ii. Dassonville *et al.: The Right to Individual Economic Freedom?*

Dassonville is a landmark ruling that occupies a significant place in the evolution of free movement law.[37] There, the Court famously defined measures having equivalent to quantitative restrictions under Article 34 TFEU to include 'all trading rules enacted by Member States which [were] capable of hindering, directly or

[29] ibid para 7.

[30] See Case C-15/15 *New Valmar BVBA v Global Pharmacies Partner Health Srl* EU:C:2016:464, para 43. See also E Spaventa, 'The Classic Freedom? The Free Movement of Goods: Old Doctrines, New Cases and Contemporary Reflections' in S Garben and I Govaere (eds), *The Internal Market 2.0* (Oxford, Hart Publishing, 2020) 103–04.

[31] Nic Shuibhne (n 5) 196.

[32] Spaventa (n 30) 102–03.

[33] G Davies, 'Understanding Market Access: Exploring the Economic Rationality of Different Conceptions of Free Movement Law' (2010) 8 *German Law Review* 671, 673.

[34] Case C-412/93 *Société d'Importation Edouard Leclerc-Siplec v TF1 Publicité SA and M6 Publicité SA* EU:C:1994:393.

[35] ibid para 39.

[36] Nic Shuibhne (n 5) 205.

[37] Case 8-74 *Procureur du Roi v Benoît and Gustave Dassonville* EU:C:1974:82.

indirectly, actually or potentially, intra-[Union] trade'.[38] This so-called *Dassonville* formula is usually conceived as the first step in the broad construction of the notion of restriction to free movement that transcends the logic underlying the principles of non-discrimination and anti-protectionism.[39] Indeed, taken at face value, its all-encompassing language subjects all forms of national market regulation to scrutiny under Article 34 TFEU, for they impact the engagement in trade.[40] It is construed as introducing the 'presumption of incompatibility'[41] of national regulatory choices that affect the exercise of economic activity and allowing only those that are objectively justified. The reference to 'indirect, potential effect' expands the breadth of Article 34 TFEU to the extent that its scope strikes down any impediment to the exercise of economic or commercial freedom in the internal market.[42] *Dassonville* is therefore understood as the authority that 'provided individual traders with a vehicle to challenge any national rule which – even potentially and indirectly – stands in their way of participating in the market on whatever terms they choose'.[43] It is true that, considered in its own historical and jurisprudential context, *Dassonville* does not exude this narrative.[44] The issue, in this case, concerned a national measure that prohibited parallel imports, the protectionist nature of which did not appear to provide the necessary context for the Court to formulate a broad approach to the notion of restriction under Article 34 TFEU.[45] Despite that, the *Dassonville* formula, which is often cited ad nauseam, has acquired a life of its own, operating as an overarching principle covering both distinctly and indistinctly applicable national rules.[46]

The Court also broadly construed the normative scope of other free movement provisions. In *Van Binsbergen*,[47] it held that restrictions under Article 56 TFEU included '*all* requirements imposed' on service providers based on their

[38] ibid para 5.

[39] See JHH Weiler, 'Epilogue: Towards a Common Law of International Trade' in JHH Weiler (ed), *The EU, the WTO, and the NAFTA: Towards a Common Law of International Trade?* (Oxford, Oxford University Press, 2001) 206. For an alternative view, see N Bernard, 'On the Art of Not Mixing One's Drinks: *Dassonville* and *Cassis de Dijon* Revisited' in L Azoulai and L Poiares Pessoa Maduro (eds), *The Past and Future of EU Law: The Classics of EU Law Revisited on the 50th Anniversary of the Rome Treaty* (Oxford, Hart Publishing, 2010) 456.

[40] MP Maduro, 'Reforming the Market or the State? Article 30 and the European Constitution: Economic Freedom and Political Rights' (1997) 3 *European Law Journal* 55, 57.

[41] N Bernard, *Multilevel Governance in the European Union* (The Hague, Kluwer Law International, 2002), 19.

[42] Weatherill (n 4) 51.

[43] Barnard (n 23) 74–75.

[44] It was subsequently confirmed in Case 82/77 *Openbaar Ministerie (Public Prosecutor) of the Kingdom of the Netherlands v Jacobus Philippus van Tiggele* ECLI:EU:C:1978:10, para 12.

[45] R Schütze, '"Re-reading" *Dassonville*: Meaning and Understanding in the History of European Law' (2018) 24 *European Law Journal* 376, 378.

[46] A Rosas, 'Life after *Dassonville* and *Cassis*: Evolution But No Revolution' in Azoulai and Poiares Pessoa Maduro (n 39) 437.

[47] Case 33-74 *Johannes Henricus Maria van Binsbergen v Bestuur van de Bedrijfsvereniging voor de Metaalnijverheid* EU:C:1974:131.

nationality or residence, which did not apply to persons established within the national territory, or 'which [might] prevent or otherwise obstruct the activities of the person providing the service' (emphasis added).[48] This was later elaborated upon in *Säger*,[49] where it was stated that Article 56 TFEU prohibited any restriction, even if it applied without distinction to all service providers, when it was '*liable to prohibit or otherwise impede* the activities of a provider of services established in another Member State where he lawfully provided similar services' (emphasis added).[50] Likewise, the Court found that Articles 45 and 49 TFEU prohibited non-discriminatory measures that were 'liable to hamper or make less attractive the exercise of fundamental freedoms guaranteed by the Treaty'.[51] This also applies to Article 63 TFEU, pursuant to which, according to the Court, a restriction on capital movements 'goes beyond the mere elimination of unequal treatment, on grounds of nationality, as between operators on the financial markets'.[52] This interpretative development appeared to stretch the boundaries of the Treaty by opening the prospect of scrutiny of any national measures, even if they were not associated with a cross-border economic activity.[53]

iii. Cassis *et al.: The Right to Choose a Regulatory Regime*

Another monumental step in setting out the breadth of individual rights flowing from free movement law was taken in *Cassis de Dijon*,[54] which concerned the compatibility with Article 34 TFEU of the national law on minimum alcohol content. In this case, the Court was faced with the exclusion of a product from a national market resulting from divergences existing between national regulatory systems.[55] The Court found that the imposition of the impugned national law was contrary to Article 34 TFEU because its effect was to promote products that met the specifications it enshrined at the expense of excluding from the national market products of other Member States which did not meet them.[56] In the absence of objective justification, the Court then famously held that there was no reason why products lawfully produced and marketed in one Member State should not be admitted in all other Member States.[57]

At an individual level, *Cassis* has had a twofold effect. First, it can be construed to bestow upon economic operators the right to choose the preferred

[48] ibid para 10.
[49] Case C-76/90 *Manfred Säger v Dennemeyer & Co Ltd* EU:C:1991:331.
[50] ibid para 12.
[51] Case C-19/92 *Dieter Kraus v Land Baden-Württemberg* EU:C:1993:125, para 32.
[52] Case C-367/98 *Commission v Portugal* EU:C:2002:326, para 44.
[53] Weatherill (n 4) 67–68.
[54] Case 120/78 *Rewe-Zentral AG v Bundesmonopolverwaltung für Branntwein (Cassis de Dijon)* EU:C:1979:42.
[55] Weatherill (n 4) 53.
[56] *Cassis de Dijon* (n 54) para 14.
[57] ibid.

national regulatory regime for production and manufacturing purposes. This effectively stems from the presumption of equivalence of national technical standards established in *Cassis*. Member States are under the duty to recognise each other's technical product standards. The individualisation of this requirement is then manifested in the ability of economic operators to penetrate any part of the internal market by having goods 'validly produced and marketed' in one Member State.[58] This was achieved by removing barriers to intra-Union trade resulting from the dual regulation by the host Member State of products that already met the equivalent legal requirements in the Member State of their origin. Therefore, economic actors saw a significant expansion of market opportunities in the internal market, for they were exempt from compliance with the technical standards of each Member State in the territory of which they wished to market their products.

However, the right to choose a preferred national regulatory regime is not absolute. The host Member State can rebut the presumption of equivalence. As the Court stated in *Cassis*, the obstacles resulting from the host Member State's regulatory choices must be accepted 'in so far as' they are justified by satisfying the so-called mandatory requirements.[59] Under the presumption of equivalence, the acceptance of the host Member State's regulatory autonomy is therefore conditional.[60] By allowing economic actors to market their products in any part of the internal market without being subjected to the technical standards of more than one Member State, *Cassis* shifted the burden of proof to the host Member State to show that the imposition of its technical requirements pursues a legitimate objective.[61] As such, economic actors only need to assert that the host Member State's regulatory choices impose or could potentially impose an additional burden. The host Member State would then have to put forward a justification subject to a high standard of proof framed by the demands of the proportionality principle.

At the same time, *Cassis* also provided market operators with ammunition to challenge any national regulatory choices – beyond technical standards – that allegedly affected the exercise of economic or commercial freedom. Read as the extension to *Dassonville*, *Cassis* is generally construed to signal the Court's willingness at that time to subject all forms of national regulation to scrutiny,[62] suggesting that they were deemed inimical to the internal market goal.[63] As the Court subsequently acknowledged, this led to 'the increasing tendency of traders

[58] Davies (n 33) 689.

[59] *Cassis de Dijon* (n 54) para 8.

[60] Weatherill (n 4) 54.

[61] I Lianos, 'Efficient Restrictions of Trade in the EU Law of the Internal Market: Trust, Distrust and the Nature of Economic Integration' (2010) 1 *CLES Working Paper Series* 1, 15.

[62] MP Maduro, 'Harmony and Dissonance in Free Movement' (2001) 4 *Cambridge Yearbook of European Legal Studies* 315, 317.

[63] Bernard (n 39) 462.

to invoke [Article 34 TFEU] as a means of challenging any rules whose effect [was] to limit their commercial freedom'.[64] The catalyst for this growing sentiment was the broad interpretation of the scope of Article 34 TFEU in the aftermath of *Cassis*. The ruling often cited in this regard is *Cinéthèque*,[65] where the Court was faced with the question of compatibility with Union law of the national law that prohibited the sale or hire in the form of videocassettes of cinematographic works shown in the cinema. The Court first acknowledged that the legislation was not discriminatory, as it applied without distinction based on the origin of videocassettes and nor did it favour the domestic production of cinematographic works.[66] Nonetheless, according to the Court, its application could create barriers to intra-Union trade resulting from the disparity of the systems operating in different Member States and the conditions attached therein.[67]

The expansion of the scope of Article 34 TFEU intensified in the infamous *Sunday Trading* saga.[68] In *Torfaen*,[69] the issue arose from the enforcement of the national rule that prohibited retail shops from being open on Sundays. Analogous to *Cinéthèque*, the Court, having found that the ban was not discriminatory based on the origin of goods, proceeded to establish whether it could be objectively justified and whether its restrictive effect did not exceed the impact intrinsic to trade rules.[70] Although the Court left it to the national court to rule on its proportionality, its reasoning indicated that a measure did not necessarily need to be discriminatory to be caught by Article 34 TFEU.[71] This was even more apparent in *Conforama*,[72] where the Court found the national rule that banned employing staff on Sundays, despite not being designed to control trade, to entail restrictive effects on the free movement of goods.[73] This is because, in the Court's words, it could pose 'negative repercussions on the volume of sales and hence on the volume of imports'.[74] Given that a broad range of national measures are susceptible to producing such an effect,[75] this reasoning appeared to propel Article 34 TFEU

[64] Joined Cases C-267/91 and C-268/91 *Criminal Proceedings against Bernard Keck and Daniel Mithouard* EU:C:1993:905, para 14.

[65] Joined Cases 60 and 61/84 *Cinéthèque SA and Others v Fédération nationale des cinémas français* EU:C:1985:329.

[66] ibid para 21.

[67] ibid para 22.

[68] For more on this, see E Sharpston, 'About that Sunday Trading Mess …' in F Amtenbrink, G Davies, D Kochenov and J Lindeboom (eds), *The Internal Market and the Future of European Integration: Essays in Honour of Laurence W Gormley* (Cambridge, Cambridge University Press, 2019).

[69] Case C-145/88 *Torfaen Borough Council v B&Q plc* EU:C:1989:593.

[70] ibid paras 14–15.

[71] Sharpston (n 68) 156.

[72] Case C-312/89 *Union départementale des syndicats CGT de l'Aisne v SIDEF Conforama, Société Arts et Meubles and Société Jima* EU:C:1991:93.

[73] ibid para 8.

[74] ibid.

[75] D Charmers, 'Repackaging the Internal Market: The Ramifications of the *Keck* Judgment' (1994) 19 *European Law Review* 385, 387.

into an instrument to determine the appropriate levels of regulation in the internal market.[76] As was later clarified in *Stoke-on-Trent*,[77] this involved subjecting all forms of national market regulation to a balancing test, whereby the pursued national interests would be weighed against the interests of ensuring the free movement of goods.[78] This approach could be construed to effectively replace the assessment of obstacles to cross-border movement with the assessment of restrictions on the exercise of economic activity.[79]

iv. Keck: *Right to Equal Market Access*

The period post-*Dassonville* and *Cassis* saw economic operators increasingly refer to Article 34 TFEU to advance their pursuit of commercial interests.[80] This led to *Keck*, which fundamentally altered the scope of this provision.[81] This ruling did not reverse either *Dassonville* or *Cassis*; instead, it limited the *Cassis* principle to measures that constitute product standards and recalibrated the *Dassonville* formula in relation to measures relating to market circumstances.[82] In doing so, *Keck* established that Article 34 TFEU was not apt to subject national regulatory choices to general scrutiny but could only operate within the confines of the demand to bring together national markets.[83] From an individual perspective, *Keck* explicitly departed from the understanding of Article 34 TFEU as a normative instrument that asserted the general right to commercial freedom at large. What emerged from this ruling was the narrow construction of this provision in terms of the right to equal market access.

The fundamental change brought about by *Keck* lies in the introduction of categorisation as an alternative legal technique to outright balancing for the purpose of demarcating the scope of Article 34 TFEU.[84] Faced with the question of compliance with this provision of the national rule that prohibited the sale at loss as a marketing method, the Court drew the infamous distinction between the so-called 'product requirements' and 'selling arrangements'. The first category includes national rules that lay down requirements to be met by goods coming from other Member States that take the form of either intrinsic or extrinsic

[76] Maduro (n 62) 319.

[77] Case C-169/91 *Council of the City of Stoke-on-Trent and Norwich City Council v B&Q plc* EU:C:1992:519.

[78] ibid para 15.

[79] PC de Sousa, 'Through Contact Lenses, Darkly: Is Identifying Restrictions to Free Movement Harder Than Meets the Eye? Comment on *Ker-Optika*' (2012) 37 *European Law Review* 79.

[80] C Pecnard and C Henin, '*Keck and Mithouard*, Two Years on: Repackaging the Free Movement of Goods' (1996) 3 *International Business Law Journal* 371, 372.

[81] *Keck and Mithouard* (n 64).

[82] Maduro (n 40) 58.

[83] S Weatherill, 'Free Movement of Goods' (2006) 55 *International & Comparative Law Quarterly* 457, 458.

[84] I Lianos, 'In Memoriam *Keck*: The Reformation of the EU Law on the Free Movement of Goods' (2015) 40 *European Law Review* 225, 227.

modifications of their characteristics.[85] In *Keck*, the Court confirmed that product requirements were caught by Article 34 TFEU, for they produced a pernicious effect on intra-Union trade and required justification on objective grounds.[86] In practice, their effect is twofold: a foreign producer would have to either pass on these costs in the sale price and risk losing out to cheaper equivalent local products or absorb these costs by reducing its profit margins.[87] Given such an extra burden,[88] foreign producers would be unable to compete based on merits with domestic producers and would likely refrain from entering the market in another Member State.[89] As confirmed in *Keck*, insofar as the intrinsic or extrinsic characteristics of a product are concerned, the host Member State does not retain the prerogative to regulate foreign products and has to trust that the regulatory standards already met in the Member State of origin are sufficient to ensure public health and consumer protection.[90]

In contrast, *Keck* introduced a conceptually and substantively different approach concerning selling arrangements. This category encompasses rules that concern, borrowing AG Tesauro's words, 'the manner in which trading activity is pursued'.[91] Previously, as the *Sunday Trading* saga paradigmatically illustrates, this category of rules fell within the scope of Article 34 TFEU and was subject to a balancing test.[92] *Keck*, however, marked a turning point. Having explicitly acknowledged the need to proceed 'contrary to what ha[d] previously been decided', the Court held that the application to products from other Member States of national rules restricting or prohibiting certain selling arrangements was not as such to hinder intra-Union trade under the *Dassonville* formula.[93] This depends on two conditions: they must be applied to all economic operators and affect the marketing of domestic products and those from other Member States in the same manner, in law and in fact.[94] Provided that these two conditions are met, national rules governing selling arrangements fall outside the scope of Article 34 TFEU as '[they are] not by nature such as to prevent [the access of foreign products] to the market or to impede [their] access any more than [they] impede the access of domestic products'.[95]

Keck signalled a fundamental shift in the nature and extent of individual rights bestowed under Article 34 TFEU. It explicitly rejected the characterisation

[85] Pecnard and Henin (n 80) 374.
[86] *Keck and Mithouard* (n 64) para 15.
[87] Pecnard and Henin (n 80) 378.
[88] There is no need to show a calculable loss. See, eg, Case 317/92 *Commission v Germany* EU:C:1994:212, para 12.
[89] Case C-457/05 *Schutzverband der Spirituosen-Industrie eV v Diageo Deutschland GmbH* EU:C:2007:576, para 33.
[90] Spaventa (n 30) 97.
[91] Opinion of AG Tesauro in *Ruth Hünermund* (n 15) para 20.
[92] See, eg, *Stoke-on-Trent and Norwich City Council* (n 77) para 15.
[93] *Keck and Mithouard* (n 64) para 16.
[94] ibid.
[95] ibid para 16.

of this provision as a normative vehicle to challenge national regulatory choices that merely limit or condition the pursuit of commercial activity within the territory of a Member State. In its reasoning, the Court first acknowledged that the prohibition of a sale promotion method restricted the volume of sales. However, unlike *Conforama*, it questioned whether it was sufficient to constitute a breach of Article 34 TFEU. The answer was negative. Compared to product requirements, the Court attributed the presumption of compatibility to the category of selling arrangements. For these rules to fall within the scope of Article 34 TFEU, it is no longer sufficient that they may impact the pursuit of commercial activity; instead, they fall foul of the Treaty only if they fail a substantively different test that is based on two interrelated elements.

First, *Keck* is generally perceived as introducing the concept of market access discrimination,[96] according to which selling arrangements breach Article 34 TFEU if they directly or indirectly discriminate against economic operators in terms of their ability to access the market of the host Member State. This test narrowed the focus of scrutiny under Article 34 TFEU by shifting it from the assessment of potential impact on intra-Union trade to the analysis of disparate impact inflicted on specific products.[97] This is reflected in the distinction drawn between 'product requirements' and 'selling arrangements', where the Court considered the former category, unlike the latter, to impede the access to the market by out-of-state producers on account of the extra regulatory burden it placed on them. Hence, the rationale underlying the discrimination-based *Keck* test is not the maintenance of untrammelled trade across national borders of Member States but fair trade within the confines of the internal market.[98]

Second, *Keck* altered the placement of the evidential burden of proof that emerged in *Cassis*.[99] This stems from the presumption of compatibility attributed to selling arrangements comprising two facets. At one end, the Court effectively refused to extend the principle of functional equivalence and mutual recognition to rules that regulate when and how a product can be sold on the market. Its approach reflects the conceptual variance existing between product requirements and selling arrangements. The former category of rules pursues the goals of either public health or consumer protection and, as such, compliance with the technical standards of the home Member State can generally provide the necessary assurances for the host Member State without the need for duplication. The category of selling arrangements encapsulates various cultural and societal constructs intrinsic to the host Member State. It concerns public interests that cannot be remedied by compliance with the law in the home Member State.[100] At the other end, under

[96] Spaventa (n 30) 102.
[97] Lianos (n 84) 228.
[98] D Edward, 'What was the *Keck* Really about?' in Amtenbrink et al (n 68) 175.
[99] J Lindeboom, 'Interpreting the EU Internal Market' in Amtenbrink et al (n 68) 90.
[100] D Wilsher, 'Does *Keck* Discrimination Make Any Sense? An Assessment of the Non-discrimination Principle within the European Single Market' (2008) 33 *European Law Review* 3, 14.

Keck, national regulators are no longer obligated to justify selling arrangements that do not concern the characteristics of a product. Instead, the burden lies on economic operators to adduce evidence of the discriminatory effect on market access. That said, they are not necessarily required to produce concrete market-based assessments as to the similarity or competitive position of products. This is paradigmatically exemplified in the post-*Keck* approach to advertising and other modalities of sale, which constitute an essential means for market penetration. In *Gourmet*,[101] the Court accepted the rebuttal of the presumption of compatibility of these rules without insisting on the precise analysis of the state of a national market.[102] Instead, it established the unequal effect of these rules based on the general comparison of their impact on out-of-state economic operators and incumbents in the host Member State. Such an effect, according to the Court, follows from the fact that a measure that imposes a complete ban on advertising or prohibits the most effective methods available to enter the market is likely to affect out-of-state producers more than domestic ones since their products are more familiar to consumers in the home Member State.[103]

Keck represents a fundamental recalibration of the philosophy that frames the reach of Article 34 TFEU. As the Court explicitly acknowledged, it was prompted by the expansive *Dassonville* formula that risked ensnaring an unlimited range of national regulatory policy choices.[104] *Keck* was meant to dispel the characterisation of Article 34 TFEU as akin to the general right to pursue commerce in the internal market that verged on, as eloquently described, 'slipping into a freewheeling rampage of economic due process'.[105] The Court demarcated the normative boundaries of the *Dassonville* formula by categorising national measures around the newly introduced concept of market access operationalised on the less intrusive (to national regulatory autonomy) notion of market equality. On this premise, a hindrance to free movement exists when a measure creates a disparity between out-of-state and in-state economic actors in the internal market; conversely, a measure is not caught if it imposes a general burden without disadvantaging any particular group of economic actors.[106] Hence, *Keck* has ossified the narrow construction of the scope of Article 34 TFEU, whereby not every measure that reduces the

[101] Case C-405/98 *Konsumentombudsmannen (KO) v Gourmet International Products AB (GIP)* EU:C:2001:135.

[102] ibid para 21.

[103] ibid.

[104] MS Jansson and H Kalimo, '*De Minimis* Meets "Market Access": Transformations in the Substance – and the Syntax – of EU Free Movement Law?' (2014) 5 *Common Market Law Review* 523, 524.

[105] A Somek, 'The Argument from Transnational Effects I: Representing Outsiders through Freedom of Movement' (2010) 16 *European Law Journal* 315, 332.

[106] G Davies, 'Between Market Access and Discrimination: Free Movement as a Right to Fair Conditions of Competition' in P Kourakos and J Snell (eds), *Research Handbook on the Law of the EU's Internal Market* (Cheltenham, Edward Elgar, 2017) 18–19.

attractiveness in economic terms of the pursuit of commercial activity in the internal market would require objective justification.[107]

B. Market Access as an Individual Right

Since *Keck*, the case law has seen the emergence of the market access test as a standalone method of assessment that is detached from equality-based reasoning.[108] This aligned the normative reach of Article 34 TFEU with that of other freedoms of movement,[109] which had already adhered to the broad concept of restriction to market access.[110] The central premise of this benchmark is that national measures, even in the absence of unequal treatment, can breach the Treaty if they affect access to the market of a Member State and, as such, would necessitate objective justification.[111] With the market access framework forming the normative foundation of the free movement law regime, the salient question is how this development defines the nature and contours of subjective entitlements derived from the freedoms of movement.

Unlike Article 34 TFEU, the broad normative reach of the Treaty's provisions on the free movement of persons and capital did not undergo substantive recalibration in line with the *Keck* categorisation. However, *Keck* contributed to the consolidation of their scope around the language of market access. In *Alpine Investments*,[112] in response to the possible application, by analogy, of the *Keck* logic to the prohibition of cold calling as a method to offer financial services, the Court was quick to find that such prohibition could not be treated similarly to measures concerning selling arrangements, since it 'directly affect[ed] access to the market in services in other Member States' by limiting offers made to potential recipients established therein.[113] The Court reached the same verdict in *Bosman* concerning the rules on the compulsory transfer fees for out-of-contract football players,[114] while in *Commission v Spain*,[115] it found that the rules on golden shares affected access to the market, as they were liable to deter investors from other Member

[107] Opinion of AG Tizzano in Case C-442/02 *CaixaBank France v Ministère de l'Économie, des Finances et de l'Industrie* EU:C:2004:187, para 58.

[108] E Spaventa, 'From Gebhard to Carpenter: Towards a (Non-)Economic European Constitution' (2004) 41 *Common Market Law Review* 743, 747.

[109] Except for Article 35 TFEU.

[110] A Tryfonidou, 'Further Steps on the Road to Convergence among the Market Freedoms' (2010) 35 *European Law Review* 36, 38.

[111] Nic Shuibhne (n 5) 234.

[112] Case C-384/93 *Alpine Investments BV v Minister van Financiën* EU:C:1995:126.

[113] ibid para 38.

[114] Case C-415/93 *Union royale belge des sociétés de football association ASBL v Jean-Marc Bosman* EU:C:1995:463, para 103.

[115] Case C-463/00 *Commission v Spain* EU:C:2003:272.

States.[116] Along the same lines, in *CaixaBank*, the prohibition of remuneration of sight accounts was deemed to affect access to the market since it denied the possibility to compete more effectively. On each occasion, it is the concept of market access that served as a benchmark to set apart the impugned national measures. This line of case law points, more clearly than before, towards the coalescence of the Treaty's provisions on the free movement of persons and capital around the prohibition of a hindrance to market access as their underlying normative framework.[117]

In the field of goods, the analogous introduction of the concept of market access, detached from the language of discrimination, materialised through the jurisprudential line on rules concerning the consumer use of a product.[118] In *Commission v Italy*,[119] the Court was faced with the compatibility with Article 34 TFEU of the national ban on towing trailers with motorbikes. Referring the *Dassonville* formula, the Court held that Article 34 TFEU encapsulated the obligation to respect *principles of non-discrimination* and *mutual recognition* and added the *principle of market access*.[120] Based on this, it was specified that Article 34 TFEU prohibited: first, measures that discriminated against out-of-state goods; second, measures that imposed a double burden on them; and, third, any other measures that hindered the access of out-of-state goods to the market of a Member State.[121] The impugned national law did not impose any technical product standards on trailers nor regulate when, where and how they could be sold. Nonetheless, the Court found that it affected the access of a product to the market by posing 'a considerable influence on the behaviour of consumers' and preventing any demand for a product, as consumers' would have no practical interest in buying it.[122] As reiterated in *Mickelsson & Roos* in relation to the law that did not ban but limited the possible use of personal watercraft,[123] this line of reasoning signalled the re-alignment of the established normative boundaries of Article 34 TFEU around the concept of market access that was devoid of the language of discrimination.[124]

Despite the initial uncertainty,[125] this new jurisprudential line did not overturn the *Keck* categorisation. It is true that the subsequent case law certainly elevated market access into an independent – and at times decisive – criterion to ascertain a

[116] ibid para 61.
[117] Davies (n 106) 17–18.
[118] J Snell, 'The Notion of Market Access: A Concept or a Slogan?' (2010) 47 *Common Market Law Review* 437, 455.
[119] Case C-110/05 *Commission v Italy (Trailers)* EU:C:2009:66.
[120] ibid para 33.
[121] ibid para 37.
[122] ibid paras 56–57.
[123] Case C-142/05 *Åklagaren v Percy Mickelsson and Joakim Roos* EU:C:2009:336.
[124] ibid para 24.
[125] See E Spaventa, 'Leaving *Keck* behind? The Free Movement of Goods after the Rulings in *Commission v Italy* and *Mickelsson and Roos*' (2009) 34 *European Law Review* 914, 922.

breach of Article 34 TFEU.[126] Yet, the Court's adherence to the broad access-based framework subsumes rather than supersedes the *Keck*-based inequality reasoning. This follows from two interrelated factors. First, the market access test qualified by the language of discrimination remains the analytical premise to assess measures governing selling arrangements,[127] though subject to the reformulated presumption.[128] Second, the general bulk of national measures so far caught by the broad market access test are the so-called residual rules that encompass those that are neither product requirements nor selling arrangements.[129] Among them are not just the rules on the consumer use of a product but also those that impose registration requirements,[130] certification requirements,[131] authorisation or approval requirements,[132] product certificate schemes[133] and general product bans.[134] Both factors suggest that selling arrangements, compared to residual rules, remain subject to a more lenient test within the broad access-based framework,[135] though the case law does not shed light on the rationale behind such distinction.[136]

While free movement law consolidates around a singular normative framework centred on the idea of market access, the meaning behind this concept remains elusive.[137] The fundamental question often raised is how, as a benchmark, it defines the normative scope of free movement law. What exactly constitutes an obstacle to market access, and what factor, or combination thereof, distinguishes rules producing such an effect from those that do not?[138] Considered at an individual level, the focus of this query concerns the parameters around which the market access principle frames the entitlement to pursue economic activities throughout the internal market. As a consequence of the judicial turnaround against the mechanical application of the *Dassonville* formula,[139] it is questionable whether

[126] See, eg, Case C-456/10 *Asociación Nacional de Expendedores de Tabaco y Timbre (ANETT) v Administración del Estado* EU:C:2012:241, para 35. See also M Jesse, 'What about Sunday Trading … ? The Rise of Market Access as an Independent Criterion under Article 34 TFEU' (2012) 3 *European Journal of Risk Regulation* 437, 440.

[127] Case C-190/20 *DocMorris NV v Apothekerkammer Nordrhein* EU:C:2021:609, para 38.

[128] Compare the Court's formulation of the *Keck* formula in the following rulings: Case C-108/09 *Ker-Optika bt v ÀNTSZ Dél-dunántúli Regionális Intézete* EU:C:2010:725, para 51; Case C-221/15 *Criminal proceedings against Etablissements Fr Colruyt NV* EU:C:2016:704, para 35.

[129] Previously this type of rule used to be subject to the *Dassonville* formula. See Case C-120/95 *Nicolas Decker v Caisse de maladie des employés privés* EU:C:1997:399, para 31; Case C-189/95 *Criminal Proceedings against Harry Franzén* EU:C:1997:504, para 69.

[130] See, eg, Case C-443/10 *Philippe Bonnarde v Agence de Services et de Paiement* EU:C:2011:641, para 26.

[131] See, eg, Case C-573/12 *Ålands vindkraft AB v Energimyndigheten* EU:C:2014:2037, para 70.

[132] See, eg, Case C-114/15 *Audace and Others* EU:C:2016:813, para 67.

[133] See, eg, Case C-484/10 *Ascafor and Asidac* EU:C:2012:113, para 56.

[134] See, eg, Case C-142/09 *Criminal Proceedings against Vincent Willy Lahousse and Lavichy BVBA* EU:C:2010:694, para 44.

[135] For a proposition for incorporating *Keck* into the broad access-based framework, see de Sousa (n 79) 88.

[136] Spaventa (n 125) 923.

[137] See, eg, Snell (n 118) 467.

[138] See also Davies (n 106) 18.

[139] R Schütze, 'Of Types and Tests: Towards a Unitary Doctrinal Framework for Article 34 TFEU?' (2016) 41 *European Law Review* 826, 830.

and to what extent the evolved concept of market access conforms to the normative standpoint developed in *Keck*.

i. A Narrow Reading of the Access-Based Framework

According to one view, the concept of market access detached from the language of discrimination aligns with the dogmatic foundation of *Keck*,[140] for the access-based framework is not intended to guarantee the untrammelled pursuit of commerce throughout the internal market,[141] morphing into an instrument of deregulatory nature. The freedoms of movement are not seen as norms that provide the right to exercise economic or commercial freedom at large, whereby every possible limitation or constraint requires objective justification. Such a construction of free movement law finds clear support among several Advocates General. It is worth considering their views in detail.

a. Market Access and Economic Freedom

The interpretative approach favoured by Advocates General supports the strict formulation of the outer boundaries of free movement law. In *Mickelson and Roos*, citing *Keck*, AG Kokott called for the exclusion of rules on product use from the scope of Article 34 TFEU, as otherwise 'individuals [might] even invoke [it] as a means of challenging national rules whose effect [was] merely to limit their general freedom of action'.[142] AG Fennelly made a similar call in *Graf*,[143] where he found that it was necessary 'if the Treaty [was] not to be exploited as a means of challenging any national rules whose effect [was] simply to limit commercial freedom'.[144] AG Maduro echoed this stance in *Marks & Spencer*, where he categorically stated that 'not every restriction on economic or commercial freedom [was] a restriction on the exercise of the freedoms of movement'.[145] In *Alfa Vita*, in turn, drawing on AG Tesauro's reasoning in *Hünermund* that Article 34 TFEU was not a provision that enshrined the right to unhindered pursuit of commerce in Member States,[146] AG Maduro asserted that '[Union] nationals [could not] draw from this provision an absolute right to economic or commercial freedom'.[147] In his words, the Court has no desire to interpret free movement law in light of the principle

[140] De Sousa (n 79) 88.
[141] Lindeboom (n 99) 87.
[142] Opinion of AG Kokott Case C-142/05 *Åklagaren v Percy Mickelsson and Joakim Roos* EU:C:2006:782, para 48.
[143] Opinion of AG Fennely in Case C-190/98 *Volker Graf v Filzmoser Maschinenbau GmbH* EU:C:1999:423.
[144] ibid para 32.
[145] Opinion of AG Maduro in *Marks & Spencer* (n 20) para 40.
[146] Opinion of AG Tesauro in *Ruth Hünermund* (n 15) paras 1 and 27.
[147] Opinion of AG Maduro in *Alfa Vita* (n 25) para 37.

of the freedom to engage in a commercial activity.[148] Along the same lines, AG Tizzano in *CaixaBank* pointed out the difficulty in describing national measures as restrictions contrary to the Treaty 'for the sole reason that they reduce[d] the *economic attractiveness* of pursuing [economic activity]' (emphasis added).[149] AG Bobek also emphasised this factor in *Krah* by pointing out that the focus on rules that merely made the exercise of the freedoms of movement 'less attractive' would be 'in urgent need of its own *Keckian* moment'.[150]

Central to this construction of free movement law is its intrinsic link to the objectives and needs of the internal market. AG Tizzano emphasised that the purpose of the Treaty was not to establish 'a market without rules' or 'a market in which rules [were] prohibited as a matter of principle, except for those necessary and proportionate to meeting imperative requirements in the public interest'.[151] This echoes AG Tesauro's characterisation of Article 34 TFEU as a provision that '[ensures] the free movement of goods in order to establish a single integrated market, eliminating therefore those national measures which in any way create an obstacle to or even mere difficulties for the movement of goods'.[152] In his view, it is not intended 'to strike down the most widely differing measures in order, essentially, to ensure the greatest possible expansion of trade'.[153] Along these lines, AG Trstenjak stated in *Idrima Tipou* that the freedoms of movement were primarily understood by the Court as 'instruments for opening up markets'.[154] AG Fennelly, in turn, defined their purpose as 'the establishment of an internal market to which products from the different Member States have both equal and, subject to qualifications in the public interest, free access'.[155] A similar conclusion was also reached by AG Maduro when he stressed that 'the Treaty provisions relating to the free movement of goods aim[ed] to guarantee the opening-up of national markets, offering producers and consumers the possibility of fully enjoying the benefits of a [Union] internal market, and not to encourage a general deregulation of national economies'.[156] Hence, according to him, the task of the Court is not to question every economic policy of Member States or to engage in challenging them.[157] The importance of constrained judicial scrutiny was also emphasised by AG Bot in *Commission v Italy*, where he expressed that 'the Court's role [was] not systematically to challenge policing measures adopted by the Member States'.[158]

[148] Opinion of AG Maduro in Case C-72/03 *Carbonati Apuani Srl v Comune di Carrara* EU:C:2004:296, para 42.

[149] Opinion of AG Tizzano in *CaixaBank* (n 107) para 58.

[150] Opinion of AG Bobek in Case C-703/17 *Adelheid Krah v Universität Wien* EU:C:2019:450, para 74.

[151] Opinion of AG Tizzano in *CaixaBank* (n 107) para 63.

[152] Opinion of AG Tesauro in *Ruth Hünermund* (n 15) para 28.

[153] ibid.

[154] Opinion of Trstenjak in Case C-81/09 *Idryma Typou AE v Ypourgos Typou kai Meson Mazikis Enimerosis* EU:C:2010:304, para 75.

[155] Opinion of AG Fennely in *Volker Graf* (n 143) para 19.

[156] Opinion of AG Maduro in *Alfa Vita* (n 25) para 37.

[157] Opinion of AG Maduro in *Marks & Spencer* (n 20) para 37.

[158] Opinion of AG Bot in *Commission v Italy (Trailers)* (n 119) para 101.

b. Access and Exercise Dichotomy

The characterisation of the freedoms of movement suggested by Advocates General based on their underlying aim of the realisation of the internal market is in congruence with the *Keck* logic and, more broadly, the division of regulatory competence between the Member States and the Union. However, it is unclear where this approach leaves the normative reach of free movement law defined by the access-based framework. If the scope of the freedoms of movement transcends the mere right to equal treatment in the internal market and does not equate to the right to economic freedom at large that subjects all forms of national regulation to scrutiny, what is then prohibited as a hindrance to market access?

According to Advocates General, the factor separating non-discriminatory rules caught by the Treaty lies in their effect on the engagement in cross-border economic activity throughout the internal market. In *Bosman*, AG Lenz argued in favour of distinguishing between measures that regulate access to an occupational activity and measures that are directed more to the exercise of that activity.[159] In his view, the former category constitutes a restriction (even if neutral), while the latter is caught only if it is discriminatory. Similarly, in *Graf*, AG Fennelly proposed the notion of 'formal restrictions on access to economic activity' that encompassed 'conditions … prescribed by law or regulation non-compliance with which constitute[d] an absolute bar to taking up the activity in question'.[160] Their imposition is sufficient on its own to establish the existence of a restriction contrary to the Treaty. In contrast, in AG Fennelly's view, when some neutral material barrier or incentive results from measures that are not intimately connected with the entry to the market or the taking up of economic activity, a prejudice to free movement must be established.[161]

AG Tizzano also suggested an analogous benchmark. He argued in *CaixaBank* that when the principle of non-discrimination was respected in the sense that the conditions for the taking-up and pursuit of economic activity were equal both in law and in fact, 'a national measure [could not] be described as a restriction on the freedom of movement of persons unless, in the light of its purpose and effects, the measure in question directly affect[ed] market access'.[162] According to him, this interpretative approach makes it possible to reconcile the objective of merging national markets into a single common market and Member States' general powers to regulate economic activities based on the exclusion from the scope of free movement law those neutral measures that merely reduce the attractiveness of pursuing a particular economic activity.[163] Echoing this concern, AG Trstenjak also offered a similar solution in *Idrima Tipou*. She argued in the

[159] Opinion of AG Lenz in Case C-415/93 *Union royale belge des sociétés de football association ASBL v Jean-Marc Bosman* EU:C:1995:293, para 205.
[160] Opinion of AG Fennely in *Volker Graf* (n 143) para 28.
[161] ibid para 31.
[162] Opinion of AG Tizzano in *CaixaBank* (n 107) para 66.
[163] ibid paras 62 and 68.

context of Article 49 TFEU that 'it would be conceivable in principle to determine the scope of the prohibition on restrictions according to whether the national provision in question establishe[d] "specific obstacles to access" or merely define[d] the "conditions applying locally"'.[164] While the prohibition of non-discriminatory restrictions would apply to the former instance, the latter would only be covered by the prohibition of direct and indirect discrimination.[165] AG Bobek drew a similar distinction in *RB v TÜV Rheinland LGA Products*,[166] where he stressed that Article 34 TFEU was aimed to ensure the free flow of goods expressed in their ability to penetrate national markets,[167] but it was not there to regulate 'the subsequent use or consumption of those goods', since once the cross-border movement had occurred, goods must comply with the rules of the host Member State, except for policies that involved a total ban or entirely prevented the use or commercialisation of certain products or their access to the market.[168]

c. The Individual Right to Compete

Based on the interpretative approach proffered by Advocates General, the freedoms of movement can be modelled into norms designed to ensure the subjective right to compete or initiate competition throughout the internal market.[169] As the Court clearly defined, the internal market involves 'the elimination of all obstacles to [intra-Union] trade in order to merge the national markets into a single market bringing about conditions as close as possible to those of a genuine internal market'.[170] Such coalescence of national markets adheres to the traditional market economy principle of free and fair competition that provides the basis for the realisation of various forms of rivalry to gain profit opportunities by offering better commodities or services in terms of quality and value.[171] The individualisation of this process is then manifested in the guarantee of the individual right to compete on merits in any national market in the Union. From this perspective, the case law can be conceptualised in a twofold proposition.

The freedoms of movement enable economic actors to initiate or participate in the interstate process of competition.[172] This is manifested in the prohibition of measures that prevent newcomers from entering the market of a Member State by imposing either discriminatory or non-discriminatory restrictions. The former

[164] Opinion of AG Trstenjak in *Idryma Typou* (n 154) para 75.
[165] ibid.
[166] Opinion of AG Bobek in Case C-581/18 *RB v TÜV Rheinland LGA Products GmbH and Allianz IARD SA* EU:C:2020:77.
[167] ibid para 64.
[168] ibid paras 65–66.
[169] For a discrimination-based argument, see Davies (n 106) 26.
[170] *Gaston Schul* (n 3) para 33.
[171] IM Kirzner, 'Entrepreneurial Discovery and the Competitive Market Process: An Austrian Approach' (1997) 35 *Journal of Economic Literature* 60, 73.
[172] ibid 62.

category stems from the principle of market equality that lays the foundation for the internal market. As a single economic sphere that involves the interaction and interchange of economic actors of diverse geographical origins, there is a need for a 'level playing field' to generate equal opportunities and fair competition.[173] In this context, the analytical focus of scrutiny is placed on the market-distorting impact of a measure that, either in object or effect, protects the competitive position of in-state incumbents or affords preference to them by disadvantaging the entry of out-of-state economic actors. This impact is caused by national regulatory choices, such as product or qualification requirements,[174] that inflict an additional burden on providers of goods or services coming from other Member States. They hamper newcomers' ability to compete on the quality or price of goods and services due to the costs incurred for meeting additional sets of regulatory standards. For the same reason, free movement law outlaws measures that restrain or thwart competition through, among other things, fixing minimum or maximum prices for goods and services,[175] completely banning advertising or long-distance sales,[176] restricting recourse to the most effective methods to gain market share[177] and, more generally, imposing conditions that are easily satisfied by incumbents in the home Member State.[178]

The protection of the right to initiate or participate in the interstate process of competition is not confined to the guarantee of market equality; it also encompasses measures that, even without disparate impact, prevent market entry or produce a similar effect in practice. Their compatibility with the Treaty is determined against the benchmark based on the individual capacity to take part in the competitive process or initiate such a process in any part of the internal market. To trigger scrutiny, there must be an intimate causal link between a measure and the inability to supply goods or services across borders to customers located in other Member States, take up employment or self-employment in other Member States, or channel investments to other Member States. This conceptualisation finds support in *Alpine Investments*, where the Court, as mentioned earlier, rejected the application by analogy of the *Keck* logic to the prohibition of cold calling as a method to offer financial services, for it 'directly affect[ed] access to the market in

[173] See also Davies (n 33) 683.

[174] See, eg, Case C-470/93 *Verein gegen Unwesen in Handel und Gewerbe Köln eV v Mars GmbH* EU:C:1995:224, para 13.

[175] See, eg, Case C-333/14 *Scotch Whisky Association and Others v The Lord Advocate and the Advocate General for Scotland* EU:C:2015:845, para 32; Case C-565/08 *Commission v Italy* EU:C:2011:188, para 51.

[176] Joined Cases C-34/95, C-35/95 and C-36/95 *Konsumentombudsmannen (KO) v De Agostini and Others* EU:C:1997:344, para 43.

[177] See, eg, Case C-322/01 *Deutscher Apothekerverband eV v 0800 DocMorris NV and Jacques Waterval* EU:C:2003:664, para 74; Case C-465/05 *Commission v Italy* EU:C:2007:781, para 125.

[178] See, eg, Joined Cases C-407/19 and C-471/19 *Katoen Natie Bulk Terminals and General Services Antwerp* EU:C:2021:107, para 59; Case C-218/19 *Adina Onofrei v Conseil de l'ordre des avocats au barreau de Paris and Others* EU:C:2020:1034, para 31; Case C-350/96 *Clean Car Autoservice GmbH and Landeshauptmann von Wien* EU:C:1998:205, para 29.

services in other Member States' by depriving operators of 'a rapid and direct technique' for marketing and for contacting potential clients established therein.[179] Further confirmation followed from *Graf*,[180] where the Court explicitly found that 'to be capable of constituting … an obstacle [contrary to Article 45 TFEU, provisions that apply without distinction] … must affect access of workers to the labour market'.[181]

It is difficult to rationalise this line of case law in discriminatory or protectionist terms. Instead, what appears to inform the Court's reasoning is the factor of complete prevention or outright block on the possibility of satisfying the existing or potential demand for a particular type of service or the possibility of availing oneself of employment opportunities in other parts of the internal market.[182] The distinction drawn by the Court makes it clear that non-discriminatory selling arrangements fall outside the scope of the Treaty precisely due to the lack of causation between the nature of market conditions that this category of measures imposes on trade and the inability to trade in itself.[183] The same logic also underlies the Court's approach to the review of rules on product use. As mentioned earlier, in *Commission v Italy*, the impugned national measure inflicted an almost total ban on the use of a product,[184] while in *Mickelson and Roos*, it had the effect of 'preventing … or … greatly restricting' it.[185] Both measures suppressed the opportunity to introduce a product to consumers and generate a demand for a product lawfully commercialised elsewhere in the internal market.[186] They rendered its sale commercially valueless by severely limiting the consumer base that might have been interested in it.[187] This reflects the Court's standpoint on the rules that subject the marketing of a product to the proof of consumer interest and even those that impose complete bans on product imports,[188] either of which disrupts the natural market interplay of supply and demand.

At the same time, the protection of the individual right to compete does not extend to non-discriminatory measures that merely condition how economic actors operate without affecting their competitive position as such. This follows from the distinction drawn between access to the interstate process of competition and the parameters that define that process. If the former aspect is not prevented or hindered, neutral measures that govern the latter are not subject to scrutiny.

[179] *Alpine Investments* (n 112) para 28.
[180] Case C-190/98 *Volker Graf v Filzmoser Maschinenbau GmbH* EU:C:2000:49.
[181] ibid para 23. See also *Bosman* (n 159) para 130.
[182] Nic Shuibhne (n 5) 238.
[183] S Weatherill, 'After *Keck*: Some Thoughts on How to Clarify the Clarification' (1996) 33 *Common Market Law Review* 887, 905.
[184] *Commission v Italy (Trailers)* (n 119) para 55.
[185] *Åklagaren v Percy Mickelsson and Joakim Roos* (n 123) para 28.
[186] Lianos (n 84) 233.
[187] Spaventa (n 125) 924.
[188] See Case 174/82 *Criminal Proceedings against Sandoz BV* EU:C:1983:213, para 4; Case 34/79 *R v Maurice Donald Henn and John Frederick Ernest Darby* EU:C:1979:295, para 12; Case C-663/18 *Criminal Proceedings against BS and CA* EU:C:2020:938, para 82.

Three lines of case law lend support to this strict reading of the Treaty. First, it is reflected in the *Keck* categorisation of product requirements and selling arrangements. The latter measures, particularly those of the so-called 'static' nature, limits or conditions the sale of goods but do not alter the competitive position of out-of-state goods compared to their in-state equivalents. As such, they produce an equal burden that all economic actors bear either by absorbing it through profit margins or passing it on to consumers through price increases.[189]

Second, although *Keck* has not been explicitly extended to other sectors of free movement law, there are instances in which the Court's reasoning aligns with the logic followed in that ruling. In *Innoventif*,[190] the national rule that did not prevent but subjected the registration of a company to the payment of the anticipated cost of publishing its objects was found to comply with Article 49 TFEU since, in the Court's view, it was not 'liable to place companies from other Member States in a less favourable factual or legal situation than companies from the Member State of establishment'.[191] This equality-based reasoning is even more apparent in *Mobistar*,[192] where the Court stated that 'measures, the only effect of which [was] to create additional costs in respect of the service in question and which affect[ed] in the same way the provision of services between Member States and that within one Member State, [did] not fall within the scope of [Article 56 TFEU]'.[193] *Volksbank România*,[194] in turn, explicitly distinguished between the concept of market entry and the process of competition itself. The Court held that the measure prohibiting certain bank charges did not render access to a national market less attractive and 'in the event of access thereto, genuinely reduce[d] the ability of the undertakings concerned to compete effectively, from the outset, against already established undertakings'.[195] A similar distinction was also made in *Commission v Italy (Insurance Fees)*, although with an opposite outcome.[196] There, the Court found that the national law imposing the obligation to contract on motor insurance providers left intact their right to access a national market as such but reduced their ability to compete effectively with incumbents.[197] This is because, according to the Court, it obliged undertakings to accept every potential customer, which would lead to significant additional costs for such undertakings in terms of rethinking their business policy and strategy due to the considerable

[189] Davies (n 106) 18–19.

[190] Case C-453/04 *innoventif Ltd* EU:C:2006:361.

[191] ibid para 39. According to the Court, the payment merely reflected the actual administrative cost of such publication. For an analogous reasoning, see Case C-70/95 *Sodemare SA, Anni Azzurri Holding SpA and Anni Azzurri Rezzato Srl v Regione Lombardia* EU:C:1997:301, para 33.

[192] Joined Cases C-544/03 and C-545/03 *Mobistar SA v Commune de Fléron* EU:C:2005:518.

[193] ibid para 31. See also *Commission v Italy* (n 175) para 49; Case C-134/03 *Viacom Outdoor Srl v Giotto Immobilier SARL* EU:C:2005:94, paras 37–39.

[194] Case C-602/10 *SC Volksbank România SA v Autoritatea Națională pentru Protecția Consumatorilor* EU:C:2012:443.

[195] ibid para 80.

[196] Case C-518/06 *Commission v Italy* EU:C:2009:270.

[197] ibid para 67.

expansion of the range of insurance services offered.[198] The difference between *Commission v Italy (Insurance Fees)* and *Volksbank România* lies in the severity of the constraint imposed on the ability to compete by exercising contractual discretion. While there was no such interference in *Volksbank România*, the impugned national measure in *Commission v Italy (Insurance Fees)* deprived undertakings of a free choice over the range of services to offer, the type of customers to contract with and the calculation of insurance premium rates. It substantially narrowed down, if not eliminated, the avenues for new market entrants to leverage against incumbents.

Third, there are measures that fall outside the scope of the Treaty for the remoteness of their effect on free movement in the internal market.[199] This finds expression in the 'effect too uncertain and indirect' doctrine,[200] the reference to which first appeared in the context of Article 34 TFEU. In *Krantz*,[201] the Court found that the national law allowing state authorities to seize movable properties to recover tax debts did not warrant the conclusion that it was liable to hinder intra-Union trade.[202] This is because the impugned national law did not seek to control trade between Member States and the possibility that potential customers would hesitate to purchase goods that were made subject to it was too uncertain and indirect.[203] The Court reiterated this test in *Peralta* as regards the prohibition against the discharge of chemical substances into the high seas.[204] The effect of such prohibition on trade between Member States was also too uncertain and indirect, for it applied without distinction to all transported chemical substances and was not aimed at regulating trade as such.[205] Based on the same terms, in *Corsica Ferries*,[206] the Court dismissed a claim brought against the national law that made it compulsory for all vessels docking at ports to use mooring services,[207] while in *BASF*,[208] it rejected the plea of incompatibility of the national law that required an official translation for patent registration.[209] The subsequent line of case law saw the criterion of 'too uncertain and indirect effect' to expand to other sectors of free movement law. The Court invoked it in *Graf* to dismiss a claim brought under

[198] ibid para 69.

[199] T Horsley, 'Unearthing Buried Treasure: Art 34 TFEU and the Exclusionary Rules' (2012) 37 *European Law Review* 734, 739.

[200] On several occasions, the Court also referred to 'too uncertain and too insignificant'. See Joined Cases C-11/06 and C-12/06 *Rhiannon Morgan and Iris Bucher* EU:C:2007:626, para 32.

[201] Case C-69/88 *H. Krantz GmbH & Co v Ontvanger der Directe Belastingen and Netherlands State* EU:C:1990:97.

[202] ibid para 11.

[203] ibid.

[204] Case C-379/92 *Criminal Proceedings against Matteo Peralta* EU:C:1994:296.

[205] ibid para 24. See also Case C-93/92 *CMC Motorradcenter GmbH v Pelin Baskiciogullari* EU:C:1993:838, para 12.

[206] Case C-266/96 *Corsica Ferries France SA v Gruppo Antichi Ormeggiatori del porto di Genova Coop. arl* EU:C:1998:306.

[207] ibid para 31.

[208] Case C-44/98 *BASF AG v Präsident des Deutschen Patentamts* EU:C:1999:440.

[209] ibid para 16.

Article 45 TFEU against the national law that denied entitlement to compensation in instances of voluntary termination of an employment contract.[210] As the Court specified, the national law was not of a kind to preclude or deter a worker from taking up employment in other Member States since the entitlement to compensation was dependent on a future and hypothetical event of involuntary redundancy.[211] In *Commission v Spain*,[212] in turn, the Court found that the impact of the refusal by a Member State to reimburse medical expenses incurred during a short stay in other Member States on the provision of tourist or educational services therein was too uncertain and indirect.[213]

The 'effect too uncertain and indirect effect' doctrine adds limits to the normative reach of free movement law. It further indicates that not every limitation or condition that structures the exercise of economic activity in the internal market is subject to scrutiny and prompts objective justification. From a functional standpoint, this criterion is premised on the causation threshold.[214] It requires a causal link between the impugned national law and the alleged effect on intra-Union movement.[215] However, the Court's application of this doctrine is informed by the presence of a specific effect that resonates with the concept of market access in a narrow sense. This stems from the fact that the exclusion of measures from the scope of free movement law pursuant to the doctrine of 'effect too uncertain and indirect effect' does not necessarily absolve them from having any impact on the engagement in economic activity in other Member States.[216] A measure may have such an impact, but it does not suffice to trigger the Treaty. In *Peralta*, the contested prohibition likely would lead to extra costs as vessels had to keep wastewater on board in special containers and move to specific installations for disposal.[217] In *Corsica Ferries*, the compulsory use of mooring services likely would lead to additional expenditure for shipping companies to transport products. The Court's characterisation of the effect produced by both measures as 'too uncertain and indirect' aligns with the understanding of free movement law as a set of normative safeguards against discriminatory treatment and market entry restrictions in the internal market. Neither of these measures was directly or indirectly discriminatory, nor did either restrict the very ability to participate in the interstate process of competition. Instead, they imposed conditions to be met by every economic actor without affecting their competitive position in the

[210] *Volker Graf* (n 180) para 25.
[211] ibid para 24.
[212] Case C-211/08 *Commission v Spain* EU:C:2010:340.
[213] ibid para 72.
[214] Nic Shuibhne (n 5) 168.
[215] Opinion of AG Pergola in Case C-44/98 *BASF AG v Präsident des Deutschen Patentamts* EU:C:1999:198, para 19.
[216] See also Horsley (n 199) 755.
[217] See Opinion of AG Lenz in Case C-379/92 *Criminal Proceedings against Matteo Peralta* EU:C:1994:191, para 6.

market. This was acknowledged by AG Fennelly, who rationalised the outcome of this line of case law based on the lack of 'a discernible effect on trade'.[218]

Therefore, from a conceptual standpoint, parallels can be drawn between the doctrine of 'effect too uncertain and indirect effect' and the rationale underlying the *Keck* test in relation to selling arrangements.[219] AG Bobek observed in *RB v TÜV Rheinland LGA Products* that both concepts shared the same logic in the sense that they excluded from the reach of Article 34 TFEU all national rules that '[did] not concern either the movement of goods or immediately subsequent or correlating steps having a clear impact on access, thus hindering access itself'.[220] Such a correlation is also prevalent in other sectors of free movement law. This follows from *Krah*, which concerned the compatibility with the Treaty of the partial recognition of professional experience acquired abroad to calculate remuneration.[221] The Court distinguished between the recognition of equivalent professional experience and professional experience, which, without being equivalent, was merely beneficial to the performance of prescribed job duties.[222] According to the Court, while the refusal to recognise the former type of experience was liable to hinder free movement as foreign workers would be dissuaded from seeking employment in other Member States, the likely impact of the refusal to recognise the latter type of experience was 'too uncertain and indirect' to constitute an obstacle to free movement.[223] As such, it was not sufficient to trigger the Treaty. This confirmed that the 'effect too uncertain and indirect effect' doctrine does not refute the existence of conditions that, in AG Tizzano's words, reduce the economic attractiveness of pursuing economic activity but excludes the existence of those that necessitate objective justification under the Treaty.

ii. A Broad Reading of the Access-Based Framework

The previous section has provided an individualist account of free movement law drawing upon the narrow construction of the access-based framework that gained much credence among several Advocates General. The central proposition of this approach is that the freedoms of movement function as instruments for the liberalisation of national markets through the prohibition of measures that discriminate against or impose restrictions on interstate movement, yet they do not extend as far as providing a platform for scrutiny of measures that condition the exercise of economic freedom at large.[224] Instead, they can be conceptualised

[218] Opinion of AG Fennely in Case C-67/97 *Anklagemyndigheden v Ditlev Bluhme* EU:C:1998:294, para 19. On the characterisation of the 'too uncertain and indirect effect' test in terms of some form of a *de minimis* test, see Jansson and Kalimo (n 104) 541.

[219] This particularly concerns 'static' selling arrangements. See, eg, Joined Cases C-401/92 and C-402/92 *Criminal Proceedings against Tankstation't Heukske vof and JBE Boermans* EU:C:1994:220.

[220] Opinion of AG Bobek in *RB v TÜV Rheinland* (n 168) para 70.

[221] Case C-703/17 *Adelheid Krah v Universität Wien* EU:C:2019:850.

[222] ibid paras 48–50.

[223] ibid para 50.

[224] Dougan (n 14) 166.

as norms that guarantee the right to initiate competition and participate in the interstate process of competition throughout the internal market. The scope of its protection encompasses regulatory choices that distort this process by creating market inequality and those that block such a process from taking place or have that effect in practice. This conceptual account of the freedoms of movement reflects their normative purpose of steering individual behaviour to achieve the internal market goal and makes it possible to balance it against the need to respect national regulatory autonomy. However, the fact also remains that market access is not a normative concept with clearly outlined limits, only lending support for the narrow conceptualisation of the freedoms of movement at an individual level. Several aspects of the Court's approach model them in broader terms to the point that they verge on the individual right to economic freedom at large in the internal market.

In the context of goods, this stems from the lack of clarity surrounding the parameters of scrutiny under the *Dassonville* formula that leaves open the prospect for its mechanical application,[225] reminiscent of the infamous *Sunday Trading* saga. Two interrelated factors are at play here. First, the uncertainty is caused by the line of reasoning that emerged in *Commission v Italy*, where the Court, in addition to the *Dassonville* formula, introduced a three-tier assessment method based on the principles of non-discrimination, mutual recognition and market access.[226] It remains unclear how these principles are meant to correlate with one another. There are instances where the Court appears to interpret this method as concretising the *Dassonville* formula, whereby any measure, irrespective of its nature, is deemed to 'hinder directly or indirectly, actually or potentially intra-Union trade', if it falls foul of at least one of these principles.[227] At the same time, there are also instances where the Court did not make any reference to this method but opted to apply the *Dassonville* formula alone to determine the compatibility of a measure with Article 34 TFEU.[228] This seems to validate the view that the three principles are not exhaustive benchmarks to frame the scope of Article 34 TFEU.[229]

Second, a similar degree of ambivalence arises from the underdetermined correlation between the three-tier assessment method outlined in *Commission v Italy* and the *Keck* approach concerning the category of selling arrangements. In one respect, the three-tier assessment method can be construed to supersede the *Keck* categorisation if it is interpreted that every impugned measure, regardless of its nature, must be tested against each of the three principles.[230] AG Bot favoured

[225] Schütze (n 45) 830.
[226] *Commission v Italy (Trailers)* (n 119) paras 33–34.
[227] See, eg, Case C-456/10 *ANETT*, para 33; Case C-385/10 *Elenca Srl v Ministero dell'Interno* EU:C:2012:634, para 23. See also Schütze (n 139) 836.
[228] See, eg, Case C-602/19 *kohlpharma GmbH v Bundesrepublik Deutschland* EU:C:2020:804, paras 38–39; Case C-573/12 *Ålands vindkraft AB v Energimyndigheten* EU:C:2014:2037, paras 66–70.
[229] LW Gormley, 'Inconsistencies and Misconceptions in the Free Movement of Goods' (2015) 40 *European Law Review* 924, 929.
[230] Schütze (n 45) 838.

this interpretation in *Scotch Whisky Association*,[231] where he inferred from the three principles outlined in *Commission v Italy* that 'a national measure [might] constitute an obstacle not only when, *as a selling arrangement*, it [was] discriminatory, in law or in fact, but also when, irrespective of its nature, it impede[d] access to the market of the Member State concerned' (emphasis added).[232] While the Court appeared to concur with AG Bot by explicitly referring to his Opinion, a contrasting viewpoint follows from *Ker-Optika* that makes a combined reference to both *Keck* and the three principles.[233] This suggests that *Keck* still applies, though it is now incorporated into the prohibition of discrimination under the three-tier assessment method, with selling arrangements only being reviewed against that benchmark alone.

A lack of clarity also remains as to the breadth of the notion of restriction in the context of other sectors of free movement law. The main contributing factor is the Court's expansive language, which while mirroring the *Dassonville* formula, is not qualified. The Court often looks at whether national measures, even in the absence of disparate impact, are liable to 'prohibit, impede or render less attractive/advantageous' the exercise of the freedoms of movement guaranteed by the Treaty.[234] At one end, such a characterisation is not attributed to every national rule or policy choice. Alongside the principle of remoteness and causation discussed above, the Court acknowledges that the scope of the Treaty is not triggered by the mere differences existing between national legal systems.[235] In *Commission v Italy*,[236] it found that 'rules of a Member State [did] not constitute a restriction within the meaning of [the Treaty] solely by virtue of the fact that other Member States appl[ied] less strict, or more commercially favourable, rules to providers of similar services established in their territory'.[237] Therefore, a Member State is not required, as held in *Sparkasse Allgäu*,[238] 'to draw up its … [legislation] on the basis of those in another Member State in order to ensure, in all circumstances, that any disparities arising from national rules [were] removed'.[239] The recognition of legal diversity permeates the Court's divergent approach over the rules governing taxation and social security,[240] which remain subject to the

[231] Opinion of AG Bot in Case C-333/14 *Scotch Whisky Association and Others v The Lord Advocate and the Advocate General for Scotland* EU:C:2015:527.

[232] ibid para 58.

[233] *Ker-Optika* (n 128) para 51.

[234] See, eg Case C-55/94 *Reinhard Gebhard v Consiglio dell'Ordine degli Avvocati e Procuratori di Milano* EU:C:1995:411, para 37.

[235] Case C-427/05 *Agenzia delle Entrate – Ufficio di Genova 1 v Porto Antico di Genova SpA* EU:C:2007:630, para 20; Joined Cases C-393/99 and C-394/99 *Hervein and Others* EU:C:2002:182, para 34; Case C-177/94 *Criminal Proceedings against Gianfranco Perfili* EU:C:1996:24, para 17.

[236] *Commission v Italy* (n 175).

[237] ibid para 49. See also Case C-371/10 *National Grid Indus BV v Inspecteur van de Belastingdienst Rijnmond/kantoor Rotterdam* EU:C:2011:785, para 62; Case C-157/07 *Finanzamt für Körperschaften III in Berlin v Krankenheim Ruhesitz am Wannsee-Seniorenheimstatt GmbH* EU:C:2008:588, para 30.

[238] Case C-522/14 *Sparkasse Allgäu v Finanzamt Kempten* EU:C:2016:253.

[239] ibid para 31.

[240] *Peralta* (n 204) para 34.

discrimination-based assessment.[241] These rules are not deemed to fall within the scope of the Treaty unless they directly or indirectly discriminate on grounds of nationality or movement.[242] For some, this form of scrutiny resonates with the *Keck* presumption.[243] Analogous to non-discriminatory modalities of sale, measures merely incurring generalised expenses on all economic actors are not construed to affect intra-Union movement.[244] At the same time, in *Tesco-Global Áruházak*,[245] AG Kokott rationalised the narrow review of tax rules by focusing on their nature and the division of regulatory competence underlying the internal market. In her view, given that taxes and duties constitute a burden per se and thereby reduce the attractiveness of establishment in another Member State, 'an examination based on non-discriminatory restrictions would … make all national taxable events subject to EU law and thereby seriously call into question the sovereignty of the Member States in tax matters'.[246] AG Kokott's reasoning reflects the parallels drawn between the exclusion of non-discriminatory taxation/social security rules from the scope of the Treaty and the similar exclusion of rules regulating the conduct of international sports tournaments.[247] Their impact whether it is on the activity of economic actors or sports athletes, derives from their very purpose and, as such, any disadvantage incurred by them is not considered to create a barrier to intra-Union movement.[248]

At the other end, national measures are assessed against the standard of 'liable to prohibit, impede or render less attractive/advantageous', the parameters of which remain ambiguous. In some instances, such an assessment seems to set a higher threshold framed around the directness of the impact on cross-border movement.[249] What appears decisive for the Court is that a national measure directly touches on cross-border movement.[250] This confines the scope of free movement law to only those non-discriminatory limitations on economic freedom that are 'directly connected to the cross-border aspect of the activity'.[251]

[241] Spaventa (n 26) 148.

[242] Case C-403/03 *Egon Schempp v Finanzamt München V* EU:C:2005:446, para 34; Case C-134/03 *Viacom Outdoor Srl v Giotto Immobilier SARL* EU:C:2005:94, para 37; Case C-18/95 *FC Terhoeve v Inspecteur van de Belastingdienst Particulieren/Ondernemingen buitenland* EU:C:1999:22, paras 40–41.

[243] V Hatzopoulos, 'Legal Aspects in Establishing the Internal Market for Services' (2007) 6 *College of Europe Research Papers in Law* 1, 10.

[244] Davies (n 106) 19.

[245] Case C-323/18 *Tesco-Global Áruházak Zrt v Nemzeti Adó- és Vámhivatal Fellebbviteli Igazgatósága* EU:C:2020:140.

[246] Opinion of AG Kokott in Case C-323/18 *Tesco-Global Áruházak Zrt v Nemzeti Adó- és Vámhivatal Fellebbviteli Igazgatósága* EU:C:2019:567, para 43.

[247] Joined Cases C-51/96 and C-191/97 *Christelle Deliège v Ligue francophone de judo et disciplines associées ASBL* EU:C:2000:199, para 64.

[248] E Spaventa, 'The Outer Limit of the Treaty free Movement Provisions: Some Reflections on the Significance of *Keck*, Remoteness and Deliège' in C Barnard and O Odudu (eds), *The Outer Limits of European Union Law* (Oxford, Hart Publishing, 2009) 270.

[249] *Alpine Investments* (n 112) para 38; *Bosman* (n 159) para 103.

[250] Snell (n 118) 452.

[251] Weatherill (n 183) 905.

This logic can be used to rationalise *Gebhard*,[252] where the Court scrutinised the national law based on Article 49 TFEU for subjecting the exercise of a legal profession using the title of *avvocato* to the requirement to register with a local bar. It also applies to *Hartlauer*,[253] where the Court held that the national law subjecting the establishment of an undertaking to prior authorisation constituted a restriction for preventing it from freely 'carrying on its activities through a fixed place of business'.[254] However, the case law does not unequivocally lend support for delimiting the scope of the Treaty's free movement of persons provisions on these terms. There is clear evidence that the Court defines it along broader lines. In *VAS Shipping*,[255] AG Hogan observed that the concept of economic, commercial or occupational activity pursued by natural or legal persons encompassed all phases and aspects of engagement in that activity, '[extending] beyond gaining an initial foothold in the market of a Member State'.[256] In *Commission v Denmark*,[257] within the framework of Article 45 TFEU, the Court, based on *Bosman* and *Graf*, held that 'the manner in which an activity [was] pursued [was] liable also to affect access to that activity'.[258] It concluded that 'legislation which relates to the conditions in which an economic activity [was] pursued [might] constitute an obstacle to the freedom of movement within the meaning of that case law'.[259] The same is evident in the context of Article 49 TFEU. In *AGET Iraklis*,[260] the Court found that the national law limiting the possibility to initiate collective redundancies was 'a serious obstacle to the exercise of the freedom of establishment'.[261] According to the Court, this freedom includes the ability to determine the nature and extent of economic activity, including the size of a fixed establishment and the number of workers required for that purpose, as well as the ability to scale down that activity or even to give it up.[262]

The broad scope of the Treaty's free movement of persons provisions also follows from the Court's approach to the modalities that govern the pursuit of a self-employed activity. Unlike the modalities of the sale of goods, which are excluded from the scope of the Treaty under *Keck* unless they are discriminatory, such a presumption of compatibility does not stretch to the modalities that

[252] Case C-55/94 *Reinhard Gebhard v Consiglio dell'Ordine degli Avvocati e Procuratori di Milano* EU:C:1995:411.
[253] Case C-169/07 *Hartlauer Handelsgesellschaft mbH v Wiener Landesregierung and Oberösterreichische Landesregierun* EU:C:2009:141.
[254] ibid para 34.
[255] Opinion of AG Hogan in Case C-71/20 *Criminal Proceedings against VAS Shipping ApS* EU:C:2021:474.
[256] ibid para 63.
[257] Case C-464/02 *Commission v Denmark* EU:C:2005:546.
[258] ibid para 37.
[259] ibid.
[260] Case C-201/15 *Anonymi Geniki Etairia Tsimenton Iraklis (AGET Iraklis)* EU:C:2016:972.
[261] ibid para 57.
[262] ibid para 53. See also Case C-255/97 *Pfeiffer Großhandel GmbH and Löwa Warenhandel GmbH* EU:C:1999:240, para 20.

relate to a self-employed activity, irrespective of whether it involves the sale of goods or provision of services.[263] In *Venturini*,[264] the Court found a restriction to the freedom of establishment in the national law that barred the sale of prescription-only medical products through para-pharmacies because it excluded their owners from certain parts of the medical products market and, as a result, 'from the accruing economic benefits'.[265] The impugned national law generally regulated the sale of prescription-only medical products and equally applied to all para-pharmacy owners without distinction. Nor did it concern the access to the market (or economic activity) as such since the setting-up of a para-pharmacy was not made contingent on prior authorisation. The Court considered neither of these factors, though it would have been expected to do so had the compatibility of the contested national law been raised in the context of Article 34 TFEU. As previously discussed, the factor of free and equal access to the market forms the core of the *Keck*-based normative framework of Article 34 TFEU. Pursuant to this, the analogous confinement of the sale of prescription-only medical products to pharmacies would likely be exculpated for not preventing or having an unequal effect on market access.[266]

These varying methods of scrutiny are rooted in the divergent strands of conceptualisation of free movement law. The narrow *Keck*-based assessment of neutral modalities of the sale of goods follows from the Court's refusal to characterise Article 34 TFEU as a normative vehicle to challenge anything limiting commercial or economic freedom at large. By extrapolating this logic to the Treaty's free movement of persons provisions, their scope can be construed to channel that very normative trait. The Court does not frame these provisions as only outlawing national rules that disadvantage out-of-state economic actors or prevent the possibility of taking up economic activity. Instead, it seems to perceive them as a platform that makes it possible to attack rules that regulate the pursuit of an employed or self-employed activity without any disparity in the impact on out-of-state and in-state economic actors.[267] What emerges from these provisions, as some scholars have already pointed out,[268] is not just the individual right to move across borders to engage in an employed or self-employed activity in other Member States but the individual right to pursue economic activity throughout the internal market free from any unjust limitations.[269] Seen through this prism, the concept of restriction contrary to the Treaty's free movement of persons provisions encompasses any measure that produces, in AG Tizzano's words, adverse repercussions on the attractiveness of pursuing economic activity in other Member States. This is not to say that such an expression of individual freedom

[263] Joined Cases C-180/98 to C-184/98 *Pavel Pavlov and Others v Stichting Pensioenfonds Medische Specialisten* EU:C:2000:428, para 75.

[264] Joined Cases C-159/12 to C-161/12 *Alessandra Venturini v ASL Varese* EU:C:2013:791.

[265] ibid paras 33–34.

[266] See, eg, Case C-418/93 *Semeraro Casa Uno and Others* EU:C:1996:242, para 24.

[267] De Cecco (n 12) 398.

[268] See, eg, Snell (n 118) 467.

[269] Spaventa (n 108) 766.

is absolute. However, any limitation imposed on it must not affect the very substance of pursuance of economic activity analogous to non-discriminatory taxation or social security policies.

II. Individual Rights under EU Competition Law

Within the framework of the Treaty, individual rights are also embedded in the provisions that ensure free and fair competition. This includes Articles 101 and 102 TFEU, which prohibit certain forms of coordinated and unilateral market conduct liable to distort the competitive process in the internal market. The individual dimension of these provisions is encapsulated in their normative capacity to produce both vertical and horizontal direct effects.[270] As the Court often reiterates, the Treaty's competition rules 'create rights for the individuals concerned' to be safeguarded by national courts.[271] As previously mentioned, this is vindicated by the availability of adequate and effective remedies, which was confirmed by the proclamation in *Courage v Crehan* that 'the full effectiveness of [the Treaty's competition rules] … would be put at risk if it were not open to any individual to claim damages for loss caused to him by a contract or by conduct liable to restrict or distort competition'.[272] However, such individualisation prompts two related queries. The first query concerns the precise nature of the subjective entitlement guaranteed by competition law. The case law and academic literature are permeated by various terms, including 'economic freedom',[273] 'commercial freedom',[274] 'freedom to compete',[275] 'freedom of competition,'[276] 'freedom of action'.[277] Despite their intrinsic connection, these expressions denote a varying degree of manifestation of the ideals of private autonomy within the framework of competition law. The second, more controversial query relates to the principal rationalisation for protecting these ideals within the framework of the Treaty's competition rules. This is intrinsically linked to the primary objectives, or a combination thereof,

[270] See, eg Case 127-73 *Belgische Radio en Televisie v SV SABAM and NV Fonior* EU:C:1974:25, para 16; Case C-282/95 P *Guérin automobiles v Commission* EU:C:1997:159, para 39.

[271] See, eg, Case C-724/17 *Vantaan kaupunki v Skanska Industrial Solutions Oy and Others* EU:C:2019:204, para 24; Case C-637/17 *Cogeco Communications Inc v Sport TV Portugal SA and Others* EU:C:2019:263, para 38; Case C-557/12 *Kone AG and Others v ÖBB-Infrastruktur AG* EU:C:2014:1317, para 20.

[272] Case C-453/99 *Courage Ltd v Bernard Crehan and Bernard Crehan v Courage Ltd and Others* EU:C:2001:465, para 26.

[273] See, eg, Case C-418/01 *IMS Health GmbH & Co OHG v NDC Health GmbH & Co KG* EU:C:2004:257, para 48.

[274] See, eg, Case T-325/01 *DaimlerChrysler AG v Commission* EU:T:2005:322, para 100.

[275] See, eg, Case T-19/92 *Groupement d'achat Edouard Leclerc v Commission* EU:T:1996:190, para 117.

[276] See, eg, Case 107/82 *Allgemeine Elektrizitäts-Gesellschaft AEG-Telefunken AG v Commission* EU:C:1983:293, para 43.

[277] See, eg, Case C-644/13 P *Villeroy & Boch SAS v Commission* EU:C:2017:59, para 51.

assigned to these sets of norms, which is one of the central points of contention among scholars whose views predominantly reflect contrasting deontological and utilitarian visions of the competitive process.

A. Jurisprudential Account

The concept of freedom is intrinsic to the operation of the Treaty's competition rules to the extent that their underlying rationale is argued to rest in its protection 'as a value in itself'.[278] While this point remains contentious,[279] these rules undoubtedly give effect to the subjective autonomy of acquiring, possessing and using economic goods and services, which can hardly be realised if economic actors deviate from the parameters of normal market behaviour. Therefore, a restriction of competition is often described in terms of a limitation imposed on the exercise of individual economic freedom. Nonetheless, what the latter concept stands for within the framework of competition law is not often elucidated.

i. Broad Construction of 'Freedom'

One strand of case law builds on the terminology that broadly manifests the ideals of private autonomy within the Treaty's competition rules. In *Hasselblad*,[280] the Court found that the 'prohibition of sales between authorised dealers provided for in a standard agreement used by an undertaking which applie[d] a selective distribution system constitute[d] a restriction of the economic freedom of such dealers and, consequently, a restriction of competition within the meaning of Article [101 TFEU]'.[281] A similar reference was also made in *Langnese*,[282] where the General Court refused to uphold the Commission's decision to deprive an undertaking, which was ordered to dismantle its network of exclusive agreements, of the benefit of block exemptions in relation to the conclusion of such agreements in the future. According to the Court, it was contrary to the principle of equal treatment to exclude certain undertakings whilst others could continue to conclude exclusive purchasing agreements. In the Court's view, this was 'liable to undermine the economic freedom of certain undertakings and create distortions

[278] W Möschel, 'Competition Policy from an Ordo-liberal Point of View' in A Peacock and T Willgerodt (eds), *German Neo-liberals and Social Market Economy* (London, Macmillan, 1989) 146.

[279] See, eg, the interchange between F Maier-Rigaud, 'On the Normative Foundations of Competition Law: Efficiency, Political Freedom and the Freedom to Compete' and H Schweitzer, 'Efficiency, Political Freedom and the Freedom to Compete – Comment on Maier-Rigaud' in D Zimmer (ed), *The Goals of Competition Law* (Cheltenham, Edward Elgar, 2012).

[280] Case 86/82 *Hasselblad (GB) Ltd v Commission* EU:C:1984:65.

[281] ibid para 46.

[282] Joined Cases T-7/93 R and T-9/93 R *Langnese Iglo GmbH and Schöller Lebensmittel GmbH & Co KG v Commission* EU:T:1993:13.

of competition on the market, contrary to the objectives of the Treaty'.[283] Along the same lines, in *Javico*,[284] the Court concluded that 'an agreement between a producer and a reseller intended to apply within the [Union] and to deprive a reseller of his commercial freedom to choose his customers by requiring him to sell only to customers established in the contractual territory [was] restrictive of competition within the meaning of Article [101 TFEU]'.[285] This reasoning was later reiterated in *Bayerische Motorenwerke*,[286] which concerned the compatibility of the clause imposed by BMW on its dealers to supply cars only to those independent leasing companies established within their territory with Article 101 TFEU. In this respect, the Court held that '[such a clause] reduce[d] each dealer's freedom of commercial action in so far as each individual dealer's choice of customer [was] confined exclusively to those leasing companies which ha[d] concluded contracts with lessees established within that dealer's contract territory'.[287] In *EPI v Commission*,[288] in turn, the Court concluded that rules regulating the exercise of a given profession did not fall, as a matter of principle, outside the scope of Article 101 TFEU merely because they were classified as 'rules of professional conduct', but could be subject to scrutiny 'by taking account of its impact on the freedom of action of the members of the profession and on its organisation and also on the recipients of the services in question'.[289]

ii. Narrow Construction of 'Freedom'

Another strand of case law narrowly construes the concept of freedom within competition law. In *Remia*,[290] the issue arose over the compatibility of the non-competition clause incorporated into a bilateral contract for the sale of business assets with Article 101 TFEU. The Court found that such a clause did not breach Article 101 TFEU since its incorporation into an agreement had the benefit of ensuring the intended effect of the transfer of business assets.[291] This is because the vendor with detailed knowledge of the transferred business would still be in a position to win back former customers immediately after the transfer and thereby drive the purchasers out of business.[292] As such, notwithstanding the

[283] ibid, 209. See also Case T-9/93 *Schöller Lebensmittel GmbH & Co KG v Commission* EU:T:1995:99, para 163.

[284] Case C-306/96 *Javico International and Javico AG v Yves Saint Laurent Parfums SA (YSLP)* EU:C:1998:173.

[285] ibid para 13. See also Case T-29/92 *SPO and Others v Commission* EU:T:1995:34, para 186; Case 85/76 *Hoffmann-La Roche & Co AG v Commission* EU:C:1979:36, para 106.

[286] Case C-70/93 *Bayerische Motorenwerke AG v ALD Auto-Leasing D GmbH* EU:C:1995:344.

[287] ibid para 19. See also Case T-286/09 *Intel Corporation v Commission* EU:T:2014:547, para 1535.

[288] Case T-144/99 *Institute of Professional Representatives before the European Patent Office v Commission* EU:T:2001:105.

[289] ibid paras 64–65.

[290] Case 42/84 *Remia BV and Others v Commission* EU:C:1985:327.

[291] ibid para 19.

[292] ibid.

limitation of the vendor's freedom, the contested clause contributed to the promotion of competition by increasing the number of undertakings in the market.[293] A similar reasoning is evident in *DLG*,[294] where the Court was asked to rule on the compatibility with Article 101 TFEU of the provision included in the statute of a purchasing association that forbade its members from obtaining supplies from its competitors. The Court found this restriction to be legitimate in light of the purpose of a purchasing association. In its view, the exclusive membership ensured 'the proper functioning of the cooperative and its contractual power in relation to producers';[295] otherwise, it would diminish the role of an association in being 'a significant counterweight to the contractual power of large producers and make way for more effective competition' by 'pursuing its objectives for the benefit of the rest of its members'.[296]

The narrow construction of the concept of 'freedom' within the scope of the Treaty's competition rules was further elaborated upon in *Wouters*.[297] The issue in that case related to the compatibility with the Treaty of the national law that prohibited lawyers from entering into contractual arrangements with accountants. The Court found that such a prohibition was not anti-competitive. To this end, it held that 'not every agreement between undertakings or every decision of an association of undertakings which restrict[ed] the freedom of action of the parties or one of them necessarily [fell] within the prohibition laid down in Article [101 TFEU]'.[298] The Court went on to state that for the purpose of the application of that provision, 'account must first of all be taken of the overall context in which the decision of the association of undertakings was taken or produce[d] its effects'.[299] This finding was later confirmed in a series of rulings. In *Meca Medina*,[300] the General Court resorted to it to determine the legality of the anti-doping regulation issued by a sports association. Unlike *Wouters*, which involved a limitation of the freedom of contract, the issue in *Medina* concerned an outright ban to engage in economic activity for a given period. However, according to the Court, such a restriction of 'freedom of action' was 'inherent in the organisation and proper conduct of competitive sport and its very purpose [was] to ensure healthy rivalry between athletes'.[301] The reasoning introduced in *Wouters* has also been applied in the instances giving rise to a mere limitation of the freedom to conduct a particular form of economic activity. In *OTOC*,[302] the Court excluded from the scope of the

[293] ibid.
[294] Case C-250/92 *Gøttrup-Klim Grovvareforening and Others and Dansk Landbrugs Grovvareselskab AmbA (DLG)* EU:C:1994:413.
[295] ibid para 34.
[296] ibid para 32.
[297] Case C-309/99 *Wouters and Others* EU:C:2002:98.
[298] ibid para 97.
[299] ibid.
[300] Case T-313/02 *David Meca-Medina and Igor Majcen v Commission* EU:T:2004:282.
[301] ibid para 45.
[302] Case C-1/12 *Ordem dos Técnicos Oficiais de Contas v Autoridade da Concorrência* EU:C:2013:127, para 93.

Treaty the conditions imposed by an association of undertakings for the provision of compulsory training for chartered accountants. This verdict was also reached in *CNG* concerning the code of conduct and the minimum level of remuneration set out by a similar body in relation to the practice of geologists.[303]

The narrower interpretation of the concept of 'freedom' in the context of the Treaty's competition rules also finds support in *Métropole télévision (M6)*,[304] where the General Court was asked to annul the Commission's decision to grant only temporary clearance to the clauses in the agreement that set out a partnership of companies aimed at providing digital satellite television for payment. The clauses granted the partnership an exclusive right to broadcast general-interest channels and the right of first refusal over special-interest channels. Considering their compatibility with the Treaty, the Court held that 'it [was] not necessary to hold, wholly abstractly and without drawing any distinction, that any agreement restricting the freedom of action of one or more of the parties [was] necessarily caught by the prohibition laid down in Article [101(1)]'.[305] It continued that 'in assessing the applicability of Article [101(1)] to an agreement, account should be taken of the actual conditions in which it function[ed], in particular the economic context in which the undertakings operate[d], the products or services covered by the agreement and the actual structure of the market concerned'.[306]

The General Court proceeded with this line of reasoning in *GlaxoSmithKline*,[307] where the dispute arose from the Commission's infringement decision against a subsidiary of the GlaxoSmithKline group for imposing a system of differentiated prices on its wholesalers based on the place of export. The Court first acknowledged that such a system 'ha[d] the effect of restricting the freedom of action of the Spanish wholesalers, in particular their freedom to choose their customers'.[308] However, citing *Wouters*, the Court continued that 'any contract concluded between economic agents operating at different stages of the production and distribution chain [had] the consequence of binding them and, consequently, of restricting them, according to the stipulated terms, in their freedom of action'.[309] The Court added that 'they [were] limited in their freedom of action since, from an economic point of view, they [were] not capable in the long term of reselling them at a lower price on the other national markets of the [Union]'.[310] That said, according to the Court, this was not sufficient to establish the breach of Article 101 TFEU because, in its words, 'it [was] still necessary to demonstrate that the limitation in question restrict[ed] competition, to the detriment of the final consumer'.[311] The Court of Justice found that the General Court had erred in law, though only in relation to

[303] Case C-136/12 *Consiglio nazionale dei geologi Autorità garante della concorrenza e del mvercato* EU:C:2013:489, para 53.
[304] Case T-112/99 *Métropole television (M6) and Others v Commission* EU:T:2001:215.
[305] ibid para 76.
[306] ibid.
[307] Case T-168/01 *GlaxoSmithKline Services Unlimited v Commission* EU:T:2006:265.
[308] ibid para 170.
[309] ibid para 171.
[310] ibid.
[311] ibid.

the emphasis placed on the impact on the final consumer when finding a restriction of competition. This follows from the reference to the *Wouters* reasoning in *API*,[312] where the referring national court enquired about the compatibility with the Treaty of the rule that determined minimum prices for road haulage services since it constrained free bargaining and curtailed the freedom to specify one of the essential elements of a contract. The Court first held that 'the legislation … making mandatory a decision of an association of undertakings which ha[d] the object or effect of restricting competition or restricting the freedom of action of the parties or of one of them [did] not necessarily fall within the prohibition laid down in Article 101(1) TFEU, read in conjunction with Article 4(3) TEU'.[313] In the light of *Wouters* and *Meca Medina*, the Court then went on to find that the restriction imposed by the impugned legislation was not limited to what was necessary to ensure the implementation of its legitimate objectives.[314]

iii. Freedom to Compete or Freedom of Competition

The case law outlined in the previous section shows that not all limitations of independent decision-making in the market trigger the Treaty's competition rules. The concept of freedom that finds expression in these norms is narrow in its nature and scope. It is best understood in terms of the ability to access the market and perform in it with the aim to compete based on merits, the success of which is measured through the proficiency to offer better-quality goods or services in an efficient manner and at lower prices.[315] Such a characterisation resonates the most with the prevalence of references to 'freedom of competition' and 'freedom to compete' in the case law.[316]

Among the earliest rulings that mention the term 'freedom of competition' is *Grundig*. In that case, the Court held that 'the principle of freedom of competition concern[ed] the various stages and manifestations of competition', in light of which Article 101 TFEU also applied to agreements that restricted the competition between distributors of products of the same make, even if it might increase the competition between producers.[317] A reference to this principle also appeared in *Deutsche Grammophon*,[318] where it was found that 'the prohibition on importation

[312] Joined Cases C-184/13 to C-187/13, C-194/13, C-195/13 and C-208/13 *API – Anonima Petroli Italiana SpA and Others v Ministero delle Infrastrutture e dei Trasporti and Others* EU:C:2014:2147.

[313] ibid para 46.

[314] ibid para 57.

[315] T Eilmansberger, 'How to Distinguish Good from Bad Competition under Article 82 EC: In Search of Clearer and More Coherent Standards for Anti-competitive Abuses' (2005) 42 *Common Market Law Review* 129, 133.

[316] For the statistics on these references, see P Akman, 'The Role of "Freedom" in EU Competition Law' (2014) 34 *Legal Studies* 183, 188.

[317] Joined Cases 56 and 58-64 *Établissements Consten SàRL and Grundig-Verkaufs-GmbH v Commission* EU:C:1966:41, 342.

[318] Case 78-70 *Deutsche Grammophon Gesellschaft mbH v Metro-SB-Großmärkte GmbH & Co KG* EU:C:1971:59.

or distribution of imported products conflict[ed] in particular with the principles [of] … free movement of goods and the institution of a system ensuring freedom of competition within the common market'.[319] More recently, in *Mauri*,[320] the Court characterised the Treaty's competition rules as normative provisions that enshrine 'the protection of the [Union's principle] of freedom of competition'.[321]

In other instances, the freedom of competition is expressed in more individual terms. In *LVM*,[322] the Court found that '[Article 101 TFEU was] designed to guarantee unfettered freedom of competition at all levels, subject to the penalties for which it provide[d]'.[323] Similarly, in *Ahlström Osakeyhtiö*,[324] AG Darmon defined a restriction of competition in terms of the effect on the exercise of the freedom of competition. In his view, a restriction of competition must be '"perceptible" or "appreciable" … the adverse effect on competition [might] be either direct or indirect and objectively or reasonably foreseeable', which in turn were the characteristics of the effect envisaged as a constituent element of interference with freedom of competition.[325] AG Tesauro shared this viewpoint in *DLG*, where he argued that 'agreements which, viewed objectively and in the abstract, ha[d] no other function than to restrict freedom of competition between the parties, or between the parties to it and third parties, in a manner considered incompatible with the [internal] market, [would] be regarded as prohibited by virtue of their object [under Article 101 TFEU]'.[326] Likewise, in *AC-Treuhand*,[327] AG Wahl submitted that 'the overall objective of the competition rules [was] to ensure that the effects of freedom of competition, which [were] the counterpart of the opening up of markets, [were] not distorted by measures, in the broadest sense of that term, which ha[d] the consequence of favouring or putting at a disadvantage certain undertakings and, ultimately, operate[d] to the detriment of consumers'.[328]

Another related line of case law manifests the competition-related notion of 'freedom' through the term 'freedom to compete'. In *TF1*,[329] the General Court found that the object of the Treaty's provisions on competition and state aid was to 'ensure freedom to compete, and [was] therefore intended to protect economic operators against measures whereby a Member State might frustrate the fundamental economic freedoms enshrined in the Treaty'.[330] Along similar

[319] ibid 496.
[320] Case C-250/03 *Giorgio Emanuele Mauri v Ministero della Giustizia* EU:C:2005:96.
[321] ibid para 1.
[322] Case C-238/99 P *Limburgse Vinyl Maatschappij (LVM) and Others v Commission* EU:C:2002:582.
[323] ibid para 494.
[324] Opinion of AG Darmon in Joined Cases 89, 104, 114, 116, 117 and 125 to 129/85 *Ahlström Osakeyhtiö and Others v Commission* EU:C:1988:258.
[325] ibid para 52.
[326] Opinion of AG Tesauro in Case C-250/92 *Gøttrup-Klim ea Grovvareforeninger v Dansk Landbrugs Grovvareselskab AmbA* EU:C:1994:249, para 16.
[327] Case C-194/14 P *AC-Treuhand AG v Commission* EU:C:2015:350.
[328] ibid para 45.
[329] Case T-17/96 *Télévision française 1 SA (TF1) v Commission* EU:T:1999:119.
[330] ibid para 50.

lines, in *Albany*,[331] AG Jacobs defined the scope of Article 101 TFEU to encompass actions that 'affect[ed] the competitive process or the freedom to compete of anyone'.[332] This term was also referred to in several rulings concerning price cartels. In *Roquette Frères*,[333] in considering the Commission's approach to establish the market effect of a cartel, the General Court found that 'account must be taken of the objective fact that, because of the price cartel, the parties specifically waived their freedom to compete with one another on prices'.[334] This suggests that a restriction of competition occurs not only when a third-party undertaking's freedom to compete is limited but also when an undertaking limits its own freedom by engaging in anti-competitive collusion.

The case law also enunciates a more specific manifestation of the freedom of competition or the freedom to compete. In *Ameyde*,[335] the Court found that the freedom of each undertaking to choose its associates freely was one of the essential elements of 'the freedom of competition'.[336] This form of freedom was also at the heart of the General Court's reasoning in *Michelin I*,[337] where the issue concerned the compatibility with Article 102 TFEU of the rebates provided by an undertaking in a dominant position. The Court held that it was necessary to consider, among other factors, whether the rebates tended to remove or restrict the buyer's freedom to choose its sources of supply,[338] since such a situation was calculated to 'prevent dealers from being able to select freely at any time in the light of the market situation the most favourable of the offers made by the various competitors and to change supplier without suffering any appreciable economic disadvantage'.[339] The General Court reiterated the importance of this factor in *Tomra* as regards exclusivity agreements.[340] It found that the obligation to obtain supplies exclusively from a particular undertaking, with or without rebates, was incompatible with the objective of undistorted competition within the internal market. This is because, in the Court's view, '[exclusivity agreements were] not based on an economic transaction which justifie[d] this burden or benefit but [were] designed to remove or restrict the purchaser's freedom to choose his sources of supply and to deny producers access to the market'.[341] In a similar vein, the Court of Justice found that it was contrary to Article 102 TFEU if a rebate

[331] Opinion of AG Jacobs in Case C-67/96 *Albany International BV v Stichting Bedrijfspensioenfonds Textielindustrie* EU:C:1999:28.

[332] ibid para 292.

[333] Case T-322/01 *Roquette Frères SA v Commission* EU:T:2006:267.

[334] ibid para 73. See also Case T-53/03 *BPB plc v Commission* EU:T:2008:254, para 300.

[335] Case C-90/76 *SRL Ufficio Henry Van Ameyde v UCI* EU:C:1977:101.

[336] ibid 1102. See also Case T-66/01 *Imperial Chemical Industries v Commission* EU:T:2010:255, para 300; Case 85/76 *Hoffmann-La Roche & Co AG v Commission* EU:C:1979:36, para 90.

[337] Case 322/81 *NV Nederlandsche Banden Industrie Michelin v Commission* EU:C:1983:313.

[338] ibid para 73.

[339] ibid para 85. See also Case C-95/04 P *British Airways plc v Commission* EU:C:2007:166, para 67; Case T-228/97 *Irish Sugar plc v Commission* EU:T:1999:246, para 214.

[340] Case T-155/06 *Tomra Systems ASA and Others v Commission* EU:T:2010:370.

[341] ibid para 209.

system 'in providing an advantage not based on any economic service justifying it ... [tended] to remove or restrict the buyer's freedom to choose his sources of supply, to bar competitors from access to the market, or to strengthen the dominant position by distorting competition'.[342]

The prevalence of both terms in the jurisprudential approach endorses the narrow characterisation of the concept of freedom within the framework of competition law. As AG Cosmas succinctly summarised in *Anic Partecipazioni*,[343] the legal interest ingrained in these provisions is not 'the untrammelled business activity of each individual undertaking but freedom of competition as a doctrine which is reflected specifically in the model of the undertaking operating independently on the market'.[344] Therefore, at a normative level, parallels can be drawn between the concept of individual rights rooted in the Treaty's free movement and competition rules. Both sets of provisions are not intended to guarantee the ability to exercise economic or commercial activity in a general sense. Instead, they ensure the ability to compete on merits in the internal market free from public regulatory barriers and the impediments of certain categories of private actors that do not conform to the parameters of normal market behaviour.[345]

B. Conceptual Account

A more controversial aspect within the framework of the competition law regime concerns the conceptual premise underlying the guarantee of the ideals of private autonomy. The salient question is whether the freedom to compete is safeguarded as an end on its own or merely as a means towards other goals. This remains a subject of contention among scholars and is predominantly fuelled by contrasting deontological and utilitarian visions of competition.[346]

i. Deontological Approach

Ordoliberalism occupies a prominent place in the deontological tradition.[347] It is closely associated with the Freiburg school of thought that greatly impacted the economic policy development in Germany in the immediate aftermath of the

[342] Case C-549/10 P *Tomra Systems ASA and Others v Commission* EU:C:2012:221, paras 71–72.

[343] Opinion of AG Cosmas in Case C-49/92 P *Commission v Anic Partecipazioni SpA* EU:C:1997:357.

[344] ibid para 41.

[345] T Eilmansberger, 'Dominance – the Lost Child? How Effects-Based Rules Could and Should Change Dominance Analysis (2006) 15 *European Competition Journal* 15, 19. For a broader normative link between the Treaty's free movement and competition rules and the freedom of competition, see W Frenz, *Handbook of EU Competition Law* (Berlin/Heidelberg, Springer, 2015).

[346] O Andriychuk, 'The Dialectics of Competition Law: Sketching the Ordo-Austrian Approach to Antitrust' (2012) 35 *World Competition* 355, 356.

[347] S Makris, 'Applying Normative Theories in EU Competition Law: Exploring Article 102 TFEU' (2014) 3 *UCL Journal of Law & Jurisprudence* 1, 37.

Second World War.[348] As such, the predominant view remains that ordoliberalism exerted a significant influence on shaping competition rules enshrined in the Treaty.[349] The core tenet of ordoliberal thinking lies in forming 'a holistic political economy and societal order'[350] that secures the social and ideological preconditions for economic liberty,[351] which is conceived as the freedom of entrepreneurs to engage in competition and seek gratification through voluntary exchanges on free markets.[352] The founders of ordoliberalism rejected the notion of a centrally planned economy due to its inefficiency and its imposition of restrictions on individual freedom.[353] In their view, private rather than governmental decision-making has to direct the flow of economic resources, as only the former process is capable of yielding a productive and reliable economic system under reduced state control.[354] Ordoliberals agreed with the fundamental tenet of classic liberalism that a competitive economic system is a necessary precondition for prosperity and individual self-realisation. However, they did not subscribe to the laissez-faire model of an almost stateless economy. In their view, it is not sufficient to protect individuals from the power of governments since an equally pernicious threat emanates even from powerful private actors. In the ordoliberal assertion, they are also capable of destroying and limiting individual economic liberty, given their inherent tendency towards cartelisation and monopolisation of markets.[355] Hence, ordoliberals proposed a 'third' way that envisaged a stronger role of the state in maintaining the institutional arrangement of economic order, expressed in the set of predefined rules that constitute and guide the market process.[356]

In ordoliberal thinking, the critical element for the functioning market is 'free, full and complete competition'.[357] As the consequence of the scarcity of goods and services,[358] it encapsulates 'an open form of supply and demand' with actions and

[348] R van den Bergh, *Comparative Competition Law and Economics* (Cheltenham, Edward Elgar, 2017) 30.

[349] C Talbot, 'Ordoliberalism and Balancing Competition Goals in the Development of the European Union' (2016) 61 *Antitrust Bulletin* 264, 271. See also A Gerbrandy, 'Rethinking Competition Law within the European Economic Constitution' (2019) 57 *Journal of Common Market Studies* 127, 129. For a counter-argument, see P Akman, 'Searching for the Long-Lost Soul of Article 82 EC' (2009) 29 *Oxford Journal of Legal Studies* 267.

[350] IH Anchustegui, 'Competition Law through an Ordoliberal Lens' (2015) 2 *Oslo Law Review* 139, 140.

[351] W Bonefeld, 'Freedom and the Strong State: On German Ordoliberalism' (2012) 17 *New Political Economy* 633, 634.

[352] ibid 38.

[353] Anchustegui (n 350) 142.

[354] DJ Gerber, 'Constitutionalizing the Economy: German Neo-liberalism, Competition Law and the "New" Europe' (1994) 42 *American Journal of Comparative Law* 25, 36.

[355] F Felice and M Vatiero, 'Ordo and European Competition Law' in L Fiorito (ed), *A Research Annual* (Bradford, Emerald Group Publishing, 2015) 152.

[356] A Ebner, 'The Intellectual Foundations of the Social Market Economy: Theory, Policy, and Implications for European Integration' (2006) 33 *Journal of Economic Studies* 206, 213.

[357] P Nedergaard, 'The Ordoliberalisation of the European Union?' (2020) 42 *Journal of European Integration* 213, 215.

[358] Anchustegui (n 350) 153.

reactions among market participants.[359] This process is conceived to foster 'the uninhibited development of individual initiative' and create alternatives among which market actors may freely choose to pursue their self-interest.[360] For ordoliberals, economic freedom is the essence of competition that is sought for its own sake.[361] Competition operates as an instrument by which individual liberty of independent decision-making is expressed and protected from abuse. Premised on this innate link, the advocates of ordoliberal thinking make two broad assertions. First, competition is a value on its own and, as such, cannot be directed towards specific objectives. This is because competition as a process would be abolished if one attempts to define its content in advance.[362] Second, the preconditions for the organisation of competition as a process can neither be found nor generated by market forces, given their tendency, if left unconstrained, to destroy the prerequisites of economic freedom.[363] Premised on historical precedents, ordoliberals recognised 'an omnipresent, strong and irrepressible urge'[364] of enterprises to prefer the private regulation of business activities and the ability to accrue economic power to eliminate competition.[365] Hence, the salient aspect of ordoliberalism is its insistence on creating a legal-institutional framework to bring order to private economic processes in a liberal environment.[366]

According to the ordoliberal school of thought, the proffered institutional framework, also often referred to as the 'economic constitution', is 'a comprehensive decision … concerning the nature … and form of the process of socio-economic cooperation … a political decision about the kind of economy a given community wants'.[367] It defines the rules of the game under which economic activities can be carried out.[368] They comprise constitutive and regulatory principles and ideals and a concomitant governmental policy aimed at implementing these normative benchmarks.[369] A societal choice to opt for the market economy system presupposes the adherence to private law order expressed in principles and ideals

[359] Felice and Vatiero (n 355) 153.
[360] E Hoppmann, 'Workable Competition: The Development of an Idea on the Norm for the Policy of Competition' (1968) 13 *Antitrust Bulletin* 61, 62.
[361] ibid.
[362] W Moschel, 'Competition as a Basic Element of the Social Market Economy' (2001) 2 *European Business Organization Law Review* 713, 713.
[363] Bonefeld (n 351) 639.
[364] W Eucken, 'The Competitive Order and its Implementation' (2006) 2 *Competition Policy International* 219, 222. The original articles appeared as W Eucken, 'Die Wettbewerbsordnung und Ihre Verwirklichung' (1949) *ORDO, Jahrbuch Fr die Ordnung von Wirtschaft und Gesellschaft* 1.
[365] Gerber (n 354) 50.
[366] VJ Vanberg, 'Ordoliberalism, Ordnungspolitik, and the Reason of Rules' (2015) 2 *European Review of International Studies* 27, 29.
[367] Gerber (n 354) 44–45.
[368] W Kerber and V Vanberg, 'Constitutional Aspects of Party Autonomy and its Limits: The Perspective of Constitutional Economics' in S Grundmann, W Kerber and S Weatherill (eds), *Party Autonomy and the Role of Information in the Internal Market* (Berlin, De Gruyter, 2001) 53.
[369] Gerber (n 354) 45.

incorporated at the constitutional level.[370] This consists of proscriptive norms such as 'private property, market price-setting, economic freedom and freedom of contract',[371] the fusion of which defines mutually compatible private domains where individuals are free to act and are protected from encroachment by other private law subjects.[372] The need for the active role of the state to closely observe the competitive process for any distortions directly flows from and is constrained by the constitutive principles and ideas underlying the market economy system.[373] Therefore, in ordoliberal understanding, the primary goal of competition law and policy is to protect the freedom of economic actors to compete in the marketplace, which is seen as the expression of individual economic liberty.[374] This entails setting positive and negative limits on the exercise of this freedom.[375] From an ordoliberal perspective, the only accepted type of competition is the so-called performance or capacity competition expressed in the form of conduct that 'makes a firm's products more attractive to consumers typically by improving their characteristics or lowering their prices'.[376] However, it is unlawful if an economic actor engages in so-called preventive competition that occurs when market conduct is 'designed to impede a rival's capacity to perform'.[377] For ordoliberals, the existence of such a power removes the legitimacy of the freedom to compete, as it leads to 'the inability to influence price or other parameters of competition'.[378] As such, the maxim that underlies the ordoliberal conception of competition law and policy is that the freedom to compete needs to be restrained to sustain its attributes.[379]

ii. Utilitarian Approach

In line with the deontological tradition, the ordoliberal approach to competition is grounded in value judgement.[380] The rightness or wrongness of market conduct depends entirely on its compliance with the constitutive rules of the market order, irrespective of its welfare implications. In ordoliberal understanding, it would be a violation of individual rights to ban conduct that the rules of the market order permit or, conversely, permit conduct that they prohibit

[370] VJ Vanberg, 'Consumer Welfare, Total Welfare and Economic Freedom: On the Normative Foundations of Competition Policy' in J Drexl, W Kerber and R Podszun (eds), *Competition Policy and the Economic Approach: Foundations and Limitations* (Cheltenham, Edward Elgar, 2012) 52.
[371] Anchustegui (n 350) 147.
[372] Vanberg (n 370) 51.
[373] C Ahlborn and C Grave, 'Walter Eucken and Ordoliberalism: An Introduction from a Consumer Welfare Perspective' (2006) 2 *Competition Policy International* 197, 201.
[374] Vanberg (n 370) 52.
[375] Anchustegui (n 350) 157.
[376] DJ Gerber, *Law and Competition in Twentieth-Century Europe: Protecting Prometheus* (Oxford, Oxford University Press, 2001) 253.
[377] ibid.
[378] Schweitzer (n 279) 177.
[379] Bonefeld (n 351) 639.
[380] Makris (n 347) 38.

on account of its efficiency or other consequences that market conduct is presumed to produce.[381] In opposition to this stands the utilitarian vision of the competition process. It is a consequentialist moral doctrine that focuses on the evaluation of social institutions exclusively based on their consequences on individuals' wellbeing.[382] The underlying premise is that the good is defined independently from the right, and the right is defined as what maximises the good.[383] From this vantage point, utilitarian thinking implies that the value of competition derives from its welfare-maximising properties.[384] Market conduct is deemed pro-competitive or anti-competitive based on its impact on welfare in the sense that it is accepted so long as it generates more good than bad regardless of its other effects.[385] The good in utilitarian thinking lies in economic efficiency, which is construed either in terms of the enhancement of total or consumer welfare. The concept of total welfare is defined as the total benefit to society. It is a measure that aggregates consumer surplus and producer surplus.[386] The concept of consumer welfare, in turn, only refers to consumer surplus expressed in the difference between what consumers would have been willing to pay and what they actually have to pay.[387]

The utilitarian approach to competition based on the consumer welfare standard came to prominence with the major rethinking and reinterpretation of the antitrust law in the US. This was led by scholars associated with the influential Chicago and post-Chicago schools of economic theory,[388] who saw an intrinsic link between competition law and economics, particularly welfare economics.[389] According to them, the adoption of the consumer welfare benchmark allows courts to establish anti-competitive market conduct by employing economic analysis in estimating whether the net effect of a particular structure, act or agreement is likely to harm consumer welfare, shown in higher prices, reduced output or lower quality.[390] The proponents of this school of thought dismissed the so-called per se approach whereby certain coordinated or unilateral forms of market conduct are presumed to restrict competition. Instead, they prescribed the assessment of

[381] Vanberg (n 370) 53.

[382] L Kaplow and S Shavell, 'Fairness versus Welfare' (2001) 114 *Harvard Law Review* 961, 1070.

[383] G Scarre, *Utilitarianism* (London, Routledge, 1996) 10.

[384] Anchustegui (n 350) 163.

[385] Makris (n 347) 36.

[386] I Lianos, 'Some Reflections on the Question of the Goals of EU Competition Law' in I Lianos and D Geradin (eds), *Handbook on European Competition Law: Substantive Aspects* (Cheltenham, Edward Elgar, 2013) 7.

[387] S Albæk, 'Consumer Welfare in EU Competition Policy' in C Heide-Jørgensen, C Bergqvistm, UB Neergaard and ST Poulsen (eds), *Aims and Values in Competition Law* (Copenhagen, DJØF Publishing, 2013) 67.

[388] See, eg, RH Bork, *The Antitrust Paradox: A Policy at War with itself* (New York, Free Press, 1978); R Posner, *Antitrust Law*, 2nd edn (Chicago, University of Chicago Press, 2001).

[389] Lianos (n 386) 4.

[390] RH Bork, 'The Goals of Antitrust Policy' (1967) 57 *American Economic Review* 242, 253.

the impact produced by market conduct that is cross-checked for its simultaneous benefits for consumers.[391] This utilitarian approach was endorsed by the US judicature that has embraced consumer welfare as a standard for finding anticompetitive market conduct.[392]

This development also exerted a considerable influence on the Commission's competition law enforcement practice, which has undergone substantial change over the last 20 years.[393] While previously the Commission primarily interpreted a restriction of competition as a restraint imposed on the freedom to compete (or market freedom),[394] its endorsement of the so-called 'more economic approach', which favours the in-depth case-by-case economic assessment of market conduct instead of a purely legalistic technique, led to a substantial shift in its interpretation and enforcement of the Treaty's competition rules.[395] While the Commission seems to oscillate between several benchmarks to establish a restriction of competition,[396] it attributes greater importance to the consumer welfare benchmark.[397] Such preponderance shown by the Commission has generated disagreements over the place of the freedom to compete within the normative framework of the Treaty's competition rules.[398] The root of discontent lies in the fact that, infused by utilitarian thinking, the consumer welfare benchmark, particularly in a pure sense, stands in stark contrast to the deontological approach (in ordoliberal terms) to the protection of market freedom. Their objectives are fundamentally different as they are based on divergent normative values.[399] Under the latter understanding, as mentioned earlier, the freedom to compete is an end in itself and not a means for the welfare of others.[400] Although consumer welfare

[391] O Andriychuk, 'Can We Protect Competition without Protecting Consumers?' (2010) 6 *Competition Law Review* 77, 81.

[392] AC Witt, *The More Economic Approach to EU Antitrust Law* (Oxford, Hart Publishing, 2016) 63.

[393] Albæk (n 387) 68. For a broader overview, see KJ Cseres, The Controversies of the Consumer Welfare Standard (2007) 3 *Competition Law Review* 121.

[394] See the Commission's approach in *Irish Sugar* (IV/34.621 and 35.059/F-3) [1997] OJ L258/1, Recital 134; *Decca Navigator System* (IV/30.979 and 31.394) [1989] OJ L43/27, Recital 11.

[395] Witt (n 392) 55.

[396] For a general overview of the available benchmarks, see G Monti, 'Article 81 EC and Public Policy' (2002) 39 *Common Market Law Review* 1057; R Nazzini, *The Foundations of European Union Competition Law: The Objective and Principles of Article 102* (Oxford, Oxford University Press, 2011); Josef Drexl, 'On the (A)Political Character of the Economic Approach to Competition Law' in Drexl, Kerber and Podszun (n 370).

[397] See R O'Donoghue and AJ Padilla, *The Law and Economics of Art 102 TFEU* (Oxford, Hart Publishing, 2013) 243. See also Articles 5 and 10 in European Commission, 'Guidance on the enforcement priorities in applying Article 82 of the EC Treaty to abusive exclusionary conduct by dominant undertakings' [2009] OJ C45/7.

[398] See, eg, LL Gormsen, 'The Conflict between Economic Freedom and Consumer Welfare in the Modernisation of Article 82 EC' (2007) 3 *European Competition Journal* 329.

[399] E Deutscher and S Makris, 'Exploring the Ordoliberal Paradigm: The Competition-Democracy Nexus' (2016) 11 *Competition Law Review* 181, 182.

[400] W Möschel, 'Competition Policy from an Ordo-liberal Point of View' in A Peacock and H Willgerodt (eds), *German Neo-liberals and the Social Market Economy* (London, Macmillan, 1989) 146.

remains a crucial factor guiding the market conduct of economic actors, it is not seen as an aim but as the result of the competition process.[401] In contrast, under the consumer welfare standard, the freedom to compete has no intrinsic value; instead, it operates as an instrument to maximise consumer well-being.[402] With such variance, a restriction of competition based on the consumer welfare standard would not necessarily constitute a restriction from the viewpoint of market freedom and vice versa. Market conduct that leads to the exclusion of less efficient competitors from the market would not necessarily be caught under the consumer welfare standard if the activity does not contribute, among other things, to lowering prices or offering better-quality products or services.[403] However, this would not sit well with the idea of ensuring market freedom, as these competitors would lose the ability to take part in the market process to acquire the necessary level of efficiency to compete.[404] This point of divergence manifests itself in the difference between the Commission's and the Court's approach to competition law enforcement.

C. Theoretical Underpinnings of the Jurisprudential Approach

Contrary to what the Commission and a considerable segment of academic literature advocate, the Court does not recognise the consumer welfare standard as the bedrock of the competition law regime. Instead, while opinions vary as to whether the Court endorses a theory of unitary objective behind the Treaty's competition rules or ascribes value-pluralistic characteristics to their normative framework,[405] the fact remains that the Court's approach conforms to the ordoliberal postulates that are underpinned by the deontological values attached to the freedom of competition and equal opportunity in the internal market.[406] The Court's stand on the competition law enforcement naturally reflects the wording of the Treaty. From the outset, protecting competition from restrictions appeared among the overarching objectives enshrined in the Treaty. The former Article 3 EC, which has now been transferred to the Protocol on the internal market and competition,[407] provided that the purpose of the then Community included 'the institution of a system ensuring that competition in the common market [was] not distorted'. Based on this provision, the Court adheres to the protection of the

[401] V Vanberg, 'Freiburg School of Law and Economics' in P Newman (ed), *The New Palgrave Dictionary of Economics*, vol 2 (London, Palgrave Macmillan, 1998) 176.

[402] See, eg, C Townley, *Article 81 EC and Public Policy* (Oxford, Hart Publishing, 2009) 177–81.

[403] Gormsen (n 398) 331–32.

[404] ibid.

[405] K Stylianou and M Iacovides, 'The Goals of EU Competition Law: A Comprehensive Empirical Investigation' (2022) 42 *Legal Studies* 620, 622.

[406] Deutscher and Makris (n 399) 197.

[407] Consolidated version of the Treaty on European Union – PROTOCOLS – Protocol (No 27) on the internal market and competition [2008] OJ C115.

competitive process that aligns with ordoliberal thinking.[408] In *Continental Can*,[409] in response to the claim that the former Article 3 EC was devoid of legal effect, the Court found that the pursuit of objectives laid down therein was indispensable for achieving the (then) Community's tasks.[410] It continued that the institution of a system of undistorted competition required a fortiori that competition must not be eliminated, for it contributed to the realisation of other Treaty's provisions and the promotion of harmonious development of economic activities throughout the then Community.[411] In *T-Mobile Netherlands*,[412] in turn, the Court reiterated AG Kokott's view that '[Article 101 TFEU], like other competition rules of the Treaty, [was] not designed only or primarily to protect the immediate interests of individual competitors or consumers, *but to protect the structure of the market and thus competition as such (as an institution)*' (emphasis added).[413]

In several instances, the Court resorted to the reasoning that only emphasised the impact on consumers. In *Deutsche Telekom*,[414] it held that '[Article 102 TFEU aimed] to protect consumers by means of undistorted competition'.[415] Along the same lines, in *Post Danmark I*,[416] the Court stated that '[Article 102 TFEU applied] to the conduct of a dominant undertaking that, through recourse to methods different from those governing normal competition on the basis of the performance of commercial operators, [had] the effect, to the detriment of consumers, of hindering the maintenance of the degree of competition existing in the market or the growth of that competition'.[417] However, this line of case law cannot be deemed to endorse the consumer welfare standard. The Court, in fact, explicitly refused to embrace consumer harm as a benchmark for finding a restriction of competition. In *GlaxoSmithKline*, the General Court resorted to the consumer welfare standard to determine the anti-competitive nature of market conduct. It first defined Article 101 TFEU as a provision that prevented undertakings from limiting competition between themselves or with third parties, thereby reducing the welfare of the final consumer.[418] As such, in the Court's view, '[the application of this provision required] an analysis designed to determine whether it [had] as its object or effect

[408] See, eg, Case C-377/20 *Servizio Elettrico Nazionale SpA and Others v Autorità Garante della Concorrenza e del Mercato and Others* EU:C:2022:379, para 47.

[409] Case 6-72 *Europemballage Corporation and Continental Can Company Inc v Commission* EU:C:1973:22.

[410] ibid para 7.

[411] ibid para 8.

[412] Case C-8/08 *T-Mobile Netherlands BV, KPN Mobile NV, Orange Nederland NV and Vodafone Libertel NV v Raad van bestuur van de Nederlandse Mededingingsautoriteit* EU:C:2009:343.

[413] ibid para 38. See also Case C-286/13 P *Dole Food Company, Inc and Dole Fresh Fruit Europe v Commission* EU:C:2015:184, para 125; Case C-450/19 *Proceedings Brought by Kilpailu- ja kuluttajavirasto* EU:C:2021:10.

[414] Case C-280/08 P *Deutsche Telekom AG v Commission* EU:C:2010:603.

[415] ibid para 180. See also Case C-478/06 *Sot Lélos kai Sia EE and Others v GlaxoSmithKline AEVE Farmakeftikon Proïonton, formerly Glaxowellcome AEVE* EU:C:2008:504, para 68.

[416] Case C-209/10 *Post Danmark A/S v Konkurrencerådet* EU:C:2012:172.

[417] ibid para 24.

[418] *GlaxoSmithKline Services Unlimited* (n 307) para 118.

the prevention, restriction or distortion of competition on the relevant market, to the detriment of the final consumer'.[419] In contrast, the Court of Justice ruled that the General Court had misapplied the law. It noted that, unlike the position taken by the General Court, there was nothing in the wording of Article 101 TFEU 'to indicate that only those agreements which deprive[d] consumers of certain advantages [might] have an anti-competitive object'.[420] This is because, like other competition rules laid down in the Treaty, this provision aims 'to protect not only the interests of competitors or of consumers, but also the structure of the market and, in so doing, competition as such'.[421]

The consumer welfare standard has also hardly gained any foothold in the case law concerning Article 102 TFEU. The proof of consumer harm may indeed operate as a deciding factor for establishing the exploitative forms of abuse.[422] However, this does not extend to the exclusionary forms of abuse, which remain subject to the freedom-based benchmark. In *British Airways*,[423] in response to the plea raised against the existence of a restriction of competition based on the lack of consumer harm, the Court held that 'Article [102 TFEU was] aimed not only at practices which [might] cause prejudice to consumers directly, but also at those which [were] detrimental to them through their impact on an effective competition structure'.[424] As a result, consumer harm is not the deciding factor for finding a restriction of competition but one among several factors to consider.[425] This is reflected in *TeliaSonera Sverige*,[426] where the Court stressed that 'the function of [the Treaty's competition rules was] precisely to prevent competition from being distorted to *the detriment of the public interest, individual undertakings and consumers*, thereby ensuring the well-being of the European Union' (emphasis added).[427]

According to the case law, the Court's approach does not conform to the instrumentalist conception of competition, the value of which exclusively lies in its quality to maximise welfare. On the contrary, in line with ordoliberal prescriptions, it attaches an intrinsic value to competition as a process and social institution that preserves a rivalrous structure in the internal market.[428] Central to this concept is an individual striving for economic self-determination and self-realisation. In this sense, the process of competition encapsulates the freedom of competition,[429]

[419] ibid para 119.
[420] Joined Cases C-501/06 P, C-513/06 P, C-515/06 P and C-519/06 P *GlaxoSmithKline Services Unlimited v Commission* EU:C:2009:610, para 63.
[421] ibid.
[422] See, eg, Case C-177/16 *Autortiesību un komunicēšanās konsultāciju aģentūra/Latvijas Autoru apvienība v Konkurences padome* EU:C:2017:689, paras 35–36.
[423] Case C-95/04 P *British Airways plc v Commission* EU:C:2007:166.
[424] ibid para 106.
[425] See, eg, Case T-705/1 *Unichem Laboratories Ltd v Commission* EU:T:2018:91, para 306; Case C-94/00 *Roquette Frères SA v Directeur General* EU:C:2002:603, para 42.
[426] Case C-52/09 *Konkurrensverket v TeliaSonera Sverige AB* EU:C:2011:83.
[427] ibid para 22.
[428] Deutscher and Makris (n 399) 197.
[429] Frenz (n 345) 176.

which the Court has elevated to a constitutional status alongside the freedoms of movement.[430] In *ADBHU*,[431] the Court unequivocally held that 'the principles of free movement of goods and freedom of competition, together with freedom of trade as a fundamental right, [were] general principles of [Union] law'.[432] Within this normative setting, the process of competition based on the autonomy of decision-making enjoyed by market actors is protected as an end on its own and not as a means to achieve welfare goals. The impairment of such autonomy can constitute a restriction of competition irrespective of whether there is a detriment to consumers. However, the Treaty's competition rules do not bestow on economic actors the direct protection of freedom of competition as such;[433] instead, they achieve this by protecting the competitive order that optimises the coordination of market conduct to ensure conformity with the parameters of 'competition on merits'.[434] The normative framework established by these rules is proscriptive rather than prescriptive.[435] It excludes or prohibits certain forms of unilateral or coordinated market conduct that deviate from the parameters of normal market behaviour while leaving economic actors with an open-ended range of behavioural options to choose from.[436]

III. Interim Conclusion

In sum, whilst formulated as prohibitions addressed to Member States and a certain category of private actors, the free movement and competition law regimes are conceived as bearers of individual rights in line with the Court's famous proclamation in *Van Gend en Loos*. These provisions form the core of the Union's economic constitution, for they aim to achieve the realisation and functioning of the internal market. The individualisation of this process can be conceptualised to manifest itself in the guarantee of market freedom understood as the right to initiate or take part in the interstate process of competition, free from, on the one hand, discriminatory and non-discriminatory public barriers, and, on the other hand, the conduct of certain category of market actors that does not fit the definition of normal market behaviour. Such homogeneous concretisation of the subjective entitlements enshrined in the Treaty's free movement and competition rules, first, reflects the degree of complementarity intrinsic to the role of these norms in the internal market and, second, aligns with the Court's vision of the internal market

[430] See Case T-170/06 *Alrosa Company Ltd v Commission* EU:T:2007:220, para 49.
[431] Case 240/83 *Procureur de la République v Association de défense des brûleurs d'huiles usagées (ADBHU)* EU:C:1985:59.
[432] ibid para 9.
[433] Frenz (n 345) 74.
[434] Drexl (n 396) 328.
[435] Vanberg (n 370) 51.
[436] ibid.

as forging separate national markets into a single economic sphere premised on the fusion of centralised and decentralised regulatory models.

Yet, the contours of the individual right derived from the free movement and competition law regimes and the parameters of its protection are not without ambiguity. At one level, in the context of free movement law, the contributing factor is the broad definition of the concept of restriction permeating the case law on the free movement of persons. This makes it difficult to accommodate the individual economic entitlement stemming from free movement law in between the extreme of the right to equal treatment and that of the right to economic freedom at large. The Court's expansive language steers the freedoms of movement towards the latter extreme. At another level, within the competition law framework, uncertainty surrounds not the nature of the safeguarded individual right but the principal rationalisation of its protection. What divides opinion in this respect is whether the freedom of competition/freedom to compete is protected as a value on its own or as a means towards other ends. At both levels, the lingering ambiguity has a profound constitutional significance that comes to light when the free movement and competition law regimes are juxtaposed (as will be shown in Chapter 5) against fundamental economic rights protected at the Union level.

4

The Union's Secondary Law and Private Autonomy

> [T]he Court has developed what Community lawyers often refer to as the doctrines of consistent interpretation of national law in the light of directives, vertical direct effect of directives and the absence of horizontal direct effect of directives. In many cases, however, those catchwords hide a more complex legal reality.[1]

While the free movement and competition rules enshrined in the Treaty on the Functioning of the European Union are instrumental to the creation and functioning of the internal market, the Union's secondary law also plays a critical role in shaping the dynamics of individual economic activities across Member States' borders. At one end, it facilitates such private initiatives. Article 114 TFEU is the primary provision that lays down the Union's competence in matters relating to the internal market. It enables the Union's institutions to enact measures that harmonise or approximate diverse national approaches to market regulation. By adding a degree of uniformity to the regulatory standards in the internal market, harmonisation measures complement the achievement of the goal of fusing national markets into a unified economic sphere pursued by the Treaty's free movement and competition rules. They can be rationalised by the need to guarantee a 'level playing field' for the maintenance of the interstate process of competition in the internal market. On the other hand, the Union's harmonisation measures, often adopted in the form of directives, impose limitations or conditions on the exercise of private autonomy. It is well known that properly implemented directives in the field of consumer, environmental or labour protection impact private parties who are subject to implementing legislation at a national level.[2] However, even in the absence of proper implementation, directives are not devoid of legal effect in a private setting. It is true that the Court continuously insists that directives do not operate as a direct source of obligations imposed on individuals and cannot be invoked against them.[3] Yet, there are several judicial avenues by which directives can, at least indirectly, affect the legal position of individuals.

[1] Opinion of AG Jacobs in Case C-443/98 *Unilever Italia SpA v Central Food SpA* EU:C:2000:57.

[2] S Weatherill, 'The Elusive Character of Private Autonomy' in D Leczykiewicz and S Weatherill (eds), *The Involvement of EU Law in Private Law Relationships* (Oxford, Hart Publishing, 2013) 15.

[3] Case 152/84 *MH Marshall v Southampton and South-West Hampshire Area Health Authority* EU:C:1986:84, para 48; Case C-91/92 *Paola Faccini Dori v Recreb Srl* EU:C:1994:292, para 20.

I. Guarantee of Private Autonomy

The Union's legislative competence under Article 114 TFEU has generated a plethora of academic commentaries.[4] For the avoidance of repetition, it is worth focusing on the salient aspects relating to this provision as a complementary tool to the Treaty's free movement and competition rules.[5] Article 114 TFEU empowers the Union's institutions to adopt 'measures for the approximation of the provisions laid down by law, regulation or administrative action in Member States which have as their object the establishment and functioning of the internal market'. This provision is a primary legal mechanism for harmonising national regulatory standards through legislative intervention that supplements their alignment by judicial principles developed through the Court's purposive interpretation of the Treaty.[6]

The Union's competence under Article 114 TFEU is not unqualified. This provision does not 'vest [in the Union] legislature a general power to regulate the internal market'.[7] In the Court's characterisation, '[harmonisation measures] referred to in [it] … must genuinely have [the object of] actually contributing to the elimination of obstacles to the free movement of goods or to the freedom to provide services, or to the removal of distortions of competition'.[8] Article 114 TFEU mandates the Union's legislator to intervene to cure disparities of national regulatory policies that are harmful to the functioning of the internal market.[9] This primarily includes those that are created by Member States exculpating their regulatory policies through accepted derogations.[10] Four threshold conditions define the scope of legislative intervention under Article 114 TFEU. First, this provision can be relied upon to remove 'differences between national laws which are such as to obstruct the fundamental freedoms and thus have a direct effect on the functioning of the internal market'.[11] Second, it can be a legal base for measures that purport to reduce differences between national laws that cause 'appreciable' distortion of competition.[12] Third, a measure enacted under Article 114 TFEU can include

[4] See, eg, I Maletić, *The Law and Policy of Harmonisation in Europe's Internal Market* (Cheltenham, Edward Elgar, 2013); K Mortelmans, 'The Relationship between the Treaty Rules and Community Measures for the Establishment and Functioning of the Internal Market: Towards a Concordance Rule' (2002) 39 *Common Market Law Review* 1303.

[5] Case C-299/19 *Techbau SpA v Azienda Sanitaria Locale AL* EU:C:2020:937, para 50.

[6] I Maletic, 'The Boundaries of the Internal Market after the Lisbon Treaty: A Closer Look at Article 95 EC' (2010) 5 *Croatian Yearbook of European Law and Policy* 19, 19.

[7] Case C-376/98 *Germany v Parliament and Council* EU:C:2000:544, para 83.

[8] Case C-491/01 *British American Tobacco (Investments) and Imperial Tobacco* EU:C:2002:741, para 60.

[9] S Weatherill, 'The Limits of Legislative Harmonization Ten Years after *Tobacco Advertising*: How the Court's Case Law Has Become a "Drafting Guide"' (2011) 12 *German Law Review* 827, 830.

[10] Opinion of AG Geelhoed in Case C-491/01 *British American Tobacco (Investments) Ltd and Imperial Tobacco Ltd* EU:C:2002:476, para 103.

[11] Case C-434/02 *Arnold André GmbH & Co KG v Landrat des Kreises Herford* EU:C:2004:800, para 30.

[12] *Germany v Parliament and Council* (n 7) para 106.

provisions necessary to ensure that certain prohibitions imposed in pursuit of the purpose of eliminating obstacles to the exercise of the freedoms of movement are not circumvented.[13] Fourth, the recourse to this provision is possible to adopt measures that 'prevent the emergence of future obstacles to trade resulting from multifarious development of national laws',[14] subject to the condition that the rise of such obstacles 'must be likely'.[15]

Considered at an individual level, harmonisation measures adopted within the confines of these four threshold conditions are anchored to the realisation of private autonomy in the internal market, for they facilitate cross-border transactions. The need for such legislative intervention arises from the discrepancy of national regulatory practices that limit or condition various aspects of private autonomy, which stands at odds with the Union's integrative objectives.[16] However, such legislative intervention does not entail a wholesale deregulatory exercise aimed at eliminating these diverging national choices – far from it. Harmonisation measures introduce uniform regulatory standards that pre-emptively or reactively deal with the concerns that prompt varying national practices in the first place. The purpose of these measures is infused by the equality-based logic that demands a 'level playing field' for economic actors operating in different Member States.[17] Harmonisation measures ensure that their competitive positions inter se are not undermined by the obligations to follow heterogeneous national regulatory standards. These measures are necessary 'to eliminate competitive distortions with an appreciable effect or restraints of trade caused by differing Member State regulations'.[18] As the Court held in *Alliance for Natural Health*,[19] the harmonisation competence under Article 114 TFEU is triggered whenever 'there [were] obstacles to trade, or it [was] likely that such obstacles [would] emerge in the future, because the Member States ha[d] taken, or are about to take, divergent measures with respect to a product or a class of products, which [brought] about different levels of protection and thereby prevent[ed] the product or products concerned from moving freely within the [Union]'.[20]

The 'level playing field' rationale is particularly at play when gauging the degree of distortion of competition caused by the discrepancy of national regulations. To trigger the harmonisation competence under Article 114 TFEU, such distortion

[13] ibid para 100.

[14] *British American Tobacco* (n 8) para 61.

[15] ibid.

[16] S Weatherill, 'Justifying Limits to Party Autonomy in the Internal Market: EC Legislation in the Field of Consumer Protection' in S Grundmann, W Kerber and S Weatherill (eds), *Party Autonomy and the Role of Information in the Internal Market* (Berlin, De Gruyter, 2001) 174.

[17] G Davies, 'Can Selling Arrangements Be Harmonised?' (2005) 30 *European Law Review* 371, 373.

[18] A von Bogdandy and J Bast, 'The European Union's Vertical Order of Competences: The Current Law and Proposals for its Reform' (2002) 39 *Common Market Law Review* 227, 244.

[19] Joined Cases C-154/04 and C-155/04 *Alliance for Natural Health v Secretary of State for Health* EU:C:2005:449.

[20] ibid para 32.

must rise to the level of 'appreciable'. In *Tobacco Advertising I*,[21] the Court attached a higher threshold to the standard of 'appreciability'. It held that undertakings in Member States that imposed fewer restrictions on tobacco advertising were at an advantage in terms of economies of scale and increase in profits, though the effects of such an advantage on competition were 'remote and indirect' to be qualified as 'appreciable'.[22] However, subsequent case law seems to set a lower threshold premised on the existence of a sole disparity between national regulations.[23] In *Tobacco Advertising II*,[24] the Court held that the difference in national rules over the sponsorship of radio programmes by tobacco companies posed 'an appreciable risk of distortions of competition' since it denied 'radio broadcasting bodies established in a Member State where a measure prohibiting sponsorship was in force the benefit of sponsorship from tobacco companies established in another Member State, where such a measure did not exist'.[25] In *Ireland v Parliament*,[26] the Court upheld Article 114 TFEU as the legal basis for a directive approximating national rules on personal data processing by finding that divergent national obligations on data retention posed significant economic implications for service providers insofar as they might involve substantial investment and operating costs.[27] In *Leitner*,[28] although not strictly on the use of Article 114 TFEU, the Court held that the harmonisation of national laws on package travel was justified by the fact that 'the existence in some Member States but not in others of an obligation to provide compensation for non-material damage would cause significant distortions of competition'.[29] In contrast to *Tobacco Advertising I*, this line of case law suggests a certain leniency on the Court's part to applying the threshold of 'appreciability'.[30]

Harmonisation aimed at reducing the disparity of national regulations can take various forms, including, as often reiterated by the Court, the requirements addressed to all Member States 'to authorise the marketing of the product or products concerned, subjecting such an obligation of authorisation to certain conditions, or even provisionally or definitively prohibiting the marketing of a product or products'.[31] While the first two actions can be construed to contribute to the realisation of the ideals of private autonomy in the internal market, harmonised bans of unsafe products may not easily fit into this equation. Such prohibitions may not perform a market-making role but fall within the outer limits of Article 114 TFEU, for they improve the functioning of the internal

[21] *Germany v Parliament and Council* (n 7).
[22] ibid para 109.
[23] K Gutman, *The Constitutional Foundations of European Contract Law: A Comparative Analysis* (Oxford, Oxford University Press, 2014) 334.
[24] Case C-380/03 *Germany v Parliament and Council* EU:C:2006:772.
[25] ibid paras 65–66.
[26] Case C-301/06 *Ireland v Parliament and Council* EU:C:2009:68.
[27] ibid para 68.
[28] Case C-168/00 *Simone Leitner v TUI Deutschland* EU:C:2002:163.
[29] ibid para 21.
[30] Gutman (n 23) 348.
[31] Case C-210/03 *Swedish Match v Secretary of State for Health* EU:C:2004:802, para 34.

market by freeing trade in products deemed less harmful by the legislature.[32] Therefore, harmonisation at the Union level can be conducive to the effective exercise of private autonomy and limit or condition it, the extent of which is discussed in the subsequent section.

II. Limitation of Private Autonomy

Directives, as a primary method of harmonisation, affect individuals through national implementation measures giving effect to them. While the impact of properly implemented directives is clear and beyond dispute, more controversial are directives that lack proper implementation. It is trite law that directives satisfying the precision and unconditionality criteria may only be invoked against Member States reneging on the obligation to transpose them into national law. However, a complex set of qualifications and exceptions is attached to this precept. Their existence is traditionally rationalised as enabling the Court to reconcile the tension between the need to preserve the specific identity of directives that is distinct from regulations and the objective of ensuring the effectiveness of Union law.[33] However, what is problematic is that these qualifications and exceptions are not immune from causing a collateral effect on a private party, which can be of the same magnitude as the impact of directives directly enforced against it. Therein lies a paradox. These qualifications and exceptions are hardly informed by the need to ensure the protection of legal certainty in private relationships,[34] while this very concern underpins the Court's insistence on the orthodox doctrine of directives having no horizontal direct effect.

A. The *Marshall* Precept and its Qualifications

Smith is another twist to the convoluted case law on the horizontal direct effect of directives.[35] This case concerned a private dispute in which a plaintiff, injured in a car accident, sued two defendants for negligence and breach of duty. However, the actual issue was more complicated than a mere personal injury action. It concerned the discrepancy existing between the directive concerning the civil liability for harm caused by motor vehicles and the defendant's insurance policy that was approved by the applicable national law.[36] Under the latter, the motor

[32] Weatherill (n 9) 837.

[33] A Dashwood, 'From *Van Duyn* to *Mangold* via *Marshall*: Reducing Direct Effect to Absurdity?' (2007) 9 *Cambridge Yearbook of European Legal Studies* 81, 82.

[34] S Prechal, *Directives in EC Law* (Oxford, Oxford University Press, 2005) 257.

[35] Case C-122/17 *David Smith v Patrick Meade and Others* EU:C:2018:631.

[36] Third Council Directive 90/232/EEC of 14 May 1990 on the approximation of the laws of the Member States relating to insurance against civil liability in respect of the use of motor vehicles [1990] OJ L129.

insurance covered only the passenger seated on the fixed seat in the front of a vehicle, excluding passengers travelling in its rear. In contrast, the directive required motor insurance to cover liability for personal injuries suffered by all passengers other than the driver.[37] Given this dissonance, the national court sought to clarify whether the national law was required to be set aside under this directive. In response, the Court gave an all-embracing ruling that took the saga of the horizontality of directives to its beginning and explained different twists along the way of its development.[38]

In *Smith*, the Court once again confirmed the *Marshall* precept of no horizontal direct effect of a directive by reiterating its familiar finding that 'it [could not] of itself impose obligations on an individual and [could not] therefore be relied upon as such against an individual'.[39] It added that 'even a clear, precise and unconditional provision of a directive seeking to confer rights on or impose obligations on individuals [could not] of itself apply in a dispute exclusively between private persons'.[40] A normative argument for this precept is grounded in the demand for legal certainty.[41] Directives cannot create obligations for individuals.[42] Their provisions can only give rise to rights that are enforceable against Member States.[43] As has often been repeated by the Court, this follows from the wording of Article 249 TFEU, pursuant to which the binding nature of a directive exists only in relation to 'each Member State to which it is addressed'.[44] This distinguishes them from regulations. The Court held that 'the effect of extending [directives] to the sphere of relations between individuals would be to recognize a power in the [Union] to enact obligations for individuals with immediate effect, whereas it [had] competence to do so only where it [was] empowered to adopt regulations'.[45] When first advanced, these strands of reasoning were not controversial. This changed with the gradual attachment of various exceptions or qualifications to the *Marshall* precept that led to much uncertainty and confusion over the normative capacity of directives to act as a source of obligations imposed on individuals.

[37] ibid Article 1.

[38] P Koutrakos, 'Is There More to Say about the Direct Effect of Directives?' (2018) 43 *European Law Review* 621, 622.

[39] *Smith* (n 35) para 42.

[40] ibid para 43.

[41] P Craig, 'The Legal Effect of Directives: Policy, Rules and Exceptions' (2009) 34 *European Law Review* 349, 353.

[42] Case C-201/02 *The Queen, on the Application of Delena Wells v Secretary of State for Transport, Local Government and the Regions* EU:C:2004:12, para 56.

[43] Joined Cases C-152/07 to C-154/07 *Arcor and Others* EU:C:2008:426, para 35.

[44] *Marshall* (n 3) para 48.

[45] *Faccini Dori* (n 3) para 24.

B. Concept of 'an Emanation of the State'

Without horizontal enforceability, directives only bind Member States. Provided that the traditional thresholds of precision and unconditionality are met, provisions of a directive can be invoked by individuals against Member States defaulting on their obligations to transpose them into national law.[46] For this reason, the definition of what constitutes a state body is an integral element in the enforcement of directives. In *Foster*,[47] the Court adopted a broad concept of the state that not only includes bodies acting in public or private capacity but equally encompasses even non-public bodies that are classed as an emanation of the state. It found that the provisions of a directive could be invoked against 'a body, whatever its legal form, which ha[d] been made responsible, pursuant to a measure adopted by the State, for providing a public service under the control of the State and ha[d] for that purpose special powers beyond those which result[ed] from the normal rules applicable in relations between individuals'.[48] In the same ruling, the Court also offered even broader characterisation by defining an emanation of the state as 'organizations or bodies which were subject to the authority or control of the State or had special powers beyond those which result[ed] from the normal rules applicable to relations between individuals'.[49] For nearly two decades, the *Foster* formula remained contentious. It was unclear whether it comprised cumulative criteria and how the criterion of 'special powers' was to be construed.

Farrell,[50] which was later confirmed in *Smith*,[51] provided some clarity to this uncertainty. In this case, the Court first held that the *Foster* formula was not intended 'to formulate a general test designed to cover all situations in which a body might be one against which the provisions of a directive capable of having direct effect might be relied upon'.[52] It then found that the *Foster* criteria '[could not be conjunctive' and, as such, a body did not need to display all the mentioned characteristics.[53] The principle underlying the concept of an emanation of the state is that organisations or bodies are distinguishable from individuals and are comparable to the state 'either because they are legal persons governed by public law that are part of the State in the broad sense, or because they are subject to the authority or control of a public body, or because they have been required, by such a body, to perform a task in the public interest and have been given, for that purpose, such special powers'.[54] A directive can, therefore, be invoked even against those

[46] Case 148/78 *Criminal Proceedings against Tullio Ratti* EU:C:1979:110, para 22.
[47] Case C-188/89 *A Foster and Others v British Gas* EU:C:1990:313.
[48] ibid para 20.
[49] ibid para 18.
[50] Case C-413/15 *Elaine Farrell v Alan Whitty and Others* EU:C:2017:745.
[51] *Smith* (n 35) para 45.
[52] *Farrell* (n 50) para 26.
[53] ibid para 28.
[54] ibid para 34.

governed by private law if they are delegated by the state to perform tasks in the public interest and possess for that purpose special powers beyond those resulting from the normal rules applicable to relations between individuals.[55]

While *Farrell* clarified the *Foster* formula, its parameters are not unshackled from uncertainty. Questions persist over their actual ambit, considered from functional and conceptional standpoints. First, *Farrell* does not elaborate on the degree to which a private law body or organisation must be under the control or authority of the state to be regarded as an emanation of the state. The case law built on *Foster* is also not very helpful. In *Rieser Internationale Transporte*,[56] a joint-stock company was deemed to be an emanation of the state for being responsible for constructing, planning, operating, maintaining and financing a motorway 'under the supervision of … public authorities'.[57] In *Sozialhilfeverband Rohrbach*,[58] this concept was found to encompass a private limited liability company whose sole shareholder was a social assistance association governed by public law.[59] Second, neither the case law pre-dating nor post-dating *Farrell* defines the concept of 'special powers'. In most instances, the emphasis seems to be placed on the specific functional characteristics of the body in question. In *Grenville Hampshire*,[60] the Court found that a body responsible for employees' claims under a supplementary occupational pension scheme was entrusted with 'special powers' manifested in '[its capacity to impose] levies on eligible supplementary occupational pension schemes and [its right] to issue those schemes with the necessary directions in connection with their winding up'.[61] Similarly, in *Farrell*, a private organisation was deemed to fall under this definition, for it '[had] the power to require all [motor vehicle] insurers to become members of it and to contribute funds for the performance of the task conferred on it by the … State'.[62]

This line of case law evinces the Court's predilection for a more contextual approach to applying the *Farrell* criteria. In one respect, such an approach may indeed be warranted, given the potential difficulties in formulating a comprehensive definition that captures all the possible expressions of the concepts of 'state control' and 'special powers'.[63] However, its substitution with the fact-specific assessment is far from ideal in terms of ensuring legal certainty.[64] Drawing a clear line separating bodies that constitute an emanation of the state can be problematic,

[55] ibid para 35.
[56] Case C-157/02 *Rieser Internationale Transporte GmbH v Asfinag* EU:C:2004:76.
[57] ibid para 27.
[58] Case C-297/03 *Sozialhilfeverband Rohrbach v Arbeiterkammer Oberösterreich and Österreichischer Gewerkschaftsbund* EU:C:2005:315.
[59] ibid para 30.
[60] Case C-17/17 *Grenville Hampshire v The Board of the Pension Protection Fund* EU:C:2018:674.
[61] ibid para 66.
[62] *Farrell* (n 50) para 40.
[63] Koutrakos (n 38) 623.
[64] ibid.

mainly because the degree of state control or the nature of special powers may vary considerably. The broad construction of both criteria under *Farrell* runs the risk of enforcing directives even against private bodies or organisations with a limited link to the state or with narrow special powers. From a conceptual point of view, such an outcome gives rise to a mismatch between the strict textual reading of Article 249 TFEU and the broader purposive interpretation of this provision. Whilst the Court continues to deny the horizontal direct effect of directives, since they are only explicitly addressed to Member States, the binding effect of directives is not limited to national organs with the required power to implement them. Instead, it also extends, through the concept of an emanation of the state, to non-state bodies that neither possess any power in relation to the implementation of directives nor have any control over that process. In that capacity, they are indistinguishable from private parties against which directives are not enforceable under the demand for legal certainty.[65] And yet, concerning them, a different balance of interests prevails that favours the effectiveness of Union law over the principle of legal certainty.

C. Duty of Consistent Interpretation

Smith also recalls and clarifies the duty resting on national courts to interpret national law as far as possible in line with directives. Such an obligation, which has its origins in the principle of sincere cooperation laid down in Article 4(3) TFEU,[66] is among the primary means for ensuring the effectiveness of directives.[67] The duty of consistent interpretation not only applies to disputes where the defendant is the state or the emanation thereof,[68] but it also concerns disputes arising between private parties.[69] In *Smith*, citing its earlier case law,[70] the Court clarified the parameters of this duty by expanding on the limits already recognised in its previous case law. It held that in the domain of private relationships, a national court '[was] not obliged, solely on the basis of EU law, to disapply the provisions of its national law which [were] contrary to … [a] directive', when it found itself unable to interpret them in a manner that was compatible with that directive.[71] In this respect, the Court set apart *Mangold* and *Kücükdeveci*-type situations by

[65] Craig (n 41) 357.

[66] See, eg, Joined Cases C-378/07 to C-380/07 *Angelidaki and Others* EU:C:2009:250, para 106; Joined Cases C-397/01 to C-403/01 *Bernhard Pfeiffer and Others v Deutsches Rotes Kreuz* EU:C:2004:584, para 110.

[67] G Betlem, 'The Doctrine of Consistent Interpretation: Managing Legal Uncertainty (2002) 22 *Oxford Journal of Legal Studies* 397, 399.

[68] Case 14/83 *Sabine von Colson and Elisabeth Kamann v Land Nordrhein-Westfalen* EU:C:1984:153, para 26.

[69] Case C-106/89 *Marleasing SA v La Comercial Internacional de Alimentacion SA* EU:C:1990:395, para 8.

[70] See Case C-441/14 *Dansk Industri* EU:C:2016:278, para 31; Case C-397/01 *Pfeiffer and Others* EU:C:2004:584, paras 113–14.

[71] *Smith* (n 35) para 49.

stating that the obligation to disapply the contravening national law only applied in instances involving directives that '[gave] concrete expression to a general principle of [Union] law'.[72] However, even within these confines, the extent to which the interpretative obligation qualifies the *Marshall* doctrine remains ambiguous.

Considered purely from a conceptual point of view, the principle of consistent interpretation is distinct from the doctrine of direct effect. Unlike the latter, the requirement of convergent construction of national law based on a directive does not generate subjective rights for individuals to claim. In this context, a directive is only used as an aid to the interpretation of national law. A national court applies national law, though it is construed according to the relevant provisions of a directive.[73] In contrast, under the doctrine of direct effect, a directive serves as a source of rights that individuals can claim. As such, it can produce a *substitutionary* effect, which, as discussed in Chapter 1, refers to the direct and immediate application of its provisions,[74] whereby individuals derive substantive rights from it instead of a national instrument that either does not exist or does not comply with its provisions.[75] As clarified by AG Léger in *Linster*,[76] for 'the ability to plead [such] substitution', a provision of a directive must confer rights by meeting the thresholds of precision and unconditionality.[77] However, no such requirement exists in the context of the interpretative obligation due to its different conceptual origin. It stems from Union and national law forming a unitary legal order based on a hierarchical structure,[78] where national law consisting of norms of lower rank ought to conform to Union law as norms of higher rank pursuant to the principle of primacy.[79] The duty of convergent construction, therefore, functions as a tool for resolving a clash either between conflicting norms regulating the same matter or between higher-ranking norms that contain the effect of the lower-ranking ones through the choice of possible methods of interpretation.[80]

Regardless of the conceptual distinction between the doctrine of direct effect and the requirement of consistent interpretation, the latter concept, even without generating invocable subjective rights, may still lead to an unexpected

[72] ibid para 48. See Case C-555/07 *Seda Kücükdeveci v Swedex GmbH & Co* EU:C:2010:21; Case C-144/04 *Werner Mangold v Rüdiger Helm* EU:C:2005:709.

[73] Betlem (n 67) 397.

[74] M Dougan, 'When Worlds Collide! Competing Visions of the Relationship between Direct Effect and Supremacy' (2007) 44 *Common Market Law Review* 931, 933.

[75] T Tridimas, 'Black, White, and Shades of Grey: Horizontality of Directives Revisited' (2001) 21 *Yearbook of European Law* 327, 330.

[76] Case C-287/98 *Grand Duchy of Luxembourg v Berthe Linster, Aloyse Linster and Yvonne Linster* EU:C:2000:468.

[77] Opinion of AG Léger in Case C-287/98 *Grand Duchy of Luxembourg v Berthe Linster, Aloyse Linster and Yvonne Linster* EU:C:2000:3, para 58.

[78] Dougan (n 74) 943.

[79] Opinion of Saggio in Joined Cases C-240/98 to C-244/98 *Océano Grupo Editorial and Others* EU:C:1999:620, para 30. See also Tridimas (n 75) 347.

[80] Betlem (n 67) 398.

burden incurred by private parties.[81] In some instances, its implications would not be dissimilar to the outcome that would occur if directives were capable of producing a horizontal direct effect.[82] However, this is not deemed to constitute (at least in theory) a discordance between the duty of consistent interpretation and the *Marshall* precept.[83] In fact, the case law suggests that some collateral obligations imposed on private parties are inevitable due to the fulfilment of convergent interpretation.[84] This is reconciled based on the lexical meaning of the *Marshall* doctrine that 'a directive may not of itself impose obligations on an individual'.[85] As such, any implication on private parties is not attributed to a directive but follows from the consistent construction of national law in light of it to ensure the effectiveness of Union law. Nonetheless, looking beyond the formalism, the reliance on a directive to interpret national law can be detrimental to one of the private parties to proceedings before a national court. What remains uncertain is the degree of collateral impact that is deemed acceptable, considering the conditional nature of the duty of consistent interpretation.

The case law is not very clear on this point. In *Marleasing*, the Court endorsed the duty of consistent interpretation in the context of the action brought by a private party, acting as a creditor, against another private party to have its articles of association declared void for having been created with the sole purpose of defrauding creditors. To this end, it relied on the national law that outlawed contracts lacking a cause or having an illegal cause. This conflicted with the relevant directive that did not envisage such a ground for contractual nullity. The Court found in favour of the defendant. Having first reiterated the duty of consistent interpretation resting on national courts, it held that this obligation precluded the interpretation of national law that would have allowed the nullity of a company to be ordered on the grounds other than those exhaustively laid down in the directive.[86] Although the defendant could not invoke the directive's provisions against the plaintiff, the reliance on them as an aid to the interpretation of national law certainly affected the legal position of the latter party, for it led to the dismissal of its nullity plea.[87] In *Dekker*,[88] a similar exercise led to a collateral effect inflicted on the legal position of a private party. Under the requirement of consistent construction of national law in light of directives, a private employer was held liable for committing sex discrimination, even though its actions did not give rise to civil liability under

[81] S Robin-Olivier, 'The Evolution of Direct Effect in the EU: Stocktaking, Problems, Projections' (2014) 12 *International Journal of Constitutional Law* 165, 179.
[82] Tridimas (n 75) 348.
[83] Craig (n 41) 358.
[84] Tridimas (n 75) 348.
[85] *Marshall* (n 3) para 48.
[86] *Marleasing* (n 69) para 9.
[87] Tridimas (n 75) 348.
[88] Case C-177/88 *Elisabeth Johanna Pacifica Dekker v Stichting Vormingscentrum voor Jong Volwassenen (VJV-Centrum) Plus* EU:C:1990:383;.

national law. The Court found that any conditions or limitations to civil liability stipulated under national law could not be applied since the wording of the relevant directive did not envisage them.[89]

Dekker, read in conjunction with *Marleasing*, suggests that the nature of a collateral effect inflicted on a private party is immaterial to the fulfilment of the duty of consistent interpretation. However, the parameters of this task became obscure in the aftermath of *Arcaro*.[90] In that case, in the context of a criminal proceeding brought against an individual for committing an environmental pollution offence, the national court sought to clarify the method of interpretation of national law without a directive impairing the legal position of an individual. The Court responded by stating that the requirement of convergent construction reached its limits '*where ... an interpretation [led] to the imposition on an individual of an obligation laid down by a directive which [had] not been transposed* or, more especially, where it [had] the effect of determining or aggravating [a criminal liability]' (emphasis added).[91] This finding led to a controversy over the contours of the interpretative duty.[92] In one respect, broadly construed, the language used by the Court in *Ancaro*, and later reiterated in *Kofoed*,[93] appears to impose a substantial limitation on this duty,[94] whereby it ceases to operate whenever it leads to an obligation imposed on an individual pursuant to an unimplemented directive.[95] The proviso added in *Arcaro* can, therefore, be argued to undo much of *Marleasing*[96] or, at the very least, minimise its potency by distinguishing between an actual obligation imposed on an individual and a mere disadvantage or detriment suffered by an individual, with only the latter being allowed.[97] In this way, *Ancaro* is at odds with *Dekker*, which imposed civil liability on a private party.[98]

However, the prevailing view supports the narrow reading of the *Arcaro* proviso. In *Kofoed*, AG Kokott found that a detriment to an individual as a consequence of reading national law in line with Union law did not militate

[89] ibid para 25. See also Case C-180/95 *Nils Draehmpaehl v Urania Immobilienservice OHG* EU:C:1997:208, para 17.

[90] Case C-168/95 *Criminal Proceedings against Luciano Arcaro* EU:C:1996:363.

[91] ibid para 41.

[92] PF Figueroa Regueiro, 'Invocability of Substitution and Invocability of Exclusion: Bringing Legal Realism to the Current Developments of the Case law of "Horizontal" Direct Effect of Directives' (2002) 7 Jean Monnet Working Paper 1, 13.

[93] Case C-321/05 *Hans Markus Kofoed v Skatteministeriet* EU:C:2007:408, para 45.

[94] Opinion of AG Jacobs in Case C-456/98 *Centrosteel v Adipol GmbH* EU:C:2000:137, para 34.

[95] P Craig, 'Directives: Direct Effect, Indirect Effect and the Construction of National Legislation' (1997) 22 *European Law Review* 519, 527.

[96] Tridimas (n 75) 348.

[97] CA Varner, 'The Effectiveness of European Community Law with Specific Regard to Directives: The Critical Step Not Taken by the European Court of Justice' (2001) 22 *Michigan Journal of International Law* 457, 471.

[98] Betlem (n 67) 406.

against the duty of consistent interpretation.[99] Referring to the existing case law,[100] she continued that 'it was lawful, by way of national provisions, that [was] to say, indirectly to apply [Union] law to the detriment of an individual'.[101] AG Jacobs made a similar observation about *Arcaro*. According to him, the proviso added in that case should be interpreted restrictively, given that it was made in the context of a criminal proceeding and was not supported by the previous case law.[102] In his view, while the process of interpretation could not determine or aggravate criminal liability, 'it [might] well lead to the imposition upon an individual of civil liability or a civil obligation which would not otherwise have existed'.[103] This narrow reading found support among other Advocates General. In *Dansk Industri*, AG Bot held that the *Arcaro* limitation should not be extended beyond criminal matters and could not be understood as precluding the interpretation of national law that would impose obligations, including the requirement to pay a severance allowance, on a private employer.[104] For AG Bot, such an obligation would not flow from the fulfilment of the interpretative obligation but 'the provision of national law, expunged of its meaning contrary to Union law'.[105] Even more broadly, AG Bobek pointed out that 'direct effect of a directive [could] be invoked against the State alone and not against private parties … by contrast, conform interpretation [found] no such limitation within the principle itself'.[106] According to him, the interpretative duty applied in the context of private litigation and, excluding criminal matters under *Arcaro*, it '[might] worsen the legal position of an individual'.[107]

Although the Court has not explicitly confirmed the narrow interpretation of the *Arcaro* proviso proffered by the Advocates General, the case law seems to endorse it. In *Oceano Groupo*,[108] the issue related to the compatibility with the right to a legal remedy enshrined in a directive of a contractual clause that conferred jurisdiction to the seller's domicile. Having found this contractual clause to be unfair insofar as it caused, contrary to the requirement of good faith, a significant imbalance in the parties' positions to the detriment of the consumer, the Court also held that '[the duty of consistent interpretation] require[d] the national court to favour the interpretation that would allow it to

[99] Opinion of AG Kokott in Case C-321/05 *Hans Markus Kofoed v Skatteministeriet* EU:C:2007:86, para 65.
[100] *Faccini Dori* (n 3) paras 25–26.
[101] Opinion of AG Kokott in *Kofoed* (n 99) para 65.
[102] Opinion of AG Jacobs in *Centrosteel* (n 94) para 34.
[103] ibid para 35.
[104] Opinion of AG Bot in Case C-441/14 *Dansk Industri (DI), Acting on Behalf of Ajos A/S v Estate of Karsten Eigil Rasmussen* EU:C:2015:776, para 76.
[105] ibid para 78.
[106] Opinion of AG Bobek in Case C-167/17 *Volkmar Kloh v An Bord Pleanála* EU:C:2018:387, para 74.
[107] ibid.
[108] Joined Cases C-240/98 to C-244/98 *Océano Grupo Editorial and Others* EU:C:2000:346.

decline of its own motion the jurisdiction conferred on it by virtue of an unfair term'.[109] While the ruling refers to *Marleasing*, there is no mention of the *Arcaro* proviso, even though it entailed the nullity of the jurisdiction clause enshrined in a contract, thus affecting the legal position of the seller. This can also be observed in *Centrosteel*,[110] where an Italian company sought payment from an Austrian company under a commercial agency contract. The latter refused to make the payment by claiming the invalidity of the contract, since the plaintiff had not been entered into the commercial agency register as required by national law, whereas the relevant directive did not provide such a requirement. The Court confirmed its previous ruling in *Bellone* by finding that the national court was bound to interpret the national law as far as possible in line with the directive, in compliance with the result pursued by it.[111] This applied even though the directive could not in itself impose obligations on individuals.[112] Once again, there was no reference to the *Arcaro* proviso.

Both rulings can be understood to support the narrow construction of the *Arcaro* proviso. While the Court's reasoning did not go beyond reiterating *Marleasing*, the rationale behind it can be discerned from the teleology of the duty of consistent interpretation. From the outset, it is necessary to distinguish between, on the one hand, *Arcaro* and *Kofoed*-type situations that involve the state invoking a provision of a directive against an individual and, on the other hand, *Marleasing*, *Oceano Grupo* and *Centrosteel*-type situations that concern a private party invoking greater rights derived from a directive, which would have been available to it had that directive been timely and properly transformed into national law. The latter factor is what prompts the interpretative duty in the first place.[113] It rectifies such an omission without waiting for the national legislator to do so.[114] As such, two claims for legal certainty are at stake: the claim of the party being denied the rights derived from an unimplemented directive and the claim of the party that relies on the national law that should have been adapted to that directive.[115] The duty of consistent interpretation aims to give effect to the state of law that ought to exist at the expense of that which ought not to. It is not material for the assessment as to whether the outcome is conducive to the legal uncertainty for another private party that finds itself penalised for acting lawfully and in good faith by complying with the applicable national law, the conflict of which with Union law is the failure of national authorities. This, however, is difficult to reconcile with the normative claim for the *Marshall* precept that is rooted in the concern for legal certainty. Such a concern is far greater in the operation of the interpretative duty than it would

[109] ibid para 32.
[110] Case C-456/98 *Centrosteel Srl v Adipol GmbH* EU:C:2000:402.
[111] ibid para 19. See Case C-215/97 *Barbara Bellone v Yokohama SpA* EU:C:1998:189.
[112] ibid para 15.
[113] Craig (n 95) 527.
[114] G de Búrca, 'Giving Effect to European Community Directives' (1992) 55 *Modern Law Review* 215, 233.
[115] Betlem (n 67) 407.

have been if directives were attributed with horizontal direct effect.[116] The former is more burdensome on private parties as they are not in control of the lawfulness of their actions. If an adverse collateral effect inflicted on a private party as a result of the fulfilment of the interpretative duty is acceptable, then, using AG Jacob's words, '[it is not] a valid criticism that enforcing directives directly against individuals would endanger legal certainty'.[117] This is even more the case given that the burden placed on an individual under the interpretative duty is heavier, for its parameters are not framed by the thresholds of precision and unconditionality. It applies to all national rules pre-dating and post-dating a directive and is subject to varying national attitudes to judicial interpretation.[118]

D. Doctrine of Incidental Direct Effect

In *Smith*, having delimited the extent of the interpretative duty by finding that a national rule did not need to be disapplied if it could not be interpreted in line with a directive, the Court also attempted to reconcile this conclusion with the case law on the incidental direct effect of directives. This doctrine refers to the invocation of a directive in a private setting against the contravening national law that incidentally leads to an immediate adverse impact on the legal position of a private party. It provides yet another qualification to the *Marshall* doctrine. Since the concept of incidental direct effect has generated extensive scholarly commentary,[119] it does not warrant an in-depth analysis. Instead, this section focuses on the parameters for the incidental direct effect of directives outlined in *Smith*. The primary aim is to ascertain the extent to which the doctrine of incidental direct effect qualifies the *Marshall* precept. Interestingly, the parameters outlined in *Smith* correspond to the main theoretical approaches proffered to bring the case law on the concept of incidental direct effect into congruence with the orthodox doctrine of directives having no horizontal direct effect.

i. Directives of Varying Nature

Smith can be construed to confine the incidental direct effect to a specific category of directives. The Court, in that case, appeared to confirm the distinction between the general instances of invocation of a directive against the application of the

[116] De Búrca (n 114) 331.

[117] Opinion of AG Jacobs in Case C-316/93 *Nicole Vaneetveld v Le Foyer SA and Le Foyer SA v Fédération des Mutualités Socialistes et Syndicales de la Province de Liège* EU:C:1994:32, para 31.

[118] Craig (n 41) 360–62.

[119] See, eg, M Lenz, 'Horizontal What? Back to Basics' (2000) 25 *European Law Review* 509; S Robin-Olivier, 'The Evolution of Direct Effect in the EU: Stocktaking, Problems, Projections' (2014) 12 *International Journal of Constitutional Law* 165; K Lenaerts and T Corthaut, 'Of Birds and Hedges: The Role of Primacy in Invoking Norms of EU Law' (2006) 31 *European Law Review* 287; M Dougan, 'The "Disguised" Vertical Direct Effect of Directives?' (2000) 59 *Cambridge Law Journal* 586.

contravening national law in a private setting and specific instances of invocation of a directive containing procedural requirements for Member States, against the application of national law incompatible with them.[120] The latter was established in *CIA Security*,[121] where the issue was raised in a tort claim brought by a private company against two private defendants to cease libelling it for unfair trading practices based on the national technical regulations that contravened the procedural rules enshrined in a directive. The Court held that the directive at issue laid down a precise obligation on Member States that individuals could rely on, and its breach constituted 'a procedural defect' rendering the national technical regulations inapplicable and unenforceable against individuals.[122] This finding was confirmed in *Unilever*,[123] which raised a similar issue but in the context of a contractual claim brought by a private company seeking payment for the supply of goods from another private company that refused to pay by claiming non-compliance with the contravening national technical regulations. The Court found that their inapplicability based on the relevant directive could be invoked in the proceedings between private parties. It also acknowledged that directives themselves could not impose obligations on individuals,[124] though it went on to conclude that the relevant directive '[did] not in any way define the substantive scope of the legal rule on the basis of which the national court must decide the case before it' and 'it [created] neither rights nor obligations for individuals'.[125] The Court applied this formula in *Smith* to conclude that the directive on motor vehicle insurance '[defined] the substantive content of a rule of law' and consequently '[could not] be relied on by one individual against another'.[126]

Smith, read in conjunction with *CIA Security* and *Unilever*, supports the approach that defines the parameters of incidental direct effect based on the classification of directives into two categories:[127] first, there are directives that concern Member States' interinstitutional relations with the Union and their exercise of public power; and, second, there are directives that regulate private relationships.[128] The possibility to invoke an unimplemented directive in a private setting, despite any collateral effect inflicted on a private party, only applies to the former category, for it comprises directives that only create obligations for Member States. This does not trigger the question of the horizontal direct effect of directives insofar as the obligations of individuals are concerned.[129] However,

[120] *Smith* (n 35) para 52.
[121] Case C-194/94 *CIA Security International v Signalson and Securitel* EU:C:1996:172.
[122] ibid para 54.
[123] Case C-443/98 *Unilever Italia SpA v Central Food SpA* EU:C:2000:496.
[124] ibid para 50.
[125] ibid para 51.
[126] *Smith* (n 35) para 54.
[127] This finds support in Opinion of AG Jacobs in *Unilever* (n 1) para 79.
[128] Dougan (n 119) 598.
[129] Opinion of AG Elmer in Case C-194/94 *CIA Security International SA v Signalson SA and Securitel SPRL* EU:C:1995:346, para 71.

such a matter arises in the context of the second category of directives since they aim to create rights and duties for individuals. Therefore, insofar as this set of directives is concerned, the denial of the horizontal direct effect of directives stands. The doctrine of the incident direct effect qualifies the *Marshall* doctrine only to the extent that the effectiveness of the provisions of Union law binding Member States is at stake.[130]

While this approach may indeed explain the rationale underlying the Court's standpoint on the invocability of a directive in *Smith* compared to *CIA Security* and *Unilever*, it does not provide a comprehensive normative account of the parameters underlying the incidental direct effect of directives. First, unlike in *Smith*, in *Bellone* for example,[131] the Court affirmed the applicability of a directive despite its scope encompassing actions of individuals.[132] While this line of case law can be subject to different forms of interpretation, it does not fit into the approach built on the categorisation of directives based on their personal and material scope.[133] Second, not all directives can easily be classified into either category. The same directive may contain certain provisions that are aimed at individuals and those that are aimed at national authorities.[134] Finally, the rationale underlying this approach is far from convincing. It is not clear why directives that are designed to reshape private relationships ought not to alter the rights and obligations of individuals, while directives that are only intended for national authorities can produce such an effect.[135]

ii. Substitution/Exclusion Dichotomy

Smith can also be read in line with the dichotomy of substitutionary and exclusionary effects, as discussed in Chapter 1. According to the proponents of this approach, this dichotomy reconciles the *Marshall* precept and the doctrine of the incidental direct effect of directives.[136] This precept prevents directives from producing a substitutionary effect,[137] expressed in its direct and immediate application instead of national law.[138] However, it does not preclude directives, even in a private setting, from causing the disapplication of inconsistent national

[130] See *CIA Security International* (n 121) para 48; *Unilever* (n 123) para 44.

[131] Case C-215/97 *Barbara Bellone and Yokohama SpA* EU:C:1998:189.

[132] ibid para 18. See also Case C-129/94 *Criminal Proceedings against Rafael Ruiz Bernáldez* EU:C:1996:143, para 24; Case C-441/93 *Panagis Pafitis and Others v Trapeza Kentrikis Ellados AE and Others* EU:C:1996:92, para 60.

[133] L Squintani and J Lindeboom, 'The Normative Impact of Invoking Directives: Casting Light on Direct Effect and the Elusive Distinction between Obligations and Mere Adverse Repercussions' (2019) 38 *Yearbook of European Law* 18, 47.

[134] Dashwood (n 33) 98.

[135] Dougan (n 74) 959.

[136] Figueroa Regueiro (n 92) 23.

[137] Dashwood (n 33) 100.

[138] Dougan (n 74) 933.

law.[139] Such an outcome is not meant to create a legal vacuum. When the national law contradicting a directive is excluded, the rights and obligations of private parties are derived from the rest of the national legal system that complies with Union law.[140] As such, any collateral impact inflicted on the legal position of private parties because of the invocation of a directive is considered to stem from the national law that subsists once the inconsistency is excluded. This is construed to align with the wording of the *Marshall* precept that 'directive may not of itself impose obligations on an individual'.[141]

This reasoning provides another rationale for the Court's separation of *Smith* from *CIA Security* and *Unilever*. According to the Court in the latter two rulings, '[the relevant directive], which created neither rights nor obligations for individuals, did not determine *the substantive content of the legal rule* on the basis of which the national court had to decide the case before it' (emphasis added).[142] By comparison, in *Smith*, according to the Court, the directive required motor insurance to cover the personal injury to all passengers, excluding the driver and '[defined] *the substantive content of a rule of law*' (emphasis added).[143] For this reason, it could not be relied upon by a traffic accident victim against a motor insurance provider. On this basis, the factor separating *Smith* from *CIA Security* and *Unilever* appears to be the source of the adverse impact inflicted on a private party. In *CIA Security* and *Unilever*, the invocation of a directive was possible since it merely excluded the contravening national law, leaving the private dispute to be decided according to the subsisting domestic legal framework. However, as explained in the next section, *Smith* also supports a different understanding of the Court's reasoning in these rulings.

Despite the attractiveness of the substitution/exclusion dichotomy as the theoretical construction of the case law,[144] its conceptual and normative characterisation of the parameters underlying the doctrine of incidental direct effect is not without reservations. It is questionable when considered from the standpoint of a private party adversely affected by the invocation of a directive against the conflicting national law. This raises two claims. First, framing the parameters of the incidental direct effect of directives based on this dichotomy seems formalistic.[145] It stems from the parallelism existing between the substitutionary and

[139] Dashwood (n 33)100.
[140] Dougan (n 74) 938.
[141] *Marshall* (n 3) para 48.
[142] *Smith* (n 35) para 53.
[143] ibid para 54.
[144] Support for this dichotomy can be found in Opinion of AG Léger in Case C-287/98 *Linster* EU:C:2000:3, para 57; and Opinion of AG Saggio in Joined Cases C-240/98 to C-244/98 *Océano Grupo* EU:C:1999:620, para 38. However, see its rejection in Opinion of AG Szpunar in Case C-261/20 *Thelen Technopark Berlin GmbH v MN* EU:C:2021:620, para 63.
[145] K Lenaerts, 'Of Birds and Hedges: The Role of Primacy in Invoking Norms of EU Law' (2006) 31 *European Law Review* 287, 305.

exclusionary effects. Both involve resolving a conflict between a directive and the national law incompatible with it, as a result of which the latter is set aside based on the solution prescribed by Union law.[146] From the perspective of a private party adversely affected by this development, it matters very little whether it is conceptualised as a mere 'modification' of the applicable national law or as an imposition of a 'new' provision of Union law.[147] In terms of the burden inflicted on it, there is no difference whether the inconsistent national law is substituted by a directive or by a residual provision of national law that reflects that directive.[148] In either eventuality, it is a directive that effectively mandates the outcome and reshapes the domestic legal system.[149] Second, within the framework of the substitution/exclusion dichotomy, a strong emphasis is placed on identifying the source of the collateral effect inflicted on a private party rather than the implications it entails. The collateral impact caused by the invocation of a directive is solely attributed to the national law that subsists. This aspect becomes apparent in light of the Court's categorisation of the collateral effect into 'direct obligations' and 'mere adverse repercussions', which is discussed below.[150]

iii. Distinction of Obligations and 'Mere Adverse Repercussions'

Smith also defined the parameters of the incidental horizontal direct effect of directives based on the degree of the collateral impact inflicted on a private party. According to this approach, the invocability of a directive in a private setting is contingent on whether its effect materialises in a direct obligation imposed on a private party or causes 'mere adverse repercussions' on its legal position.[151] *Smith* suggests that the *Marshall* doctrine of no horizontal direct effect prevents the invocation of a directive only when it places a direct obligation on a private party. This resonates with how the Court distinguished *Smith* from *CIA Security* and *Unilever* by finding that the directive in the latter two instances could be invoked in a private setting, for it 'created neither rights nor *obligations* for individuals' (emphasis added).[152] While this conclusion, on its own, may appear to reflect the specific 'regulatory' or 'public law' nature of a directive for being concerned with the interinstitutional relationship between Member States and the Union,[153] a different picture emerges if it is viewed in conjunction with *Wells*.[154]

[146] Dougan (n 74) 939.
[147] Craig (n 41) 368.
[148] Dashwood (n 33) 103.
[149] Craig (n 41) 368.
[150] See the distinction drawn in *Wells* (n 42) para 57; *Unilever* (n 123) paras 45–52; Case C-192/94 *El Corte Inglés SA v Cristina Blázquez Rivero* EU:C:1996:88, para 17; *Pfeiffer and Others* (n 70) para 108.
[151] Squintani and Lindeboom (n 133) 39.
[152] *Smith* (n 35) para 53.
[153] Dougan (n 119) 959. See also Dashwood (n 33) 98.
[154] *Wells* (n 42).

In *Wells*, the issue related to the claim brought by an individual challenging the validity of a permit granted to a private undertaking by a public authority without carrying out the environmental impact assessment required by the relevant directive. It was argued that the invocation of the directive in this context would lead to 'inverse direct effect', obliging a Member State, contrary to the *Marshall* doctrine, to deprive a private party of its rights at the request of another party.[155] The Court rejected this proposition. It found that, under the *Marshall* doctrine, 'an individual [might] not rely on a directive against a Member State where it [was] a matter of a State obligation directly linked to the performance of *another obligation* falling, pursuant to that directive, on a third party' (emphasis added).[156] However, referring to *CIA Security* and *Unilever*, the Court then added that '*mere adverse repercussions* on the rights of a third party, even if the repercussions are certain, [did] not justify preventing an individual from invoking the provisions of a directive against the Member State concerned' (emphasis added).[157]

This approach conceptually differs from the substitution/exclusion dichotomy that focuses solely on the source of the collateral impact instead of the implications of invoking a directive on the substance of a private dispute.[158] This is reflected in *Smith*, where the underlying benchmark used to distinguish between 'direct obligations' and 'mere adverse repercussions' appears to be the capacity of a directive '[to] determine the *substantive content of the legal rule on the basis of which the national court [has] to decide the case before it* and consequently create '*obligations* for individuals' (emphasis added).[159] This capacity, albeit formulated differently, is also expressed in *Wells*, where the invocability of a directive was made conditional on its '[direct link] to the performance of [an] *obligation* falling … on a third party' (emphasis added).[160] Thus, the analytical inquiry prompted by both rulings is whether a directive directly impacts the norm to be applied to resolve a private dispute, regardless of whether it is a provision of national law or the relevant directive.[161]

An affirmative answer to this inquiry is likely to trigger the *Marshall* doctrine. This was the case in *Smith*, where the Court denied the possibility for a rear-seat passenger, a victim of a car accident, to claim indemnity for personal injuries from a motor insurance company based on the provisions of an unimplemented directive.[162] This is also evident in *Faccini Dori*,[163] where a consumer, based on

[155] ibid para 55.
[156] ibid para 56.
[157] ibid para 57 (emphasis added). See also Case C-244/12 *Salzburger Flughafen GmbH v Umweltsenat* EU:C:2013:203, paras 46-47; Case C-508/14 *Český telekomunikační úřad v T-Mobile Czech Republic a.s. and Vodafone Czech Republic a.s.* EU:C:2015:657, para 47; Joined Cases C-152/07 to C-154/07 *Arcor and Others*, para 36.
[158] Squintani and Lindeboom (n 133) 51.
[159] *Smith* (n 35) 53.
[160] *Wells* (n 42) para 56.
[161] Squintani and Lindeboom (n 133) 60.
[162] *Smith* (n 35) para 55.
[163] *Faccini Dori* (n 3).

the *Marshall* doctrine, could not directly invoke the right of cancellation provided in the relevant unimplemented directive, instead of national law, to exonerate itself from the liability to pay under the contract agreed with a trader away from business premises.[164] Similarly, in *Pfeiffer*,[165] the *Marshall* doctrine was found to preclude employees from relying directly on the relevant unimplemented directive setting a 48-hour maximum working week instead of national law, to claim reimbursement for their overtime work.[166] In this line of case law, the relevant directive, if successfully invoked, would have governed the substantive issue in the proceedings between private parties (uncompensated victim–insurer, consumer–trader, employee–employer) by bestowing on one party a specific right while imposing a corresponding obligation on another party. This would be difficult to reconcile with the *Marshall* doctrine.

An analogous outcome does not arise in the so-called triangular situations, where the invocation of an unimplemented directive by an individual, despite the collateral effect on another private party, does not trigger the *Marshall* doctrine. The distinguishing factor is that triangular situations involve an additional set of normatively-laden factual circumstances in parallel to the civil proceedings between private parties.[167] Within this framework, a directive invoked by an individual is not deemed to impose an obligation on another party since it does not modify the substantial issue of the private proceedings as such but affects the norm that governs that additional set of factual circumstances. Although the latter may indeed prejudice the position of a private party, this would constitute what the Court defines as 'merely adverse repercussions'.[168] In *CIA Security*, although a tort claim brought by a private company against two private defendants was horizontal in kind, the issue was vertical in substance.[169] The private company could invoke the relevant directive, which met the thresholds of precision and unconditionality, against the application of the contravening national technical standards. However, that directive did not concern the substance of the private dispute over unfair commercial practices. While invoking the directive may have frustrated the defendants' claims as part of those proceedings, they were not confronted with any actual obligation not envisaged by the existing domestic law.

Inasmuch as this approach comes very close to offering a comprehensive account of the case law, an attempt to rationalise the parameters of the indirect horizontal effect of directives in line with the distinction drawn between 'direct obligations' and 'mere adverse repercussions' is not without uncertainty. This dichotomy rests on a rigid separation whereby a directive that impacts the substantive content

[164] ibid para 25.
[165] *Pfeiffer and Others* (n 70).
[166] ibid paras 104–09.
[167] Squintani and Lindeboom (n 133) 54–55.
[168] *Wells* (N 42) para 57.
[169] Dougan (n 119) 602.

of the norm governing a private dispute is to always result in direct obligations imposed on a private party, whilst a directive transforming a different norm is to always lead to 'mere adverse repercussions' inflicted on a private party. Only in the first instance does invoking a directive trigger the *Marshall* doctrine; hence it is prohibited. On the face of it, the dichotomy of 'direct obligations' and 'mere adverse repercussions' centres on the impact of invoking directives. However, this effect-based reasoning appears to be more formulaic than substantive. This is because the nature and degree of the burden placed on a private party due to invoking a directive does not play a role as such.

This is evident when juxtaposing *Faccini Dori* and *Unilever*. Although both concerned a private contract agreed between two parties, a directive could only be invoked in *Unilever*. In this case, unlike *Faccini Dori*, there was no direct obligation imposed on a private party because of the invoked directive affecting the substance of a private dispute. However, contrasting the collateral impact in these rulings reveals that the defendant in *Unilever* suffered as much from the invoked directive as the seller would have done in *Faccini Dori* had the directive been recognised to produce a horizontal direct effect.[170] Although the black letter of the relevant directive did not define the substantive rule applicable to the contractual dispute, it did affect its substance by binding the defendant to the duties not recognised under the existing domestic law.[171] The effect was even more burdensome since the defendant had no control over its legal destiny for not being aware of the Member State's failure to comply with the invoked directive.[172] As pointed out by AG Jacobs, it lost out not because of its own failure to comply with the obligations under Union law but because of the Member State's conduct.[173] Yet, under the present dichotomy, such a detrimental effect would constitute a 'mere adverse repercussion' that cannot prevent an individual from relying on an unimplemented directive against a defaulting Member State.

Considered separately, the verdict in *Unilever* is hardly objectionable as it is vindicated by the need to ensure the effectiveness of Union law.[174] However, what is problematic is the lack of prominence of this principle in *Faccini Dori*, especially where the directive, despite aiming to reshape private relationships, was prevented from having precisely that effect.[175] Instead, it was decided by giving effect to the objective of preserving the specific identity of directives.[176] The difference in the underlying rationale is explained by characterising *Faccini Dori* as concerning a

[170] Tridimas (n 75) 345.

[171] M Dougan, 'Case C-443/98, *Unilever Italia v. Central Food*, Judgment of the Court of Justice of 26 September 2000, [2000] ECR I-7535. Full Court' (2001) 38 *Common Market Law Review* 1503, 1508; R Schütze, 'Direct Effects and Indirect Effects of Union Law' in R Schütze and T Tridimas (eds), *Oxford Principles of European Union Law* (Oxford, Oxford University Press, 2018) 283.

[172] Craig (n 41) 367.

[173] Opinion of AG Jacobs in *Unilever* (n 1) para 101.

[174] For more on this, see Dashwood (n 33) 82.

[175] Dougan (n 74) 959.

[176] Dashwood (n 33) 82.

typical horizontal situation and *Unilever* as involving a 'triangular' situation that raises the vertical direct effect of directives.[177] However, as already argued, given that Member States are the sole addressees of directives, an individual invoking provisions enshrined in them would always raise the issue of vertical direct effect, irrespective of the context in which it is done.[178] For this reason, notwithstanding the substantive scope of the relevant directive, even *Faccini Dori* can technically be construed to form a triangular situation that fits into the extended vertical direct effect framework, whereby the claimant would be deemed to rely on the unimplemented directive against the defaulting Member State and the burden imposed on the defendant seller to cancel the claimant's subscription to a language course would be construed as a 'mere adverse repercussion' not preventing the invocation of the directive.[179] Hence, even if the distinction drawn between 'direct obligations' and 'mere adverse repercussions' may provide an accurate descriptive account of the case law, it remains difficult to square the circle between the doctrine of incidental horizontal direct effect and the *Marshall* precept without disregarding the nature and degree of collateral impact inflicted on a private party.

E. Directives and General Principles of Law

Another matter dealt with by *Smith* is the interplay between directives and general principles of Union law that is generally considered to qualify the *Marshall* doctrine. In response to the referring court's query on the relevance of the *Mangold* line of reasoning to adjudicating the private dispute, the Court found that a directive not giving concrete expression to general principles of law did not oblige national courts to set aside the contravening national law.[180] In one respect, this finding confirms the limited normative capacity of directives in a private setting compared to the general principles of law that can confer rights and obligations on individuals. However, this finding also appears to allude to the intrinsic link between directives that give concrete expression to general principles of law and the horizontal direct effect of the latter source of Union law. It is possible to discern three elements to the interplay between directives and horizontally applicable general principles of law, which can be argued to substantiate the claims of further dilution of the *Marshall* precept.

i. Directives as a Source of General Principles of Law

Directives as instruments of the Union's secondary law form part of the normative landscape from which general principles of law are extrapolated. While the

[177] Squintani and Lindeboom (n 133) 27.
[178] Dougan (n 74) 960.
[179] ibid.
[180] *Smith* (n 35) para 49.

Court is commonly known to 'discover' these norms from 'constitutional traditions common to the Member States'[181] and 'international instruments',[182] it also resorts to inductive reasoning based on the statutory guidance by anchoring the parameters for the recognition of a general principle of law to the framework of the Union's primary and secondary law.[183] In *Fag og Arbejde*,[184] the Court refused to recognise non-discrimination on grounds of obesity as a general principle of law due to the lack of a relevant provision enshrined in the Treaty.[185] In *Jippes*,[186] in turn, the Court found that the protection of animal welfare could not constitute a general principle of law since it did not form part of the objectives of the Treaty, nor was it supported by the Union's secondary law.[187] The latter factor was also reiterated in *Audiolux*, which elaborated upon the applicable criteria.[188] On the one hand, according to the Court, for a legal postulate to constitute a general principle of Union law, it is not sufficient that the Union's secondary law lays down certain provisions related to it; instead, it must be ascertained whether '[the provisions of the Union's secondary law] give any conclusive indications of the existence of such a principle'.[189] On the other hand, the Court's reasoning in *Audiolux* suggests that a general principle of Union law can only be derived from the binding provisions of the Union's secondary law.[190] However, their binding nature may not be sufficient to recognise a general principle of Union law. This follows from *Dominquez*, where the Court, despite finding the binding effect of the entitlement to a paid annual leave, only defined it as 'a particularly important principle of European Union social law'.[191]

ii. Directives as a 'Trigger' for General Principles of Law

Despite lacking the normative capacity to produce a horizontal direct effect, directives nevertheless act as a trigger for the application of general principles of Union law in a private setting. This is because, as discussed in Chapter 1, the field of application of the latter set of norms is confined to areas falling 'within the scope

[181] Case 1/70 *Internationale Handelsgesellschaft mbH v Einfuhr- und Vorratsstelle für Getreide und Futtermittel* EU:C:1970:114, para 4.

[182] Case 4/73 *Nold, Kohlen- und Baustoffgroßhandlung v Commission* EU:C:1974:51, para 13.

[183] See also C Semmelmann, 'General Principles of EU Law: The Ghost in the Platonic Heaven in Need of Conceptual Clarification' (2013) 2 *Pittsburgh Papers on the European Union* 1, 19.

[184] Case C-354/13 *Fag og Arbejde (FOA) v Kommunernes Landsforening* EU:C:2014:2463.

[185] ibid para 40. See also Case C-13/05 *Sonia Chacón Navas v Eurest Colectividades SA* EU:C:2006:456, para 56.

[186] Case C-189/01 *Jippes and Others* EU:C:2001:420.

[187] ibid para 76.

[188] Case C-101/08 *Audiolux SA ea v Groupe Bruxelles Lambert SA (GBL) and Others and Bertelsmann AG and Others* EU:C:2009:626.

[189] ibid para 34.

[190] ibid. According to the Court, even the reference to the term 'general principles' is not sufficient on its own.

[191] Case C-282/10 *Maribel Dominguez v Centre informatique du Centre Ouest Atlantique and Préfet de la région Centre* EU:C:2012:33, para 16.

of Union law' and, as such, they do not apply autonomously but require 'the direct intermediary of some other acts or provisions of Union law' to bring a situation at hand within the ambit of Union law.[192] Directives operate as a trigger for the application of a general principle of law when there is a provision of national law that is either meant to implement them or deals with a matter governed by them. This begs the question of whether a directive can fulfil the same role even in the absence of national law.[193]

There is no clear answer to this in the case law, though one can tentatively draw on two rulings. In one respect, as discussed in Chapter 1, in *HK Danmark v Experian*,[194] the Court applied the principle of non-discrimination on grounds of age to assess the alleged discriminatory treatment arising from the occupation pension scheme stipulated in a private employment contract. Although the Court identified the national legislation implementing Directive 2000/78 the situation also came within the scope of Union law because the occupation pension scheme at hand fell within the scope of that directive.[195] Given the presence of the national implementation measure, one can only speculate whether the latter factor alone would have sufficed to trigger the application of the general principle of non-discrimination on grounds of age. The hesitation is also fuelled by *Audiolux*, where the national court queried about the existence of the general principle of Union law on the equal treatment of shareholders and its applicability to a private relationship. AG Trstenjak concluded that there was no such general principle in Union law, and even if there was one, it could not be invoked against a private party.[196] The Advocate General continued that the latter point was not affected by the *Mangold* line of case law since it only related to situations involving the compatibility of national law with the requirements of Union law.[197] The Court concurred with AG Trstenjak, though without addressing the second query raised by the national court. Thus, neither rulings confirms the capacity of directives to trigger the application of general principles of law in a private setting in the absence of national law, though they also do not necessarily deny it.

iii. Directives as an 'Instantiator' of General Principles of Law

The final element of the interplay of directives and general principles of Union law is expressed in the intrinsic link between them in terms of their substantive scope in a private setting. This is evident in *Kücükdeveci* and *Dansk Industri*,

[192] M Dougan, 'Judicial Review of Member State Action under the General Principles and the Charter: Defining the "Scope of Union Law"' (2015) 52 *Common Market Law Review* 1201, 1202.

[193] E Spaventa, 'The Horizontal Application of Fundamental Rights as General Principles of Union Law' in A Arnull, C Barnard, M Dougan and E Spaventa (eds), *A Constitutional Order of States: Essays in Honour of Alan Dashwood* (Oxford, Hart Publishing, 2011) 204.

[194] Case C-476/11 *HK Danmark Acting on Behalf of Glennie Kristensen v Experian A/S* EU:C:2013:590.

[195] ibid para 22.

[196] Opinion of AG Trstenjak in Case C-101/08 *Audiolux SA ea v Groupe Bruxelles Lambert SA (GBL) and Others and Bertelsmann AG and Others* EU:C:2009:410, para 120.

[197] ibid para 122.

where the Court consistently referred not just to 'the general principle of non-discrimination on grounds of age', but also to that principle 'as given expression in Directive 2000/78'. This can be construed to denote the degree of generality inherent in that principle and, for that matter, most general principles of Union law,[198] which requires further substantiation by the Union's secondary law. The Court explicitly emphasised this in *Audiolux*, where it found that the general principle of equal treatment '[could] not itself rise to a particular obligation' or 'determine the specific situation to which such an obligation [related]' and therefore required 'specific expression'.[199] As further specified in *Dansk Industri*, a directive fulfils this by establishing a more precise framework to facilitate the practical implementation of the general principle of equal treatment and setting various possible exceptions to its scope.[200]

In light of the *Marshall* doctrine, the interplay of general principles of Union law and directives established in the *Mangold* line of reasoning exhibits peculiar dynamics between a horizontally applicable provision of Union law and a horizontally inapplicable one. The problematic aspect lies in the fact that a directive that cannot apply to private relationships produces such an effect through a general principle of law. One can attempt to reconcile this effect with the *Marshall* doctrine by interpreting a general principle of law, rather than a directive, as an actual source of any adverse impact inflicted on an individual.[201] To some extent, this finds support in *Dansk Industri*, where the Court held that 'the scope of the protection conferred by the directive [did] not go beyond that afforded by [the general principle]'.[202] However, this suggests a formalistic construction of their interplay. Even if a general principle of law is the applicable law, it is a directive that informs the substance of it,[203] constituting its practical aspect.[204] The obligations read into a general principle of law are based on the specific provisions enshrined in a directive.[205] The latter norm can, therefore, be construed to serve as a de facto standard of review,[206] which stands at odds with the *Marshall* doctrine,[207] for it poses a risk to legal certainty in a private setting.[208]

[198] J Bengoetxea, 'General Legal Principles Navigating Space and Time' in U Bernitz, X Groussot and F Schulyok (eds), *General Principles of EU Law and European Private Law* (Alphen aan den Rijn, Kluwer, 2013) 48.

[199] *Audiolux* (n 188) paras 57–58.

[200] *Dansk Industri* (n 70) para 23.

[201] Craig (n 41) 373.

[202] *Dansk Industri* (n 70) para 23.

[203] E Muir, 'Of Ages in – and Edges of – EU Law' 48 (2011) *Common Market Law Review* 39, 57.

[204] Opinion of AG Maduro in Case C-303/06 *S Coleman v Attridge Law and Steve Law* EU:C:2008:61, para 8.

[205] Craig (n 41) 373.

[206] M de Mol, 'The Novel Approach of The CJEU on the Horizontal Direct Effect of the EU Principle of Non-discrimination: (Unbridled) Expansionism of EU Law?' (2011) 18 *Maastricht Journal of European and Comparative Law* 109, 126.

[207] Opinion of AG Mazák in Case 411/05 *Félix Palacios de la Villa v Cortefiel Servicios SA* EU:C:2007:106, para 130.

[208] Opinion of AG Sharpston in Case C-427/06 *Birgit Bartsch v Bosch und Siemens Hausgeräte (BSH) Altersfürsorge GmbH* EU:C:2008:297, para 31.

III. Interim Conclusion

In sum, considerable uncertainty lingers over the legal impact of directives in private relations. It stems from the complexity of qualifications and exceptions attached to the *Marshall* doctrine. First, directives are enforceable against a private body or organisation classed as an emanation of the state so long as it is subject to state control or performs public tasks based on special powers. Second, an additional burden can be inflicted on a private party from the fulfilment by national courts of their duty of harmonious interpretation of national law in line with directives. Third, adverse collateral impact on a private party can occur when directives are invoked against the application of the contravening national law. Lastly, the impact on private relations cannot be excluded when directives operate as a trigger for the application of general principles of Union law. The main challenge posed by these qualifications and exceptions lies in the difficulty of squaring the circle between the *Marshall* doctrine and the invocation of directives via additional judicial avenues that can undoubtedly lead to obligations imposed on private parties. Paradoxically, the Court justifies the *Marshall* doctrine by the need to ensure legal certainty in private relationships, though this concern hardly informs the set of qualifications and exceptions attached to it.

5

Coexistence and Intersection*

The European Union is based on a free market economy, which implies that undertakings must have the freedom to conduct their business as they see fit.[1]

The Union's legal system builds on two expressions of the ideals of private autonomy. First, these ideals are manifested in fundamental economic rights that are recognised *qua* general principles of Union Law and are enshrined in the Charter. Second, they are embodied in the Treaty's free movement and competition rules and the Union's secondary law that complements them. These sets of provisions generate two-dimensional interaction reflecting their intrinsically linked yet distinct normative structures. In one respect, there is a degree of convergence between them that implies their coexistence in a symbiotic relationship. Given the difference in their scope of application, this warrants a clear framework that sets out the parameters of their coexistence and complementarity. At the same time, despite the degree of overlap between them, fundamental economic rights and the Treaty's free movement and competition rules substantially diverge. They are vested with distinctive normative purposes, which demand limiting their respective spheres of application.

I. Normative Convergence

The normative convergence of the Treaty's free movement and competition rules with fundamental economic rights is expressed in their functional correlation. These provisions form the core of the economic constitution of the Union, for they operate as an essential catalyst for the dynamism of private economic initiatives across national borders.[2] They guarantee market freedom understood as the right

* This chapter draws on R Babayev, 'Private Autonomy at Union Level: On Art 16 CFREU and Free Movement Rights' (2016) 53 *Common Market Law Review* 979; R Babayev, 'Duality of Economic Freedom Protection in the Interplay of Article 16 CFR and Article 102 TFEU' (2020) 45 *European Law Review* 693.

[1] Opinion of AG Wahl in Case C-201/15 *Anonymi Geniki Etairia Tsimenton Iraklis (AGET Iraklis)* EU:C:2016:429, para 1.

[2] P-C Müller-Graff, 'Basic Freedoms: Extending Party Autonomy across Borders' in S Grundmann, W Kerber and S Weatherill (eds), *Party Autonomy and the Role of Information in the Internal Market* (Berlin, De Gruyter, 2001) 133.

to initiate and participate in the interstate process of competition, untrammelled by disproportionate national regulations and destructive strategies of private actors with unilateral or combined market power. Whether providing goods and services, taking up employment or self-employment, or channelling investments in the internal market, each process naturally entails the exercise of individual autonomy of economic action. Clear parallels, therefore, exist between fundamental economic rights and the Treaty's free movement and competition rules. However, the contours and perimeters of their symbiotic coexistence are ill-defined and require clarification.

A. The Interplay of Fundamental Economic Rights and Fundamental Freedoms

The exercise of the freedoms of movement is intrinsically intertwined with the exercise of fundamental economic rights protected at the Union level.[3] Articles 49 and 56 TFEU apply to any form of engagement in economic activity. It is defined as 'any activity consisting in offering goods and services on a given market',[4] which is exercised in conformity with 'normal market conditions'[5] and is not 'provided for nothing',[6] though it does not need to generate a profit.[7] Analogous economic considerations are prevalent in the context of goods and capital but with a caveat. Although the definition of 'goods' carries a strong economic connotation,[8] Articles 34 and 35 TFEU apply 'irrespective of whether the goods concerned are being transported across borders for sale or resale, or rather for personal use or consumption'.[9] These provisions are triggered whenever the exercise by a proprietor of the right to use and dispose of possession has a cross-border dimension. This equally extends to Article 63 TFEU, within the framework of which the Court tends to focus more on the capital than on its owner or holder,[10] with no specific individual requirements to meet.[11]

[3] G Comparato and H-W Micklitz, 'Regulated Autonomy between Market Freedoms and Fundamental Rights in the Case Law of the CJEU' in U Bernitz, X Groussot and F Schulyok (eds), *General Principles of EU Law and European Private Law* (Alphen aan den Rijn, Kluwer Law International 2013) 122.

[4] Joined Cases C-180/98 to C-184/98 *Pavel Pavlov and Others v Stichting Pensioenfonds Medische Specialisten* EU:C:2000:428, para 75.

[5] Opinion of AG Jacobs in Case 344/87 *I. Bettray v Staatssecretaris van Justitie I Bettray v Staatssecretaris van Justitie* EU:C:1989:113, para 32.

[6] Case C-179/14 *Commission v Hungary* EU:C:2016:108, para 154.

[7] Case C-301/14 *Pfotenhilfe-Ungarn eV v Ministerium für Energiewende* EU:C:2015:589, para 48; Case C-281/06 *Hans-Dieter Jundt and Hedwig Jundt v Finanzamt Offenburg* EU:C:2007:816, para 33.

[8] Case C-299/19 *Techbau SpA v Azienda Sanitaria Locale AL* EU:C:2020:937, para 51.

[9] Case C-267/16 *Albert Buhagiar and Others v Minister for Justice* EU:C:2018:26, para 67. See also Case C-18/88 *Régie des télégraphes et des téléphones v GB-Inno-BM SA* EU:C:1991:474, para 8; Case 215/87 *Heinz Schumacher v Hauptzollamt Frankfurt am Main-Ost* EU:C:1989:111, para 22.

[10] Case C-326/07 *Commission v Italy* EU:C:2009:193, para 35.

[11] C Barnard, *The Substantive Law of the EU: The Four Freedoms*, 5th edn (Oxford, Oxford University Press, 2016) 523.

Given this inherent link, the immediate question is how the freedoms of movement and fundamental economic rights coexist from a normative standpoint. Contrasting perspectives have been put forward at a conceptual level. Some contend that the freedoms of movement operate as a means to extend across internal frontiers of Member States the realm of subjective autonomy and private initiative traditionally protected by fundamental economic rights.[12] Others, however, construe the freedoms of movement as conceptually and normatively distinct,[13] for they do not embody or guarantee fundamental economic rights.[14] The crux of the query in this context lies in the extent to which the functional convergence between the freedoms of movement and fundamental economic rights translates into the overlap in their normative scope. The case law reveals several phases in the evolution of the intersection between these sets of provisions that can be stratified into three stages.

i. Stage 1: Separate Spheres of Application

At the outset, the outer boundaries of fundamental economic rights recognised *qua* general principles of Union law were not fully unlocked. As discussed in Chapter 1, the genesis of these normative provisions can be traced back to the system of economic dirigisme introduced for the establishment and functioning of the internal market. Consequently, their sphere of application remained confined to the then Community's policy enactment without necessarily extending to Member States.[15] Support for this understanding flowed from *Cinéthèque*,[16] where the Court refused to review the compliance with fundamental rights of the national measure that prohibited the sale and marketing of cinematographic works in the form of videocassettes during the year they were being shown in the cinemas. The claimants challenged this measure on two accounts for its incompatibility with Article 34 TFEU and the freedom of expression enshrined in the ECHR. The Court, first, found that the measure created 'barriers to intra-Union trade in videocassettes because of the disparities between the systems operated in the different Member States and between the conditions for the release of cinematographic works in the cinemas of those States'.[17] However, in the Court's view,

[12] See, eg, S Grundmann, 'Information, Party Autonomy and Economic Agents in European Contract Law' (2002) 39 *Common Market Law Review* 269, 270; Müller-Graff (n 2) 133.

[13] See, eg, G Davies 'Freedom of Movement, Horizontal Effect, and Freedom of Contract' (2012) 2 *European Review of Private Law* 805, 810.

[14] See, eg, JW Rutgers, 'The European Economic Constitution, Freedom of Contract and the DCFR' (2009) 5 *European Review of Contract Law* 95, 95.

[15] D Chalmers, 'Looking Back at ERT and its Contribution to the EU Fundamental Rights Agenda' in L Azoulai and L Poiares Pessoa Maduro (eds), *The Past and Future of EU Law: The Classics of EU Law Revisited on the 50th Anniversary of the Rome Treaty* (Oxford, Hart Publishing, 2010) 140.

[16] Joined Cases 60 and 61/84 *Cinéthèque SA and Others v Fédération nationale des cinémas français* EU:C:1985:329.

[17] ibid para 22.

such a restriction was justified by the need to encourage the creation of cinematographic works irrespective of their origin.[18] The Court refused to address the second claim. It held that 'although it [was] true that it [was] the duty of this Court to ensure observance of fundamental rights in the field of [Union] law, it [had] no power to examine the compatibility with [the ECHR] of national legislation which [concerned], as in this case, an area which [fell] within the jurisdiction of the national legislator'.[19]

Viewed solely on its own merits, *Cinéthèque* could be read in two overlapping ways. On the one hand, it appeared to endorse a decentralised system for the enforcement of fundamental rights protection in the Union. This would imply a division of competence between the Court and national courts whereby only the latter would be responsible for reviewing national law for its compliance with fundamental rights. On the other hand, it suggested that fundamental economic rights, and fundamental rights in general, recognised as general principles of Union law did not intersect with the freedoms of movement. This is because only against the latter norms was the Court prepared to test the consonance of national measures in the internal market context. If they did not constitute a restriction of the freedoms of movement or were exculpated according to available derogations, either outcome would signal the limits to Union law.[20]

ii. Stage 2: ERT*: General Principles and the Charter*

The *Cinéthèque* dictum, at least in the understanding mentioned above, was short-lived. The Court reformulated its approach in *ERT*,[21] which, together with *Wachauf*,[22] widened the projection of the Union's system of fundamental rights protection to national law.[23] As is well known, while *Wachauf* employed the language of constraint on national *implementing* measures, *ERT* extended fundamental rights to national measures *derogating* from the Treaty's free movement provisions. This added a new dimension to the coexistence and interplay of fundamental economic rights and the freedoms of movement.

The issue in *ERT* concerned the compatibility of a national television monopoly with the Treaty's free movement provisions and the freedom of expression

[18] ibid para 23.

[19] ibid para 26. See also Case 12/86 *Meryem Demirel v Stadt Schwäbisch Gmünd* EU:C:1987:400, para 28.

[20] This view was endorsed by AG Jacobs writing extra-judicially. See FG Jacobs, 'Human Rights in the European Union: The Role of the Court of Justice' (2001) 26 *European Law Review* 331, 337. See also Lord Goldsmith, 'A Charter of Rights, Freedoms and Principles' (2001) 38 *Common Market Law Review* 1201, 1205.

[21] Case C-260/89 *Elliniki Radiophonia Tiléorassi AE (ERT) and Panellinia Omospondia Syllogon Prossopikou v Dimotiki Etairia Pliroforissis and Sotirios Kouvelas and Nicolaos Avdellas and Others* EU:C:1991:254.

[22] Case 5/88 *Hubert Wachauf v Bundesamt für Ernährung und Forstwirtschaft* EU:C:1989:321.

[23] PC Villalón, '"All the Guidance", *ERT* and *Wachauf*' in Azoulai and Poiares Pessoa Maduro (n 15) 163.

proclaimed in the ECHR. In this opinion, AG Lenz did not deem it necessary to consider the latter claim. Based on the *Cinéthèque* dictum, he held that 'it [was] not primarily the Court … which [was] called upon to judge alleged or actual infringements by the Member States of the human rights protected by that Convention … [and] in particular, it [did] not fall to the Court to examine the compatibility of the rules of the Member States with the Convention on Human Rights'.[24] However, the Court took a different view by reaching a verdict opposite to that decided in *Cinéthèque*. It first reiterated that 'it had no power to examine the compatibility with the ECHR of national rules which [did] not fall within the scope of Union law'.[25] Yet, according to the Court, this was not the case whenever a Member State resorted to Treaty-based derogations to justify a national measure restricting the freedoms of movement. Such justification 'must be interpreted in the light of the general principles of law and in particular of fundamental rights', denoting that a national rule could fall under the exceptions provided in the Treaty 'only if they are compatible with the fundamental rights the observance of which is ensured by the Court'.[26]

At first, the Court's rationale to distinguish *ERT* from *Cinéthèque* appeared to lie in their technical difference.[27] While *Cinéthèque* concerned an indistinctly applicable measure that fell outside the scope of Union law, *ERT* involved a discriminatory measure that fell within the scope of Union law since its justification was based on the explicit derogation contained in the Treaty. However, in *Familiapress*,[28] the Court affirmed the *ERT* doctrine in the context of the justification of a national measure under mandatory requirements,[29] effectively proclaiming the reversal of the *Cinéthèque* dictum. The normative reach of fundamental rights recognised *qua* general principles of law is replicated within the framework of the Charter. Before acquiring a legally binding force, it was not clear whether the Charter incorporated the *ERT* doctrine.[30] The source of uncertainty stemmed from the fact that the *ERT* doctrine did not explicitly find its way into the wording of the Charter. As is well known, Article 51 CFR limits the scope of the Charter to 'Member States only when they are implementing Union law', though the Explanations to the Charter refer to Member States' obligation to respect fundamental rights 'when they act in the scope of Union law' by specifically citing *ERT*. The clarification to this conundrum followed

[24] Opinion of AG Lenz in Case C-260/89 *ERT* EU:C:1991:26, para 50.

[25] *ERT* (n 21) para 42.

[26] ibid para 43.

[27] J Snell, 'Fundamental Rights Review of National Measures: Nothing New under the Charter?' (2015) 21 *European Public Law* 285, 289.

[28] Case C-368/95 *Vereinigte Familiapress Zeitungsverlags- und vertriebs GmbH v Heinrich Bauer Verlag* EU:C:1997:325.

[29] ibid para 24.

[30] See, eg, PM Huber, 'The Unitary Effect of the Community's Fundamental Rights: The *ERT*-Doctrine Needs to Be Reviewed' (2008) 14 *European Public Law* 323, 331–32.

from *Pfleger*,[31] where the Court confirmed the *ERT* doctrine and found that 'the use by a Member State of exceptions provided for by EU law in order to justify an obstruction of a fundamental freedom guaranteed by the Treaty must … be regarded … as "implementing Union law" within the meaning of Article 51(1) of the Charter'.[32]

ERT extended the normative remit of fundamental rights within the Union's legal order. While before, they exclusively operated as judicial constraints on the Community/Union policy-making, including their national implementation, in *ERT*, they came to be applied by the Court as norms setting out the parameters of national law.[33] This development added a level of intricacy and complexity to what initially was mere abstract normative parallelism between the Treaty's free movement provisions and fundamental economic rights recognised *qua* general principles of law and enshrined in the Charter. The *ERT* doctrine aligned their respective spheres of application to the point that a national measure compromising a cross-border economic activity in breach of the freedoms of movement is exculpated only if it can be shown to comply with fundamental economic rights. Therefore, both sets of provisions can concurrently apply to the impugned national law, which, as a result, becomes subject to scrutiny against two normative standards. The immediate question in this context is how such a double review system aligns with the allocation of competence between the Union and Member States. Notwithstanding what the supplementary application of fundamental economic rights to the national measures derogating from the Treaty may suggest,[34] it is difficult to argue that the double review system transforms the remit of the Union's supervision over the traditional areas of national competence. This stems from the parameters of restriction and justification tests set out in the case law.

In *ERT* situations, the judicial review based on fundamental economic rights is constrictive in its form. There are two facets to it. First, the Court's approach reflects the conceptual parallelism between fundamental economic rights and the freedoms of movement. As pointed out earlier, while they do not necessarily fuse, both sets of provisions nonetheless give effect to the ideals of private autonomy. A restriction of the freedoms of movement equally compromises the freedom to conduct business, the right to property or the freedom to choose an occupation.[35] Conversely, a constraint of the latter three norms can also limit the exercise of freedoms of movement.[36] Hence, against the growing tendency of national courts to seek to ascertain the compatibility of national measures with the Charter alongside the freedoms of movement, the Court generally favours following a restrictive approach. There are instances where the Court

[31] Case C-390/12 *Robert Pfleger and Others* EU:C:2014:281.

[32] ibid para 36.

[33] Villalón (n 23) 163.

[34] For criticism of the rationale behind the *ERT* doctrine, see, eg, J Coppell and A O'Neill, 'The European Court of Justice: Taking Rights Seriously?' (1992) 29 *Common Market Law Review* 689.

[35] See, eg, *Robert Pfleger and Others* (n 31) para 60.

[36] See, eg, Case C-518/06 *Commission v Italy* EU:C:2009:270, para 66.

found no need to conduct scrutiny of national measures for compliance with fundamental economic rights under the Charter for their normative convergence with the freedoms of movement. In *Sokoll-Seebacher*,[37] a national court specifically enquired whether Article 16 CFR and Article 49 TFEU precluded the national rule that did not lay down sufficiently precise criteria for opening a new pharmacy. The Court limited its assessment solely to Article 49 TFEU. It held that the specific reference to 'Union law' in the wording of Article 16 CFR must be understood as meaning that this provision referred to Article 49 TFEU and, as such, the impugned national measure should be assessed under the latter Treaty provision alone.[38] Similarly, in *Gardella*,[39] the Court opted not to apply Article 15 CFR by focusing on Article 52(2) CFR and confirming that Article 15(2) CFR itself reiterated inter alia the free movement of workers guaranteed by Article 45 TFEU.[40] Along the same lines, in *AV*,[41] the Court defined Articles 15 and 16 CFR as provisions recognising 'rights that [were] the subject of provisions in the EU Treaties – that [was] to say … Article 49 TFEU – [as such] those rights must be exercised, in accordance with Article 52(2) of the Charter, "under the conditions and within the limits defined by those Treaties"'.[42]

In instances of possible infringements of fundamental economic rights, the Court also tends to confine itself to merely confirming by analogy the outcome of the review of the impugned national measure against the Treaty's free movement provisions. In *Berlington Hungary*,[43] it held that '[a national rule that was] restrictive from the point of view of Article 56 TFEU [was] also capable of limiting the right to property enshrined in Article 17 of the Charter'.[44] In *PI*,[45] in turn, the closure of commercial premises without authorisation that constituted a restriction of Article 49 TFEU was also found to entail a limitation of the freedom to conduct business enshrined in Article 16 CFR.[46] Hence, given their normative overlaps, a separate examination of whether an impugned national law infringes a fundamental economic right seems unwarranted. Indeed, in *Global Starnet*,[47] the Court held that 'examination of the restriction represented by national legislation from the point of view of Articles 49 and 56 TFEU also cover[ed] possible limitations of the exercise of the rights and freedoms laid down in Articles 15 to 17 of the Charter so that a separate examination of the

[37] Case C-367/12 *Susanne Sokoll-Seebacher* EU:C:2014:68.

[38] ibid paras 21–23.

[39] Case C-233/12 *Simone Gardella v Istituto nazionale della previdenza sociale (INPS)* EU:C:2013:449.

[40] ibid para 39. See also Case C-284/15 *Office national de l'emploi (ONEm) v* EU:C:2016:220, para 33.

[41] Case C-465/18 *AV and BU v Comune di Bernareggio* EU:C:2019:1125.

[42] ibid para 29.

[43] Case C-98/14 *Berlington Hungary Tanácsadó és Szolgáltató kft and Others v Magyar Állam* EU:C:2015:386.

[44] ibid para 90.

[45] Case C-348/09 *PI v Oberbürgermeisterin der Stadt Remscheid* EU:C:2012:300.

[46] ibid para 65.

[47] Case C-322/16 *Global Starnet Ltd v Ministero dell'Economia e delle Finanze and Amministrazione Autonoma Monopoli di Stato* EU:C:2017:985.

freedom to conduct a business [was] not necessary'.[48] Generally, in neither of the existing *ERT* rulings, strictly considered, did the Court seem to face an issue that could not have been resolved solely according to the review based on free movement law if not for the reference to fundamental economic rights made by either a national court or the Commission.

Second, the parameters of the *ERT*-type application of fundamental economic rights are also framed by the scope of possible exemptions attributed to these rights. Much like the freedoms of movement, the guarantee of fundamental economic rights is not unfettered. Both sets of norms envisage legitimate forms of interference in the general interest. Besides, due to the normative overlaps between them, there is a clear convergence of public interest grounds capable of justifying a restriction of either form of individual entitlement. Therefore, in most *ERT* situations, the Court tends to either subject an impugned national law to the justification test based on the combined reading of Article 52 CFR and the established derogations to free movement law or extend by analogy the outcome of the latter exercise to Article 52 CFR.[49] In *AGET Iraklis*,[50] the Court considered whether the national framework of collective redundancies, which restricted the freedom of establishment and the freedom to conduct business, was capable of being justified on the grounds of employee protection.[51] In *Berlington Hungary*, in turn, the Court merely found that 'an unjustified or disproportionate restriction of the freedom to provide services under Article 56 TFEU [was] also not permitted under Article 52(1) of the Charter, in relation to Article 17 thereof'.[52]

However, the apparent convergence of public interest grounds capable of justifying a restriction of fundamental economic rights and the freedoms of movement comes with a caveat. It is well documented that the Court applies a strict interpretation of derogations from free movement law, at least when dealing with Member States invoking the express derogations enshrined in the Treaty.[53] Compared to this practice, the exercise of fundamental economic rights, regardless of whether they are recognised *qua* general principles of law or enshrined in the Charter, is subject to a wide set of limitations. This is particularly evident in the context of the freedom to engage in economic activity. Before the Charter's adoption, the standard formula followed by the Court was that this freedom protected as a general

[48] ibid para 50, See also Joined Cases C-407/19 and C-471/19 *Katoen Natie Bulk Terminals NV and General Services Antwerp NV v Belgische Staat and Middlegate Europe NV v Ministerraad* EU:C:2021:107, para 56.

[49] See, eg, Joined Cases C-52/16 and C-113/16 *'SEGRO' Kft v Vas Megyei Kormányhivatal Sárvári Járási Földhivatala* EU:C:2018:157, para 128.

[50] Case C-201/15 *Anonymi Geniki Etairia Tsimenton Iraklis (AGET Iraklis)* EU:C:2016:972.

[51] ibid para 79. See also *PI* (n 45) para 81.

[52] *Berlington Hungary* (n 43) para 90.

[53] See, eg, Case 72/83 *Campus Oil Ltd and Others v Minister for Industry and Energy and Others* EU:C:1984:256, para 37; Case C-337/06 *Bayerischer Rundfunk and Others v GEWA – Gesellschaft für Gebäudereinigung und Wartung mbH* EU:C:2007:786, para 64; Case C-47/02 *Albert Anker, Klaas Ras and Albertus Snoek v Bundesrepublik Deutschland* EU:C:2003:516, para 60.

principle of Union law, 'far from constituting an unfettered prerogative, must be viewed in the light of the social function of the activities protected thereunder'.[54] Its recognition in the Charter, in turn, explicitly subjects it to 'Union law and national laws and practices', based on which the Court narrowly construes its normative boundaries. In *Sky Österreich*,[55] the Court found that 'the freedom to conduct a business [might] be subject to a broad range of interventions on the part of public authorities which [might] limit the exercise of economic activity in the public interest'.[56] The apparent dissonance in the breadth of possible derogations from fundamental economic rights and the freedoms of movement implies divergent parameters of scrutiny. If a national measure is exculpated pursuant to fundamental economic rights, it may not necessarily be so under the freedoms of movement. Conversely, if it is exculpated based on the derogations to the freedoms of movement, this would also hold true in the context of fundamental economic rights, rendering any further review all but redundant.

iii. Stage 3: The Independent Application of Fundamental Economic Rights

In *ERT* situations, the scope of free movement law can be understood to delimit the breadth of the Union's supervision of national policy choices based on fundamental economic rights. It is the legitimisation of an infringement of the Treaty that triggers and frames the assessment of conformity of an impugned national measure with those rights. Consequently, although the *ERT* doctrine aligned the sphere of application of fundamental rights with that of the Treaty's free movement provisions, it did not attribute an independent value to the review pursuant to them. However, such a construction of the *ERT* doctrine has come under question with the recent ruling in *Commission v Hungary* that marks the third stage in the evolution of the intersection between the Treaty's free movement provisions and fundamental economic rights.[57] The issue, in that case, arose from the infringement action brought for the first time by the Commission against Hungary for the failure to comply with the Charter by enacting the legislation that extinguished the rights of usufruct over agricultural land created by contract between any individuals except close family members. The significance of this proceeding did not lie in the impugned national law as such since the Court in *SEGRO* already declared it to be incompatible with the Treaty.[58] Instead, as

[54] Case 44/79 *Liselotte Hauer v Land Rheinland-Pfalz* EU:C:1979:290, para 7. See also Case 265/87 *Hermann Schräder HS Kraftfutter GmbH & Co KG v Hauptzollamt Gronau* EU:C:1989:303, para 15; Case C-177/90 *Ralf-Herbert Kühn v Landwirtschaftskammer Weser-Ems* EU:C:1992:2, paras 16 and 17.

[55] Case C-283/11 *Sky Österreich GmbH v Österreichischer Rundfunk* EU:C:2013:28.

[56] ibid para 46.

[57] Case C-235/17 *Commission v Hungary* EU:C:2019:432.

[58] '*SEGRO*' (n 49) para 94.

AG Saugmandsgaard Øe pointed out, it stems from the fact that the Commission sought a separate examination of the possible infringement of Article 17 CFR.[59] This raised a constitutional query of whether an independent fundamental rights review aligns with the allocation of competence between the Union and Member States laid down in the Treaty and what implications this normative development ultimately poses.

a. The AG's Opinion and the Court's Ruling

According to the Commission's submission, the need for separate assessment under Article 17 CFR lay in the broader scope of this provision compared to the freedoms of movement. Against this premise, the response of the Court can be construed in two ways. In one respect, the Court did not seem to endorse the Commission's claim since it reviewed the compatibility of the impugned national law solely within the periphery of the *ERT* doctrine. The Court first found that the extinguishment of rights to usufruct over agricultural land lawfully acquired by nationals of Member States other than Hungary restricted, because of its very subject matter, the right of the persons concerned under Article 63 TFEU. The Court then proceeded to establish whether the contested national law could be justified by overriding and proportionate reasons and, as part of that, according to *ERT*, whether it complied with fundamental rights, particularly Article 17 CFR. However, viewed from a different angle, the approach taken by the Court conveys a different narrative that does not necessarily diverge from the Commission's characterisation of the ultimate remit of the fundamental rights review via the *ERT* route. As formulated by AG Saugmandsgaard Øe, the Commission's submission rested on the idea of restrictions on the freedoms of movement acting as a 'gateway' to the field of application of the Charter by triggering the scope of Union law, based on which the Court acquires jurisdiction to conduct an independent fundamental rights review.[60] Two overlapping factors in the Court's reasoning appear to reflect this approach.

First, as mentioned earlier, the compatibility of the impugned national law raised in *Commission v Hungary* had already been addressed in the previous case law. The factual circumstances in that ruling did not in any way differ from those concerned in *SEGRO*. Yet, despite the lack of a new substantive reason warranting a fresh assessment on its merits, the Court felt the need to undertake one. It did so by merely reiterating, in a rather lengthy way, the reasoning and finding provided in *SEGRO* that the contested national law breached Article 63 TFEU and rejected the same grounds for justification submitted by the Hungarian government therein.[61] Second, much like *Commission v Hungary*, *SEGRO* already raised

[59] Opinion of AG Saugmandsgaard Øe in Case C-235/17 *Commission v Hungary* EU:C:2018:971, para 75.
[60] ibid para 98.
[61] *Commission v Hungary* (n 57) para 58.

the question of the conformity of the impugned national law with Article 17 CFR, though it met with a different response from the Court. In that case, having dismissed the submitted grounds for justification and having acknowledged the lack of compensation for the total loss of rights of usufruct,[62] the Court saw no necessity for further examination under the Charter.[63] This stands in stark contrast to *Commission v Hungary*, which also provides the assessment of whether the extinguishment of usufruct rights constituted the deprivation of possession within the meaning of Article 17 CFR and whether it was objectively justified, albeit with a reference to the same grounds considered under Article 63 TFEU.[64] Thus, although the contested national law was twice found to constitute an unjustified restriction of Article 63 TFEU, the Court still found the need to examine the existence of an infringement of Article 17 CFR, thereby transcending the *ERT* framework.

In *Commission v Hungary*, the Court did not follow the advice of AG Saugmandsgaard Øe, who argued against the separate examination of the impugned national law under Article 17 CFR. In AG Saugmandsgaard Øe's view, doubts over such a fundamental rights review are rooted in the intention of the Charter's drafters. Already in *SEGRO*, he argued that the exclusion of the applicability of the Charter in the present context followed from the very wording of Article 51(1) CFR,[65] under which for the Charter's provisions to apply to national measures, the latter must fall within the scope of Union law.[66] According to AG Saugmandsgaard Øe, in circumstances when the scope of Union law is triggered solely because of a restriction of the freedoms of movement, fundamental rights may only be relied on via either the *Schmidberger* route,[67] 'where [these] rights are called on to serve as a shield in order to defend the legislation concerned', or the *ERT* route, 'where [these] rights cause the loss of a shield raised in order to defend the legislation concerned'.[68] While both routes concern the existence of justification, in the former instance, a fundamental right is sought to support the justification ground submitted by a Member State, whereas, in the latter instance, it operates as a means to reject the justification ground relied on by a Member State. For AG Saugmandsgaard Øe, in the *ERT* route, 'fundamental rights are applied not independently, but in the context of the justification of a restriction of the freedoms of movement'.[69] Otherwise, as the Advocate General observed, it would run counter to Article 51(2) CFR, which stipulates that 'the Charter does not extend

[62] '*SEGRO*' (n 49) para 91.

[63] ibid para 128.

[64] *Commission v Hungary* (n 57) paras 67–89 and 123–29.

[65] Opinion of AG Saugmandsgaard Øe in Joined Cases C-52/16 and C-113/16 *'SEGRO' Kft v Vas Megyei Kormányhivatal Sárvári Járási Földhivatala* EU:C:2017:410, para 138.

[66] Case C-617/10 *Åklagaren v Hans Åkerberg Fransson* EU:C:2013:105, para 21.

[67] Case C-112/00 *Eugen Schmidberger, Internationale Transporte und Planzüge v Republik Österreich* EU:C:2003:333, paras 69–79. In this case, the Austrian government relied on the protection of rights to freedom of expression and freedom of assembly to justify a restriction of the free movement of goods caused by the closure of a major transit route resulting from a demonstration.

[68] Opinion of AG Saugmandsgaard Øe in '*SEGRO*' (n 65) paras 128–29.

[69] ibid para 134.

the field of application of Union law beyond the powers of the Union or establish any new power or task for the Union, or modify powers and tasks as defined in the Treaties'.[70] In AG Saugmandsgaard Øe's opinion, such an outcome would give rise to conceptual, institutional and substantive complexities. First, in his words, requiring Member States to respect fundamental rights to that extent would have the effect of limiting 'the regulatory and policy approaches available in those Member States, while the power of the EU to set the boundaries of what is possible [would increase] correspondingly'.[71] Second, a more institutional question arising in this context concerns 'the extent to which the Court has the jurisdiction to take the place of national constitutional courts or ECtHR in monitoring the legislation and actions of the Member States in the light of fundamental rights'.[72]

b. The *Lex Generalis/Lex Specialis* Relationship

The position advocated by AG Saugmandsgaard Øe not only stems from the wording of Article 51(2) CFR but also finds support in the Charter's characterisation of fundamental economic rights contained therein as *lex specialis* to the Treaty's free movement provisions. This rests on a combination of two factors. First, an important determinant is the wording of the Charter's provisions that enshrine fundamental economic rights. Article 15 CFR states that 'every citizen of the Union has the freedom to seek employment, to work, to exercise the right of establishment and to provide services in any Member State'. As the Court confirmed,[73] the Explanations to the Charter elaborate that Article 15 CFR relates to the Treaty's provisions on the freedom of movement of workers, freedom of establishment and freedom to provide services. Article 16 CFR, in turn, recognises the freedom to conduct business 'in accordance with Union law'. In line with the Explanations to the Charter, the latter reference is clarified to mean that the right under this provision 'is to be exercised with respect for Union law and national legislation and [as such] it may be subject to the limitations provided for in Article 52(1) of the Charter'. On the other hand, the prevalence attached to the freedoms of movement in the review of national law emanates from Article 52(2) CFR, which stipulates that 'rights recognised by this Charter for which provision is made in the Treaties shall be exercised under the conditions and within the limits defined by those Treaties'. According to the Explanations to the Charter, this provision refers to rights that are already expressly guaranteed in the Treaty and, as such, 'remain subject to the conditions and limits applicable to the Union law on which they are based, and for which provision is made in the Treaties'.

For the *lex generalis* character of fundamental economic rights, the *in concreto* assessment pursuant to them of national measures already found to restrict the

[70] Opinion of AG Saugmandsgaard Øe in *Commission v Hungary* (n 59) para 69.
[71] ibid para 68.
[72] ibid.
[73] *PI* (n 45) para 53.

freedoms of movement would lose its normative proprium. This was echoed by AG Saugmandsgaard Øe in *Commission v Hungary*, where he argued that the separate examination of the impugned national law based on Article 17 CFR 'would in any event be *superfluous*'[74] and would not offer any added value to the individuals concerned, since they were already protected by Article 63 TFEU.[75] This was in response to the Commission's claim that while the separate analysis under Articles 15 and 16 CFR was not justified due to their normative convergence with the freedoms of movement, Article 17 CFR was broader in its content.[76] AG Saugmandsgaard Øe found this reasoning unconvincing. According to him, 'the right to property is an economic right which, like the freedom to choose an occupation and the freedom to conduct a business, is protected under freedoms of movement, and therefore their respective contents overlap, if not completely, to a large extent at least'. As such, in his view, the finding of interference with the rights guaranteed by Article 63 TFEU and Article 17 CFR and the possibility for its objective justification '[would] be based on the same factors, leading to an outcome which is essentially identical'.[77] Indeed, this kind of normative parallelism does not emerge in the context of the *ERT* review based on other fundamental rights that do not substantively align with the freedoms of movement. *ERT* itself was concerned with the conformity with the freedom of expression protected in the ECHR of the grounds that were claimed to justify the national television monopoly found to be in breach of Article 56 TFEU. The same right was at stake in *Familiapress*,[78] where the Court emphasised the need to determine whether the national prohibition of selling publications with a prize competition was proportionate to the aim of maintaining press diversity.[79] Contrasted against the freedom to conduct business or the freedom to choose an occupation, the freedom of expression is anchored to normative concerns that are extraneous to the freedoms of movement, for it is not infused with the vision of market building.

c. Normative Limits to the *ERT* Review?

Given the *lex generalis* character attributed to fundamental economic rights in the Charter, the separate *in concreto* assessment pursuant to them carries the risk of altering the parameters of the *ERT* review. This was echoed by AG Saugmandsgaard Øe in *SEGRO*, where he inferred two limits to the *ERT* framework, within which the respect for fundamental rights is incorporated into the conditions that need to be satisfied when invoking derogations from the Treaty. First, the Charter's rights

[74] Opinion of AG Saugmandsgaard Øe in *Commission v Hungary* (n 59) para 114.
[75] ibid para 123.
[76] ibid para 115.
[77] ibid para 120.
[78] Case C-368/95 *Vereinigte Familiapress Zeitungsverlags- und vertriebs GmbH v Heinrich Bauer Verlag* EU:C:1997:325.
[79] ibid para 27.

cannot be applied autonomously where a national measure restricting the freedoms of movement is not in any event justified on objective grounds.[80] In his view, there is no need for a fundamental rights review if no overriding public interests can exculpate an impugned national measure. Second, the Charter cannot be applied autonomously when such a measure does not entail any restriction of the freedoms of movement.[81] According to the Advocate General, this specifically concerns the *Keck*-type situations, where conducting an independent fundamental rights review would mean that all forms of national law, even those that do not infringe the freedoms of movement as such, might be censured under the Charter in all cross-border factual circumstances coming within the scope of those freedoms.[82] This outcome would manifestly be at odds with Article 6(1) TFEU and Article 51(2) CFR that preclude the extension of the powers of the Union outlined in the Treaties.

Both limits to the *ERT* framework identified by AG Saugmandsgaard Øe find support in the case law, though the endorsement that stems from it is not without its doubts. Insofar as the first limit is concerned, the Court generally adheres to the *ERT* parameters, albeit with variations,[83] by framing the fundamental rights prerequisite as one among other limitations on Member States' ability to derogate from the Treaty. It is, therefore, triggered at the justification stage, where the Court must be persuaded that a national measure seeking to benefit from written or unwritten exemption clauses is in the general interest and is proportionate to the objective pursued.[84] This rests on the fact that while Member States retain the power to deviate in certain circumstances from the freedoms of movement guaranteed in the Treaty, the exercise of that power is circumscribed by the criteria derived from Union law, including the respect for fundamental rights recognised therein.[85] Within these confines, a fundamental rights review presupposes the existence of legitimate aims capable of justifying barriers to free movement and the chosen means to be suitable and proportionate to achieve them. In the absence of either factor, such a review loses its pertinence since the impugned national law cannot, in any event, be exculpated.

However, the case law does not unequivocally corroborate the above-mentioned line of inference. Some doubts arise from *Pfleger*, where the issue concerned the justification of the national law that prohibited the unauthorised

[80] Opinion of AG Saugmandsgaard Øe in '*SEGRO*' (n 65) para 135.

[81] ibid.

[82] ibid para 137.

[83] There is inconsistency in the sequence of the Court's engagement with the fundamental rights question in *ERT* scenarios. Contrast, eg, *AGET Iraklis* (n 50) paras 61 et seq; *Berlington Hungary* (n 43) paras 61 et seq; *Global Starnet Ltd* (n 47) paras 39 et seq.

[84] JHH Weiler and NJS Lockhardt, '"Taking Rights Seriously" Seriously: The European Court of Justice and its Fundamental Rights Jurisprudence – Part I' (1995) 32 *Common Market Law Review* 51, 77.

[85] Opinion of AG Sharpston in Case C-390/12 *Robert Pfleger and Others* EU:C:2013:747, para 45. For a counter-argument, see Snell (n 27) 299.

operation of game machines contrary to Article 56 TFEU. The Court first referred to the need, based on *ERT*, to assess the derogation from the freedom to provide services for its compliance with the Charter.[86] Yet, having acknowledged that the impugned national law neither pursued the purported aim nor was proportionate to it, the Court proceeded to separately examine the existence of an infringement of Articles 15–17 CFR.[87] As AG Saugmandsgaard Øe pointed out, while the Court ruled out the need for the *in concreto* assessment based on the Charter, the judgment casts doubt over 'whether an alleged infringement of the Charter may be examined independently of the question of a breach of the freedoms of movement'.[88] Indeed, such vacillation was further augmented by the approach followed in *Commission v Hungary*. As mentioned earlier, in *SEGRO*, the Court already found that the national law extinguishing the usufruct rights over agricultural land was indirectly discriminatory and explicitly rejected the justification pleas for not being suitable and proportionate to the aims pursued. Nevertheless, even though it was apparent that the same impugned national law could not, in any event, be exculpated in *Commission v Hungary*, the Court still subjected it to what can be construed as the separate *in concreto* assessment of its compatibility with Article 17 CFR and possible justification under Article 52 CFR.

The ambivalence emerging from *Pfleger* and *Commission v Hungary* also sits uneasily with the AG Saugmandsgaard Øe's second limit to the *ERT* review. It finds support in *Pelckmans*,[89] which related to the compatibility with Article 34 TFEU and Articles 15–16 CFR of the national law that provided for compulsory closure of shops once a week. The Court found no breach of Article 34 TFEU by characterising the impugned measure as a non-discriminatory selling arrangement pursuant to *Keck*.[90] Doing so meant that the measure did not fall within the scope of Union law and, as such, did not trigger the applicability of the Charter. With the general language used in this ruling, the Court seemed to distance itself from its earlier approach in *Karner*,[91] though it did not expressly refer to the latter case.[92] Much like *Pelckmans*, the issue in *Karner* concerned the national rule on advertising, which the Court found to constitute a selling arrangement that complied with the conditions of universality and neutrality laid down by *Keck*, though this was not the end of the matter. The Court continued with the *in concreto* assessment of whether the national measure breached the freedom of expression enshrined in Article 10 ECHR.[93] This suggested that a separate fundamental rights review of national law was possible even when it was deemed to fall outside the scope of free movement law. The conflicting verdicts in *Pelckmans* and *Karner* can be

[86] *Robert Pfleger and Others* (n 31) para 35.
[87] ibid paras 56–60.
[88] Opinion of AG Saugmandsgaard Øe in *Commission v Hungary* (n 59) para 94.
[89] Case C-483/12 *Pelckmans Turnhout NV v Walter Van Gastel Balen NV and Others* EU:C:2014:304.
[90] ibid para 24.
[91] Case C-71/02 *Herbert Karner Industrie-Auktionen GmbH v Troostwijk* EU:C:2004:181.
[92] See also Snell (n 27) 286.
[93] *Karner* (n 91) para 49.

reconciled, albeit with a reservation,[94] by construing the former ruling to overrule the latter and endorse the second limit to the *ERT* review identified by AG Saugmandsgaard Øe.[95] If *Pelckmans* confirms the second limitation to the *ERT* framework, it is unclear how it squares with *Commission v Hungary*. Taken at face value, they may not seem to contradict one another as their legal circumstances are different. Unlike *Commission v Hungary*, the applicability of the Charter was not triggered in *Pelckmans* because the impugned national law was not a restriction pursuant to *Keck*. That said, *Commission v Hungary* leaves the prospect open for the application of the Charter independently of the question of compatibility with the Treaty's free movement provisions. Based on a careful reading of both rulings, such dissonance can also be presented as symptomatic of the dichotomy of instrumentalist and individual-centric dimensions underlying free movement law.

(1) Instrumentalism: The Traits of Normative Divergence

Pelckmans can be construed to signal the normative distinctiveness between free movement law, or at least Article 34 TFEU, and fundamental economic rights. As pointed out earlier, there is a functional similarity between these sets of provisions in terms of the protection and guarantee of the ideals of private autonomy. Articles 15–17 CFR operate as normative shields safeguarding the individual liberty of economic action against public and private forms of intervention.[96] The freedoms of movement, in turn, enable the exercise of such liberty across the borders of Member States. They presuppose and entail the engagement in economic activity or choice of occupation and the exercise of the freedom of contract and property ownership. However, despite the common normative underpinning shared by the freedoms of movement and fundamental economic rights, the generally accepted narrative is that these sets of provisions do not assimilate. They are understood to have distinct normative purposes that frame the extent to which these provisions manifest the ideals of private autonomy.[97]

Being drawn from the 'constitutional traditions common to Member States',[98] Articles 15–17 CFR express the liberal notion of private autonomy enshrined in national legal systems.[99] Within this conceptual domain, much like its national counterpart, these norms focus directly on the 'performative or entrepreneurial'

[94] One may wonder whether the difference in the verdicts in *Pelckmans* and *Karner* was, in fact, prompted by the normative variance existing between the fundamental rights concerned in these rulings, whereby an additional review is not necessarily excluded if the matter concerns a fundamental right that is normatively distinct from the freedoms of movement.

[95] Snell (n 27) 286.

[96] See, eg, Case C-70/10 *Scarlet Extended v SABAM* EU:C:2011:771; Case C-360/10 *SABAM v Netlog* EU:C:2012:85; Case C-426/11 *Mark Alemo-Herron and Others v Parkwood Leisure Ltd* EU:C:2013:521.

[97] F de Cecco, 'Fundamental Freedoms, Fundamental Rights, and the Scope of Free Movement Law' (2014) 15 *German Law Journal* 383, 394.

[98] Case C-4/73 *J Nold, Kohlen- und Baustoffgroßhandlung v Commission* EU:C:1974:51, para 13.

[99] R Babayev, 'Private Autonomy at Union Level: On Art 16 CFREU and Free Movement Rights' (2016) 53 *Common Market Law Review* 979, 981.

side of the right to individual self-determination.[100] Their purposive role as a normative source is to safeguard the individual liberty to express one's free will and rational choices in endeavours for personal self-realisation and self-satisfaction.[101] These values form a constituent part of the political, economic and social construction of the polity committed to market economy principles.[102] Vested with a human/civil rights dimension under the Charter, Articles 15–17 CFR protect private autonomy for its intrinsic value as an end in itself. They are not limited in their personal scope but encompass everyone so long as a situation is governed by Union law.[103]

In comparison, the freedoms of movement are not traditionally seen to display similar attributes, notwithstanding their characterisation by the Court as 'fundamental rights' or 'fundamental principles'.[104] This stems from the normative purpose of these provisions that is generally understood to lie elsewhere. These freedoms protect and facilitate the ability to supply goods or services across borders of Member States, engage in an employed or self-employed activity in other Member States or make capital investments in other Member States.[105] However, these private economic initiatives are not safeguarded as an intrinsic value as such; instead, they are instilled with the element of 'instrumentality'.[106] The freedoms of movement play a fundamental role in the establishment and proper functioning of the internal market. They lay the foundation of the legal and regulatory platform, which, in the Court's own words, 'must be understood as being intended to eliminate all barriers … to … [intra-Union] trade' and are 'an indispensable instrument for the realisation of a market without internal frontiers'.[107]

Viewed in this light, *Pelckmans* can be read to reflect the difference in the perimeters of manifestation of the ideals of private autonomy that are intrinsic to Article 34 TFEU and Articles 15–16 CFR. In that ruling, by exculpating the national law on shop closure based on the twofold *Keck* test, the Court once again distanced itself from the characterisation of Article 34 TFEU 'as a means of challenging any rules whose effect is to limit … commercial freedom'.[108] This would not have been possible had the Court conducted an independent review under Article 16 CFR, according to which the impugned national law would have likely

[100] M Everson and C Gonçalez, 'Article 16' in S Peers, T Harvey, J Kenner and A Ward (eds), *The EU Charter of Fundamental Rights: A Commentary* (Oxford, Hart Publishing, 2014), 438.

[101] See, eg, Case C-314/12 *UPC Telekabel Wien GmbH v Constantin Film Verleih* EU:C:2014:192, para 49.

[102] See Case C-9/99 *Echirolles Distribution SA v Association du Dauphine* EU:C:2000:532, para 25.

[103] See, eg, Case C-225/17 P *Islamic Republic of Iran Shipping Lines and Others v Council* EU:C:2019:82, para 102; Case T-510/18 *Khaled Kaddour v Council of the European Union* EU:T:2020:436, para 166.

[104] See, eg, Case C-222/86 *Unectef v Heylens* EU:C:1987:442, para 14; *Schmidberger* (n 67) para 51.

[105] See also D Charmers, 'Repackaging the Internal Market: The Ramifications of the *Keck* Judgment' (1994) 19 *European Law Review* 385, 392.

[106] De Cecco (n 97) 385.

[107] Case C-265/95 *Commission v France* EU:C:1997:595, para 30; *Schmidberger* (n 67) para 56.

[108] Joined Cases C-267/91 and C-268/91 *Criminal Proceedings against Bernard Keck and Daniel Mithouard* EU:C:1993:905, para 14.

entailed a constraint on the exercise of the freedom to engage in commercial or economic activity in the internal market, prompting the need for objective justification.[109] The focal point of scrutiny under this provision is the impact of a policy measure on an individual, with public interest considerations only coming into play at the stage when the justification of a restraint is considered.[110] By contrast, the substance of Article 34 TFEU, viewed through the prism of *Keck*,[111] does not rest on the value intrinsic to the guarantee of the individual liberty of economic action as such.[112] It is imbued by the internal market rationale built on the idea of the unhindered flow of goods across borders of Member States rather than the notion of individual traders' economic or commercial freedom at large. The effect on the latter is only brought into focus when it can be shown that a restriction inflicted on that freedom creates a barrier to the cross-border movement of goods.[113] Given this normative distinction, a separate review based on Article 16 CFR in the *Keck/Pelckmans*-type situations, according to *ERT*, would lead to a shift in the legal boundaries of Union law set out by the Court. It would turn back time by breathing new life into the all-encompassing interpretation of the scope of Article 34 TFEU that originated in *Dassonville* and culminated in the *Sunday Trading* saga.[114]

(2) Individual-Centrism: The Traits of Normative Assimilation?

If the logic behind the decision in *Pelckmans* is imbued by the instrumentalist orientation underlying Article 34 TFEU, the conflicting verdicts in *Pfleger* and *Commission v Hungary* can be rationalised by the growing individual-centric re-alignment of the Treaty's provisions on the free movement of persons. Their evolution has followed a different path that has led to the development and adoption, in both judicial and academic circles, of a non-instrumentalist conception that is detached from the ideals of 'market citizen'.[115] These provisions are no longer perceived as a means for opening up or liberalisation of national markets. Instead, they are explicated as norms that also contain a constitutional dimension whereby their beneficiaries' right to exercise economic activity in other Member

[109] See to this effect Case C-391/92 *Commission v Greece* EU:C:1995:199, para 15. See also Case C-565/08 *Commission v Italy* EU:C:2011:188, para 49; Case C-602/10 SC *Volksbank România SA v Autoritatea Naţională pentru Protecţia Consumatorilor* EU:C:2012:443, para 74.

[110] De Cecco (n 97) 399.

[111] Despite a few rulings that suggested otherwise, *Keck* remains good law. See the latest confirmation in Case C-190/20 *DocMorris NV v Apothekerkammer Nordrhein* EU:C:2021:609, para 38.

[112] For a broader analysis along these lines, see MP Maduro, 'Reforming the Market or the State? Article 30 and the European Constitution: Economic Freedom and Political Rights' (1997) 3 *European Law Journal* 55, 67.

[113] De Cecco (n 97) 398.

[114] See, eg, Case C-145/88 *Torfaen Borough Council v B&Q plc* EU:C:1989:593; Case C-169/91 *Council of the City of Stoke-on-Trent and Norwich City Council v B&Q plc* EU:C:1992:519.

[115] J Snell, 'And Then There were Two: Products and Citizens in Community Law' in T Tridimas and P Nebbia (eds), *European Union Law for the Twenty-First Century: Internal Market and Free Movement Community Policies*, vol 2 (Oxford, Hart Publishing, 2004) 67.

States is protected as an end in itself.[116] Characterised in this way, these provisions connote deeper normative assimilation with Articles 15 and 16 CFR. Indeed, support for such a link is explicitly offered in the textual formulation of Article 15 CFR, which referring to the free movement of workers, services and establishment, provides that 'every citizen of the Union has the freedom to seek employment, to work, to exercise the right of establishment and to provide services in any Member State'. The ideals underlying the individual liberty of economic action equally surface in the linguistic framing of the Treaty's provisions on persons, for they, unlike those on goods or capital,[117] have identifiable rights holders.[118] This begs the question of whether the Treaty's free movement of persons provisions and Articles 15 and 16 CFR can indeed be conceptualised as mutually reinforcing norms within the Union's legal order. There are two aspects to this query.

In one respect, these norms can be juxtaposed against one another in terms of their material scope. Undoubtedly, the language of market access that the Court tends to adhere to across all sectors of free movement law may appear to set the Treaty's free movement of persons provisions apart from Articles 15 and 16 CFR. Based on this approach, the scope of the former provisions can be narrowly framed to outlaw only non-discriminatory restrictions on taking-up of an employed or self-employed activity without affecting those that condition the pursuit of such a venture.[119] In AG Trstenjak's words, the delimitation of their scope in this manner reflects the Court's understanding of 'the fundamental freedoms primarily as instruments for opening up markets',[120] inscribing an instrumental value to the subjective entitlement derived from them. However, this does not quite capture the whole picture. As discussed in Chapter 3, the crux of the issue lies in the fact that the case law on persons does not entirely conform to the access-based logic derived from the *Keck* doctrine.

The concept of restriction, in the absence of discrimination, is not limited to rules that hinder the possibility of gaining an initial foothold in the market but also extends to those that relate to the actual pursuit of an employed or self-employed activity.[121] The rationale for their assessment seems to rest not on the

[116] E Spaventa, 'From Gebhard to Carpenter: Towards a (Non-)Economic European Constitution' (2004) 41 *Common Market Law Review* 743, 772.

[117] Article 34 TFEU equally extends to third-country goods that are put in free circulation in a Member State, while Article 63 TFEU covers capital movements directed to and from third countries. See, eg, Case C-101/05 *Skatteverket v A* EU:C:2007:804, para 39; Case 41-76 *Donckerwolke and Others v Procureur de la République and Others* EU:C:1976:182, para 18.

[118] A Tryfonidou, 'Further Steps on the Road to Convergence among the Market Freedoms' (2010) 35 *European Law Review* 36, 38.

[119] Case C-415/93 *Union royale belge des sociétés de football association ASBL v Jean-Marc Bosman* EU:C:1995:463, para 103. See also Case C-384/93 *Alpine Investments BV v Minister van Financiën* EU:C:1995:126, para 38.

[120] Opinion of AG Trstenjak in Case C-81/09 *Idryma Typou AE v Ypourgos Typou kai Meson Mazikis Enimerosis* EU:C:2010:304, para 75.

[121] Opinion of AG Hogan in Case C-71/20 *Criminal Proceedings against VAS Shipping ApS* EU:C:2021:474, para 63.

existence of an actual barrier to cross-movement but on what AG Tizzano described, 'the sole reason that they reduce the economic attractiveness of pursuing that activity'.[122] Framed as such, the normative domains of the Treaty's free movement of persons provisions and Articles 15 and 16 CFR become rather difficult to demarcate both in terms of what constitutes and what does not constitute a limitation to the exercise of individual entitlements they guarantee. First, their assimilation can be observed in *PI*, where a national court made a request for a preliminary ruling on the compatibility with Union law of the national law that allowed the closure of a commercial establishment with an immediate effect on the suspicion of practising an illegal professional activity. The law was neither discriminatory nor related to market access as such. Yet, the Court held that it constituted a restriction on the freedom of establishment and the freedom to conduct business due to the negative consequences it could pose 'on the turnover and continuation of the professional activity'.[123] Second, the convergence between the Treaty's free movement of persons provisions and Articles 15 and 16 CFR follows from the common limits to their scope. Neither is understood to outlaw non-discriminatory rules that subject economic actors to tax or social security obligations. In both instances, this can be explained by construing the collection of tax or social contributions as not affecting the pursuit of economic activity per se, notwithstanding their effect on the attractiveness and profitability of one's engagement in such an activity. However, the possibility of tax or social contribution of an excessive nature triggering scrutiny, at least in theory, cannot altogether be excluded.[124]

At the same time, these sets of provisions can be contrasted in terms of their 'territorial' or 'geographical' reach. As is well known, the Treaty's provisions on persons only apply to situations that contain a cross-border element, expressed in the movement of individuals from one Member State to another for employment, establishment and the provision or receipt of services.[125] In this context, these provisions differ from Articles 15 and 16 CFR in two overlapping respects. First, under the cross-border requirement, these provisions do not cover the so-called 'static' actors who, having not exercised the freedoms of movement, are engaged or wish to engage in an economic activity where all factual elements are located 'within one and the same Member State'.[126] They are not allowed to invoke the Treaty against the rules of that Member State, unlike foreign actors operating there. Viewed through this prism, the scope of protection under the freedoms

[122] Opinion of AG Tizzano in Case C-442/02 *CaixaBank France v Ministère de l'Économie, des Finances et de l'Industrie* EU:C:2004:187, para 58.

[123] Case C-230/18 *PI v Landespolizeidirektion Tirol* EU:C:2019:383, paras 60 and 65.

[124] E Spaventa, *Free Movement of Persons in the European Union: Barriers to Movement in Their Constitutional Context* (Alphen aan den Rijn, Kluwer Law International, 2007) 148. See also, *Berlington Hungary* (n 43) para 40.

[125] See, eg, Case 175/78 *The Queen v Vera Ann Saunders* EU:C:1979:88, para 11; Case C-180/83 *Hans Moser and Land Baden-Württemberg* EU:C:1984:233, para 18.

[126] Opinion of AG Sharpston in Case C-34/09 *Gerardo Ruiz Zambrano v Office national de l'emploi (ONEm)* EU:C:2010:560, para 137.

of movement is narrower compared to Articles 15 and 16 CFR, which make it possible to challenge any limitation on the individual liberty of economic action, irrespective of a claimant's nationality or place of establishment, so long as the situation falls within the scope of Union law.[127] Second, the cross-border requirement can also be construed to separate these sets of norms at a conceptual level. As AG Wahl alluded to in *Venturini*,[128] this requirement stresses the instrumentality inherent in the normative purpose of the freedoms of movement.[129] It intrinsically ties them to the realisation of the internal market goal of fusing national markets into a unified economic sphere,[130] premised on the dynamism of individual economic activities across national borders.[131] This endorses the traditional understanding, entrenched in the division of regulatory competence between the Union and Member States,[132] that the freedoms of movement do not guarantee the right to economic or commercial freedom at large for its intrinsic value.

However, it is indisputable that the gradual expansion of the scope of free movement law has led to the diminution of factual constellations that are materially deemed to be 'purely internal'.[133] The fact that a situation is 'confined in all respects within a single Member State'[134] does not automatically render the freedoms of movement inapplicable. On the contrary, the Court considers their scope to be triggered when, among other factors,[135] the cross-border effect of the impugned national law cannot be ruled out even in purely internal situations if it is 'far from inconceivable' that natural and legal persons from other Member States can be made subject to it while making use of their freedoms.[136] The problem with this logic is that the existence of a 'potential' intra-Union element is inherent in the very construction of the internal market.[137] With the freedoms of movement programmed to champion private economic initiatives in various forms across frontiers, it is difficult to establish with certainty that national law, particularly in the context of the Treaty's provisions on services, is incapable of having any effect

[127] For their invocation in the context of a single Member State, see, eg, Case C-540/16 *UAB 'Spika' and Others* EU:C:2018:565; Case C-534/16 *Finančné riaditeľstvo Slovenskej republiky v BB construct sro* EU:C:2017:820; Case C-447/15 *Ivo Muladi v Krajský úřad Moravskoslezského kraj* EU:C:2016:533.

[128] Opinion of AG Wahl in Joined Cases C-159/12 to C-161/12 *Alessandra Venturini v ASL Varese and Others* EU:C:2013:529.

[129] ibid para 27.

[130] S Weatherill, *The Internal Market as a Legal Concept* (Oxford, Oxford University Press, 2017) 49.

[131] SI Sánchez, 'Purely Internal Situations and the Limits of EU Law: A Consolidated Case Law or a Notion to Be Abandoned?' (2018) 14 *European Constitutional Law Review* 7, 9.

[132] N Nic Shuibhne, *The Coherence of EU Free Movement Law: Constitutional Responsibility and the Court of Justice* (Oxford, Oxford University Press, 2013) 118.

[133] Sánchez (n 131) 11.

[134] Case C-464/15 *Admiral Casinos & Entertainment AG v Balmatic Handelsgesellschaft mbH and Others* EU:C:2016:500, para 21.

[135] For other possible exceptions, see, eg, Case C-268/15 *Fernand Ullens de Schooten v État belge* EU:C:2016:874.

[136] See, eg, Case C-470/11 *SIA Garkalns v Rīgas dome* EU:C:2012:505, para 21; Joined Cases C-570/07 and C-571/07 *José Manuel Blanco Pérez and María del Pilar Chao Gómez* EU:C:2010:300, para 40; Case 286/81 *Criminal Proceedings against Oosthoek's Uitgeversmaatschappij BV* EU:C:1982:438, para 9.

[137] Spaventa (n 124) 153.

whatsoever on that process due to the hypothetical 'lack' of individual interest in making use of these freedoms.[138] As AG Bobek pointed out in this context, 'cross-border potentiality remains at the level of a reasonably conceivable hypothesis ... [as] the fact that, for example, some recipients of a service are likely to come from another Member State is enough to engage the rules of the Treaty on services'.[139] Therefore, taken at face value, service providers can effectively derive from the Treaty, to use AG Szpunar's words, 'a right akin to an economic fundamental right'[140] to challenge any rules of the Member State of establishment that prevent the very existence of a domestic market for a particular type of service.[141]

Support in the case law for such conceptualisation of the Treaty's free movement of persons provisions is not unequivocal. This is reflected in *Visser*,[142] where the claimant challenged the compatibility with Union law of the national retail zoning plan restrictions. Notwithstanding the purely internal context, the Court confirmed that the Services Directive applied to the issue at stake.[143] It held that the aim to achieve 'a genuine internal market in services' required 'the elimination of obstacles which [were] encountered by providers in becoming established in the Member States, whether in their own Member State or in another Member State, and which [were] liable to affect adversely their ability to supply services to recipients located throughout the European Union'.[144] However, the applicability of the freedoms of movement became a whole different story. First, the Court continued to emphatically adhere to the cross-border requirement.[145] It made abundantly clear that the scope of the Services Directive transcended that of the freedoms of movement, which remain inapplicable to the circumstances confined to a single Member State.[146] Second, while confirming this doctrine, the Court, without any explanation, did not resort to the 'far from inconceivable' logic. It is unclear why Article 49 TFEU was not deemed to be applicable when the possibility cannot be excluded that a natural and legal person from another Member State would have been interested in taking up a retail activity and, as a result, would have been subject to the impugned planning restrictions. Such an approach further adds to

[138] R Grimbergen, 'How Boundaries Have Shifted: On Jurisdiction and Admissibility in the Preliminary Ruling Procedure' (2015) 8 *Review of European Administrative Law* 39, 58.

[139] Opinion of Bobek in Case C-581/18 *RB v TÜV Rheinland LGA Products GmbH and Allianz IARD S.A* EU:C:2020:77, para 30.

[140] Opinion of AG Szpunar in Case C-311/19 *BONVER WIN, a s v Ministerstvo financí ČR* EU:C:2020:640, para 62.

[141] Spaventa (n 124) 101. See also the Court's reasoning in Case C-405/98 *Konsumentombudsmannen (KO) v Gourmet International Products AB (GIP)* EU:C:2001:135.

[142] Joined Cases C-360/15 and C-31/16 *College van Burgemeester en Wethouders van de gemeente Amersfoort v X BV and Visser Vastgoed Beleggingen BV v Raad van de gemeente Appingedam* EU:C:2018:44.

[143] Directive 2006/123/EC of the European Parliament and of the Council of 12 December 2006 on services in the internal market [2006] OJ L376.

[144] *Visser* (n 142) para 105.

[145] ibid para 101.

[146] ibid.

the conspicuous elusiveness surrounding the 'far from inconceivable' logic, which operates without clearly outlined parameters.[147]

d. Patterns of Cross-Fertilisation

The preceding section demonstrated that the Treaty's free movement of persons provisions and Articles 15–17 CFR do not fully fuse. However, the degree of their normative assimilation ensures conceptual and functional cross-fertilisation between them that blurs the dichotomy of individual-centric and instrumentalist paradigms underlying their coexistence. There are two intertwined facets in the dynamics of this process.

From one perspective, the individual-centric realignment of the Treaty's provisions on the free movement of persons can be construed to trace its normative legitimacy to the coalescence of Union citizenship and fundamental (economic) rights guaranteed in the Charter.[148] It is a truism that Union citizenship, introduced by the Maastricht Treaty, resulted in a profound change in the legal status of Member States' nationals. The Court encapsulated its normative potential when it ruled that 'Union citizenship [was] destined to be the fundamental status of nationals of the Member States'.[149] As highlighted by AG Cosmas, the intrinsic value of such status lies in the acquisition of a 'specific right [by Member State nationals] … irrespective of whether the enjoyment of this right is accompanied by the promotion of other [Union] aspirations or objectives'.[150] For AG Colomer, in turn, the creation of Union citizenship, with the corollary of the freedom to move and reside, represents 'a considerable qualitative step forward in that it separates that freedom from its functional or instrumental elements … and raises it to the level of a genuinely independent right inherent in the political status of the citizens of the Union'.[151] It is generally perceived that this development led to the metamorphosis of the free movement of persons provisions into norms that, while remaining driven by the creation and maintenance of the internal market, form an integral part of the spectrum of rights bestowed on Union citizens by

[147] Opinion of AG Wahl in Joined Cases C-159/12 to C-161/12 *Alessandra Venturini v ASL Varese* EU EU:C:2013:529, para 20. Contrast the reasoning in *José Manuel Blanco Pérez* (n 136) and Joined Cases C-419/12 and C-420/12 *Crono Service scarl and Others and Anitrav* EU:C:2014:81. For more on this, see H Voogsgeerd, 'More Autonomy for Member States in So-Called "Purely Internal Situations"?' (2019) 2 *ETE Law Journal* 43; J Krommendijk, 'Wide Open and Unguarded Stand Our Gates: The CJEU and References for a Preliminary Ruling in Purely Internal Situations' (2017) 18 *German Law Journal* 1359.

[148] De Cecco (n 97) 384.

[149] Case C-184/99 *Rudy Grzelczyk v Centre public d'aide sociale d'Ottignies-Louvain-la-Neuve* EU:C:2001:458, para 31. For more on this see, eg, D Thym, 'The Judicial Deconstruction of Union Citizenship' in D Thym (ed), *Questioning EU Citizenship: Judges and the Limits of Free Movement and Solidarity in the EU* (Oxford, Hart Publishing, 2017).

[150] Opinion of AG Cosmas in Case C-378/97 *Criminal Proceedings against Florus Ariël Wijsenbeek* EU:C:1999:144, para 84.

[151] Opinion of AG Ruiz-Jarabo Colomer in Joined Cases C-11/06 and C-12/06 *Rhiannon Morgan and Iris Bucher* EU:C:2007:174, para 25.

virtue of holding the nationality of Member States.[152] In this capacity, these provisions can be understood as conferring upon every Union citizen the right to freely pursue economic or commercial activity in an interstate setting as the specific expression of fundamental economic rights guaranteed as general principles of Union law and codified in Articles 15 and 16 CFR.[153] This is vindicated by the Court's analytical methodology within the framework of the free movement of persons provisions that often 'demonstrates a tendency towards protecting individuals'[154] rather than the traditional concerns of market integration as such.[155]

From the opposite perspective, the individual dimension to the Treaty's free movement of persons provisions augments the sphere of applicability of the Charter's rights as an integral aspect of the protection of the rule of law in the Union. This can be viewed from two angles. First, within the traditional *ERT* framework, a fundamental rights review is triggered whenever a Member State seeks justification for derogating from the freedoms of movement. Thus, while such scrutiny remains contingent on the infringement of these freedoms, the broader their normative reach, the greater the likelihood of fundamental rights applying to impugned national measures. This transpires from the juxtaposition of *Pelckmans* with *Pfleger* and *Commission v Hungary*. The former ruling narrowly constructed the scope of Article 34 TFEU. By endorsing the *Keck* doctrine, it further affirmed that a restraint of a trader's freedom to exercise economic or commercial activity by the prescribed modalities of sale is not, in itself, prima facie relevant for the question of compatibility with Article 34 TFEU, so long as there is no barrier to cross-border movement.[156] This substantially limits the prospect of the *ERT* review under Articles 15–17 CFR within the framework of Article 34 TFEU. In contrast, *Pfleger* and *Commission v Hungary* seem to be informed by the broader concept of restriction embedded in the free movement of persons provisions that, as discussed in Chapter 3, have not been subject to normative recalibration in line with *Keck* that rendered a limit on the pursuit of economic/commercial freedom insufficient to trigger their scope without the disparate impact to market entry.[157] Instead, their scope is imbued by the value intrinsic to the guarantee of Union citizens' ability to exercise this freedom throughout the internal market, which opens up the normative landscape that is innately conducive to triggering the applicability of the Charter.

[152] Tryfonidou (n 118) 41.

[153] Snell (n 115) 69.

[154] Opinion of AG Ruiz-Jarabo Colomer in Case C-228/07 *Jörn Petersen v Landesgeschäftsstelle des Arbeitsmarktservice Niederösterreich* EU:C:2008:281, para 17.

[155] De Cecco (n 97) 399.

[156] S Weatherill, 'After *Keck*: Some Thoughts on How to Clarify the Clarification' (1996) 33 *Common Market Law Review* 887, 905. The author stated that such an exclusion is rationalised based on the absence of a direct connection between a limit of commercial freedom and the cross-border aspect of the activity.

[157] Joined Cases C-267/91 and C-268/91 *Criminal Proceedings against Bernard Keck and Daniel Mithouard* EU:C:1993:905, para 14.

Second, the scope of the free movement of persons provisions framed by their individual-centric dimension also leads to a qualitative leap in the enforcement of fundamental rights enshrined in the Charter, particularly Articles 15–17 CFR. In *Pfleger* and *Commission v Hungary*, the Court resorted to the independent application of the Charter in addition to the claim based on the Treaty.[158] It distinguished the question of compliance with fundamental economic rights and enforced the Charter in a substantive sense by subjecting the impugned national measure itself to extra scrutiny rather than its exculpation from the freedoms of movement. This can be construed to mark a departure from the traditional *ERT* doctrine that intrinsically attaches a fundamental rights review to the question of compliance with the Treaty.[159] This jurisprudential development poses a question of constitutional significance as to the boundaries of national regulatory discretion. Specifically, it is unclear whether, within the *ERT* framework, the independent application of the Charter readily reconciles with its normative boundaries set out in Article 6(1) TEU and Article 52(1) CFR.

In *Commission v Hungary*, the Court did not share this concern but seemed to concur with the Commission's submission that the substantive application of the Charter finds its normative justification in the protection of Union citizens exercising Treaty-based freedoms. According to the Commission, for individuals affected by national law, the finding of an infringement of these rights is then 'a realisation of [the respect for] rule of law'.[160] According to this characterisation, the enforcement of this principle does not represent a shift in the division of competence between the Union and Member States. This is because the independent enforcement of fundamental rights remains contingent on the actual or likely infringement of the Treaty's free movement provisions and is therefore constricted to their sphere of application. However, it remains to be seen how far the Court is prepared to stretch this link to enforce the principle of the rule of law and what it is ready to accept as a trigger for the substantive application of the Charter.[161] For AG Saugmandsgaard Øe, there is a risk that an actual or likely restriction of the freedoms of movement may not be necessary. According to the concerns he raised in *SEGRO*, the examination of an infringement of the Charter independently of an infringement of the freedoms of movement could mean that 'all national legislation, even legislation that does not restrict those freedoms, might be censured in the light of the Charter when it is challenged in a factual situation coming within the scope of those freedoms, that is to say, in

[158] X Groussot, N Kirst and P Leisure, '*Segro* and its Aftermath: Between Economic Freedoms, Property Rights and the "Essence of the Rule of Law"' (2019) *2 Nordic Journal of European Law* 69, 83.

[159] Opinion of AG Saugmandsgaard Øe in *Commission v Hungary* (n 59) para 90.

[160] ibid para 99.

[161] On the enforcement of this principle, see also Case C-156/21 *Hungary v European Parliament and Council* EU:C:2022:97; Case C-64/16 *Associação Sindical dos Juízes Portugueses v Tribunal de Contas* EU:C:2018:117.

any cross-border situation'.[162] Such an outcome would be difficult to align with Article 6(1) TEU and Article 52(1) CFR.

B. The Interplay of Competition Rules and Fundamental Economic Rights

Normative overlaps equally exist between the Treaty's competition rules and fundamental economic rights protected at the Union level. Analogous to free movement law, the underlying premise is their common normative underpinning expressing the ideals of private autonomy. Both sets of provisions give effect to the liberty to acquire, possess and use economic goods and services as per one's will and interests to achieve self-realisation and self-fulfilment in economic terms. This kind of convergence between the Treaty's competition rules and fundamental economic rights equally instigates a query related to their coexistence and intersection with one another. Specifically, it is questionable what type of interplay these sets of provisions bring about from normative and functional standpoints and within what parameters this occurs or ought to occur.

i. Perimeters of Normative Overlaps

The normative nexus between the Treaty's competition rules and fundamental economic rights finds its clear expression within the framework of Article 16 CFR. The Explanations to the Charter state that this provision is premised on the amalgamation of several principles recognised in case law,[163] including the freedom to exercise economic or commercial activity, contractual freedom, and the principle of free competition.[164] At an individual level, the explicit reference to 'the principle of free competition' signals the existence of an intrinsic link between the right to engage in economic or commercial activity and the ability to compete in the market. Indeed, the principle of free competition is a prerequisite for effective engagement in business.[165] The realisation of this activity is predicated on the market conditions that make it possible to succeed on merits based on price, quality or innovation. Within the Union's legal system, they are ensured by Articles 101 and 102 TFEU that prohibit coordinated and unilateral forms of private conduct distorting competition by deviating from the parameters of normal market behaviour. The

[162] Opinion of AG Saugmandsgaard Øe in '*SEGRO*' (n 65) para 137.

[163] See, eg, Case 11-70 *Internationale Handelsgesellschaft mbH v Einfuhr- und Vorratsstelle fur Getreide und Futtermittel* EU:C:1970:114; Case C-230/78 *SpA Eridania-Zuccherifici nazionali and SpA Società Italiana per l'Industria degli Zuccheri* EU:C:1979:216.

[164] See *AGET Iraklis* (n 50) para 67.

[165] T Eilmansberger, 'How to Distinguish Good from Bad Competition under Article 82 EC: In Search of Clearer and More Coherent Standards for Anti-competitive Abuses' (2005) 42 *Common Market Law Review* 129, 133.

constitutional safeguard of the individual entitlement enshrined in Article 16 CFR is therefore not only contingent on the legal framework that guarantees a competitive market structure but also warrants an unwavering institutional commitment to it. The contours of such interrelation are framed by the idiosyncratic elements underlying the normative nexus between the Treaty's competition rules and fundamental economic rights. It is worth considering them first.

a. Varying Manifestation of the Freedom of Economic Action

The normative correlation of the Treaty's competition rules with fundamental economic rights suggests a degree of functional affinity existing between them. However, this does not necessarily assimilate these provisions from a normative standpoint. The first, perhaps obvious, distinguishing factor is the extent to which the Treaty's competition rules and fundamental economic rights give effect to the ideals of private autonomy. Article 16 CFR, as discussed in Chapter 2, is the first provision to expressly 'constitutionalise'[166] the entitlement to engage in individual or corporate business activities at the Union level.[167] It is broader in scope.[168] It affords protection against both public and private forms of intervention.[169] According to the Court's expansive definition, it includes 'the right for any business to be able to freely use, within the limits of its liability for its own acts, the economic, technical and financial resources available to it'.[170] A similar characterisation can be attributed to Article 17 CFR. As pointed out in Chapter 2, this provision 'constitutionalises' the protection of the right to own property in the Union *acquis*. It encapsulates a bundle of rights,[171] including the entitlement to use property, dispose of it and bequeath it.

In contrast, the Treaty's competition rules do not protect these individual entitlements in the same sense. Instead, the regulatory framework based on them aims to ensure that market actors adhere to the parameters of 'competition on merits'. These rules outlaw unilateral or coordinated conduct that is likely to have a demonstrable effect on free and fair competition among private actors in the internal market. Such prohibition guarantees the ability to exercise the freedom to compete or market freedom.[172] It is expressed in an undertaking's ability to access the market and operate in it, the success of which is measured

[166] X Groussot, GT Pétursoon and J Pierce, 'Weak Right, Strong Court: The Freedom to Conduct Business and the EU Charter of Fundamental Rights' in S Douglas-Scott and N Hatzis (eds), *Research Handbook on EU Law and Human Rights* (Cheltenham, Edward Elgar, 2017) 342.

[167] *Sky Österreich* (n 55) para 43. See also Case C-477/14 *Pillbox 38 (UK) Ltd, Trading as Totally Wicked v Secretary of State for Health* EU:C:2016:324, para 155.

[168] See, eg, *Finančné riaditeľstvo Slovenskej republiky* (n 127) para 35.

[169] See, eg, *Scarlet Extended v SABAM* (n 96) para 46.

[170] Case C-314/12 *UPC Telekabel Wien GmbH v Constantin Film Verleih* EU:C:2014:192, para 48.

[171] D Sheehan, *The Principles of Personal Property Law*, 2nd edn (Oxford, Hart Publishing, 2017) 6.

[172] See Opinion of AG Bot in Case C-201/09 P *ArcelorMittal Luxembourg SA v Commission* EU:C:2011:190, fn 60.

through the proficiency to offer better-quality goods or services in an efficient manner and at lower prices.[173] Contrasted with fundamental economic rights, the Treaty's competition rules narrowly manifest the ideals of private autonomy. Undoubtedly, the freedom to compete constitutes an integral part of the right to engage in economic or commercial activity, and it is far from easy to draw a clear line between them. However, their normative spheres do not fully overlap. As succinctly put by AG Cosmas, the Treaty's competition rules are not concerned with the guarantee of 'the untrammelled business activity of each individual undertaking', but its ability to 'operat[e] *independently* on the market' (emphasis added).[174] This is, in some way, reflected in the Court's finding that 'the Treaty intended in Article [101 TFEU] to leave untouched *the internal [organisation] of an undertaking* and to render it liable to be called in question, by means of Article [102 TFEU], only in cases where it reaches such a degree of seriousness as to amount to an abuse of a dominant position' (emphasis added).[175]

b. Divergent Normative Purposes

Another factor separating the Treaty's competition rules and fundamental economic rights is the difference in their normative purpose. As previously mentioned, drawn from the 'constitutional traditions common to Member States',[176] fundamental economic rights mirror the liberal concept of private autonomy enshrined in national legal systems.[177] In contrast, the very purpose of the Treaty's competition rules is inherently shaped by the internal market goal. This follows from the wording of Articles 101 and 102 TFEU that the anti-competitiveness of coordinated or unilateral forms of market conduct is determined by reference to the internal market. These provisions do not provide a legal basis for the regulation of competition as such,[178] but only to the extent necessary to maintain the free and fair competitive structure in the internal market.[179] This interpretation is supported by the wording of Article 3 TFEU, which provides that the Union shall have exclusive competence to establish 'the competition rules necessary for the functioning of the internal market'. In addition, it is reflected in the degree of complementarity existing between the free movement and competition law

[173] Eilmansberger (n 165) 133.

[174] Opinion of AG Cosmas in Case C-49/92 P *Commission v Anic Partecipazioni SpA* EU:C:1997:357, para 41.

[175] Joined Cases 56 and 58-64 *Établissements Consten SàRL and Grundig-Verkaufs-GmbH v Commission* EU:C:1966:41, 340).

[176] *Nold* (n 98) para 13.

[177] Babayev (n 99) 987.

[178] R Nazzini, *The Foundations of European Union Competition Law: The Objective and Principles of Article 102* (Oxford, Oxford University Press, 2011) 113.

[179] Opinion of AG Kokott in Case C-95/04 P *British Airways plc v Commission* EU:C:2006:133, para 68.

regimes in terms of the overarching aim vested in them. The Court famously proclaimed that the Treaty's competition rules were designed to abolish barriers between Member States and prevent undertakings from reconstructing such barriers and restoring the national divisions in the internal market.[180] In the same vein, the intrinsic link to the internal market project stems from the correlation between the Treaty's competition rules and the competition law of Member States. As held by the Court, these two legal systems consider the barriers to competition 'from different points of view': whereas the former provisions regard it in light of 'obstacles which may result for trade between Member States', 'each body of national legislation proceeds on the basis of the considerations peculiar to it'.[181]

For this reason, it is no coincidence that some consider the ultimate objective of the Treaty's competition rules to be the pursuit of the long-term social welfare goal ingrained in the philosophy of the internal market.[182] This resonates with the Court's characterisation of the function served by the Treaty's competition rules as 'ensuring the well-being of the European Union' that encompasses the welfare of 'the public interest, individual undertakings and consumers'.[183] Hence, there is an element of 'instrumentality' instilled in the expression of the ideals of private autonomy within the framework of the Treaty's competition rules.[184] Much like the Treaty's free movement provisions, they are also programmed to operate as a medium to steer individual behaviour to forge national markets into one single economic area.[185] Hence, contrasted against fundamental economic rights that manifest the autonomous notion of the individual liberty of economic action, the Treaty's competition rules express its operationalised variation.

ii. *The Contours of Normative Interplay*

The Treaty's competition rules and fundamental economic rights, particularly Article 16 CFR, form a symbiotic relationship. With the concept of effective competition constituting an intrinsic component of the freedom to engage in economic or commercial activity protected under the Charter, the Treaty's competition rules are integral to its constitutional guarantee. Concurrently, securing the independence of economic actors' decision-making capacity is the prerequisite for the maintenance of a competitive process in the market.[186] It is the endowment

[180] Joined Cases 56 and 58-64 *Consten and Grundig v Commission* EU:C:1966:41, 341.
[181] Case 14-68 *Walt Wilhelm and Others v Bundeskartellamt* EU:C:1969:4, para 3.
[182] Nazzini (n 178) 116.
[183] Case C-52/09 *Konkurrensverket v TeliaSonera Sverige AB* EU:C:2011:83, para 22. See also Case C-94/00 *Roquette Frères SA v Commission* EU:C:2002:603, para 42.
[184] De Cecco (n 97) 385.
[185] G Comparato, 'Private Autonomy and Regulation in the EU Case-Law' in H-W Micklitz, Y Svetiev and G Comparato (eds), 'European Regulatory Private Law: The Paradigms Tested' (2014) 4 *European University Institute Working Papers* 11.
[186] E Deutscher and S Makris, 'Exploring the Ordoliberal Paradigm: The Competition-Democracy Nexus' (2016) 11 *Competition Law Review* 181, 198.

of the right to engage in economic activity and the right to choose an occupation or profession that leads to competition.[187] Therefore, the guarantee of the individual liberty of economic action and the protection of free and fair competition are two sides of the same coin. Although not yet explicitly elucidated in the case law, this exposition is supported by the Court's continuous adherence to the deontological framing of the scope of the Treaty's competition rules around the pluralism of economic actors, market freedom, equality of opportunity and fairness.[188] As discussed in Chapter 3, this stands in stark contrast to the Commission's embracement of the more economic approach that focuses on welfare-maximising factors.

The Court's approach can first be discerned from its characterisation of the objectives pursued by the Treaty's competition rules. Its understanding in this respect is infused by a multitude of values that encompass not only the concept of market freedom but also the process of competition considered on its own. In the early rulings, the Court held that Articles 101 and 102 TFEU must be applied in light of the aim of '[instituting] … a system ensuring that competition in the common market [was] not distorted, and … the task of promoting throughout the community harmonious development of economic activities'.[189] However, the subsequent case law saw a more expansive definition of the aim pursued by the Treaty's competition rules. In *TeliaSonera Sverige*,[190] as mentioned earlier, the Court found that 'the function of those rules [was] precisely to prevent competition from being distorted to the detriment of the public interest, individual undertakings and consumers, thereby ensuring the well-being of the European Union'.[191] In *GlaxoSmithKline*,[192] in turn, the Court defined the aim of Article 101 TFEU to include the protection of 'not only the interests of competitors or of consumers, but also the structure of the market and, in so doing, competition as such'.[193] This finding echoed the Court's definition of Article 102 TFEU as a provision that 'aimed not only at practices which [might] cause prejudice to consumers directly, but also at those which are detrimental to them through their impact on an effective competition structure'.[194]

[187] E-J Mestmacker, 'The Development of German and European Competition Law with Special Reference to the EU Commission's Article 82 Guidance of 2008' in LF Pace (ed), *European Competition Law: The Impact of the Commission's Guidance on Article 102* (Cheltenham, Edward Elgar, 2011) 28.

[188] See, eg, Case C-462/99 *Connect Austria Gesellschaft für Telekommunikation GmbH v Telekom-Control-Kommission, and Mobilkom Austria AG* EU:C:2003:297, paras 80–88; Case 322/81 *NV Nederlandsche Banden Industrie Michelin v Commission* EU:C:1983:313, para 73.

[189] Joined Cases 6 and 7-73 *Istituto Chemioterapico Italiano SpA and Commercial Solvents Corporation v Commission* EU:C:1974:18, para 32. See also Case 85/76 *Hoffmann-La Roche & Co AG v Commission* EU:C:1979:36, para 125.

[190] *Konkurrensverket v TeliaSonera Sverige AB* (n 184).

[191] ibid para 22.

[192] Joined Cases C-501/06 P, C-513/06 P, C-515/06 P and C-519/06 P *GlaxoSmithKline Services Unlimited v Commission* EU:C:2009:610.

[193] ibid para 63.

[194] Case C-202/07 P *France Télécom SA v Commission* EU:C:2009:214, para 105.

Notwithstanding their consistent recurrence throughout the case law, the meaning attached to the concepts of 'competitive structure of the market' and 'competition as such' is hardly defined. These terms are inherently interlinked to the point that they appear to be synonymous, enabling their interchangeable use.[195] Indeed, the Court's reference to 'competition as such' is likely to denote the process of dynamic rivalry among market participants.[196] As a set of behavioural patterns, this process contributes to the transfer of property rights, the division of labour, the efficient allocation of resources and the promotion of the well-being of consumers.[197] 'A competitive structure of the market', in turn, is likely to concern the state of the market at a specific point in time,[198] expressed in terms of the number of economic actors present in the market, their market share and the level of market concentration.[199]

The sustained reference to both terms suggests that the Court attributes an intrinsic value to the process of competition. It is perceived as an institution that must be safeguarded as an end in itself.[200] Such protection is not warranted because of the welfare-maximising properties of competition. Instead, its value derives more from the need to preserve a degree of rivalry among independent private actors that reciprocally constrain their exercise of economic freedom and power.[201] The protection of competition in this sense presupposes the guarantee of economic plurality,[202] with the freedom of action and choice of economic actors being an indispensable element of it.[203] In other words, the protection of the effective competitive process is a direct corollary of securing the individual liberty of economic action and the independent decision-making of competitors.[204] Indeed, the catalysts behind competition are self-interest and profit maximisation, which underpin constitutionally guaranteed fundamental economic rights in a political system based on market economy principles.[205] These factors drive market actors to achieve superior business performance by anticipating and satisfying consumer demand with the most efficient and innovative use of scarce resources.[206] While such a process is characteristically pervaded

[195] Nazzini (n 178) 15.
[196] Deutscher and Makris (n 186) 198.
[197] Mestmacker (n 187) 47.
[198] Nazzini (n 178) 15.
[199] AC Witt, *The More Economic Approach to EU Antitrust Law* (Oxford, Hart Publishing, 2016) 265.
[200] See Opinion of AG Kokott in Case C-8/08 *T-Mobile Netherlands BV and Others v Raad van bestuur van de Nederlandse Mededingingsautoriteit* EU:C:2009:343, para 58.
[201] Deutscher and Makris (n 186) 198.
[202] A Ezrachi, 'The Goals of EU Competition Law and the Digital Economy' (2018) *BEUC Discussion Paper*, 15.
[203] P Behrens, 'The "Consumer Choice" Paradigm in German Ordoliberalism and its Impact upon EU Competition Law' (2014) *Europa-Kolleg Hamburg, Institute for European Integration, Discussion Paper* 1/14, 23.
[204] Deutscher and Makris (n 186) 198.
[205] Mestmacker (n 187) 25.
[206] Eilmansberger (n 165) 133.

by uncertainty and spontaneity,[207] this can be disrupted by the temptations of self-interest of certain private actors wishing to restrict or control competition through unilateral or coordinated forms of market conduct.[208] The legal framework established by competition law aims to eliminate such urges.[209] It sets out the rules of the game and ensures interdependence among market actors through constraints they mutually exert on each other.[210]

The value of economic pluralism embedded in the pursuit of an effective competition structure underlies the Court's characterisation of competitive harm under Articles 101 and 102 TFEU. In one respect, there is a substantial body of case law on Article 101 TFEU that defines a restriction of competition based on the ability of competitors to exercise market freedom. Viewed in this context, this provision first ensnares barriers to market entry. In *Langnese Iglo*,[211] the Court ruled that to determine whether the exclusive purchasing agreements fell within the scope of Article 101 TFEU, it was necessary to consider whether 'those agreements cumulatively [had] the effect of denying access to that market for new domestic and foreign competitors'.[212] In *Cementhandelaren*,[213] in turn, it was held that 'the prohibition by the association on all sales to resellers who [were] not authorized by it [made] it more difficult for producers or sellers from other member states to be active in or penetrate the [national] market'.[214] Similarly, the scope of Article 101 TFEU is triggered by the limitations imposed on competitors' ability to exercise independent decision-making in the market. This includes deciding whom to sell to and where to sell. In *Hasselblad*,[215] the Court concluded that 'a prohibition of sales between authorized dealers constitute[d] a restriction of their economic freedom and, consequently, a restriction of competition'.[216] In *CRAM and Rheinzink*,[217] it found export clauses included in an agreement '[to] constitute, by its very object, a restriction on competition … [for they limited] the freedom of the dealer to market the goods where he wish[ed] and allow[ed] the two producers to prevent parallel imports within the common market'.[218]

[207] As eloquently put by Hayek, competition, viewed systematically, is 'a procedure for discovering facts which, if the procedure did not exist, would remain unknown or at least would not be used'. See FA Hayek, 'Competition as a Discovery Procedure', MS Snow (trans) (2002) 5 *Quarterly Journal of Austrian Economics* 9, 9.

[208] Mestmacker (n 187) 26.

[209] ibid.

[210] Deutscher and Makris (n 186) 198.

[211] Case T-7/93 *Langnese Iglo GmbH and Schöller Lebensmittel GmbH & Co KG v Commission* EU:T:1995:98.

[212] ibid para 99.

[213] Case 8-72 *Vereeniging van Cementhandelaren v Commission* EU:C:1972:84.

[214] ibid para 30.

[215] Case 86/82 *Hasselblad (GB) Ltd v Commission* EU:C:1984:65.

[216] ibid para 46.

[217] Joined Cases 29/83 and 30/83 *Compagnie Royale Asturienne des Mines SA and Rheinzink GmbH v Commission* EU:C:1984:130.

[218] ibid para 24.

The value of economic pluralism is even more discernible in the context of Article 102 TFEU. It is manifested in the outlawing of actions taken by a market actor holding a dominant position that result in the elimination of competitors in the market and thereby further reinforcement of its position by having recourse to means 'other than those within the scope of competition on the merits'.[219] The case law reveals two aspects of such prohibition. In one respect, in *Intel II*,[220] the Court confirmed that Article 102 TFEU did not 'seek to ensure that competitors less efficient than the undertaking with the dominant position should remain on the market' and that 'not every exclusionary effect [was] necessarily detrimental to competition'.[221] As such, Article 102 TFEU would not be triggered if 'competition on merits' engaged by a dominant undertaking 'lead[s] to the departure from the market or the marginalisation of competitors that are less efficient and so less attractive to consumers from the point of view of, among other things, price, choice, quality or innovation'.[222] This factor underpins the so-called 'as efficient competitor test' developed by the Court to distinguish an anti-competitive exclusion from exclusion as a result of 'competition on merits'. However, the application of this test does not necessarily exculpate the abusive market conduct that prevents access to the market by new entrants that have not yet reached the necessary level of efficiency. This is reflected in *Post Danmark II*,[223] where the Court acknowledged that the satisfaction of the 'as efficient competitor test' was not obligatory, for it might not always be relevant given the structure of the market.[224] Where a dominant undertaking holds a very large market share and the market is, therefore, protected by high barriers, 'the emergence of an as-efficient competitor [is] practically impossible'.[225] Under these conditions, according to the Court, 'the presence of a less efficient competitor might contribute to intensifying the competitive pressure on that market and, therefore, to exerting a constraint on the conduct of the dominant undertaking'.[226]

The conceptualisation of competition as an institution framed by the pluralism of economic actors and private interests, equality of opportunity and fairness underpins the normative nexus between the Treaty's competition rules and fundamental economic rights. Ingrained in the protection of human dignity and, specifically, civil rights, the latter set of norms traditionally serves as a defensive weapon aimed at protecting natural or legal persons against the abuse of state power.[227] They epitomise the ethos of a free market economy and the spirit of free

[219] Case T-228/97 *Irish Sugar plc v Commission* EU:T:1999:246, para 111.
[220] Case C-413/14 P *Intel Corp Inc v European Commission* EU:C:2017:632.
[221] ibid paras 133–34.
[222] ibid para 134.
[223] Case C-23/14 *Post Danmark A/S v Konkurrencerådet* EU:C:2015:651.
[224] ibid para 59.
[225] ibid.
[226] ibid para 60.
[227] H Collins, 'On the (In)Compatibility of Human Rights Discourse and Private Law' in H Micklitz (ed), *Constitutionalization of European Private Law* (Oxford, Oxford University Press, 2014) 28.

enterprise and entrepreneurship that espouse the ideal that private rather than governmental decision-making must direct the flow of economic resources, the division of labour and the transfer of ownership. However, threats to the effective exercise of the individual liberty of economic action do not vanish with full state compliance with fundamental economic rights in the absence of compelling reasons to the contrary. Private actors with unilateral or combined market power can equally eliminate or adversely affect the exercise of fundamental economic rights by causing market foreclosures. The inclusion of competition rules in the Treaty reflects the reality of such risks. These provisions guarantee equal market opportunities by prohibiting forms of market conduct that deviate from the parameters of normal market behaviour and thus cause harm to the competitive process in the internal market.[228] As the Explanations to the Charter suggest, this functionally correlates to the realisation of the freedom enshrined in Article 16 CFR, which the Court endows with the attributes of the right to business equality and, more importantly, free and fair competition.[229]

This constitutional bond forged between fundamental economic rights, particularly Articles 16 and 17 CFR, and the Treaty's competition rules is likely to be severed if consumer-oriented welfare considerations exclusively guide the scope of the latter set of provisions. Under this approach, as previously discussed, the Treaty's competition rules would outlaw unilateral or coordinated forms of market conduct only when they cause consumer harm, irrespective of their adverse effect on competitors' exercise of market freedom. The latter would only come into play if there were a detriment to consumers. However, such conditionality is at odds with the normative premise underlying Article 16 CFR. As a human/civil right, market freedom, constituting the core element of the right to engage in economic activity, warrants protection as a value that reflects, first and foremost, the interests of its beneficiaries.[230] Imbued with liberal ideals,[231] it is meant to channel motives of individual self-interest and incentives, regardless of whether they may or may not benefit consumers. Yet, this characterisation does not necessarily dismiss the value of the latter factor. Consumers' well-being is enhanced by the rivalry that naturally occurs because of market actors making use of their economic autonomy.[232] They thrive by anticipating and satisfying consumers' needs in the most efficient ways, ultimately leading to a variety of goods and services available to them.[233] Hence, consumers' freedom of choice is a direct corollary of exercising

[228] Case C-202/88 *France v Commission* EU:C:1990:64, para 51.
[229] Everson and Gonçalez (n 100) 449.
[230] See R Zäch, 'Freedom to Compete and the More Economic Approach: Limits Imposed by Law' (2009) 40 *International Review of Intellectual Property and Competition Law* 623, 626.
[231] AT Peacock, *The Political Economy of Economic Freedom* (Cheltenham, Edward Elgar, 1997) 3.
[232] P Behrens, 'The Ordoliberal Concept of "Abuse" of a Dominant Position and its Impact on Article 102 TFEU' in F di Porto and R Podszun (eds), *Abusive Practices in Competition Law* (Cheltenham, Edward Edgar, 2018) 10.
[233] Peacock (n 231) 6.

the individual liberty of autonomous economic action, ensured by the system of free and fair competition.

II. Normative Divergence

While fundamental economic rights and the Treaty's free movement and competition rules coexist in a symbiotic relationship,[234] the divergence of their normative purposes adds a layer of complexity to their interplay by raising the prospect of a material conflict between them. For a start, the application and enforcement of the Treaty's free movement and competition rules in pursuit of the internal market goal can lead to limitations or conditions imposed on the exercise of fundamental economic rights. This would prompt the need to delimit their respective spheres of application. On the one hand, it is unclear what kind of private actions give rise to a breach of the Treaty, while on the other hand, there is uncertainty over the extent to which the ideals of private autonomy can exculpate the actions of private actors from the scope of the Treaty. Queries along these lines have generated a vast amount of commentary in the literature, though considered predominantly from the perspective of fundamental economic rights recognised as general principles of Union law.[235] With the passage of the Charter into the tier of the Union's primary law, Articles 15–17 CFR offer a new platform for private actors to assert their interests in the process of enforcement of the Treaty's free movement and competition rules. They add a human/civil rights dimension to the counterbalance of the ideals of private autonomy against the Treaty's guarantee of market freedom in the internal market. Several conceptual and analytical concerns emerge in this context.

A. The Main Points of Conflict

As previously mentioned, the free movement and competition law regimes are 'functionalised' to operate as a medium to steer individual behaviour to forge separate national markets into a single economic sphere.[236] The attainment of this goal envisages certain obligations that are enforceable even against private

[234] See also V Trstenjak and E Beysen, The Growing Overlap of Fundamental Freedoms and Fundamental Rights in the Case-Law of the CJEU' (2013) 38 *European Law Review* 293, 311.

[235] See, eg, H Schepel, 'Freedom of Contract in Free Movement Law: Balancing Rights and Principles in European Public and Private Law' (2013) 5–6 *European Review of Private Law* 1211; K Cseres, 'Competition and Contract Law' in AS Hartkamp, MW Hesselink, EH Hondius, C Mak and CE du Perron (eds), *Towards a European Civil Code*, 4th edn (Alphen aan den Rijn, Kluwer Law International, 2011); Davies (n 13); M Mataija, 'The Public–Private Distinction, Autonomy and Free Movement: Unpacking the Assumptions' (2013) 13 *Global Jurist* 23.

[236] Comparato (n 185) 11.

actors. Therefore, within the framework of the free movement and competition law regimes, the ideals of private autonomy are simultaneously protected and delimited. As a result, the outer boundaries of these regimes can spread into the private realm and trigger the protective safeguards provided by fundamental economic rights.

i. Conflict of Fundamental Economic Rights and Fundamental Freedoms

The root of a possible material conflict of fundamental economic rights with the freedoms of movement lies in the gradual expansion of the horizontal reach of the latter set of provisions. As discussed in Chapter 1, this process rests on two strands. First, as confirmed in *TopFit*,[237] free movement law applies when 'a group or organisation exercise *a certain power* over individuals and is in a position *to impose on them conditions* which adversely affect the exercise of the fundamental freedoms guaranteed under the Treaty' (emphasis added).[238] Second, in instances not involving private or non-public bodies with regulatory or quasi-regulatory powers, the Court's approach so far has been twofold. It expressly excluded a private contract from the scope of Article 34 TFEU by finding that the obligation arising from it could not be regarded as a barrier to trade under Article [34] of the Treaty 'since it was not imposed by a Member State but agreed between individuals'.[239] In contrast, the Court recognised the full direct horizontal effect of the principle of non-discrimination on grounds of nationality under Article 45 TFEU by finding that 'the prohibition of discrimination [on the ground of nationality] applied equally to all agreements intended to regulate paid labour collectively, as well as to contracts between individuals'.[240]

On the face of it, the horizontal direct effect attributed to free movement law may be limited in its reach. In most instances, it is confined to private actors exerting some power over others that cannot be circumvented by exercising private autonomy.[241] However, the fact remains that the case law does not provide a clear outline of the extent to which the freedoms of movement apply to private conduct.[242] As AG Trstenjak pointed out in *Fra.bo*,[243] this increases the risk of

[237] Case C-22/18 *TopFit eV and Daniele Biffi v Deutscher Leichtathletikverband eV* EU:C:2019:497.

[238] ibid para 39. See also Case C-411/98 *Angelo Ferlini v Centre hospitalier de Luxembourg* EU:C:2000:530, para 50.

[239] Case C-159/00 *Sapod Audic v Eco-Emballages SA* EU:C:2002:343, para 74.

[240] Case C-281/98 *Roman Angonese v Cassa di Risparmio di Bolzano SpA* EU:C:2000:296, para 34.

[241] R Babayev, 'Contractual Discretion and the Limits of Free Movement Law' (2015) 23 *European Private Law Review* 875, 882.

[242] H Schepel, 'Constitutionalising the Market, Marketising the Constitution, and to Tell the Difference: On the Horizontal Application of the Free Movement Provisions in the EU Law' (2012) 18 *European Law Journal* 177, 177.

[243] Case C-171/11 *Fra.bo SpA v Deutsche Vereinigung des Gas- und Wasserfaches eV (DVGW)* EU:C:2012:176.

a clash with fundamental economic rights.[244] Indeed, an obligation imposed on private actors to take a certain action or refrain from certain actions to ensure free movement in the internal market poses a limitation to the realisation of the individual liberty of economic action.[245] This raises the likelihood of those private actors resorting to fundamental economic rights now codified in the Charter as a platform to challenge the enforcement of the Treaty's free movement provisions, which would necessitate a fair balance being struck between these norms. The need for such an exercise is perceptible when juxtaposing *Angonese* and *Alemo-Herron*.[246] In the former ruling, according to the Court, the *effet utile* and uniformity of the prohibition of discrimination on grounds of nationality justified subjecting a private employer's recruitment policy to scrutiny under Article 45 TFEU. In the latter, in turn, the Court emphasised that the inability of an employer to take part in collective bargaining reduces its contractual freedom 'to the point that such a limitation [was] liable to adversely affect the very essence of its freedom to conduct a business'. Undoubtedly, *Angonese* and *Alemo-Herron* relate to different substantive matters. Nonetheless, the same factual situation can trigger both categories of interests described. As a result, the pertinent question is not whether but how the Treaty's free movement provisions and fundamental economic rights must be reconciled with each other and what analytical framework is most suited to this end.

ii. Conflict of Fundamental Economic Rights and Competition Rules

While the freedoms of movement, despite producing some form of horizontal direct effect, are predominantly concerned with restrictions of a public nature, the primary addressees of the Treaty's competition rules are private actors. As previously discussed, these provisions ensure a free and fair competitive structure in the internal market that is a prerequisite for equal market opportunities.[247] They establish a normative framework aimed at the realisation of market freedom manifested in the ability to buy or sell goods and services at quantities and prices of one's choice by exercising the autonomy to enter into binding agreements and the discretion to exchange property ownership.[248] This normative framework consists of a set of external constraints on the engagement with certain forms of unilateral and coordinated market conduct that risk eliminating competition in the internal market. Article 101 TFEU prohibits undertakings from entering into different forms of price-fixing or market-sharing agreements.[249] Article 102 TFEU,

[244] ibid para 56.
[245] Davies (n 13) 813.
[246] *Mark Alemo-Herron and Others* (n 96).
[247] Opinion of AG Kokott in *British Airways* (n 179) para 68.
[248] Cseres (n 235) 205–06.
[249] See, eg, Case C-591/16 *PH Lundbeck A/S and Lundbeck Ltd v Commission* EU:C:2021:243; Case C-70/93 *Bayerische Motorenwerke AG v ALD Auto-Leasing D GmbH* EU:C:1995:344; Case C-53/69 *Sandoz AG v Commission Sandoz AG v Commission* EU:C:1972:74.

in turn, limits the choice of market strategies or tactics available to dominant market actors.[250] The range of constraints prescribed by these provisions can undoubtedly touch on the ability to choose trading partners and agree to contractual terms, the discretion to decide the pricing structure of products and the way they are sold, or the entitlement to bear the fruits of investments.[251] As such, enforcing a competitive market structure comes at the cost of limitations and conditions imposed on the exercise of individual entitlements guaranteed by fundamental economic rights. As AG Kokott and AG Jacobs pointed out,[252] this raises the need for careful balancing between the interests protected by the effective enforcement of competition law and the interests of individual undertakings.

The case law marks the importance attached to fundamental economic rights in the process of competition law enforcement. However, the Court does not always explicitly equilibrate the opposing interests at stake. This is evident in instances involving the exercise of contractual and property rights. In one respect, a series of decisions uphold the respect for the freedom of contract as an individual entitlement, setting the normative boundaries of the Treaty's competition rules. In *Dimosia*,[253] the Court considered this freedom to constitute 'the emanation of people's freedom to act', the guarantee of which was 'essential' 'in a Union that [was] committed to respecting the principle of an open market economy where competition [was] free'.[254] As such, it is not only that the Treaty's competition rules provide the regulatory framework for the exercise of individual contractual autonomy, but the extent of their enforcement also has to conform to the value intrinsic to the freedom of contract.[255] As confirmed in *Bayer*,[256] the enforcement of this principle cannot lead to the obligation to supply imposed on an undertaking. According to the Court, while the refusal to supply may, in certain circumstances, form part of an anti-competitive agreement, the immediate compliance with such an obligation risks depriving an undertaking of 'its independence in defining certain crucial elements in its business policy'.[257]

The endorsement of the freedom of contract has not always attracted the same degree of attention. This is evident from the difference in the approaches followed by the General Court and the Court of Justice in *Alrosa*,[258] where

[250] See, eg, Case 322/81 *NV Nederlandsche Banden Industrie Michelin v Commission* EU:C:1983:313.

[251] See, eg, Case C-441/07 P *Commission v Alrosa Company Ltd* EU:C:2010:377; *Irish Sugar plc v Commission* (n 219); Case C-7/97 *Oscar Bronner GmbH & Co KG v Mediaprint Zeitungs- und Zeitschriftenverlag GmbH* EU:C:1998:569; Case C-62/86 *AKZO Chemie BV v Commission* EU:C:1991:286.

[252] Opinion of AG Kokott in Case C-441/07 P *Commission v Alrosa Company Ltd* EU:C:2009:55, para 3; Opinion of AG Jacobs in Case C-7/97 *Bronner GmbH & Co KG v Oscar Bronner GmbH & Co KG v Mediaprint Zeitungs- und Zeitschriftenverlag GmbH* EU:C:1998:264, para 57.

[253] Case T-421/09 RENV *Dimosia Epicheirisi Ilektrismou AE (DEI) v Commission* EU:T:2016:748.

[254] ibid para 131 (author's translation).

[255] Case T-128/98 *Aéroports de Paris v Commission* EU:T:2000:290, para 82.

[256] Case T-41/96 *Bayer AG v Commission* EU:T:1996:68.

[257] ibid para 54.

[258] Case T-170/06 *Alrosa Company Ltd v Commission* EU:T:2007:220; Case C-441/07 P *Commission v Alrosa Company Ltd* EU:C:2010:377.

the issue concerned the Commission decision that rendered binding, under Regulation 1/2003 the individual commitment made by an undertaking under investigation to cease any contractual relations with a third party for an indefinite period.[259] The General Court ruled that the infringement measure was disproportionate, having identified less onerous solutions than the absolute prohibition of any future contractual relations between the parties concerned.[260] The Court of Justice disagreed with this verdict. It first found that the principle of proportionality did not fully apply in the context of the commitment procedure under Regulation 1/2003. It then concluded that the General Court had erred in law by conducting a proportionality review and substituting its own assessment of complex economic circumstances for that of the Commission, thus encroaching on its discretion in this area.[261] This form of judicial deference received widespread criticism for emasculating the proportionality review and jeopardising the rule of law within the framework of Regulation 1/2003.[262] Indeed, the Court's hands-off approach set no meaningful limit to the remedial discretion available to the Commission in adopting commitment decisions,[263] the nature of which instinctively requires a delicate balancing of the protection of competition in the internal market and the respect for contractual freedom of third parties.[264] The need for symmetry between these interests was confirmed in *Groupe Canal+*,[265] which in some way, at least partially, reversed *Alrosa*. In that case, the Court ruled that the Commission's decision to bind an undertaking under investigation to its commitment not to apply certain contractual clauses vis-a-vis a third party, without the analogous commitment expressed by the latter, interfered with the contractual freedom of that third party.[266] Although *Groupe Canal+* did not technically deviate from the letter of *Alrosa*,[267] it confirmed that the principle of proportionality applied to the interests of third

[259] Council Regulation (EC) No 1/2003 of 16 December 2002 on the implementation of the rules on competition laid down in Articles 81 and 82 of the Treaty [2003] OJ L1.

[260] *Alrosa Company Ltd v Commission* (n 258) para 103.

[261] *Commission v Alrosa Company Ltd* (n 258) para 67.

[262] F Wagner-von Papp, 'Best and Even Better Practices in Commitment Procedures after *Alrosa*: The Dangers of Abandoning the "Struggle for Competition Law"' (2012) 49 *Common Market Law Review* 929, 937. See also F Cengiz, 'Judicial Review and the Rule of Law in the EU Competition Law Regime after *Alrosa*' (2011) 7 *European Competition Journal* 127, 129.

[263] R Stones, 'Commitment Decisions in EU Competition Enforcement: Policy Effectiveness v the Formal Rule of Law' (2019) 38 *Yearbook of European Law* 361, 391.

[264] Opinion of AG Pitruzzella in Case C-132/19 P *Groupe Canal+ v Commission* EU:C:2020:355, para 116.

[265] Case C-132/19 P *Groupe Canal + v Commission* EU:C:2020:1007.

[266] ibid para 107.

[267] N Dunne, 'Challenging Competition Commitment Decisions: *Groupe Canal+*' (2021) 58 *Common Market Law Review* 1229, 1232. According to the author, the Court in *Alrosa* indeed held that the interests of third parties must be taken into consideration, though this appeared to be little more than lip service, considering the breadth of discretion afforded to the Commission and the effect of its decision on the business model of the third party.

parties by prompting the Commission to ensure that their contractual rights were not rendered nugatory.[268]

Similarly, a correlation exists between the interest of undistorted competition and the value of property ownership. Conceptually, the Treaty's competition rules ensure a 'level playing field' for the realisation of market freedom through the undisturbed exercise of property rights.[269] They regulate the behaviour of market actors by placing certain limits on the exercise of ownership rights. This is because, much like the freedom of contract, a misuse of the right to property by a certain category of market actors can give rise to the distortion of competition in the internal market. Such a possibility exists when an undertaking holding a dominant position refuses to grant other competitors access to a specific asset, thereby abusing its position and posing a severely negative impact on the competitive process. However, forcing on an undertaking (even one in a dominant position) a duty to grant access to an asset, supply or deal does not come without legal limits. Its overzealous enforcement risks encroaching upon the right to property and the freedom of contract of an undertaking in question.[270] The tension of this sort is particularly prevalent in instances involving an undertaking's invention that is protected as intellectual property or infrastructure built and used for its own business purposes.[271] As AG Jacobs explained in *Bronner*,[272] penalising the refusal to make available an asset in either situation is detrimental to the liberty to freely dispose of property as per one's wishes and needs, not to mention the ability to choose trading partners since a direct result of this step is that a proprietor would be compelled to relinquish ownership rights by offering its asset to competitors.[273] Such an outcome negates the concept of competition as a dynamic process for individual self-realisation that allows a market actor to reserve for its own use and to profit from its innovation and investment. There will be no incentive left if a market actor is bound to share the benefits of its innovation and investment at the mere request of a competitor.[274] For this very reason, as discussed below, the Court applies additional conditions, first formulated in *Bronner*, to strike a balance between the protection of free competition and the respect for ownership.[275]

[268] *Groupe Canal + v Commission* (n 265) para 106.

[269] Cseres (n 235) 205.

[270] V Hagenfeldt, *EC Competition Law: The Essential Facilities Doctrine* (Norderstedt, GRIN Verlag, 2009) 4. See also Case 238/87 *AB Volvo v Erik Veng (UK) Ltd* EU:C:1988:477, para 8; Case T-151/01 *Der Grüne Punkt-Duales System Deutschland GmbH v Commission* EU:T:2007:154, paras 182–83.

[271] See, eg, Case C-42/21 P *Lietuvos geležinkeliai AB v Commission* EU:C:2023:12; Case C-152/19 P *Deutsche Telekom AG v Commission* EU:C:2021:238; Case C-307/18 *Generics (UK) Ltd and Others v Competition and Markets Authority* EU:C:2020:52; Case T-65/98 *Van den Bergh Foods Ltd v Commission* EU:T:2003:281.

[272] *Oscar Bronner* (n 251).

[273] Opinion of AG Jacobs in Case C-7/97 *Oscar Bronner* EU:C:1998:264, para 56.

[274] ibid para 57. See also Case T-814/17 *Lietuvos geležinkeliai AB v Commission* EU:T:2020:545, para 90.

[275] For the application of the *Bronner* criteria, see, eg, Case C-165/19 P *Slovak Telekom, a s v Commission* EU:C:2021:239; Case C-295/12 P *Telefónica SA and Telefónica de España SAU v Commission* EU:C:2014:2062.

B. Reconciliation of the Interests at Stake

The process of resolving a possible conflict of fundamental economic rights with the Treaty's free movement and competition rules can be viewed from two perspectives. First, a more conventional approach, rooted in the public law-based concept of proportionality, sees both Treaty-based provisions as a means to achieve 'a collective good',[276] expressed in the construction of a supranational polity built on the internal market. This approach focuses on whether the countervailing policy concern is sufficient justify the interference with a protected fundamental right.[277] This would be so if the enforcement of either set of provisions, considered within their normative framework, meets the proportionality requirement that consists of three tests of suitability, necessity and proportionality in a narrow sense. Second, as previously discussed, the Treaty's free movement and competition rules are also construed as privately enforceable individual rights.[278] On this premise, the intersection of these sets of provisions and fundamental economic rights assumes a different character. This change stems from the switch from the public domain to the private realm, traditionally distinguished by the equality of private actors.[279] The idea of equality, in this sense, presupposes the existence of countervailing rights, interests and policies on both sides that require weighing up one against the other.[280] Unlike the first approach, the focus rests on the extent to which the effective realisation of one requires a limitation imposed on another and vice versa. The case of interference with the respective rights of each side needs to be assessed concurrently according to the test of proportionality. This 'double proportionality' review ensures that due weight and equal consideration are accorded to the opposing interests at stake. The case law explicitly recognises both analytical approaches. However, the Court tends to favour the first method by often confining the proportionality assessment to the benchmarks developed within the free movement and competition law regimes.

i. Balancing under Free Movement Law

In conflicts between the freedoms of movement and fundamental rights, the Court strives to find an equilibrium between the competing interests at stake,[281] though it does not always employ the same methodology to this end.[282] *Schmidberger* stands out for embracing the double test of proportionality. In this case, the Court was

[276] De Cecco (n 97) 401.
[277] Collins (n 227) 49.
[278] See, eg, *Roman Angonese* (n 240); Case C-453/99 *Courage v Crehan* EU:C:2001:465.
[279] M Flaherty, 'Private Law and its Normative Influence on Human Rights' in K Barker and D Jensen (eds), *Private Law: Key Encounters with Public Law* (Cambridge, Cambridge University Press, 2013) 217.
[280] Collins (n 227) 50.
[281] This section draws on Babayev (n 99).
[282] See also Trstenjak and Beysen (n 234) 312.

asked to rule on whether a restriction on the free movement of goods in the form of a 30-hour blockage of a motorway was justified by the freedom of expression. In aligning this right with Article 34 TFEU, the Court did not confine its analysis to the question of whether the restriction of intra-Union trade, which resulted from the exercise of the freedom of expression, was proportionate to the protection of that right.[283] Instead, it also examined at whether 'an outright ban on the demonstration would have constituted unacceptable interference with that right'.[284] In the Court's words, the imposition of stricter conditions over the location and duration of the demonstration would lead to an excessive restriction, depriving the freedom of expression of a substantial part of its scope.[285] The Court concluded that 'an action of that type usually entail[ed] inconvenience for non-participants, in particular as regards free movement, but the inconvenience [might] in principle be tolerated provided that the objective pursued [was] essentially the public and lawful demonstration of an opinion'.[286] The reasoning in this ruling mirrored the two analytical parameters identified by AG Trstenjak in *Commission v Germany* for the reconciliation of the freedoms of movement law and fundamental rights.[287] First, such an exercise must rest on the presumption that the realisation of both interests at stake constitutes a legitimate objective.[288] Second, the fair balancing of opposing interests must ensure that 'the restriction by a fundamental right on a fundamental freedom [does not] go beyond what is appropriate, necessary and reasonable to realise that fundamental right … [and conversely], the restriction on a fundamental right by a fundamental freedom [does not] go beyond what is appropriate, necessary and reasonable to realise the fundamental freedom'.[289]

However, unlike *Schmidberger*, the case law shows a strong predilection for a conceptually and analytically different method, whereby the Court generally tends to conduct a balancing exercise by restricting its reasoning to the frame of limitations prescribed by the Treaty's free movement provisions and the specific conditions attached thereof. As is widely known, the freedoms of movement are not absolute. They can be departed from based on either the express derogations laid down in the Treaty or judge-made mandatory requirements, subject to the proportionality assessment. The main problem with this approach is that the existing justification regime is not equipped to weigh pure private interests against the internal market objective. This stems from the fact that it is primarily, if not exclusively, tailored to meet the interests of Member States, who remain the primary

[283] *Schmidberger* (n 67) para 89.
[284] ibid.
[285] ibid para 90.
[286] ibid para 91.
[287] Opinion of AG Trstenjak in Case C-271/08 *Commission v Germany* EU:C:2010:183.
[288] ibid para 188.
[289] ibid para 190.

addressees of free movement law.[290] The expansion of its horizontal reach has not been followed by the corresponding extension of available justification grounds that adequately reflect the interests of private actors.

Two factors are problematic in this context. First, it is questionable whether private actors can invoke the existing justification grounds or whether they are reserved for Member States. In *Bosman*, in response to the objection by the Union of European Football Associations (UEFA) that only Member States could rely on the Treaty-based derogations, the Court held that 'there [was] nothing to preclude individuals from relying on justifications on grounds of public policy, public security or public health'.[291] The Court added that 'neither the scope nor the content of those grounds of justification [was] in any way affected by the public or private nature of the rules in question'.[292] Yet, the opposite follows from *Laval*,[293] where the issue concerned, among other things, the possibility of a trade union engaging in a collective action to invoke the Treaty-based derogations. The Court responded negatively by stating that 'not being bodies governed by public law', trade unions could not avail themselves of the public policy exception.[294] This, however, only seems to concern the Treaty-based derogations without extending to the category of mandatory requirements. In *Viking*,[295] having found that a collective action taken by a trade union was a restriction on the freedom of establishment, the Court also conceded that such a restriction might 'in principle, be justified by an overriding reason of public interest, such as the protection of workers'.[296] It follows that within the current justification regime, private actors can at least have recourse to specific public interest grounds under the category of mandatory requirements. Indeed, in *Wouters*,[297] in response to the question on the compatibility with Articles 49 and 56 TFEU of the prohibition of multi-disciplinary partnerships between lawyers and accountants, the Court held that it would, in any event, appear to be justified by the need 'to ensure the proper practice of the legal profession'.[298] In *Angonese*, in turn, the Court acknowledged that the language requirements imposed by a private actor such as a private bank could be justified, provided that they 'were

[290] C Barnard, 'Derogations, Justifications and the Four Freedoms: Is State Interest Really Protected?' in C Barnard and O Odudu, *The Outer Limits of European Union Law* (Oxford, Hart Publishing, 2009) 273.

[291] *Bosman* (n 119) para 86.

[292] ibid.

[293] C-341/05 *Laval un Partneri Ltd v Svenska Byggnadsarbetareförbundet* EU:C:2007:809.

[294] ibid para 84.

[295] Case C-438/05 *International Transport Workers' Federation and Finnish Seamen's Union v Viking Line ABP and OÜ Viking Line Eesti* EU:C:2007:772.

[296] ibid para 90. See also D Wyatt, 'Horizontal Effect of Fundamental Freedoms and the Right to Equality after *Viking* and *Mangold*, and the Implications for Community Competence' (2008) 4 *Croation Yearbook of European Law and Policy* 1, 31. However, according to the author, the protection of workers can also be deemed to constitute a private economic interest.

[297] Case C-309/99 *Wouters and Others* EU:C:2002:98.

[298] ibid para 122.

based on objective factors unrelated to the nationality of the persons concerned and … were in proportion to the aim legitimately pursued',[299] for instance, a specific linguistic policy.[300] Similarly, in *Olympique Lyonnais*,[301] the restriction on the free movement of young football players was justified according to 'the objective of encouraging the recruitment and training of young players'.[302]

Yet, the availability of the category of mandatory requirements to private actors comes with an important caveat. There are not many public interest grounds that private actors can invoke. Moreover, it is neither reasonable nor realistic to expect that, considering that these actors predominantly pursue their own private interests of an economic nature rather than being motivated by broader public-oriented concerns. This brings us to another limitation of the existing justification regime. According to the well-established case law, it does not encompass purely economic reasons. As held in *Commission v Italy*, the grounds under Article 36 TFEU are 'directed to eventualities of a non-economic kind'.[303] Member States cannot rely on this provision to plead 'the economic difficulties caused by the elimination of barriers to [intra-Union] trade'.[304] The same also holds true for the category of mandatory requirements. In *Verkooijen*,[305] the Court confirmed that 'aims of a purely economic nature [could not] constitute an overriding reason in the general interest justifying a restriction of a fundamental freedom guaranteed by the Treaty'.[306] Although the Court gave effect to economic considerations coupled with other public concerns,[307] it has yet to consider them as sufficient grounds on their merit. The rationale behind this limitation rests upon the idea that economic concerns of Member States are not significant enough to outweigh the aims pursued by the Treaty. Although this reasoning seems persuasive enough in relation to Member States, extending it by analogy to private actors is contentious because the primary motive of their activity is imbued by the sense of self-realisation in economic terms.

[299] *Roman Angonese* (n 240) para 42.

[300] S de Vries and R van Mastrigt, 'The Horizontal Direct Effect of the Four Freedoms: From a Hodgepodge of Cases to a Seamless Web of Judicial Protection in the EU Single Market?' in U Bernitz, X Groussot and F Schulyok (eds), *General Principles of EU Law and European Private Law* (Alphen aan den Rijn, Kluwer, 2013) 271. See also Case C-202/11 *Anton Las v PSA Antwerp NV* EU:C:2013:239, para 25; Case C-424/97 *Salomone Haim v Kassenzahnärztliche Vereinigung Nordrhein* EU:C:2000:357, para 60.

[301] Case C-325/08 *Olympique Lyonnais v Olivier Bernard and Newcastle UFC* EU:C:2010:143.

[302] ibid para 45.

[303] Case 7-61 *Commission v Italy* EU:C:1961:31, p 329. See also Case 352/85 *Bond van Adverteerders and Others v The Netherlands State* EU:C:1988:196, para 34; Case C-288/89 *Stichting Collectieve Antennevoorziening Gouda and Others v Commissariaat voor de Media* EU:C:1991:323, para 11.

[304] Case 72/83 *Campus Oil Ltd and Others v Minister for Industry and Energy and Others* EU:C:1984:256, para 35.

[305] Case C-35/98 *Staatssecretaris van Financiën v B.G.M. Verkooijen* EU:C:2000:294.

[306] ibid para 48. See also Case C-398/95 *Syndesmos ton en Elladi Touristikon kai Taxidiotikon Grafeion v Ypourgos Ergasias* EU:C:1997:282, para 23.

[307] See, eg, Case C-544/11 *Helga Petersen and Peter Petersen v Finanzamt Ludwigshafen* EU:C:2013:124, para 50.

Therefore, the balancing within the confines of the justification regime prescribed by the Treaty's free movement provisions substantially differs from the approach followed in *Schmidberger*. Unlike the latter alternative, the former juristic method does not give effect to equal ranking between the freedoms of movement and fundamental rights that need to be brought into balance by ascertaining the proportionality of opposing restrictions.[308] The assessment under this method is one-sided, as it does not attribute equal weight and due consideration to both interests at stake. Contrasted against *Schmidberger*, *Viking*, for instance, does not reflect upon the substance of the right to strike and appears to undermine the significance of its recognition as a fundamental right.[309] As mentioned earlier, the exercise of the right to strike was not deemed sufficient on its own to justify a restriction of the freedom of establishment. Furthermore, the Court did not even assess the importance of that right in the collective bargaining process; instead, it focused on its restrictive effect and insisted on other means 'less restrictive of freedom of establishment'.[310] Lastly, there was no consideration of the circumstances where the exercise of the right to strike would require, in the sense of *Schmidberger*, tolerance of limitations imposed on the exercise of the freedom of establishment. The shortcomings of this methodology, combined with the lack of consistent application of the *Schmidberger* technique in the case law, make recourse to fundamental economic rights now enshrined in the Charter inevitable.

ii. Balancing under Competition Law

The case law also demonstrates the Court's tendency to equilibrate the Treaty's competition rules and fundamental economic rights within the derogation regime prescribed by the former set of provisions. Compared to free movement law, this is not necessarily problematic on its own since the reconciliation of the opposing interests within the normative prescriptions of Articles 101 and 102 TFEU, albeit not entirely immune from ambiguities, is not marred by the asymmetry of the horizontality that is intrinsic to their scope and the exclusively public nature of the available justification grounds. There are two factors at play. Despite certain overlaps with free movement law, the Treaty's competition rules were, from the outset, designed as norms primarily addressed to private actors. While the wording of the Treaty's competition rules may not contain explicit references to the protection of the freedom of contract or the right to property, these principles undoubtedly qualify the extent of their enforcement. This is more evident within the framework of Article 102 TFEU. The Court gives effect to these individual rights either

[308] Collins (n 227) 50.
[309] ACL Davies, 'One Step Forward, Two Steps Back? The *Viking* and *Laval* Cases in the ECJ' (2008) 37 *Industrial Law Journal* 126, 141.
[310] *Viking* (n 295) para 87.

directly or through specifically formulated conditions that delimit the extent of competition law enforcement.[311] In the *Bronner* line of case law, the Court aligned the fundamental nature of the right to property and the freedom of contract with the interests of undistorted competition in the internal market by applying the indispensability criterion. The obligation of a dominant undertaking to grant access to the infrastructure or service developed for its own needs is limited to a narrow set of circumstances where such access is '*indispensable* to carrying on the rival's business' (emphasis added).[312] As AG Jacobs explained in *Bronner*, the rationale for this criterion lies in 'the desire, from a legal point of view, to protect the right of an undertaking to choose its trading partners and freely to dispose of its property ... and, from an economic point of view, in the long term, to promote competition, in the interest of consumers, by allowing a company to retain for its own use facilities which it has developed'.[313] That said, the *Bronner* formula is not all-embracing. As recently confirmed in *Google Shopping*,[314] it does not apply to 'every issue of, or partly of, access';[315] instead, the normative reach of Article 102 TFEU is calibrated through the prescribed system of justification.

Despite the silence in the textual formulation of Article 102 TFEU, the Commission and the Court recognise the possibility of justifying market conduct liable to breach this provision.[316] Unlike Article 101 TFEU, the justification under Article 102 TFEU operates more as a 'denial defence' mechanism directed against a prima facie case of abuse of a dominant position.[317] As AG Jacobs stated in *Syfait*, based on the wording of this provision, 'the two-stage analysis suggested by the distinction between an abuse and its objective justification is ... somewhat artificial' because 'the very fact that conduct is characterised as an "abuse" suggests that a negative conclusion has already been reached'.[318] Hence, dominant market actors can invoke justification only to displace the presumption of abuse by exonerating their conduct from the scope of Article 102 TFEU.[319] The normative framework of this provision envisages, broadly construed, three types of justification. The first two are based on objective factors such as efficiency and public policy considerations. In *British Airways*, the Court held that '[in] the assessment of the economic justification of [a rebate system, granted by a dominant market actor] ... it [had] to be determined whether the exclusionary effect arising from such a

[311] *Aéroports de Paris v Commission* (n 255) para 51.

[312] *Oscar Bronner* (n 251) para 38.

[313] Opinion of AG Jacobs in *Oscar Bronner* (n 273) paras 56–62.

[314] Case T-612/17 *Google LLC, Formerly Google Inc. and Alphabet, Inc v Commission* EU:T:2021:763.

[315] ibid para 230. See also Case C-295/12 P *Telefónica SA and Telefónica de España SAU v Commission* EU:C:2014:2062, para 75; *Konkurrensverket v TeliaSonera Sverige AB* (n 183) paras 55–58.

[316] However, this was not the Court's initial approach; see, eg, Joined Cases T-191/98, T-212/98 to T-214/98 *Atlantic Container Line AB and Others v Commission* EU:T:2003:245, para 1112.

[317] V Brisimi, *The Interface between Competition and the Internal Market: Market Separation under Art 102 TFEU* (Oxford, Hart Publishing, 2016) 72.

[318] Opinion of AG Jacobs in Case C-53/03 *Synetairismos Farmakopoion Aitolias & Akarnanias (Syfait) and Others v GlaxoSmithKline plc and GlaxoSmithKline AEVE* EU:C:2004:673, para 72.

[319] *Intel* (n 220) para 140. See also Nazzini (n 178) 290.

system, which [was] disadvantageous for competition, [might] be counterbalanced, or outweighed, by advantages in terms of efficiency which also [benefited] the consumer'.[320] This is reflected in the Commission's Guidance that specifies the actual conditions for a successful plea of the efficiency-based justification.[321] The Guidance paper also refers to the possibility for public policy grounds that are non-economic, such as health and safety reasons, to justify exclusionary conduct,[322] though the extent to which they can counter the finding of an infringement of Article 102 TFEU is unclear. In one respect, in both *Hilti* and *Tetra Pak II*,[323] the Court rejected the pleas made pursuant to public health and consumer protection, stating that the remedy for these objectives must lie in the appropriate legislation and regulation[324] rather than be up to dominant market actors to decide.[325] On the contrary, a different conclusion follows from *Wouters*, in which the Court found no infringement of Article 101 TFEU if a restriction of competition stemmed from the pursuit of a regulatory objective by an undertaking.[326] It is not inconceivable, under specific circumstances,[327] for the Court to extend this line of reasoning to Article 102 TFEU.[328]

Even though both efficiency and public policy considerations provide the normative basis for balancing in the context of Article 102 TFEU, the immediate interests of dominant undertakings are primarily reflected in the third form of justification that is premised on the concept of 'competition on merits'. It is well established that a market actor reaching the threshold of dominance is not in itself a recrimination.[329] Article 102 TFEU does not prevent market actors from acquiring, on their own merits, such a position in the market.[330] It merely ensures that they refrain from having recourse to market strategies or tactics that fall outside the parameters of 'competition on merits',[331] depriving their competitors

[320] *British Airways* (n 179) para 86. See also *Konkurrensverket v TeliaSonera Sverige AB* (n 183) para 76.

[321] European Commission, Guidance on the enforcement priorities in applying Article 82 of the EC Treaty to abusive exclusionary conduct by dominant undertakings [2009] OJ C45/7, para 30.

[322] ibid para 29.

[323] Case T-30/89 *Hilti AG v Commission* EU:T:1991:70; Case T-83/91 *Tetra Pak International SA v Commission* EU:T:1994:246.

[324] *Tetra Pak* (n 323) para 84.

[325] *Hilti* (n 323) para 118.

[326] *Wouters* (n 297) paras 97–109. See also Joined Cases C-427/16 and C-428/16 *CHEZ Elektro Bulgaria AD v Yordan Kotsev* EU:C:2017:890, para 54; Case C-184/13 *API – Anonima Petroli Italiana SpA and Others v Ministero delle Infrastrutture e dei Trasporti and Others* EU:C:2014:2147, para 55.

[327] See Case C-250/92 *Gøttrup-Klim ea Grovvareforeninger v Dansk Landbrugs Grovvareselskab AmbA* EU:C:1994:413, paras 50–51.

[328] See M Mataija, *Private Regulation and the Internal Market: Sports, Legal Services, and Standard Setting in EU Economic Law* (Oxford, Oxford University Press, 2016) 96; E Rousseva, 'The Concept of "Objective Justification" of an Abuse of a Dominant Position: Can it Help to Modernise the Analysis under Article 82 EC?' (2006) 2 *Competition Law Review* 27, 41.

[329] *Michelin* (n 250) para 57. See also *Intel* (n 220) para 133.

[330] Case T-235/18 *Qualcomm, Inc v Commission* EU:T:2022:358, para 349.

[331] *Irish Sugar plc v Commission* (n 219) para 111.

or non-competitors of access to market opportunities.[332] Dominant market actors, therefore, retain the ability to compete on merits.[333] They are entitled to protect their commercial interests when they are threatened by competitors or new market entrants offering lower prices or better trading terms.[334] The exclusionary effect of such conduct would not necessarily breach the Treaty. This is because 'competition on the merits may, by definition, lead to the departure from the market or the marginalisation of competitors that are less efficient and so less attractive to consumers from the point of view of, among other things, price, choice, quality or innovation'.[335]

However, as a concept, 'competition on merits' remains elusive. It is difficult to define in abstract terms what constitutes competitive market behaviour and what factors separate it from anti-competitive market conduct. A query along these lines was raised in *Servizio Elettrico Nazionale and Others*,[336] where the national court requested clarification over means that come within the scope of 'competition on merits' for establishing an infringement of Article 102 TFEU. To determine whether the conduct of a dominant undertaking conforms to the parameters of 'competition on merits', the Court highlighted the criterion of material and rational impossibility of a hypothetical, equally efficient competitor to imitate the conduct in question. Under this criterion, two categories of market practices fall outside the scope of 'competition on merits'. First, this concept does not encompass 'any practice the implementation of which holds no economic interest for a dominant undertaking, except that of eliminating competitors'.[337] This concerns practices such as loyalty rebates, predatory pricing or margin squeezes.[338] In terms of their effect, they substantially differ from the market conduct that reduces a dominant undertaking's costs, increases efficiency and broadens consumer choice through the introduction of new goods or services or the improvement of their quality.[339] In *Qualcomm*,[340] the General Court set aside the Commission's decision that Qualcomm's exclusivity payments for the supply of chipsets to Apple produced a foreclosure effect. According to the General Court, the Commission failed to demonstrate that these payments denied Qualcomm's rivals the possibility to compete for Apple's

[332] See, eg, Case T-111/96 *ITT Promedia NV v Commission* EU:T:1998:183, para 138; Case T-203/01 *Manufacture française des pneumatiques Michelin v Commission* EU:T:2003:250, paras 54 and 97.

[333] *Hoffmann-La Roche* (n 189) para 6.

[334] *Atlantic Container Line* (n 316) para 28. See also *Irish Sugar plc v Commission* (n 219) para 112.

[335] Case C-680/20 *Unilever Italia Mkt Operations Srl v Autorità Garante della Concorrenza e del Mercato* EU:C:2023:33, para 37.

[336] Case C-377/20 *Servizio Elettrico Nazionale SpA and Others v Autorità Garante della Concorrenza e del Mercato and Others* EU:C:2022:379.

[337] ibid para 77.

[338] See, eg, Case C-549/10 P *Tomra Systems and Others v Commission* EU:C:2012:221; Case T-201/11 Si.mobil *telekomunikacijske storitve dd v Commission* EU:T:2014:1096; Case C-202/07 P *France Télécom SA v Commission* EU:C:2009:214.

[339] Opinion of AG Rantos in Case C-377/20 *Servizio Elettrico Nazionale SpA and Others v Autorità Garante della Concorrenza e del Mercato and Others* EU:C:2021:998, para 62.

[340] *Qualcomm, Inc v Commission* (n 330).

business. This is because, even without these payments, Apple had no incentive to switch to Qualcomm's competitors, for they could not satisfy Apple's exacting technical and scheduling requirements.[341] Therefore, in the General Court's verdict, Apple sourcing chipsets from Qualcomm and not from its competitors fell within the parameters of competition on merits without producing an anticompetitive foreclosure effect.[342]

Second, the concept of 'competition on merits' does not cover a practice that a hypothetical, equally efficient competitor cannot adopt due to an undertaking's reliance on the use of resources or means inherent in holding a dominant position.[343] This relates to the refusal by a dominant undertaking to grant access to the infrastructure that its competitors cannot replicate or when such access is made more difficult.[344] In *Google Shopping*, Google challenged the Commission's finding that it abused its dominant position by self-favouring its comparison-shopping service. Among Google's pleas was the submission that promoting the positioning and display of its comparison-shopping service was part of the quality improvement in its general search engine that constituted 'competition on merits' and hence could not be treated as abusive. The General Court rejected this argument. It ruled that such a practice could not fall within the scope of 'competition on merits' due to its economic irrationality and apparent inconsistency with the intended purpose of a general search engine.[345] The General Court concluded that there was 'a certain form of abnormality' in Google's practice since the value of the infrastructure at stake lay 'in its capacity to be open to results from external (third-party) sources … which [enriched and enhanced] the credibility of the search engine as far as the general public [was] concerned'.[346] On this premise, according to the General Court, Google's promotion of its comparison-shopping service and the demotion of competing services by an adjustment algorithm could not be considered as a method falling within the scope of 'competition on merits'.

Compared to the other two forms of defence, the concept of 'competition on merits' stands at the heart of what amounts to abuse of a dominant position within the meaning of Article 102 TFEU. It can be characterised as an objective standard that operates at the stage of establishing the presumption of abuse and not just its rebuttal. Setting out the contours of 'competition on merits' mirrors the determination of the constituent elements of abusive conduct. However, while the concept of 'competition on merits' gives effect to the immediate interests of undertakings under investigation, it is not without its challenges. First, as mentioned earlier, it is difficult to define in advance specific market practices

[341] ibid para 414.
[342] ibid.
[343] *Servizio Elettrico Nazionale* (n 336) para 78.
[344] Opinion of AG Rantos in *Servizio Elettrico Nazionale* (n 339) para 71.
[345] *Google* (n 314) para 184.
[346] ibid para 178.

that correspond to 'competition on merits'. As AG Rantos pointed out in *Servizio Elettrico Nazionale and Others*, its abstract nature expresses an economic ideal against which the current competition law enforcement favours the analysis of the anti-competitive effect of market conduct over the one based on its form.[347] Second, 'competition on merits' as a 'defence' has only been accepted in limited circumstances.[348] The reason lies in the conditions attached. To invoke it, a dominant undertaking must demonstrate that its market conduct is suitable, necessary and proportionate to the threat emanating from its competitors or new market entrants.[349] What these conditions entail lacks sufficient clarity,[350] which is problematic given that they tread a fine line between an intention to abuse a dominant position and a mere response to the challenges posed by competitors or new market entrants.[351]

iii. Balancing under the Charter

The previous two sections focused on the Court's established practice to resolve the normative conflicts arising from the extent of enforcement of the Treaty's free movement and competition rules against private actors. From a conceptual standpoint, it was shown that the analytical approach solely framed around the set of derogations prescribed by the Treaty often entails somewhat one-sided and even asymmetrical proportionality assessment. Undoubtedly, it is the nature of the infringed norm that directs and frames the scrutiny around the set of limitations allowed in relation to that norm and the specific conditions attached thereof. However, the intersection between fundamental economic rights and the Treaty's free movement and competition rules shapes a different normative landscape within which they must be reconciled. While intrinsically linked, they generate two opposing claims for the protection of individual rights, where each raises the need to delimit the respective sphere of application of the opposing norm at stake. As identified by AG Trstenjak in *Commission v Germany*, the effective realisation of fundamental economic rights constitutes a legitimate objective that prompts limits to the enforcement of the Treaty's free movement and competition rules.[352] Conversely, the effective realisation of market freedom pursued by the latter provisions is a legitimate reason to restrict the exercise of fundamental economic rights.[353] Such a clash of claims resonates, to a considerable degree, with traditional private law disputes that are adjudicated premised on the presumption

[347] Opinion of AG Rantos in *Servizio Elettrico Nazionale* (n 339) para 55.
[348] C Simpson, 'Dominant Firms and Selective Discounting in the EU: When is "Meeting Competition" a Defence?' (2016) 12 *European Competition Journal* 1, 12.
[349] Case 27/76 *United Brands Company and United Brands Continentaal BV v Commission* EU:C:1978:22, paras 189–90.
[350] The Guidance on Article 102 TFEU does not even mention this form of justification.
[351] G Monti, *EC Competition Law* (Cambridge, Cambridge University Press, 2007) 206–07.
[352] Opinion of AG Trstenjak in *Commission v Germany* (n 287) para 188.
[353] ibid.

of competing interests and policies existing on both sides of the argument that carry equal weight and warrant due consideration.[354] Measured against this, the reconciliation of fundamental economic rights with the Treaty's free movement and competition rules requires the concurrent assessment of interference with each provision based on the proportionality principle.

As pointed out above, the double test of proportionality is not extraneous to the case law, despite the Court's inconsistency in applying it since *Schmidberger*. In the present context, with the Lisbon Treaty in force, one limb of this test would trigger the protective safeguards built in Articles 15-17 CFR taken in conjunction with the justification regime laid out in Article 52(1) CFR. This combination offers private actors a new additional platform to assert their rights. Alongside the general principles of Union law, it assumes the role of ensuring that no deficit occurs in the protection of fundamental economic rights when enforcing Union law. In particular, under Article 52(1) CFR, the legitimacy of every form of interference with the Charter, regardless of its nature, must flow from the satisfaction of a set of benchmarks. According to this provision, any limitation 'must be provided for by law', 'must respect the essence of [the Charter's rights or freedoms]' and, 'subject to the principle of proportionality', 'may only be made if [it is] necessary and genuinely [meets] objectives of general interest recognised by the Union or the need to protect the rights and freedoms of others'. Much like the Treaty's free movement rules, Article 52(1) CFR mandates proportionality analysis as a juristic method to balance the interests protected as fundamental rights in the Charter and other interests or countervailing policy considerations.

However, there is conceptual and substantive distinctiveness to the justification regime under Article 52 CFR. It also enshrines the requirement that any limitation on the right protected by the Charter must respect the essence of that right. This clause purports the existence of an inalienable core of a right that cannot be limited by any reason. Whilst much has been written on the proportionality principle and its parameters, the essence of a right has received very little attention. The value added by this concept is that it epitomises the fundamental characteristics of constitutional rights. In comparison, it is normatively alien to the freedoms of movement, not to mention the Treaty's competition rules even when considered in the capacity of privately enforceable rights. Indeed, the Court often employs the terminology of 'fundamental rights' or 'fundamental principles' when dealing with the Treaty's free movement and competition rules.[355] Yet, such fundamentality does not carry the same connotation. Within the framework of constitutional rights, it encapsulates their universality that is historically shaped by the common

[354] Collins (n 227) 50.

[355] See, eg, Case 240/83 *Procureur de la République v Association de défense des brûleurs d'huiles usagées (ADBHU)* EU:C:1985:59, para 9.

European constitutional tradition.[356] It is also intrinsic, in its substance, to the respect for human dignity.[357] In contrast, the entitlement to unhindered interstate movement and competition is not fundamental in a similar sense. This is because the Treaty's free movement and competition rules are grounded in the specific political and legal context developed at the Union level.[358] Their fundamentality is expressed in the enforcement of commitments undertaken by Member States within the internal market framework.[359] This difference prompts two interrelated queries. First, it is questionable how the essence clause under Article 52 CFR fits the parameters of the double test of proportionality if the latter were to serve as a formula to balance the interests protected by fundamental economic rights and those served by the Treaty's free movement and competition rules. Second, as a rights protection instrument, it is unclear what constitutes the essence of fundamental economic rights codified in the Charter.

a. The Concept of 'Essence' under Article 52(1) CFR

The respect for the essence of a right as a limitation on the restrictions of fundamental rights is an attribute of the constitutional compact formed in Europe in the post-war period.[360] This concept traces its origin to the German Basic Law that influenced its incorporation into the constitutions of other Member States.[361] Even though the essence clause is not expressly recognised in the text of the ECHR, it has attained prominence in the case law of the Strasbourg Court.[362] Finally, the inclusion of the essence clause in Article 52(1) CFR reflects the body of the case law existing before the introduction of the Charter. The Explanations to the Charter expressly quote the passage in *Karlsson*, which reiterated the finding in *Nold* that 'the rights thereby guaranteed, far from constituting unfettered prerogatives, must be viewed in the light of the social function … [and] if necessary, be subject to certain limits justified by the overall objectives pursued by the community, *on condition that the substance of these rights is left untouched*' (emphasis added).[363]

[356] T Tridimas and G Gentile, 'The Essence of Rights: An Unreliable Boundary?' (2019) 20 *German Law Journal* 794, 812. According to the authors, a different picture emerges within the framework of EU citizenship case law.

[357] H Voogsgeerd, 'The EU Charter of Fundamental Rights and its Impact on Labor Law: A Plea for a Proportionality-Test "Light"' (2012) *Goettingen Journal of International* Law 293, 296.

[358] De Cecco (n 97) 386.

[359] W Sauter and H Schepel, *State and Market in European Union Law: The Public and Private Spheres of the Internal Market before the EU Courts* (Cambridge, Cambridge University Press, 2019) 11.

[360] Tridimas and Gentile (n 356) 795.

[361] K Lenaerts, 'Limits on Limitations: The Essence of Fundamental Rights in the EU' (2019) 20 *German Law Journal* 779, 780.

[362] For its place in the case law of the ECtHR, see S van Drooghenbroeck and C Rizcallah, 'The ECHR and the Essence of Fundamental Rights: Searching for Sugar in Hot Milk?' (2019) 20 *German Law Journal* 904.

[363] *Nold* (n 98) para 14; Case 44/79 *Liselotte Hauer v Land Rheinland-Pfalz* EU:C:1979:290, para 23.

As the case law suggests, the concepts of 'essence' and 'substance' are coterminous and may be used interchangeably.[364]

The conceptualisation of the notion of essence is a delicate and complex task that does not admit an easy answer. Conflicting legal theories exist about its meaning and function. One of the main points of contention is whether the essence of rights should be understood in absolute or relative terms. This query finds its roots in the divergent understandings of the character of rights as constitutional norms and, concomitantly, the contrasting models of adjudication within the human rights space. Some contend that constitutional rights are deontological constraints that represent the correct standards of moral and legal reasoning and, as such, cannot be balanced against any other normative factors.[365] Dworkin famously conceptualised rights as '*trumps* over some background justification for a political decision that states a goal for the community as a whole' (emphasis added).[366] Habermas, in turn, described rights as 'firewalls' that constrain legislative choices.[367]

In contrast, others define constitutional rights as norms possessing a teleological structure that requires balancing in any and all instances of their application.[368] Alexy, for example, claims that what the right holder has by virtue of having rights is not a subjective entitlement that takes priority over any other countervailing concerns.[369] In his understanding, which is unfused by teleology and deontology,[370] most rights are 'principles' and 'principles' are 'optimisation commands', which require 'the realisation of something to the greatest extent possible given the legal and factual possibilities'.[371] The infringement of a right only serves to trigger the proportionality-focused balancing of colliding principles based on the weight attached to each side.[372]

According to these conceptions of rights, the characterisation of their essence varies considerably. At one end, the so-called absolutist theory is premised on the idea that fundamental rights as norms consist of two integral components: a nucleus that must remain free from interference and a periphery, the protection of which can be reconciled with opposing reasons.[373] For the proponents of this

[364] On the use of the term 'essence' to denote the 'substance' of a right, see Opinion of AG Trabucchi in Case 4/73 *Nold* EU:C:1974:27, 515.

[365] G Pavlakos, 'Constitutional Rights, Balancing and the Structure of Autonomy' (2011) 24 *Canadian Journal of Law and Jurisprudence* 129, 129.

[366] R Dworkin, 'Rights as Trumps' in J Waldron (ed), *Theories of Rights* (Oxford, Oxford University Press, 1984) 153.

[367] J Habermas, *Between Facts and Norms: Contributions to a Discourse Theory of Law and Democracy* (Cambridge, MA, MIT Press, 1996) 258–59.

[368] Pavlakos (n 365) 129.

[369] R Alexy, 'Individual Rights and Collective Goods' in CS Nino (ed), *Rights* (Dartmouth, Aldershot, 1992) 166.

[370] Pavlakos (n 365).

[371] R Alexy, *A Theory of Constitutional Rights* (Oxford, Oxford University Press, 2009) 47.

[372] M Kumm, 'Institutionalising Socratic Contestation: The Rationalist Human Rights Paradigm, Legitimate Authority and the Point of Judicial Review' (2007) 1 *European Journal of Legal Studies* 153, 161.

[373] Lenaerts (n 361) 786.

approach, the notion of the essence of a right and proportionality are distinct, non-overlapping categories that mutually exclude one another.[374] No proportionality inquiry is to be carried out in relation to the interference with the essence of a right, for it can never be overridden by other considerations.[375] A measure is unlawful once it is established that the essence of a right has been compromised.[376] The respect for the essence thus creates a limit to the pursuit of countervailing interests without the proportionality-based balancing.[377] The sphere to which proportionality applies ends where the boundary of a right's nucleus begins.[378] This is because the supporters of this approach see no independent value in the concept of essence and in its role of preventing certain limitations if it is not possible to define the essence of a right separately from proportionality. For them, therefore, the inviolability of the inner core of a right and putting it beyond balancing constitute a '*sine qua non*' for the constitutionality of interference with a right.[379]

At the other end, the so-called relativist theory constructs the notion of essence as a somewhat redundant concept.[380] It is based on the premise that any interference with a fundamental right, including those that touch its core, can only be determined by employing the proportionality principle.[381] Under this view, a right's nucleus is not immune from affliction but permits balancing the essence of a right with countervailing interests and considerations.[382] For the advocates of this approach, the notion of essence is seated in relativity, whereby it only becomes apparent when viewed against its background.[383] It exists in symbiosis with proportionality to the point that there are partial overlaps between them, expressed in the fact that finding a breach of essence depends on a balancing exercise.[384] A right's nucleus is what is deemed to remain once it is established whether interference is proportional to the societal needs, requirements and aspirations.[385] The relativist theory conceptualises a fundamental right as a progressive entitlement, whereby the greater the infliction, the greater the need for

[374] M Brkan, 'In Search of the Concept of Essence of EU Fundamental Rights Through the Prism of Data Privacy' (2017) 1 *Maastricht University Faculty of Law Working Papers* 1, 22.

[375] Tridimas and Gentile (n 356) 803.

[376] Lenaerts (n 361) 781.

[377] J Rivers, 'Proportionality and Variable Intensity of Review' (2006) 65 *Cambridge Law Journal* 174, 184.

[378] I Leijten, *Core Socio-economic Rights and the European Court of Human Rights* (Cambridge, Cambridge University Press, 2017) 123.

[379] Tridimas and Gentile (n 356) 803.

[380] M Brkan, 'The Essence of the Fundamental Rights to Privacy and Data Protection: Finding the Way through the Maze of the CJEU's Constitutional Reasoning' (2019) 20 *German Law Journal* 864, 867.

[381] M Husovec, 'The Essence of Intellectual Property Rights under Article 17(2) of the EU Charter' (2019) 20 *German Law Journal* 840, 847.

[382] Tridimas and Gentile (n 356) 803.

[383] G van der Schyff, 'Cutting to the Core of Conflicting Rights: The Question of Inalienable Cores in Comparative Perspective' in E Brems (ed), *Conflicts between Fundamental Rights* (Antwerp, Intersentia, 2008) 134.

[384] Brkan (n 374) 4.

[385] Van der Schyff (n 383) 135.

justification.[386] For the advocates of this approach, fundamental rights gain unequally in strength as the intensity of interference increases, since a very serious form of interference can hardly ever be exculpated by raising the weight of the justifying reasons.[387]

The language and structure of Article 52(1) CFR lend more support for the absolutist approach. This provision sets out the essence clause and other preconditions as cumulative requirements to the extent that the failure to meet either would render any limitation unlawful.[388] In its first sentence, Article 52(1) CFR requires that any limitation on the exercise of fundamental rights must be provided for by law and must respect their essence, while the principle of proportionality is only mentioned in the second sentence. This suggests that the respect for essence is designed as a stand-alone test preceding the proportionality-based inquiry. Its autonomous input is manifested in the progressive assessment within the framework of Article 52(1) CFR, whereby the determination of a breach of essence comes first, followed by proportionality analysis in the absence of such a breach.[389]

The absolutist approach is also reflected in the practice of the Court,[390] despite the lack of systematic engagement with the essence clause that is prevalent in the case law.[391] *Schrems* was the first ruling to recognise a breach of the essence of a fundamental right protected under the Charter without recourse to the proportionality assessment.[392] In that case, the Court found that the legislation allowing authorities 'to have access on a generalised basis to the content of electronic communications' constituted a violation of the essence of the fundamental right to respect for private life as guaranteed by Article 7 CFR.[393] Likewise, the Court held that the legislation that did not provide 'any possibility for an individual to pursue legal remedies in order to have access to personal data relating to him, or to obtain the rectification or erasure of such data' did not respect the essence of the fundamental right to effective judicial protection under Article 47 CFR.[394] A similar verdict was also reached in *LM*,[395] where the Court concluded that the executing judicial authority is permitted to refrain from giving effect to the European arrest warrant if there was a real risk that the person in respect of whom it was

[386] Tridimas and Gentile (n 356) 803.

[387] M Klatt and M Meister, 'Proportionality: A Benefit to Human Rights? Remarks on the I·CON Controversy' (2012) 10 *International Journal of Constitutional Law* 687, 691.

[388] Tridimas and Gentile (n 356) 803.

[389] Brkan (n 374) 22.

[390] See, eg, Joined Cases C-203/15 and C-698/15 *Tele2 Sverige AB v Post- och telestyrelsen and Secretary of State for the Home Department v Tom Watson and Others* EU:C:2016:970; Case C-291/12 *Michael Schwarz v Stadt Bochum* EU:C:2013:670.

[391] See also Tridimas and Gentile (n 356) 803.

[392] Case C-362/14 *Maximillian Schrems v Data Protection Commissioner* EU:C:2015:650.

[393] ibid para 94.

[394] ibid.

[395] Case C-216/18 PPU *LM (Minister for Justice and Equality (Deficiencies in the System of Justice)* EU:C:2018:586.

issued suffered a breach of the right to an independent tribunal. This is because 'the requirement of judicial independence forms part of the *essence of the fundamental right to a fair trial*, a right which is of cardinal importance as a guarantee that all the rights which individuals derive from EU law will be protected and that the values common to the Member States ... in particular the value of the rule of law, will be safeguarded' (emphasis added).[396]

Within the framework of fundamental economic rights, the case law also endorses the role of essence as a stand-alone requirement distinct from the proportionality assessment. This follows from the Court's tendency to separate the essence test from other prescribed preconditions under Article 52(1) CFR by strictly following the wording of this provision. In *Sky Österreich*,[397] the Court held that a measure limiting the ability of the holder of exclusive broadcasting rights to decide freely on the price to charge interfered with the freedom under Article 16 CFR. In terms of its possible justification within the framework of Article 52 CFR, it ruled that the measure did not affect the core content of the freedom to conduct a business before proceeding with the proportionality assessment. In *Alemo-Herron*,[398] in turn, the Court found a breach of essence contrary to Article 16 CFR. It concluded that the inability of the transferee of employment contracts to participate in collective bargaining negotiations reduced its contractual freedom to the point of adversely affecting the very essence of its freedom to conduct business.[399] Unlike *Sky Österreich*, this finding was not followed by the proportionality assessment against the legitimate grounds of employee protection. This line of case law, read in conjunction with *Schrems*, identifies a twofold structure to fundamental rights consisting of a core and a periphery. Any compromise of the core of a right cannot be exculpated on any grounds by balancing competing interests under the proportionality assessment.[400] Such an exercise is reserved for when a limitation of the periphery of a right is at stake, provided that its essence is unaffected.

At the same time, the adherence of the Court to this approach is not unequivocal. The Court does not always analytically engage with the concept of essence. Sometimes, the reference to it is made *in passim* only to outline the preconditions under Article 52(1) CFR.[401] On other occasions, the Court primarily focuses on the proportionality assessment by either combining it with the essence test or not mentioning the latter at all.[402] In *Association Kokopelli*,[403] the Court

[396] ibid para 48. See also Joined Cases C-245/19 and C-246/19 *État luxembourgeois v B and Others* EU:C:2020:795, para 69.

[397] *Sky Österreich* (n 55).

[398] ibid para 44.

[399] *Mark Alemo-Herron and Others* (n 96).

[400] ibid para 35.

[401] Tridimas and Gentile (n 356) 807. See Case C-101/12 *Herbert Schaible v Land Baden-Württemberg* EU:C:2013:661, para 27.

[402] See, eg, Case C-729/18 P *VTB Bank PAO, Formerly VTB Bank OAO v Council* EU:C:2020:499, para 80; Case C-501/18 *BT v Balgarska Narodna Banka* EU:C:2021:249, para 109; Case C-611/12 P *Jean-François Giordano v Commission* EU:C:2014:2282, para 49.

[403] Case C-59/11 *Association Kokopelli v Graines Baumaux* SAS EU:C:2012:447.

held that the Union's regime for vegetable seeds was capable of restricting traders' freedom to pursue their professional activity.[404] Without any reference to the essence of Article 16 CFR, it then moved on to the issue of justification by ruling that the obstacle at stake was not disproportionate in terms of impairing the right to exercise that freedom.[405] Likewise, in *Deutsches Weintor*,[406] the Court appeared to conflate the essence test with the proportionality assessment. There, it held that the prohibition of health claims in advertising restricted the freedom to pursue economic activity, though it was not disproportionate and hence did not in any way affect the substance of the freedom under Article 16 CFR.[407] The reasoning in both rulings was premised on the formula long established by the Court, according to which restrictions imposed on rights recognised in the Union cannot constitute 'a disproportionate and intolerable interference, impairing the very substance of those rights'.[408] On the face of it, this formula integrates the concept of 'substance', which coincides with that of 'essence',[409] into the proportionality consideration. It transforms the requirement to respect the substance/essence of a right from the 'limit of limits' that defines the validity of the interference with a right to a prerequisite that sets a minimum threshold in the proportionality assessment. However, on a deeper level, this formula alludes to the convergence in the interpretative process under both essence and proportionality requirements. Their separation may be maintained conceptually, though its practical realisation is rather complex. It is not often possible to determine the essence of a right without engaging in balancing based on the proportionality analysis.[410] A measure going beyond the acceptable level of limitation imposed on the exercise of a right would certainly be disproportionate, though it would also affect its essence.[411]

b. The Essence of Individual Economic Rights

The extent of the enforcement of the Treaty's free movement and competition rules for achieving the internal market goal cannot deprive individuals of the inviolable core of the right to property, the freedom of contract or the freedom to engage in economic or commercial activity. This begs the question of how the essence of a fundamental right is to be distinguished from its periphery. The case law does not provide any concrete criteria as the Court often abstains from

[404] ibid para 78.
[405] ibid para 79.
[406] Case C-544/10 *Deutsches Weintor eG v Land Rheinland-Pfalz* EU:C:2012:526.
[407] ibid para 54.
[408] See Case 44/79 *Liselotte Hauer v Land Rheinland-Pfalz* EU:C:1979:290, para 23.
[409] Case T-187/11 *Mohamed Trabelsi and Others v Council* EU:T:2013:273, para 81.
[410] Tridimas and Gentile (n 356) 804.
[411] S Peers and S Prechal, 'Scope and Interpretation of the Rights and Principles' in S Peers, T Harvey, J Kenner and A Ward (eds), *The EU Charter of Fundamental Rights: A Commentary* (Oxford, Hart Publishing, 2014) 1480.

engaging in the normative delimitation of the interests recognised as fundamental rights.[412] Instead, it defines the requirement to respect the essence of a right to mean that the right 'is not called into question as such'.[413] The Court's language suggests that the essence of a right is compromised when the impugned limitation empties that right of its content to the point of calling its very existence into doubt.[414] Indeed, AG Trabucchi defined the concept of essence to consist '*in the recognition of the existence of the rights themselves*, but not, as regards their exercise, in the recognition of all the powers which [could] make up the content of those rights' (emphasis added).[415] AG Trabucchi also added that the exercise and particular composition of rights were 'without doubt subject to the evolution of rules whose respect for the right [was] unassailable only so far as concern[ed] the essence of the right, which alone [was] regarded as inviting fundamental protection'.[416] A breach of essence, thus, occurs when a fundamental right no longer offers any practical value,[417] leaving the right holder devoid of protection.[418] On this premise, for the enforcement of the Treaty's free movement and competition rules to compromise the essence of fundamental economic rights, there must be an inimical effect on the realisation of the essential attributes that frame their nature as distinct fundamental rights.[419] This invites a further question of what constitutes their essential attributes and what constitutes interference in this context.

To address this query, the following two sections focus on the essence of the right to property and the freedom to conduct business. Although the essence clause equally extends to Article 15 CFR, the likelihood of the enforcement of the Treaty's free movement and competition rules affecting the freedom to choose an occupation protected by this provision seems minimal. This is based on two overlapping factors. First, from a normative perspective, Article 15 CFR is intrinsically connected to Article 16 CFR. In *Spain v Commission*,[420] the Court confirmed that 'freedom to conduct a business ... coincide[d] with freedom to pursue an occupation'.[421] Therefore, it is not surprising that Articles 15 and 16 CFR are often

[412] *Nold* (n 98) 110.

[413] Case C-537/16 *Garlsson Real Estate and Others v Commissione Nazionale per le Società e la Borsa* EU:C:2018:193, para 45; Case C-524/15 *Luca Menci* EU:C:2018:197, para 43; Case C-129/14 PPU *Zoran Spasic* EU:C:2014:586, para 58.

[414] Lenaerts (n 361) 784.

[415] Opinion of AG Trabucchi in *Nold* (n 364) 515.

[416] ibid.

[417] Brkan (n 374) 16. This seems to underlie the divergent verdicts in *Maximillian Schrems* (n 392) and *Tele2 Sverige* (n 390); Joined Cases C-293/12 and C-594/12 *Digital Rights Ireland Ltd v Minister for Communications, Marine and Natural Resources and Others and Kärntner Landesregierung and Others* EU:C:2014:238.

[418] Case C-484/14 *Tobias Mc Fadden v Sony Music Entertainment Germany GmbH* EU:C:2016:689, para 88.

[419] Tridimas and Gentile (n 356) 804.

[420] Joined Cases C-184/02 and C-223/02 *Spain and Finland v Parliament and Council* EU:C:2004:497.

[421] ibid para 51.

applied in tandem, and there are even instances where the Court gave preference to scrutiny under the latter provision.[422] Second, notwithstanding the overlaps between them, Articles 15 and 16 differ in terms of the extent of their conceptual and structural alignment with the Treaty's free movement and competition rules. On the one hand, as mentioned previously, Article 15 CFR explicitly refers to the Treaty's free movement provisions by guaranteeing every Union citizen 'the freedom to seek employment, to work and to exercise the right of establishment in any Member State'.[423] On the other hand, as AG Bobek pointed out in *Lidl*,[424] unlike Article 16 CFR, which concerns already established forms of business and occupation, Article 15 CFR applies to natural persons and is concerned with their access to work and choice of occupation.[425] Hence, it is difficult to envisage the enforcement of the freedoms of movement impinging on the essence of this individual entitlement, as they are designed to facilitate such private initiatives across borders in the internal market.

(1) The Essence of the Right to Property

The essence of the right to property can be conceptualised to encapsulate what an owner has by virtue of his or her entitlement to possession protected by law. A restriction that fails to meet the requirement to respect the essence of this right is unlawful per se and cannot be justified on objective grounds.[426] This prompts the question of what degree of harm to ownership would lead to a breach of the essence of the right to property. Article 17 CFR proclaims that 'everyone has the right to own, use, dispose of and bequeath his or her lawfully acquired possessions'. Although this range of attributes associated with ownership lacks a precise definition, it is reasonable to construe them to form the essential components of the right to property. They represent the constituent elements without which ownership protection ceases to provide any value to its right holder. Support for this reading, albeit not explicitly, can be found in the case law. The Court generally tends to frame the breach of the essence of the right to property in terms of the degree of availability of the attributes now specified by Article 17 CFR.[427] According to its approach, such a breach occurs when an owner is denied the possibility to exercise 'autonomously and for his benefit' rights 'with an asset value creating, under the legal system, an established legal position'.[428] Under this characterisation, for the

[422] See, eg, *PI* (n 45) paras 54–55.

[423] See Case C-166/20 *BB v Lietuvos Respublikos sveikatos apsaugos ministerija* EU:C:2021:554, para 31.

[424] Opinion of AG Bobek in Case C-134/15 *Lidl GmbH & Co KG v Freistaat Sachsen* EU:C:2016:169.

[425] ibid para 27.

[426] P Oliver and C Stothers, 'Intellectual Property under the Charter: Are the Court's Scales Properly Calibrated?' (2017) 54 *Common Market Law Review* 517, 536.

[427] This follows from the case law on the freezing of assets. See, eg, Case T-510/18 *Khaled Kaddour v Council* EU:T:2020:436, para 169; Case T-153/15 *Mohamad Hamcho and Hamcho International v Council* EU:T:2016:630, para 122. See also separately Case C-393/19 *Criminal Proceedings against OM* EU:C:2021:8, paras 59–68.

[428] Case C-398/13 P *Inuit Tapiriit Kanatami and Others v Commission* EU:C:2015:535, para 60.

enforcement of the Treaty to fall foul of the requirement to respect the essence of the right to property, it must lead to the loss of the intrinsic value of ownership.

In the context of competition law, this assertion finds support in the dichotomy drawn by the Court between the existence of property rights and their exercise. In *Consten and Grundig*,[429] the Court held that the enforcement of Article 101 TFEU did not affect the grant of intellectual property rights under national law but only limited their exercise to the extent necessary to give effect to the prohibition of an anti-competitive agreement.[430] A distinction along these lines can also be observed in *Slovak Telekom*, which identified two categories of refusal to grant access to infrastructure. In that case, the Court found that it would be detrimental to the right to property to force a dominant undertaking to provide access to the infrastructure it had developed for its own needs.[431] However, according to the Court, when a dominant undertaking grants access to its infrastructure but subjects it to unfair conditions, competition enforcement measures 'will … be less detrimental' to the right to property.[432] The existence/exercise dichotomy did not take long to find its way into free movement law. Its applicability was confirmed in *Deutsche Grammophon*,[433] where the issue concerned the compatibility with the Treaty of the injunction obtained by a proprietor prohibiting a third party from selling or marketing its intangible assets. Considered in the context of Article 34 TFEU, the Court first conceded that the Treaty envisaged the protection of industrial and commercial property as an exception to the prohibition of restrictions on the free movement of goods. However, the Court continued that while the Treaty '[did] not affect the *existence* of rights … with regard to industrial and commercial property, the *exercise* of such rights [might] nevertheless fall within the prohibitions laid down by the Treaty' (emphasis added).[434] In particular, the Court elaborated that the Treaty admitted derogations only to safeguard rights which constituted 'the specific subject-matter of [industrial and commercial property]'.[435] It follows that in the context of the enforcement of the Treaty's free movement and competition rules, a possible breach of the essence of a proprietary right depends on the overall extent to which the exercise of that right is restricted and still subsists. Although the applicable parameters are not always clear-cut, two overlapping strands of reasoning can be drawn from the Court's practice based on the concepts of deprivation and control of proprietary rights.

[429] Joined Cases 56 and 58-64 *Établissements Consten SàRL and Grundig-Verkaufs-GmbH v Commission* EU:C:1966:41.

[430] ibid, 345. See also Case 24-67 *Parke, Davis and Co v Probel, Reese, Beintema-Interpharm and Centrafarm* EU:C:1968:11, 72.

[431] *Slovak Telekom* (n 275) para 46. See also *AB Volvo* (n 270) para 8.

[432] ibid para 51.

[433] Case 78-70 *Deutsche Grammophon Gesellschaft mbH v Metro-SB-Großmärkte GmbH & Co KG* EU:C:1971:59.

[434] ibid para 11.

[435] ibid.

In one strand of case law, a breach of essence is found in the interference that leads to deprivation.[436] Such intrusion causes the dispossession of property by taking away the ownership over it from the proprietor.[437] This covers the instances of expropriation and nationalisation, the legality of which under Article 17 CFR is contingent on fair compensation being paid in good time for the loss sustained.[438] Deprivation can also occur without the formal transfer of property so long as a measure nullifies the essential attributes of ownership.[439] In *Biovilac*,[440] the Court found that a measure divesting an owner of its property and preventing or limiting the freedom to put it into use encroached upon the substance of the right to property.[441] In one respect, such an effect takes place when the existence of the right to property is challenged. In *HOLD Alapkezelő*,[442] the Court held that the contested measure would constitute the deprivation of property contrary to Article 17 CFR if it called into question employees' right to property over company shares.[443] A similar effect is seen when an owner is denied the entitlement to reap the rewards from property ownership. In *Wachauf*,[444] the Court described the rule that deprived a tenant farmer of 'the fruits of his labour and his investments' as incompatible with the protection of fundamental rights in the Union.[445] This reasoning is also reflected in *YS v NK*,[446] where the Court ruled that the limitation of only part of the total pension amount did not affect the essence of the right to property.[447] *A contrario*, it is clear that withholding the whole or substantial part of a pension entitlement would not satisfy the essence test. Along the same lines, in *Generics*,[448] the Court held that a measure rendering it 'practically impossible' to carry out economic activities constituted the disproportionate and unacceptable interference with the very substance of the right to property.[449] However, according to the Court, not every restriction on production necessitated by an economic situation would infringe on the essence of the right to property, even if it affects the profitability or the very existence of an undertaking.[450]

[436] Case C-686/18 *OC ea and Others v Banca d'Italia and Others* EU:C:2020:567, para 89.
[437] See, eg, Case C-238/20 *'Sātiņi-S' SIA* EU:C:2022:57, para 31.
[438] *Commission v Hungary* (n 57) para 87.
[439] See Case C-277/10 *Martin Luksan v Petrus van der Let* EU:C:2012:65, para 70.
[440] Case 59/83 *SA Biovilac NV v European Economic Community* EU:C:1984:380.
[441] ibid para 22.
[442] Case C-352/20 *HOLD Alapkezelő Befektetési Alapkezelő Zrt v Magyar Nemzeti Bank* EU:C:2022:606.
[443] ibid para 72.
[444] Case 5/88 *Hubert Wachauf v Bundesamt für Ernährung und Forstwirtschaft* EU:C:1989:321.
[445] ibid paras 18–19.
[446] Case C-223/19 *YS v NK (Occupational Pensions of Managerial Staff)* EU:C:2020:753.
[447] ibid para 92.
[448] Case C-368/96 *The Queen v The Licensing Authority Established by the Medicines Act 1968 ex parte Generics (UK)* EU:C:1998:583.
[449] ibid para 85.
[450] Case 258/81 *Metallurgiki Halyps AE v Commission* EU:C:1982:422, para 13. See also Joined Cases 172 and 226/83 *Hoogovens Groep BV v Commission* EU:C:1985:355, para 29.

Another strand of case law distinguishes between the deprivation of ownership and the controls imposed on an owner over the use of property. The latter category does not deny the peaceful enjoyment of property but merely limits the extent to which ownership entitlements can be exercised.[451] This form of interference is not considered to breach the essence of the right to property. In *Kuhn*,[452] a measure was not found to affect the substance of the right to property if economic operators could engage in other ways of utilising their property.[453] Similarly, in *Booker*,[454] the Court made it clear that a measure leading to the destruction and slaughter of fish to prevent the spread of disease did not deprive the owners of using their fish farms but enabled them to continue to carry out their activities.[455] The same logic is also evident in *Schräder*,[456] where a cereal processor could not plead the breach of the right to property as it only bore an administrative and accounting charge in connection to the payment or transfer of a levy instead of carrying the pecuniary burden of paying the levy itself.[457]

To establish a breach of the essence of the right to property, the difference between the deprivation of ownership and the control of its use appears to lie in the degree of interference. The Court's practice suggests that the interference which leaves an owner some ability to exercise rights over a possession, even to a limited extent, is to be considered as a control of property use rather than its deprivation. However, drawing a clear line demarcating these categories is not without its difficulties and tensions. It is questionable whether the essence test under Article 17 CFR envisages a higher threshold by requiring that all ownership entitlements specified therein be irrevocably nullified. Support for this supposition follows from the line of case law concerning the compatibility with Article 17 CFR of sanctions authorising the freezing of funds and other economic resources.[458] There, the Court held that such measures did not constitute the deprivation of property but a restriction on the exercise of property rights. This was based on several factors, including the duration of sanctions, the intent behind them and the availability of some form of access to property. In *Kadi*,[459] the General Court stated that the freezing of funds was a *temporary* precautionary measure that, unlike confiscation, did not intend to deprive an owner or affect the very substance of the right of property, but only the use thereof.[460] However, as the General Court

[451] Case C-44/89 *Georg von Deetzen v Hauptzollamt Oldenburg* EU:C:1991:401, para 29.
[452] Case C-177/90 *Ralf-Herbert Kühn v Landwirtschaftskammer Weser-Ems* EU:C:1992:2.
[453] ibid para 17.
[454] Joined Cases C-20/00 and C-64/00 *Booker Aquacultur Ltd and Hydro Seafood GSP Ltd v The Scottish Ministers* EU:C:2003:397.
[455] ibid para 80.
[456] Case 265/87 *Hermann Schräder HS Kraftfutter GmbH & Co KG v Hauptzollamt Gronau* EU:C:1989:303.
[457] ibid para 16.
[458] See, eg, Case T-154/15 *Aiman Jaber v Council* EU:T:2016:629, para 121; Case T-579/11 *Tarif Akhras v Council* EU:T:2015:97, para 150.
[459] Case T-315/01 *Yassin Abdullah Kadi v Council and Commission* EU:T:2005:332.
[460] ibid para 248.

subsequently acknowledged, this conclusion would be called into question if an owner was unable to access its property for nearly 10 years.[461] Furthermore, in *Boucha Al Assad*,[462] the Court established the legality of the freezing of funds by emphasising the fact that the impugned measure allowed the possibility to use them to meet essential needs or meet certain commitments and to gain specific authorisations to thaw those funds, other financial assets or other economic resources.[463]

In contrast, a somewhat mixed approach can be discerned from the case law of the ECtHR. In *Sporrong*,[464] the dispute concerned the compatibility with Article 1 of Protocol I to the ECHR of the expropriation permits issued over the applicants' property that were continuously renewed and were subsequently revoked while being in force for more than 20 years. The ECtHR first acknowledged that although the right to property lost some of its substance, it did not disappear. The owners were not deprived of their properties as such but could continue to utilise them and the possibility of selling them remained during that period.[465] Nevertheless, according to the Court's verdict, the law in force still infringed Article 1 of Protocol I to the ECHR since it did not strike a fair balance between the protection of the right to property and the requirements of general interest by being inflexible and leaving owners in complete uncertainty and unable to fully enjoy their possession.[466] This conclusion implies that the essence of the right to property can still be violated even with the availability of some ownership entitlements. However, a conflicting interpretation follows from *Phocas v France*,[467] where the ECtHR also found the interference with the substance of the right to property against similar factual circumstances. According to its reasoning, a threat of expropriation or restriction on the building undoubtedly created an obstacle to its continuous use in all its forms.[468] Despite that, the ECtHR reached an opposite conclusion to that in *Sporrong*. It found no infringement of Article 1 of Protocol I to the ECHR based on the owner's conduct over the possible purchase of the property by the state.[469] This suggests that the nullification of all ownership entitlements may affect the essence of the right, but it would not necessarily be incompatible with Article 1 of Protocol I to the ECHR. Such an approach is difficult to reconcile with the essence of rights representing their indefeasible inner core, respect for which is the logical consequence of their characterisation as 'fundamental'.[470]

[461] Case T-85/09 *Yassin Abdullah Kadi v Commission* EU:T:2010:418, para 150.
[462] Case T-202/12 *Bouchra Al Assad v Council* EU:T:2014:113.
[463] ibid para 118.
[464] *Sporrong and Lönnroth v Sweden* App No 7151/75 (ECtHR, 18 December 1984).
[465] ibid para 63.
[466] ibid paras 70–73.
[467] *Phocas v France* App No 17869/91 (ECtHR, 23 April 1996).
[468] ibid para 59.
[469] ibid para 60.
[470] Tridimas and Gentile (n 356) 803.

(2) The Essence of the Freedom to Conduct Business

The definitional uncertainty equally surrounds the concept of essence within the framework of the freedom to conduct business protected under Article 16 CFR. Despite the growing body of case law, the Court has yet to comprehensively map the core elements that form its very essence and what the required respect for it entails under Article 52 CFR. As pointed out in Chapter 2, its standard reasoning often only consists of an almost mechanical reference to the Explanations to the Charter that the protection afforded by Article 16 CFR covers the freedom to exercise economic or commercial activity, freedom of contract and the principle of free competition. Nonetheless, specific characteristics of the individual entitlements provided by Article 16 CFR occasionally appear in the case law. The Court defined this provision as a norm that conferred on its right holder the liberty to '[pursue] industrial or commercial activities for profit within the European Union'.[471] In *UPC Telekabel Wien*,[472] it added that Article 16 CFR included 'the right for any business to be able to freely use, within the limits of its liability for its own acts, the economic, technical and financial resources available to it'.[473] Contractual discretion is integral to the effectuation of this right. The Court attributed to Article 16 CFR the role of protecting 'the freedom to choose with whom to do business and the freedom to determine the price of a service'.[474] The emphasis placed on these individual entitlements suggests that they, even if not exhaustively, encapsulate the essential content of the freedom to conduct business. Without them, the legal protection afforded by Article 16 CFR becomes devoid of any practical value. Indeed, the Court's approach to the requirement to respect the essence under this provision revolves, broadly considered, around the distinction between the existence of the aforementioned individual entitlements and their exercise.[475] This follows from two distinct yet overlapping patterns emerging from the case law.

According to one line of reasoning, the essence under Article 16 CFR, read in conjunction with Article 52 CFR, is breached when a measure calls into question the freedom to conduct business. Such an outcome can be expressed in two ways. Broadly considered, this encompasses circumstances where an individual is denied the right to engage in economic or commercial activity of one's own choice.[476] In *Marshall*,[477] the Court rejected the claim that the Union's measure on the conservation of fishery resources affected the substance of the right to exercise

[471] Case T-215/15 *Mykola Yanovych Azarov v Council* EU:T:2016:49, para 91.
[472] Case C-314/12 *UPC Telekabel Wien GmbH v Constantin Film Verleih* EU:C:2014:192.
[473] ibid para 48.
[474] Joined Cases C-798/18 and C-799/18 *Federazione nazionale delle imprese elettrotecniche ed elettroniche (Anie) and Others* EU:C:2021:280, para 57. See also Case C-277/16 *Polkomtel sp z o. v Prezes Urzędu Komunikacji Elektronicznej* EU:C:2017:989, para 50.
[475] Case C-306/93 *SMW Winzersekt GmbH v Land Rheinland-Pfalz* EU:C:1994:407, para 24. See also Case T-113/96 *Edouard Dubois et Fils SA v Council and Commission* EU:T:1998:11, para 75.
[476] *OC ea and Others* (n 436) para 89.
[477] Case C-370/88 *Procurator Fiscal v Andrew Marshall* EU:C:1990:392.

a professional activity.[478] This was because the claimants retained the freedom to fish and were only subject to the requirement to use authorised nets. Similarly, in *Pillbox 38*,[479] although the Court found that the prohibition imposed on the promotion of electronic cigarettes and refill containers interfered with the freedom to conduct business, it did not affect its essence, for it did not prevent economic operators from manufacturing and marketing those products.[480] It follows that a mere limitation imposed on the exercise of an economic activity does not breach the essence of the freedom to conduct business under Article 16 CFR.[481] Instead, for such an effect to materialise, an intrusion with this freedom must render the right holder's ability to take up and pursue an economic activity 'practically impossible'.[482] In *Spika*,[483] the Court alluded to a breach of the essence of the freedom to conduct business when finding that the applicable method of allocation of fishing opportunities entailed 'the complete closure of the market in question'.[484] The same logic applies when an impugned measure results in the closure of an undertaking.[485]

More specifically, the essence of the freedom to conduct business is breached when an individual is denied the right to exercise the freedom of contract. This was upheld in *Alemo-Herron*, where the Court found such a breach because the new employer was deprived of the ability to either 'assert its interests effectively in a contractual process [or] negotiate the aspects determining changes in working conditions for its employees with a view to its future economic activity'.[486] Although *Alemo-Herron* provoked much controversy over the protection of employee rights,[487] the Court reiterated its position in the subsequent case law.[488] In *Asklepios Kliniken*,[489] it decided that the essence of the freedom to conduct business under Article 16 CFR was not breached as the impugned national law, unlike

[478] ibid para 28.

[479] *Pillbox 38 (UK) Ltd* (n 167).

[480] ibid para 161. See also Case T-52/09 *Nycomed Danmark ApS v European Medicines Agency (EMA)* EU:T:2011:738, para 92.

[481] Case 234/85 *Staatsanwaltschaft Freiburg v Franz Keller* EU:C:1986:377, para 9.

[482] *Generics* (n 448) para 85.

[483] Case C-540/16 *UAB 'Spika' and Others* EU:C:2018:565.

[484] ibid para 38. See also Case T-251/18 *International Forum for Sustainable Underwater Activities (IFSUA) v Council* EU:T:2020:89, para 154.

[485] Joined Cases 154, 205, 206, 226 to 228, 263 and 264/78, 39, 31, 83 and 85/79 *SpA Ferriera Valsabbia and Others v Commission* EU:C:1980:81, para 89.

[486] *Mark Alemo-Herron and Others* (n 96) para 35.

[487] See, eg, S Weatherill, 'Use and Abuse of the EU's Charter of Fundamental Rights: on the Improper Veneration of "Freedom of Contract"' (2014) 10 *European Review of Contract Law* 167; J Prassl, 'Freedom of Contract as a General Principle of EU law? Transfers of Undertakings and the Protection of Employer Rights in EU Labour Law' (2013) 42 *Industrial Law Journal* 434.

[488] See Case C-328/13 *Österreichischer Gewerkschaftsbund v Wirtschaftskammer Österreich – Fachverband Autobus-, Luftfahrt- und Schifffahrtsunternehmungen* EU:C:2014:2197, paras 29–30. See also Case C-344/18 *ISS Facility Services NV v Sonia Govaerts and Atalian NV, Formerly Euroclean NV* EU:C:2020:239, para 26.

[489] Joined Cases C-680/15 and C-681/15 *Asklepios Kliniken Langen-Seligenstadt GmbH v Ivan Felja and Asklepios Dienstleistungsgesellschaft mbH v Vittoria Graf* EU:C:2017:317.

in *Alemo-Herron*, provided the possibility for a new employer in a similar context to adjust working conditions 'either consensually or unilaterally'.[490] Equally, in *AGET Iraklis*, the Court found no effect on the essence of the freedom to conduct business in the national law that sets out a framework for carrying out collective redundancies.[491]

However, on both levels, the distinction drawn between the existence of an individual entitlement and the limitation of its exercise is not always apparent. This stems from the fact that the Court also defines Article 16 CFR as a provision that safeguards the right holder from being exposed to an undue and unfair burdens[492] of a financial and non-financial nature.[493] The problem with such a characterisation is that it does not rest on clearly defined analytical parameters. An extensive financial and non-financial burden can be framed to deny the right holder the freedom to engage in economic activity or the freedom of contract. At the same time, it can equally constitute a limitation imposed on the exercise of either individual entitlement. Such uncertainty would likely lead to an uneasy equilibrium between Article 16 CFR and the extent of enforcement of the Treaty's free movement and competition rules.

One strand of case law narrowly defines the scope of Article 16 CFR to the extent that any additional burden imposed on the right holder of this provision is not deemed to deprive the freedom to conduct business of its essence. In *Fedesa*,[494] the Court upheld the validity of the Union's measure prohibiting the use of certain hormones in livestock farming. Referring to the protection of public health, it rejected the claim that it caused considerable financial losses for traders. In *EMA*,[495] based on the same ground, the Court concluded that the cost of obtaining market authorisation for a pharmaceutical product was not unlawful, despite restricting the right of pharmaceutical companies to freely conduct their business.[496] In the same manner, in *McDonagh*,[497] the Court was not convinced by the plea that the requirement to provide care for air passengers in the event of cancellation or long delays would deprive air carriers of the 'fruits of their labour and of their investment'.[498] The rationale underlying these verdicts lay in the degree of gravity carried by the relevant justification grounds,

[490] ibid para 24.
[491] *AGET Iraklis* (n 50) para 88.
[492] Everson and Gonçalez (n 100) 453.
[493] See, eg, Case C-430/17 *Walbusch Walter Busch GmbH & Co KG v Zentrale zur Bekämpfung unlauteren Wettbewerbs Frankfurt am Main eV* EU:C:2019:47, para 46; C-101/12 *Herbert Schaible v Land Baden-Württemberg* EU:C:2013:661, para 82.
[494] Case C-331/88 *The Queen v Minister of Agriculture, Fisheries and Food and Secretary of State for Health ex parte Fedesa and Others* EU:C:1990:391.
[495] Case T-52/09 *Nycomed Danmark ApS v European Medicines Agency (EMA)* EU:T:2011:738.
[496] ibid para 91.
[497] Case C-12/11 *Denise McDonagh v Ryanair Ltd* EU:C:2013:43.
[498] ibid para 59. See also *Case C-11/11 Air France v Heinz-Gerke Folkerts and Luz-Tereza Folkerts* EU:C:2013:106, para 46; Joined Cases C-581/10 and C-629/10 *Emeka Nelson and Others v Deutsche Lufthansa AG and TUI Travel plc and Others v Civil Aviation Authority* EU:C:2012:657, para 81.

which, in the Court's view, were capable of validating 'even substantial negative economic consequences for certain economic operators'.[499] Such a burden was not deemed to be at odds with the requirement to respect the substance of the freedom to conduct business or excessive enough to trigger the essence test under Article 52 CFR. The greater weight attached to the justification grounds resonates with the language of Article 16 CFR that the freedom to conduct business is recognised in accordance with Union law and national law and practices. Indeed, the Court often reiterates that this provision 'may … be subject to a broad range of interventions on the part of public authorities which may, in the public interest, limit the exercise of economic activity'.[500]

At the same time, this jurisprudential line does not necessarily allege the complete disregard of the interests of the right holder under Article 16 CFR. The Court tends to distinguish between different levels of burden by considering that certain economic and non-economic consequences can breach the essence of the freedom to conduct business. At one end of the spectrum are measures that are deemed to pose a minimal effect on the ability to exercise economic activity or contractual freedom. In *Schaible*,[501] the Court disagreed with the claim that, for preventing infectious diseases, the obligation to identify livestock individually using electronic eartags was sufficiently excessive to breach Article 16 CFR.[502] In *YS v NK*, as mentioned earlier, it held that the employer's obligation to pay a lower pension than the contractually agreed amount respected the essence of the freedom of contract because it only led to 'a very small part of the occupational pensions' to be withheld.[503] At the other end of the spectrum stand measures whose financial or non-financial repercussions are viewed to pose a risk to the essence of the freedom to conduct business. In *Walbusch Walter Busch*,[504] the Court found that the obligation to provide a standard form through which consumers could exercise the right of withdrawal from a distance selling contract was liable to impose 'an unsupportable burden' on a trader.[505] Similarly, in *Airhelp*,[506] the Court ruled that granting air passengers the entitlement to claim compensation in the event of cancellations or long delays would

[499] See Case C-570/19 *Irish Ferries Ltd v National Transport Authority* EU:C:2021:664, para 98; Case C-579/19 *The Queen, on the Application of Association of Independent Meat Suppliers and Cleveland Meat Company Ltd v Food Standards Agency* EU:C:2021:665, para 97; Case C-58/08 *The Queen, on the Application of Vodafone Ltd and Others v Secretary of State for Business, Enterprise and Regulatory Reform* EU:C:2010:321, para 69.

[500] Case C-124/20 *Bank Melli Iran v Telekom Deutschland GmbH* EU:C:2021:1035, para 82.

[501] Case C-101/12 *Herbert Schaible v Land Baden-Württemberg* EU:C:2013:661.

[502] ibid para 61.

[503] *YS v NK* (n 446) para 89.

[504] Case C-430/17 *Walbusch Walter Busch GmbH & Co KG v Zentrale zur Bekämpfung unlauteren Wettbewerbs Frankfurt am Main eV* EU:C:2019:47.

[505] ibid para 46. See also Case C-179/21 *absoluts-bikes and more- GmbH & Co KG v the-trading-company GmbH* EU:C:2022:353, para 40.

[506] Case C-28/20 *Airhelp Ltd v Scandinavian Airlines System Denmark – Norway – Sweden* EU:C:2021:226.

cause 'serious economic harm' for air carriers, as it could be 'exploited for the purposes of industrial action'.[507] Considered on their own merits, these decisions are hardly contentious. They can be understood to reflect the dichotomy between the core and periphery of a right ingrained in the structure of Article 52 CFR. Separating these constituting elements requires measuring the intensity and gravity of the burden inflicted on the right holder. However, what remains problematic is the uncertainty related to the parameters against which the Court carries out such an exercise. Contrasting the approaches in the case law reveals an incongruence in the characterisation of some forms of burden as breaching the essence of Article 16 CFR while exempting others.

The *Alemo-Herron*-line of interpretation clearly contrasts the reasoning followed in *EMA* and *McDonagh*. In *Alemo-Herron*, as mentioned earlier, the Court found that the obligation of a new employer, in the event of a transfer of an undertaking, to accept collectively agreed terms without taking part in their negotiations adversely affected the essence of the freedom to conduct business,[508] for it reduced its contractual freedom and exposed it to extra costs in terms of wage increase as a result of the 'inevitable differences in working conditions [between the public and private sectors]'.[509] However, unlike *EMA* and *McDonagh*, the Court did not deem it necessary to consider whether the importance of employee protection could justify such negative financial implications. The same is true about the verdict given in *Achbita*,[510] where the issue concerned the legality of dismissal on account of an employee's insistence on wearing an Islamic headscarf at work. The Court found that, an employer could invoke, pursuant to the freedom to conduct business, its policy of neutrality as a legitimate aim capable of justifying such dismissal.[511] As part of the proportionality assessment, it then added that forcing an employer to seek alternative measures to dismissal must not lead to an extra burden being imposed on it.[512] This point was explicitly reinforced in *WABE*.[513] In the context of similar factual circumstances, it was held that the inability to pursue a policy of neutrality would undermine an employer's freedom to conduct business as 'it would suffer adverse consequences', given the nature of its activities.[514] In both *Achbita* and *WABE*, the Court was therefore quick to indicate a possible breach of essence under Article 16 CFR but did not make any reference to the formula, endorsed in *EMA* and *McDonagh*, that the importance of a legitimate

[507] ibid para 84.
[508] *Mark Alemo-Herron and Others* (n 96) para 35.
[509] ibid para 27.
[510] Case C-157/15 *Samira Achbita and Centrum voor gelijkheid van kansen en voor racismebestrijding v G4S Secure Solutions NV* EU:C:2017:203.
[511] ibid para 38.
[512] ibid para 43.
[513] Joined Cases C-804/18 and C-341/19 *IX v WABE eV and MH Müller Handels GmbH v MJ* EU:C:2021:594.
[514] ibid para 67.

interest, in the form of employee protection, might justify even substantial negative economic consequences for economic operators.

The oddity that stems from this juxtaposition is not that the verdicts in *Alemo-Herron*, *Achbita* and *WABE* should have unequivocally gone in favour of the employees concerned. Such an outcome would have curtailed an employer's freedom to shape the content of binding contractual obligations or formulate a business policy, given the nature of its economic activity, which, according to the Court, breaches the essence of the freedom to conduct business. Instead, the crux of the issue lies in the interpretative line followed to reach this conclusion, particularly viewed against the Court's general tendency to equate the denial of a right with the breach of its essence. In the present context, it did not engage in detail with the question of whether and to what extent the possible additional financial burden being imposed on an employer risked nullifying the carrying out of its business altogether. This is particularly evident in *Alemo-Herron*, where the effect on essence was taken at face value or, at least, the threshold for its breach was set substantially lower than in other instances. In *Sky Österreich*, the Court ruled that a measure limiting the ability of the holder of exclusive broadcasting rights to decide freely on the price to charge interfered with the freedom under Article 16 CFR. Yet, in its view, this was insufficient to affect the core content of the freedom to conduct business because the impugned measure did not 'prevent a business activity from being carried out as such'. In contrast, this was found to be so in *Alemo-Herron*, even though it involved a similar constraint imposed on the exercise of contractual freedom and incurred a comparable economic burden. Indeed, were a new employer to accept the already existing collective agreement, the cost of the slight increase in hourly employee wages would not have been any greater than the costs concerned in *Sky Österreich*. Notwithstanding this, the intrusion into contractual freedom and the possible additional financial burden sufficed to breach the essence of the freedom to conduct business. This finding was not subject to the extra stipulation the Court made in *Sky Österreich* that an intrusion had to render the very engagement in business either impossible or difficult in practice. Hence, whilst an additional financial or non-financial burden inflicted on the right holder can lead to a breach of the essence of the freedom to conduct business, the parameters for measuring this effect remain questionable.

III. Interim Conclusion

The coexistence and intersection of the Treaty's free movement and competition rules with fundamental economic rights consist of a two-dimensional form of interaction. At one level, there is a degree of convergence between these sets of provisions expressed in their functional correlation of giving effect to the ideals of private autonomy in the Union's legal order. However, the locus of such convergence varies. The alignment of the Treaty's free movement provisions and fundamental economic rights does not generally translate into the overlap in their scope of application. This is rooted in the predominantly instrumentalist orientation of free movement law that deviates from the deontological nature of fundamental economic rights. That said, the gradual individual-centric re-alignment of the Treaty's provisions on persons, which stems from the Court's broad definition of their scope, generates the dynamics of cross-fertilisation between them and fundamental economic rights, thus blurring the divergence of their normative scope. Likewise, the Treaty's competition rules and fundamental economic rights do not coincide in their normative scope, yet there is a deep conceptual affinity between them. The constitutional safeguard of fundamental economic rights warrants the guarantee of a competitive process, which is reflected in its protection as an institution framed around the pluralism of economic actors and private interests. On another level, the degree of convergence between the Treaty's free movement and competition rules with fundamental economic rights does not necessarily exclude the prospect of a material conflict between them, considering their divergent normative purposes. As is widely agreed, the resolution for such a clash lies in applying the double test of proportionality whereby both the limitations in the enforcement of the Treaty's free movement and competition rules and the restrictions of fundamental economic rights are deemed legitimate so long as they are proportionate. Despite the attractiveness of this analytical technique, it is submitted that the concept of the essence of fundamental rights enshrined in the Charter poses conceptual and functional challenges to framing the parameters of the double test of proportionality. The role of the essence clause in the reconciliation of conflicting values remains somewhat underdeveloped, as the Court has yet to systematically define and explain it. Equally, what this clause entails is uncertain, given the complexity surrounding the characterisation of the inviolable substance of most rights protected under the Charter.

Conclusion

Conscious of its spiritual and moral heritage, the Union … places the individual at the heart of its activities.[1]

Private autonomy stood at the epicentre of the evolution of two constitutional paradigms underlying the European integration process. At one end, the ideals of private autonomy pervaded the Court's famous equation of the prohibitions addressed to Member States in the Treaty with specific individual rights that sowed the seeds of the directly enforceable freedoms of movement which, complemented by the competition rules, accelerated the fusion of the national markets into a single economic sphere. At another end, the ideals of private autonomy occupied the forefront of the jurisprudential genesis of the Union's fundamental rights doctrine through the medium of unwritten general principles of law that provided much-warranted legitimacy to the authority of the Union's legal order. These constitutional paradigms have matured along related yet diverse normative pathways that shape the normative value attached to private autonomy in the Union's legal system. The present study has aimed to explore this process by examining the coexistence, intersection and cross-fertilisation of these constitutional paradigms. This offers a new and different perspective to understanding the idiosyncratic nature of the normative claim for private autonomy in the Union's legal order by drawing the contours of protection afforded to individuals therein.

The guarantee of private autonomy in the normative edifice of the Union has three distinct traits. The first trait is that the Union's legal order epitomises an intricate combination of varying forms of manifestation and limitation of private autonomy framed by a tangled web of complexity attached to their coexistence and interaction that generates a set of legal tensions and conflicting forces. The ideals of private autonomy are protected by fundamental economic rights, such as the right to property, the freedom of contract and the right to pursue economic or professional activity. First and foremost, they operate as a limit to the powers delegated to the Union's institutions. The respect for these rights, alongside other categories of rights, constitutes a precondition for the legality of any acts of the Union, whether legislative or administrative. However, fundamental economic rights are not absolute prerogatives and, as such, their exercise can be limited by the Union's secondary law. Therein lies two sources of tension. It arises from the impact of unimplemented directives in the private domain. Although the Court maintains

[1] Preamble to the Charter of Fundamental Rights of the European Union [2012] OJ C326/391.

that directives cannot produce a direct effect between private parties, this orthodox doctrine is at odds with several judicial avenues through which directives are still enforceable in this setting. Likewise, the analogous dilution of the orthodox doctrine can be observed in the context of directives acting as a trigger for the horizontal application of general principles of law that limit or condition the exercise of private autonomy.

At the same level, another source of tension discussed in this volume concerns the constitutional guarantees of an economic and non-economic nature that qualify the expressions of private autonomy. Two sets of norms belong to this category. First, it includes the general principle of equality that is structured by 'market' and social dimensions. The former aspect serves the market integration objective and is manifested in the prohibition of non-discrimination on grounds of nationality, which can produce a direct effect between private parties. The social dimension of the general principle of equality, in turn, is expressed in the expansion of the principle of non-discrimination to new grounds such as age and is driven by the value of 'interpersonal equality'. Second, the exercise of private autonomy is equally conditioned by the constitutional guarantees of a non-economic nature enshrined in the Charter that apply in the private domain. However, their enforcement against private parties is conditional on meeting specific normative requirements, which are not immune to conceptual and methodological challenges.

The Treaty's free movement and competition rules constitute the second category of norms that express the ideals of private autonomy within the Union's legal system. Whilst formulated as prohibitions addressed to Member States and certain categories of private actors, they are conceived as bearers of individual rights. These sets of provisions are integral to the establishment and proper functioning of the internal market, for they enable private economic activities across borders of Member States by outlawing, respectively, national barriers to free movement and certain forms of market conduct by private actors with unilateral or combined market power. However, both aspects conjure up several forms of tension. In the context of free movement law, this flows from two layers of uncertainty: the first concerns the extent to which private economic activities with an interstate link can be conditioned by national regulatory autonomy, while the second relates to the capacity of the freedoms of movement to impose direct obligations that are enforceable among private parties. In the context of competition law, tension primarily emanates from the ambiguity concerning the principal rationalisation for enforcing this set of provisions. The welfare-oriented approaches are at odds with the constitutional significance embedded in the guarantee of free and fair competition in the market. Both layers of uncertainty are prone to cause a material conflict between the free movement and competition law regimes and fundamental economic rights despite the symbiotic relationship interweaving these two sets of norms.

The second trait is that beneath the surface of these tensions lies the disparity in the degree of normative weight attributed to the ideals of private autonomy, compounded by the lack of a clear systematic approach to defining the contours of protection they warrant. Two interwoven trends are prevalent in the case law. At times, the Court's verdict appears to be, either explicitly or implicitly, informed by the ideals of private autonomy, while at other times, its reasoning does not seem to give them due consideration. The case law related to the horizontal reach of free movement law is emblematic of both approaches. In one respect, the Court endorses contractual freedom by exempting the sale of goods agreements from scrutiny while subjecting the expression of contractual preferences in employment relationships to the requirement of non-discrimination on grounds of nationality. Despite their apparent difference, both approaches can be argued to stem from the same logic of a private party's predisposition to effectively conduct independent decision-making in the market. It is deemed limited in employment relationships due to employees' weak bargaining position or, more generally, in private relationships involving private actors with regulatory powers enabling them to assert some form of dominance that cannot be circumvented by exercising private autonomy. However, a different picture emerges from the Court's tendency to reconcile the interests sheltered by private autonomy and those pursued by free movement law exclusively within the confines of the derogations prescribed by the Treaty. This analytical method often leads to one-sided and asymmetrical proportionality assessment, which deviates from the traditional adjudication of private disputes that rests on balancing competing interests and policies that must carry equal weight on both sides of the argument.

The same double-edged approach is equally pervasive in relation to the normative reach of the Union's secondary law, particularly directives, within the realm of private relations. The Court's continuous adherence to the orthodox doctrine of no horizontal direct effect of directives reflects the concerns for private autonomy. Directives on their own are not considered as a source of individual rights and obligations, for they are only addressed to Member States that are required to implement them in national law. However, this orthodox doctrine is subject to a complex set of qualifications and exceptions that allow for the enforcement of directives in a private setting. They operate regardless of the adverse collateral effect inflicted on private parties to the point that their implications would be no different than if directives were horizontally enforceable between private parties. In one respect, the case law can be construed to lend support for the narrow construction of these qualifications and exceptions. An attempt can be made to reconcile them with the orthodox doctrine based on the dichotomy drawn between the substitutionary and exclusionary effects of a directive or the dichotomy of direct obligation or 'mere adverse repercussions' of a directive. However, a distinction along these lines seems rather formalistic and rigid. It does not make it possible to square the circle between the orthodox doctrine and its exceptions and qualifications without disregarding the nature and degree of the collateral impact inflicted on private parties.

The paucity of judicial solicitude towards concerns of private autonomy is also apparent in the context of general principles of law and the Charter's provisions deemed directly enforceable between private parties. While the horizontality attributed to these provisions is not unconditional, the boundaries of such capacity do not reflect the normative claim for private autonomy recognised by law. This specifically concerns instances where general principles of law and the Charter's provisions are deemed applicable in a private domain for setting aside the national law conflicting with Union law. It is undisputed that such an outcome finds its rationale in the need to ensure the effectiveness of legal protection bestowed on individuals under Union law. However, invalidating or setting aside the conflicting national law pursuant to general principles of law and the Charter's provisions is not without its repercussions in a private setting. At one end, such an outcome entitles a private party to a remedy against another party who, despite acting in good faith by following the applicable national law, is held liable for the failure committed by national authorities. At another end, despite the financial or non-financial burden such a remedy entails, the case law is silent on the capacity of a private party to bring a claim for state liability against the national authorities responsible for the failure to comply with Union law.

The third trait is that the concept of private autonomy in the Union's legal order is hardwired with deontological and instrumentalist instincts, the correlation of which exhibits the evolutionary dynamics of the market integration project. Fundamental economic rights embody the deontological value of private autonomy. Drawn from 'constitutional traditions common to Member States', these rights manifest and protect the individual capacity for autonomous economic action as an end in itself rather than as a means to other ends. Their recognition as general principles of law and subsequent codification in the Charter led to the inception and development of individual safeguards that were absent in the original Treaty. This development ossified the constitutional commitment to market economy principles at the Union level. When contrasted against these rights, a different manifestation of private autonomy emerges in the context of the free movement and competition law regimes. They can be defined as a set of provisions infused by the instrumentalist value attached to private autonomy. Their normative purpose does not lie in the protection of individual cross-border economic initiatives as a value on their own, for they predominantly serve the internal market goal. These provisions are programmed to operate as a medium to steer individual behaviour for forging national markets into a single economic area and ensuring its smooth functioning.

Such a juxtaposition of the free movement and competition law regimes with fundamental economic rights allows us to discern the contours of individual rights derived from the former set of provisions in line with the Court's vision of 'a new legal order' outlined in *Van Gen en Loos*. Two contrasting perspectives emerge in this exercise. It is possible to submit a narrow individualist account of the free movement and competition law regimes that draws upon the restrictive interpretation of these provisions proffered by several Advocates General. Unlike Articles 15–17 CFR, the Treaty's free movement and competition rules do not bestow the right to economic or commercial freedom at large. Instead, they are homogeneously conceptualised to guarantee market freedom understood as the subjective right to initiate or take part in the interstate process of competition throughout the internal market, free from, on the one hand, discriminatory and non-discriminatory national measures and, on the other hand, the impediments of private actors with unilateral or combined market power that do not conform to the parameters of normal market conduct. This approach has several advantages. From a broad standpoint, it aligns with the Court's vision of creating a single economic area that operates as a platform to unlock and accelerate interstate competition – whether this is in relation to the sale of goods or provision of services, securing employment or making investments – for achieving lasting economic and societal prosperity in the Union. From a more specific standpoint, this approach makes it possible to concretise the reach of the Treaty's free movement and competition provisions based on the degree of complementarity intrinsic to their normative purpose. At one end, the concept of the right to initiate and participate in the interstate process of competition individualises the access-based framework underlying free movement law without morphing it into an instrument of a deregulatory nature. At another end, it individualises the guarantee by competition law of a 'level playing field' in the internal market by regulating the conduct of private actors with unilateral or combined market power.

The individualist account of free movement law developed in this volume is not without nuance. Unlike Article 34 TFEU, the scope of the Treaty's free movement of persons provisions has not undergone *Keck*-like normative recalibration but has evolved along a different path. This follows from the Court's continuous tendency to broadly define the concept of restriction under these provisions, which is not solely amenable to the rationalisation in terms of market integration. Instead, the case law evinces the growing individual-centric re-alignment of the Treaty's free movement of persons provisions, expressed in the metamorphosis of these provisions from the instruments that serve the liberalisation of national markets to the norms with a constitutional dimension that protect the ability of rights holders to exercise economic activity in an interstate setting as an end on its own. This finds legitimacy in the coalescence of Union citizenship and fundamental rights guaranteed in the Charter. Seen through this lens, there is deeper normative assimilation between the Treaty's free movement of persons provisions and fundamental economic rights, which is bound to blur the dichotomy of deontological and instrumentalist paradigms underlying their coexistence and will likely shift the dynamics of the internal market bargain struck between the Union's institutions and Member States.

BIBLIOGRAPHY

Ahlborn, C and Grave, C, 'Walter Eucken and Ordoliberalism: An Introduction from a Consumer Welfare Perspective' (2006) 2 *Competition Policy International* 197

Akman, P, 'Searching for the Long-Lost Soul of Article 82 EC' (2009) 29 *Oxford Journal of Legal Studies* 267

——. 'The Role of "Freedom" in EU Competition Law' (2014) 34 *Legal Studies* 183

Albæk, S, 'Consumer Welfare in EU Competition Policy' in C Heide-Jørgensen, C Bergqvistm, UB Neergaard and ST Poulsen (eds), *Aims and Values in Competition Law* (Copenhagen, DJØF Publishing, 2013)

Alexy, R, 'Individual Rights and Collective Goods' in CS Nino (ed), *Rights* (Dartmouth, Aldershot, 1992)

——. *A Theory of Constitutional Rights* (Oxford, Oxford University Press, 2009)

Anchustegui, IH, 'Competition Law through an Ordoliberal Lens' (2015) 2 *Oslo Law Review* 139

Andriychuk, O, 'Can We Protect Competition without Protecting Consumers?' (2010) 6 *Competition Law Review* 77

——. 'The Dialectics of Competition Law: Sketching the Ordo-Austrian Approach to Antitrust' (2012) 35 *World Competition* 355

Antinori, MR, 'Does Lochner Live in Luxembourg? An Analysis of the Property Rights Jurisprudence of the European Court of Justice' (1994) 18 *Fordham International Law Journal* 1778

Ashiagbor, D, 'Article 15: Freedom to Choose an Occupation and Right to Engage in Work, and Article 29: Right of Access to Placement Services' in S Peers, T Hervey, J Kenner and A Ward (eds), *The EU Charter of Fundamental Rights: A Commentary* (Oxford, Hart Publishing, 2014)

Babayev, R, 'Contractual Discretion and the Limits of Free Movement Law' (2015) 23 *European Review Private Law* 875

——. 'Private Autonomy at Union Level: On Art 16 CFREU and Free Movement Rights' (2016) 53 *Common Market Law Review* 979

Barnard, C, 'Derogations, Justifications and the Four Freedoms: Is State Interest Really Protected?' in C Barnard and O Odudu, *The Outer Limits of European Union Law* (Oxford, Hart Publishing, 2009)

——. *The Substantive Law of the EU: The Four Freedoms*, 5th edn (Oxford, Oxford University Press, 2016)

Basedow, J, 'General Principles of European Private Law and Interest Analysis: Some Reflections in the Light of *Mangold* and *Audiolux*' (2016) 24 *European Review of Private Law* 331

Becker, F, 'Market Regulation and the "Right to Property" in the European Economic Constitution' (2007) 26 *Yearbook of European Law* 255

Behrens, P, 'The "Consumer Choice" Paradigm in German Ordoliberalism and its Impact upon EU Competition Law' (2014) *Europa-Kolleg Hamburg, Institute for European Integration, Discussion Paper* 1/14

——. 'The Ordoliberal Concept of "Abuse" of a Dominant Position and its Impact on Article 102 TFEU' in F di Porto and R Podszun (eds), *Abusive Practices in Competition Law* (Cheltenham, Edward Edgar, 2018)

Bengoetxea, J, 'General Legal Principles Navigating Space and Time' in U Bernitz, X Groussot and F Schulyok (eds), *General Principles of EU Law and European Private Law* (Alphen aan den Rijn, Kluwer, 2013)

Bernard, N, 'Discrimination and Free Movement in EC Law' (1996) 45 *International and Comparative Law Quarterly* 82

——. *Multilevel Governance in the European Union* (The Hague, Kluwer, 2002)
——. 'On the Art of Not Mixing One's Drinks: *Dassonville* and *Cassis de Dijon* Revisited' in L Azoulai and L Poiares Pessoa Maduro (eds), *The Past and Future of EU Law: The Classics of EU Law Revisited on the 50th Anniversary of the Rome Treaty* (Oxford, Hart Publishing, 2010)
Betlem, G, 'The Doctrine of Consistent Interpretation: Managing Legal Uncertainty (2002) 22 *Oxford Journal of Legal Studies* 397
Beyer-Katzenberger, M, 'Judicial Activism and Judicial Restraint at the Bundesverfassungsgericht: Was the *Mangold* Judgment of the European Court of Justice an Ultra Vires Act?' (2011) 11 *ERA Forum* 517
Bogg, AL, 'Only Fools and Horses: Some Sceptical Reflections on the Right to Work' in V Mantouvalou (ed), *The Right to Work: Legal and Philosophical Perspectives* (Oxford, Hart Publishing, 2017)
Bonefeld, W, 'Freedom and the Strong State: On German Ordoliberalism' (2012) 17 *New Political Economy* 633
Bork, RH, 'The Goals of Antitrust Policy' (1967) 57 *American Economic Review* 242
——. *The Antitrust Paradox: A Policy at War with itself* (New York, The Free Press, 1978)
Brisimi, V, *The Interface between Competition and the Internal Market: Market Separation under Art 102 TFEU* (Oxford, Hart Publishing, 2016)
Brkan, M, 'In Search of the Concept of Essence of EU Fundamental Rights through the Prism of Data Privacy' (2017) 1 *Maastricht University Faculty of Law Working Papers* 1, 22
——. 'The Essence of the Fundamental Rights to Privacy and Data Protection: Finding the Way through the Maze of the CJEU's Constitutional Reasoning' (2019) 20 *German Law Journal* 864
Buendia Sierra, JL, 'Writing Straight with Crooked Lines: Competition Policy and Services of General Economic Interest in the Treaty of Lisbon' in A Biondi, P Eeckhout and S Ripley (eds), *EU Law after Lisbon* (Oxford, Oxford University Press, 2012)
Cengiz, F, 'Judicial Review and the Rule of Law in the EU Competition Law Regime after *Alrosa*' (2011) 7 *European Competition Journal* 127
Chalmers, D, 'Looking Back at ERT and its Contribution to the EU Fundamental Rights Agenda' in L Azoulai and L Poiares Pessoa Maduro (eds), *The Past and Future of EU Law: The Classics of EU Law Revisited on the 50th Anniversary of the Rome Treaty* (Oxford, Hart Publishing, 2010)
Charmers, D, 'Repackaging the Internal Market: The Ramifications of the *Keck* Judgment' (1994) 19 *European Law Review* 385
Charmers, D and Barroso, L, 'What *Van Gend en Loos* Stands for' (2014) 12 *International Journal of Constitutional Law* 105
Cherednychenko, O, 'Rediscovering the Public/Private Divide in EU Private Law' (2019) 26 *European Law Journal* 27
Cole, M, 'Does the EU Commission Really Hate the US? Understanding the Google Decision through Competition Theory' (2019) 44 *European Law Review* 468
Collins, H, 'On the (In)Compatibility of Human Rights Discourse and Private Law' in H Micklitz (ed), *Constitutionalization of European Private Law* (Oxford, Oxford University Press, 2014)
——. 'Is There a Human Right to Work?' in V Mantouvalou (ed), *The Right to Work: Legal and Philosophical Perspectives* (Oxford, Hart Publishing, 2017)
Comparato, G, 'Private Autonomy and Regulation in the EU Case-Law' in H-W. Micklitz, Y Svetiev and G Comparato (eds), 'European Regulatory Private Law: The Paradigms Tested' (2014) 4 *European University Institute Working Papers* 11
Comparato, G and Micklitz, H-W, 'Regulated Autonomy between Market Freedoms and Fundamental Rights in the Case Law of the CJEU' in U Bernitz, X Groussot and F Schulyok (eds), *General Principles of EU Law and European Private Law* (Alphen aan den Rijn, Kluwer, 2013)
Coppell, J and O'Neill, A, 'The European Court of Justice: Taking Rights Seriously?' (1992) 29 *Common Market Law Review* 689
Craig, P, 'Directives: Direct Effect, Indirect Effect and the Construction of National Legislation' (1997) 22 *European Law Review* 519
——. 'The Legal Effect of Directives: Policy, Rules and Exceptions' (2009) 34 *European Law Review* 349

——. 'General Principles of Law: Treaty, Historical, and Normative Foundations' in KS Ziegler, PJ Neuvonen and V Moreno-Lax (eds), *Research Handbook on General Principles of EU Law: Constructing Legal Orders in Europe* (Cheltenham, Edward Edgar, 2022)
Cseres, KJ, 'The Controversies of the Consumer Welfare Standard' (2007) 3 *Competition Law Review* 121
——. 'Competition and Contract Law' in AS Hartkamp, MW Hesselink, EH Hondius, C Mak and CE du Perron (eds), *Towards a European Civil Code*, 4th edn (Alphen aan den Rijn, Kluwer, 2011)
Dashwood, A, 'From *Van Duyn* to *Mangold* via *Marshall*: Reducing Direct Effect to Absurdity?' (2007) 9 *Cambridge Yearbook of European Legal Studies* 81
Davies, ACL, 'One Step Forward, Two Steps Back? The Viking and Laval Cases in the ECJ' (2008) 37 *Industrial Law Journal* 126
Davies, B, '*Internationale Handelsgesellschaft* and Miscalculation at the Inception' in F Nicola and B Davies (eds), *EU Law Stories: Contextual and Critical Histories of European Jurisprudence* (Cambridge, Cambridge University Press, 2017)
Davies, G, 'Can Selling Arrangements Be Harmonised?' (2005) 30 *European Law Review* 371
——. 'Understanding Market Access: Exploring the Economic Rationality of Different Conceptions of Free Movement Law' (2010) 8 *German Law Review* 671
——. 'Freedom of Movement, Horizontal Effect, and Freedom of Contract' (2012) 3 *European Review of Private Law* 805
——. 'Between Market Access and Discrimination: Free Movement as a Right to Fair Conditions of Competition' in P Kourakos and J Snell (eds), *Research Handbook on the Law of the EU's Internal Market* (Cheltenham, Edward Elgar, 2017)
De Búrca, G, 'Giving Effect to European Community Directives' (1992) 55 *Modern Law Review* 215
De Cecco, F, 'Fundamental Freedoms, Fundamental Rights, and the Scope of Free Movement Law' (2014) 15 *German Law Journal* 383
De Mol, M, 'The Novel Approach of The CJEU on the Horizontal Direct Effect of the EU Principle of Non-discrimination: (Unbridled) Expansionism of EU Law?' (2011) 18 *Maastricht Journal of European and Comparative Law* 109
De Sousa, PC, 'Through Contact Lenses, Darkly: Is Identifying Restrictions to Free Movement Harder Than Meets the Eye? Comment on *Ker-Optika*' (2012) 37 *European Law Review* 79
De Vries, S, and van Mastrigt, R, 'The Horizontal Direct Effect of the Four Freedoms: From a Hodgepodge of Cases to a Seamless Web of Judicial Protection in the EU Single Market?' in U Bernitz, X Groussot and F Schulyok (eds), *General Principles of EU Law and European Private Law* (Alphen aan den Rijn, Kluwer, 2013)
Deakin, S, 'Article 15: Freedom to Choose an Occupation and Right to Engage in Work' in F Dorssemont, K Lörcher, S Clauwaert and M Schmitt (eds), *The Charter of Fundamental Rights of the European Union and the Employment Relation* (Oxford, Hart Publishing, 2019)
Deutscher, E and Makris, S, 'Exploring the Ordoliberal Paradigm: The Competition-Democracy Nexus' (2016) 11 *Competition Law Review* 181
Donaldson, T, *Corporations and Morality* (Englewood Cliffs, NJ, Prentice Hall, 1982)
Dougan, M, 'The "Disguised" Vertical Direct Effect of Directives?' (2000) 59 *Cambridge Law Journal* 586
——. 'Case C-443/98, *Unilever Italia v. Central Food*, Judgment of the Court of Justice of 26 September 2000, [2000] ECR I-7535. Full Court' (2001) 38 *Common Market Law Review* 1503
——. 'When Worlds Collide! Competing Visions of the Relationship between Direct Effect and Supremacy' (2007) 44 *Common Market Law Review* 931
——. 'Legal Developments' (2010) 48 *Journal of Common Market Studies* 163
——. 'In Defence of *Mangold*?' in A Arnull, C Barnard, M Dougan and E Spaventa (eds), *A Constitutional Order of States: Essays in Honour of Alan Dashwood* (Oxford, Hart Publishing, 2011)
——. 'The Impact of the General Principles of Union Law upon Private Relationships' in D Leczykiewicz and S Weatherill (eds), *The Involvement of EU Law in Private Law Relationships* (Oxford, Hart Publishing, 2013)

——. 'Judicial Review of Member State Action under the General Principles and the Charter: Defining the "Scope of Union Law"' (2015) 52 *Common Market Law Review* 1201

Drexl, J, 'Competition Law as Part of the European Constitution' in A von Bogdandy and J Bast (eds), *Principles of European Constitutional Law* (Oxford, Hart Publishing, 2009)

——. 'On the (A)Political Character of the Economic Approach to Competition Law' in J Drexl, W Kerber and Podszun, R, (eds), *Competition Policy and the Economic Approach: Foundations and Limitations* (Cheltenham, Edward Elgar, 2012)

Dunne, N, 'Challenging Competition Commitment Decisions: *Groupe Canal+*' (2021) 58 *Common Market Law Review* 1229

Dworkin, R, *Taking Rights Seriously* (Cambridge, MA, Harvard University Press, 1977)

——. 'Rights as Trumps' in J Waldron (ed), *Theories of Rights* (Oxford, Oxford University Press, 1984)

Ebner, A, 'The Intellectual Foundations of the Social Market Economy: Theory, Policy, and Implications for European Integration' (2006) 33 *Journal of Economic Studies* 206

Editorial Comments, 'The Scope of Application of the General Principles of Union Law: An Ever-Expanding Union?' (2010) 47 *Common Market Law Review* 1589

Edward, D, 'What was the *Keck* Really About?' in F Amtenbrink, G Davies, D Kochenov, and J Lindeboom (eds), *The Internal Market and the Future of European Integration: Essays in Honour of Laurence W Gormley* (Cambridge, Cambridge University Press, 2019)

Eilmansberger, T, 'How to Distinguish Good from Bad Competition under Article 82 EC' (2005) 42 *Common Market Law Review* 129

Eilmansberger, T, 'Dominance: The Lost Child? How Effects-Based Rules Could and Should Change Dominance Analysis' (2006) 15 *European Competition Journal* 15

Elkan, D, Holdgaard, R and Schaldemose, GK, 'From Cooperation to Collision: The ECJ's *Ajos* Ruling and the Danish Supreme Court's Refusal to Comply' (2018) 55 *Common Market Law Review* 17

Eriksson, A, 'European Court of Justice: Broadening the Scope of European Nondiscrimination Law' (2009) 7 *International Journal of Constitutional Law* 731

Eucken, W, 'Die Wettbewerbsordnung und Ihre Verwirklichung' (1949) *ORDO, Jahrbuch Fr die Ordnung von Wirtschaft und Gesellschaft* 1

——. 'The Competitive Order and its Implementation' (2006) 2 *Competition Policy International* 219

Everling, U, 'Will Europe Slip on Bananas? The Bananas Judgment of the Court of Justice and National Courts' (1996) 33 *Common Market Law Review* 401

Everson, M and Gonçalez,C, 'Article 16' in S Peers, T Harvey, J Kenner and A Ward (eds), *The EU Charter of Fundamental Rights: A Commentary* (Oxford, Hart Publishing, 2014)

Ezrachi, A, 'The Goals of EU Competition Law and the Digital Economy' (2018) *BEUC Discussion Paper*, 15.

Felice, F and Vatiero, M, 'Ordo and European Competition Law' in L Fiorito (ed), *A Research Annual: Research in the History of Economic Thought and Methodology* (Bradford, Emerald Group Publishing, 2015)

Figueroa Regueiro, PF, 'Invocability of Substitution and Invocability of Exclusion: Bringing Legal Realism to the Current Developments of the Case-Law of "Horizontal" Direct Effect of Directives' (2002) 7 *Jean Monnet Working Paper* 1

Flaherty, M, 'Private Law and its Normative Influence on Human Rights' in K Barker and D Jensen (eds), *Private Law: Key Encounters with Public Law* (Cambridge, Cambridge University, 2013)

Fontanelli, F, Some Reflections on the General Principles of the EU and on Solidarity in the Aftermath of *Mangold* and *Kücükdeveci*' (2011) 17 *European Public Law* 225

Fornasier, M, 'The Impact of EU Fundamental Rights on Private Relationships: Direct or Indirect Effect?' (2015) 23 *European Review of Private Law* 29

Franziou, E, 'Case C-176/12 *Association de Médiation Sociale*: Some Reflections on the Horizontal Effect of the Charter and the Reach of Fundamental Employment Rights in the European Union' (2014) 10 *European Constitutional Law Review* 332

——. '(Most of) the Charter of Fundamental Rights is Horizontally Applicable' (2019) 15 *European Constitutional Law Review* 306

Gerber, DJ 'Constitutionalizing the Economy: German Neo-liberalism, Competition Law and the "New" Europe' (1994) 42 *American Journal of Comparative Law* 25

——. *Law and Competition in Twentieth-Century Europe: Protecting Prometheus* (Oxford, Oxford University Press, 2001)

Gerbrandy, A, 'Rethinking Competition Law within the European Economic Constitution' (2019) 57 *Journal of Common Market Studies* 127

Glazer, EM, 'Rule of (Out)Law: Property's Contingent Right to Exclude' (2008) 156 *University of Pennsylvania Law Review* 331

Lord Goldsmith, 'A Charter of Rights, Freedoms and Principles' (2001) 38 *Common Market Law Review* 1201

Gormley, LW, 'Inconsistencies and Misconceptions in the Free Movement of Goods' (2015) 40 *European Law Review* 924

Gormsen, LL, 'The Conflict between Economic Freedom and Consumer Welfare in the Modernisation of Article 82 EC' (2007) 3 *European Competition Journal* 329

Grimbergen, R, 'How Boundaries Have Shifted: On Jurisdiction and Admissibility in the Preliminary Ruling Procedure' (2015) 8 *Review of European Administrative Law* 39

Groussot, X, *General Principles of Community Law* (Groningen, Europa Law Publishing, 2006)

Groussot, X, Kirst, N and Leisure, P, '*Segro* and its Aftermath: Between Economic Freedoms, Property Rights and the "Essence of the Rule of Law"' (2019) 2 *Nordic Journal of European Law* 69

Groussot, X, Lech, L and Petursson, GT, 'The Reach of EU Fundamental Rights on Member State Action after Lisbon' in S de Vries, U Bernitz and S Weatherill (eds), *The Protection of Fundamental Rights in the EU after Lisbon* (Oxford, Hart Publishing, 2013)

Groussot, X, Pétursoon, GT and Pierce, J, 'Weak Right, Strong Court: The Freedom to Conduct Business and the EU Charter of Fundamental Rights' in S Douglas-Scott and N Hatzis (eds), *Research Handbook on EU Law and Human Rights* (Cheltenham, Edward Elgar, 2017)

Grundmann, S, 'Information, Party Autonomy and Economic Agents in European Contract Law' (2002) 39 *Common Market Law Review* 269

Gutman, K, *The Constitutional Foundations of European Contract Law: A Comparative Analysis* (Oxford, Oxford University Press, 2014)

Gutmann, T, 'Some Preliminary Remarks on a Liberal Theory of Contract' (2013) 76 *Law and Contemporary Problems* 39

Habermas, J, *Between Facts and Norms: Contributions to a Discourse Theory of Law and Democracy* (Cambridge, MA, MIT Press, 1996)

Hancox, E, 'The Meaning of "Implementing" EU Law under Article 51(1) of the Charter: *Åkerberg Fransson*' (2013) 50 *Common Market Law Review* 1411

Harding, C, Kohl, U and Salmon, N, *Human Rights in the Market Place: The Exploitation of Rights Protection by Economic Actors* (Abingdon, Routledge, 2016)

Hartkamp, AS, 'The Effect of the EC Treaty in Private Law: On Direct and Indirect Horizontal Effects of Primary Community Law' (2010) 18 *European Review of Private Law* 527

——. 'The General Principles of EU Law and Private Law' (2011) 75 *Rabels Zeitschrift für ausländisches und internationales Privatrecht* 241

Harvey, P, 'The Right to Work and Basic Income Guarantees: Competing or Complementary Goals? (2005) 2 *Rutgers Journal of Law & Urban Policy* 8

Hatzopoulos, V, 'Legal Aspects in Establishing the Internal Market for Services' (2007) 6 *College of Europe Research Papers in Law* 1

——. *Regulating Services in the European Union* (Oxford, Oxford University Press, 2012)

Hayek, FA, *The Constitution of Liberty* (London, Routledge & Kegan Paul, 1963)

——. 'Competition as a Discovery Procedure', translated by MS Snow (2002) 5 *Quarterly Journal of Austrian Economics* 9

Holdgaard, R, Elkan, D and Schaldemose, GK, 'From Cooperation to Collision: The ECJ's *Ajos* Ruling and the Danish Supreme Court's Refusal to Comply' (2018) 55 *Common Market Law Review* 17

Hoppmann, E, 'Workable Competition: The Development of an Idea on the Norm for the Policy of Competition' (1968) 13 *Antitrust Bulletin* 61
Horsley, T, 'Unearthing Buried Treasure: Art 34 TFEU and the Exclusionary Rules' (2012) 37 *European Law Review* 734
Huber, PM, 'The Unitary Effect of the Community's Fundamental Rights: The *ERT*-Doctrine Needs to Be Reviewed' (2008) 14 *European Public Law* 323
Husovec, M, 'The Essence of Intellectual Property Rights under Article 17(2) of the EU Charter' (2019) 20 *German Law Journal* 840
Jacobs, FG 'Human Rights in the European Union: The Role of the Court of Justice' (2001) 26 *European Law Review* 331, 337
Jansson, MS and Kalimo, H, 'De Minimis Meets "Market Access": Transformations in the Substance – and the Syntax – of EU Free Movement Law?' (2014) 5 *Common Market Law Review* 523
Jesse, M, 'What about Sunday Trading … ? The Rise of Market Access as an Independent Criterion under Article 34 TFEU' (2012) 3 *European Journal of Risk Regulation* 437
Joerges, C, 'The Law in the Process of Constitutionalizing Europe' (2002) 4 *EUI Working Paper LAW* 1
Kaplow, L and Shavell, S, 'Fairness versus Welfare' (2001) 114 *Harvard Law Review* 961
Kerber, W and Vanberg, V, 'Constitutional Aspects of Party Autonomy and its Limits: The Perspective of Constitutional Economics' in S Grundmann, W Kerber and S Weatherill (eds), *Party Autonomy and the Role of Information in the Internal Market* (Berlin, De Gruyter, 2001)
Kingreen, T, 'Fundamental Freedoms' in A von Bogdandy and J Bast (eds), *Principles of European Constitutional Law* (Oxford, Hart Publishing, 2009)
Kirzner, IM, 'Entrepreneurial Discovery and the Competitive Market Process: An Austrian Approach' (1997) 35 *Journal of Economic Literature* 60
Klatt, M and Meister, M, 'Proportionality: A Benefit to Human Rights? Remarks on the I·CON Controversy' (2012) 10 *International Journal of Constitutional Law* 687
Koutrakos, P, 'Is There More to Say about the Direct Effect of Directives?' (2018) 43 *European Law Review* 621
Krommendijk, J, 'Principled Silence or Mere Silence on Principles? The Role of the EU Charter's Principles in the Case Law of the Court of Justice' (2015) 11 *European Constitutional Law Review* 321
——. 'Wide Open and Unguarded Stand Our Gates: The CJEU and References for a Preliminary Ruling in Purely Internal Situations' (2017) 18 *German Law Journal* 1359
Kuipers, JJ, *EU Law and Private International Law: The Interrelationship in Contractual Obligations* (Leiden, Martinus Nijhoff, 2012)
Kumm, M, 'Institutionalising Socratic Contestation: The Rationalist Human Rights Paradigm, Legitimate Authority and the Point of Judicial Review' (2007) 1 *European Journal of Legal Studies* 153
——. '*Internationale Handelsgesellschaft*, *Nold* and the New Human Rights Paradigm' in L Azoulai and L Poiares Pessoa Maduro (eds), *The Past and Future of EU Law: The Classics of EU Law Revisited on the 50th Anniversary of the Rome Treaty* (Oxford, Hart Publishing, 2010)
Landes, WM and Posner, R, 'Trademark Law: An Economic Perspective' (1987) 30 *Journal of Law and Economics* 265
Lazzerini, N, '(Some of) the Fundamental Rights Granted by the Charter May Be a Source of Obligations for Private Parties: *AMS*' (2014) 51 *Common Market Law Review* 907
——. 'The Horizontal Application of the General Principles of EU Law: Nothing Less Than Direct Effect' in K Ziegler, P Neuvonen and V Moreno-Lax (eds), *Research Handbook on General Principles of EU Law* (Cheltenham, Edward Elgar, 2022)
Leczykiewicz, D, 'Horizontal Application of the Charter of Fundamental Rights' (2013) 38 *European Law Review* 479
——. 'Horizontal Effect of Fundamental Rights: In Search of Social Justice or Private Autonomy in EU Law?' in U Bernitz, X Groussot and F Schulyok (eds), *General Principles of EU Law and European Private Law* (Alphen aan den Rijn, Kluwer, 2013)
——. 'The Judgment in Bauer and the Effect of the EU Charter of Fundamental Rights in Horizontal Situations' (2020) 16 *European Review of Contract Law* 323

Leible, S, 'Fundamental Freedoms and European Contract Law' in S Grundmann (ed), *Constitutional Values and European Contract Law* (Alphen aan den Rijn, Kluwer, 2008)

Leijten, I, *Core Socio-economic Rights and the European Court of Human Rights* (Cambridge, Cambridge University Press, 2017)

Lenaerts, K, 'Exploring the Limits of the EU Charter of Fundamental Rights' (2012) 8 *European Constitutional Law Review* 375

——. 'In Vielfalt geeint: Grundrechte als Basis des europäischen Integrationsprozesses' (2015) 42 *Europaische grundrechte zeitschrift* 353

——. 'Limits on Limitations: The Essence of Fundamental Rights in the EU' (2019) 20 *German Law Journal* 779

Lenaerts, K and Corthaut, T, 'Of Birds and Hedges: The Role of Primacy in Invoking Norms of EU Law' (2006) 31 *European Law Review* 287

Lenz, M, 'Horizontal What? Back to Basics' (2000) 25 *European Law Review* 509

Lewandowski, W, 'The Implications of the Recent Jurisprudence of the Court of Justice of the European Union for the Protection of the Fundamental Rights of Athletes and the Regulatory Autonomy of Sporting Federations' (2020) 25 *Tilburg Law Review* 55

Lianos, I, 'Efficient Restrictions of Trade in the EU Law of the Internal Market. Trust, Distrust and the Nature of Economic Integration' (2010) 1 *CLES Working Paper Series* 1

——. 'Some Reflections on the Question of the Goals of EU Competition Law' in I Lianos and D Geradin (eds), *Handbook on European Competition Law: Substantive Aspects* (Cheltenham, Edward Elgar, 2013)

——. 'In Memoriam *Keck*: The Reformation of the EU Law on the Free Movement of Goods' (2015) 40 *European Law Review* 225

Lindeboom, J, 'Interpreting the EU Internal Market' in F Amtenbrink, G Davies, D Kochenov and J Lindeboom, *The Internal Market and the Future of European Integration: Essays in Honour of Laurence W. Gormley* (Cambridge, Cambridge University Press, 2019)

Lock, T, 'Rights and Principles in the EU Charter of Fundamental Rights' (2019) 56 *Common Market Law Review* 1201

Lockhart, NJS and Weiler, JHH, '"Taking Rights Seriously" Seriously: The European Court and its Fundamental Rights Jurisprudence – Part I' (1995) 32 *Common Market Law Review* 51

Lourenco, L, 'Rights and Principles in the Charter and the General Principles of EU law: "We're One, But We're Not the Same"?' (2018) 5 *e-Pública* 72

Maduro, MP 'Reforming the Market or the State? Article 30 and the European Constitution: Economic Freedom and Political Rights' (1997) 3 *European Law Journal* 55

——. 'Harmony and Dissonance in Free Movement' (2001) 4 *Cambridge Yearbook of European Legal Studies* 315

Maher, I, 'The Legal Dimension in EU Integration' in AM El-Agraa, *The European Union Economics and Policies*, 9th edn (Cambridge, Cambridge University Press, 2011)

Maier-Rigaud, F, 'On the Normative Foundations of Competition Law: Efficiency, Political Freedom and the Freedom to Compete' in D Zimmer (ed), *The Goals of Competition Law* (Cheltenham, Edward Elgar, 2012)

Makris, S, 'Applying Normative Theories in EU Competition Law: Exploring Article 102 TFEU' (2014) 3 *UCL Journal of Law & Jurisprudence* 1

Maletić, I, 'The Boundaries of the Internal Market after the Lisbon Treaty: A Closer Look at Article 95 EC' (2010) 5 *Croatian Yearbook of European Law and Policy* 19

——. *The Law and Policy of Harmonisation in Europe's Internal Market* (Cheltenham, Edward Elgar, 2013)

Mancini, GF and Keeling, DT, 'Democracy and the European Court of Justice' (1994) 57 *Modern Law Review* 175

Mataija, M, 'The Public–Private Distinction, Autonomy and Free Movement: Unpacking the Assumptions' (2013) 13 *Global Jurist* 23

——. *Private Regulation and the Internal Market: Sports, Legal Services, and Standard Setting in EU Economic Law* (Oxford, Oxford University Press, 2016)
Mendes, J, 'Bounded Discretion in EU Law: A Limited Judicial Paradigm in a Changing EU' (2017) 80 *Modern Law Review* 443
Merrill, TW, 'Property and the Right to Exclude' (1998) 77 *Nebraska Law Review* 730
Mestmacker, E-J, 'The Development of German and European Competition Law with Special Reference to the EU Commission's Article 82 Guidance of 2008' in LF Pace (ed), *European Competition Law: The Impact of the Commission's Guidance on Article 102* (Cheltenham, Edward Elgar, 2011)
Micklitz, HW, 'Social Justice and Access Justice in Private Law' (2011) 2 *EUI Working Paper LAW* 1
Monti, G, 'Article 81 EC and Public Policy' (2002) 39 *Common Market Law Review* 105
Mortelmans, K, 'The Relationship between the Treaty Rules and Community Measures for the Establishment and Functioning of the Internal Market: Towards a Concordance Rule' (2002) 39 *Common Market Law Review* 1303
Möschel, W, 'Competition Policy from an Ordo-liberal Point of View' in A Peacock and T Willgerodt (eds), *German Neo-liberals and Social Market Economy* (London, Macmillan, 1989)
——. 'Competition as a Basic Element of the Social Market Economy' (2001) 2 *European Business Organization Law Review* 713
Muir, E, 'Of Ages in – and Edges of – EU Law' 48 (2011) *Common Market Law Review* 39
——. 'Pursuing Equality in the EU' in D Chalmers and A Arnull (eds), *The Oxford Handbook of European Union Law* (Oxford, Oxford University Press, 2015)
Müller-Graff, P-C, 'Basic Freedoms: Extending Party Autonomy across Borders' in S Grundmann, W Kerber and S Weatherill (eds), *Party Autonomy and the Role of Information in the Internal Market* (Berlin, De Gruyter, 2001)
Naraine, G, 'Dignity, Self-Realization and the Spirit of Service: Principles and Practices of Decent Work' in D Peccoud (ed), *Philosophical and Spiritual Perspectives on Decent Work* (Geneva, International Labour Office, 2004)
Nazzini, R, *The Foundations of European Union Competition Law: The Objective and Principles of Article 102* (Oxford, Oxford University Press, 2011)
Nedergaard, P, 'The Ordoliberalisation of the European Union?' (2020) 42 *Journal of European Integration* 213
Neuwahl, NA 'The Treaty on European Union: A Step Forward for the Protection of Human Rights?' in NA Neuwahl and A Rosas (eds), *The European Union and Human Rights* (The Hague, Martinus Nijhoff, 1995)
Nic Shuibhne, N, *The Coherence of EU Free Movement Law: Constitutional Responsibility and the Court of Justice* (Oxford, Oxford University Press, 2013)
Nickel, JW, *Making Sense of Human Rights*, 2nd edn (London, Wiley-Blackwell, 2006)
Nielsen, NK 'The Protection of Fundamental Rights in the Law of the European Union' (1994) 63 *Nordic Journal of International Law* 213
Nolte, G, 'General Principles of German and European Administrative Law: A Comparison in Historical Perspective' (1994) 57 *Modern Law Review* 191
O'Donoghue, R and Padilla, AJ, *The Law and Economics of Art.102 TFEU* (Oxford, Hart Publishing, 2013)
Oliver, P, 'What Purpose Does Article 16 of the Charter Serve?' in U Bernitz, X Groussot and F Schulyok (eds), *General Principles of EU Law and European Private Law* (Alphen aan den Rijn, Kluwer, 2013)
Oliver, P and Stothers, C, 'Intellectual Property under the Charter: Are the Court's Scales Properly Calibrated?' (2017) 54 *Common Market Law Review* 517
Papadopoulos, T, 'Criticising the Horizontal Direct Effect of the EU General Principle of Equality' (2011) 4 *European Human Rights Law Review* 438
——. *EU Law and the Harmonization of Takeovers in the Internal Market* (Alphen aan den Rijn, Kluwer, 2010)

Pavlakos, G, 'Constitutional Rights, Balancing and the Structure of Autonomy' (2011) 24 *Canadian Journal of Law and Jurisprudence* 129

Peacock, AT, *The Political Economy of Economic Freedom* (Cheltenham, Edward Elgar, 1997)

Pecnard, C and Henin, C, '*Keck* and *Mithouard*, Two Years on: Repackaging the Free Movement of Goods' (1996) 3 *International Business Law Journal* 371

Peers, S, 'Supremacy, Equality and Human Rights: Comment on *Kucukdeveci* (C-555/07)' (2010) 35 *European Law Review* 849

Peers, S and Prechal, S, 'Article 52: Scope and Interpretation of Rights and Principles' in S Peers, T Harvey, J Kenner and A Ward (eds), *The EU Charter of Fundamental Rights: A Commentary* (Oxford, Hart Publishing, 2014)

——. 'Scope and Interpretation of the Rights and Principles' in S Peers, T Harvey, J Kenner and A Ward (eds), *The EU Charter of Fundamental Rights: A Commentary* (Oxford, Hart Publishing, 2014)

Penner, JE, 'The "Bundle of Rights" Picture of Property' (1996) 43 *Los Angeles Law Review* 711

Pescatore, P, 'Fundamental Rights and Freedoms in the System of the European Communities' (1970) 18 *American Journal of Comparative Law* 343

——. 'Public and Private Aspects of European Community Competition Law' (1986) 10 *Fordham International Law Journal* 373

Posner, R, *Antitrust Law*, 2nd edn (Chicago, Chicago University Press, 2001)

Prassl, J, 'Freedom of Contract as a General Principle of EU Law? Transfers of Undertakings and the Protection of Employer Rights in EU Labour Law' (2013) 42 *Industrial Law Journal* 434

Prechal, S, *Directives in EC Law* (Oxford, Oxford University Press, 2005)

——. 'Competence Creep and General Principles of Law' (2010) 3 *Review of European Administrative Law* 5

Rasmussen, H, *On Law and Policy in the European Court of Justice: A Comparative Study in Judicial Policymaking* (Dordrecht, Martinus Nijhoff, 1986)

Rivers, J, 'Proportionality and Variable Intensity of Review' (2006) 65 *Cambridge Law Journal* 174

Robin-Olivier, S, 'The Evolution of Direct Effect in the EU: Stocktaking, Problems, Projections' (2014) 12 *International Journal of Constitutional Law* 165

Rodrigues, JNC, 'The Incorporation of Fundamental Rights in the Community Legal Order' in L Azoulai and L Poiares Pessoa Maduro (eds), *The Past and Future of EU Law: The Classics of EU Law Revisited on the 50th Anniversary of the Rome Treaty* (Oxford, Hart Publishing, 2010)

Rosas, A, 'Life after *Dassonville* and *Cassis*: Evolution But No Revolution' in L Azoulai and L Poiares Pessoa Maduro (eds), *The Past and Future of EU Law: The Classics of EU Law Revisited on the 50th Anniversary of the Rome Treaty* (Oxford, Hart Publishing, 2010)

Rousseva, E, 'The Concept of "Objective Justification" of an Abuse of a Dominant Position: Can it Help to Modernise the Analysis under Article 82 EC?' (2006) 2 *Competition Law Review* 27

Rubin, P and Klumpp, T, 'Property Rights and Capitalism' in DC Mueller (ed), *The Oxford Handbook of Capitalism* (Oxford, Oxford University Press, 2012)

Ruffert, M, 'The Right to Pursue a Freely Chosen Occupation' in D Ehlers (ed), *European Fundamental Rights and Freedoms* (Berlin, De Gruyter, 2007)

Rutgers, JW, 'The European Economic Constitution, Freedom of Contract and the DCFR' (2009) 5 *European Review of Contract Law* 95

Sánchez, SI, 'Purely Internal Situations and the Limits of EU Law: A Consolidated Case Law or a Notion to Be Abandoned?' (2018) 14 *European Constitutional Law Review* 7

Sarkin, J and Koenig, M, 'Developing the Right to Work: Intersecting and Dialoguing Human Rights and Economic Policy' (2011) 33 *Human Rights Quarterly* 1

Sauter, W, 'Proportionality in EU Law: A Balancing Act?' (2013) 15 *Cambridge Yearbook of European Legal Studies* 439

Sauter, W and Schepel, H, *State and Market in European Union Law: The Public and Private Spheres of the Internal Market before the EU Courts* (Cambridge, Cambridge University Press, 2019)

Schepel, H, 'Constitutionalising the Market, Marketising the Constitution, and to Tell the Difference: On the Horizontal Application of the Free Movement Provisions in the EU Law' (2012) 18 *European Law Journal* 177

——. 'Freedom of Contract in Free Movement Law: Balancing Rights and Principles in European Public and Private Law' (2013) 5–6 *European Review of Private Law* 1211

Scheuner, U, 'Fundamental Rights in European Community Law and in National Constitutional Law: Recent Decisions in Italy and in the Federal Republic of Germany' (1975) 12 *Common Market Law Review* 171

Schiek, D, 'Constitutional Principles and Horizontal Effects: *Kücükdeveci* Revisited' (2010) 1 *European Labour Law Journal* 368

——. *Economic and Social Integration: The Challenge for EU Constitutional Law* (Cheltenham, Edward Edgar, 2012)

Schmid, C, 'Multi-level Constitutionalism and Constitutional Conflicts Interconnecting the National, European and International Economic Constitutions in the Banana Dispute' (PhD thesis, European University Institute, 2001)

Schmidt, M, 'The Principle of Non-discrimination in Respect of Age: Dimensions of the ECJ's *Mangold* Judgment' (2005) 7 *German Law Journal* 505

Schultz, V, 'Life is Work' (2000) 100 *Columbia Law Review* 1881

Schütze, R, 'Of Types and Tests: Towards a Unitary Doctrinal Framework for Article 34 TFEU?' (2016) 41 *European Law Review* 826

——. 'Direct Effects and Indirect Effects of Union Law' in R Schütze and T Tridimas (eds), *Oxford Principles of European Union Law* (Oxford, Oxford University Press, 2018)

——. '"Re-reading" *Dassonville*: Meaning and Understanding in the History of European Law' (2018) 24 *European Law Journal* 376

Schweitzer, H, 'Efficiency, Political Freedom and the Freedom to Compete: Comment on Maier-Rigaud' in D Zimmer (ed), *The Goals of Competition Law* (Cheltenham, Elgar Edward, 2012)

Sharpston, E, 'About that Sunday Trading Mess …' in F Amtenbrink, G Davies, D Kochenov, and J Lindeboom (eds), *The Internal Market and the Future of European Integration: Essays in Honour of Laurence W Gormley* (Cambridge, Cambridge University Press, 2019)

Sheehan, D, *The Principles of Personal Property Law*, 2nd edn (Oxford, Hart Publishing, 2017)

Simpson, C 'Dominant Firms and Selective Discounting in the EU: When is "Meeting Competition" a Defence?' (2016) 12 *European Competition Journal* 1

Snell, J, 'And Then There were Two: Products and Citizens in Community Law' in T Tridimas and P Nebbia (eds), *European Union Law for the Twenty-First Century: Internal Market and Free Movement Community Policies*, vol 2 (Oxford, Hart Publishing, 2004)

——. 'The Notion of Market Access: A Concept or a Slogan?' (2010) 47 *Common Market Law Review* 437

——. 'Fundamental Rights Review of National Measures: Nothing New under the Charter?' (2015) 21 *European Public Law* 285

Somek, A, 'The Argument from Transnational Effects I: Representing Outsiders through Freedom of Movement' (2010) 16 *European Law Journal* 315

——. *Engineering Equality: An Essay on European Anti-discrimination Law* (Oxford, Oxford University Press, 2011)

Sommeregger, G, 'The Horizontalization of Equality: The German Attempt to Promote Non-discrimination in the Private Sphere via Legislation' in A Sajó and R Uitz (eds), *The Constitution in Private Relations: Expanding Constitutionalism* (Utrecht, Eleven International Publishing, 2005)

Spaventa, E, 'From *Gebhard* to Carpenter: Towards a (Non-)Economic European Constitution' (2004) 41 *Common Market Law Review* 743

——. *Free Movement of Persons in the European Union: Barriers to Movement in Their Constitutional Context* (Alphen aan den Rijn, Kluwer, 2007)

——. 'Leaving *Keck* Behind? The Free Movement of Goods after the Rulings in *Commission v Italy* and *Mickelsson and Roos*' (2009) 34 *European Law Review* 914

——. 'The Outer Limit of the Treaty Free Movement Provisions: Some Reflections on the Significance of Keck, Remoteness and Deliège' in C Barnard and O Odudu (eds), *The Outer Limits of European Union Law* (Oxford, Hart Publishing, 2009)

——. 'The Horizontal Application of Fundamental Rights as General Principles of Union Law' in A Arnull, C Barnard, M Dougan and E Spaventa (eds), *A Constitutional Order of States: Essays in Honour of Alan Dashwood* (Oxford, Hart Publishing, 2011)

——. 'The Classic Freedom? The Free Movement of Goods: Old Doctrines, New Cases and Contemporary Reflections' in S Garben and I Govaere (eds), *The Internal Market 2.0* (Oxford, Hart Publishing, 2020)

Sprankling, JG, *The International Law of Property* (Oxford, Oxford University Press, 2014)

Squintani, L and Lindeboom, J, 'The Normative Impact of Invoking Directives: Casting Light on Direct Effect and the Elusive Distinction between Obligations and Mere Adverse Repercussions' (2019) 38 *Yearbook of European Law* 18

Stern, JY, 'What is the Right to Exclude and Why Does it Matter?' in J Penner (ed), *Property Theory: Legal and Political Perspectives* (Cambridge, Cambridge University Press, 2018)

Stylianou, K and Iacovides, M, 'The Goals of EU Competition Law: A Comprehensive Empirical Investigation' (2022) 42 *Legal Studies* 620

Talbot, C, 'Ordoliberalism and Balancing Competition Goals in the Development of the European Union' (2016) 61 *Antitrust Bulletin* 264

Thorson, B, *Individual Rights in EU Law* (Cham, Springer International, 2016)

Thüsing, G and Horler, S, 'Annotation to Case C-555/07, *Seda Kücükdeveci v Swedex*, Judgment of the Court (Grand Chamber) of 19 January 2010' (2010) 47 *Common Market Law Review* 1161

Thym, D, 'The Judicial Deconstruction of Union Citizenship' in D Thym (ed), *Questioning EU Citizenship: Judges and the Limits of Free Movement and Solidarity in the EU* (Oxford, Hart Publishing, 2017)

Townley, C, *Article 81 EC and Public Policy* (Oxford, Hart Publishing, 2009)

Tridimas, T, 'The Principle of Proportionality in Community Law: From the Rule of Law to Market Integration' (1996) 31 *Irish Jurist* 83

——. 'Black, White, and Shades of Grey: Horizontality of Directives Revisited' (2001) 21 *Yearbook of European Law* 327

——. T, *General Principles of EU Law* (Oxford, Oxford University Press, 2006)

——. 'The General Principles of Law: Who Needs Them?' (2015) 52 *Les Cahiers de Droit* 419

Tridimas, T and Gentile, G, 'The Essence of Rights: An Unreliable Boundary?' (2019) 20 *German Law Journal* 794

Trstenjak, V and Beysen, E, The Growing Overlap of Fundamental Freedoms and Fundamental Rights in the Case-Law of the CJEU' (2013) 38 *European Law Review* 293

Tryfonidou, A, 'Further Steps on the Road to Convergence among the Market Freedoms' (2010) 35 *European Law Review* 36

Van den Bergh, R, *Comparative Competition Law and Economics* (Cheltenham, Edward Elgar, 2017)

Van der Schyff, G, 'Cutting to the Core of Conflicting Rights: The Question of Inalienable Cores in Comparative Perspective' in E Brems (ed), *Conflicts between Fundamental Rights* (Antwerp, Intersentia, 2008)

Van Drooghenbroeck, S and Rizcallah, C, 'The ECHR and the Essence of Fundamental Rights: Searching for Sugar in Hot Milk?' (2019) 20 *German Law Journal* 904

Van Eijken, H and de Vries, S, 'Deepening and Widening of the Protection of Fundamental Rights of European Citizens vis-à-vis Non-state, Private Actors' in R Buikema, A Buyse and ACGM Robben (eds), *Cultures, Citizenship and Human Rights* (Abingdon, Routledge, 2019)

Vanberg, V, 'Freiburg School of Law and Economics' in P Newman (ed), *The New Palgrave Dictionary of Economics*, vol 2 (London, Palgrave Macmillan, 1998)

——. 'Consumer Welfare, Total Welfare and Economic Freedom: On the Normative Foundations of Competition Policy' in J Drexl, W Kerber and R Podszun (eds), *Competition Policy and the Economic Approach: Foundations and Limitations* (Cheltenham, Edward Elgar, 2012)

——. 'Ordoliberalism, Ordnungspolitik, and the Reason of Rules' (2015) 2 *European Review of International Studies* 27

Varner, CA, 'The Effectiveness of European Community Law with Specific Regard to Directives: The Critical Step Not Taken by the European Court of Justice' (2001) 22 *Michigan Journal of International Law* 457

Veneziani, B, 'Article 16: Freedom to Conduct a Business' in F Dorssemont, K Lörcher, S Clauwaert and M Schmitt (eds), *The Charter of Fundamental Rights of the European Union and the Employment Relation* (Oxford, Hart Publishing, 2019)

Villalón, PC, '"All the Guidance", *ERT* and *Wachauf*' in L Azoulai, L Poiares Pessoa Maduro (eds), *The Past and Future of EU Law: The Classics of EU Law Revisited on the 50th Anniversary of the Rome Treaty* (Oxford, Hart Publishing, 2010)

Von Bogdandy, A and Bast, J, 'The European Union's Vertical Order of Competences: The Current Law and Proposals for its Reform' (2002) 39 *Common Market Law Review* 227

Von Danwitz, T, 'Questionnaire', seminar on the Charter of Fundamental Rights of the European Union (The Hague, 2011)

Voogsgeerd, H, 'The EU Charter of Fundamental Rights and its Impact on Labor Law: A Plea for a Proportionality-Test "Light"' (2012) *Goettingen Journal of International* Law 293

——. 'More Autonomy for Member States in So-Called "Purely Internal Situations"?' (2019) 2 *Elte Law Journal* 43

Wagner-Von Papp, F, 'Best and Even Better Practices in Commitment Procedures after Alrosa: The Dangers of Abandoning the "Struggle for Competition Law"' (2012) 49 *Common Market Law Review* 929, 937

Walkila, S, *Horizontal Effect of Fundamental Rights in EU Law* (Groningen, Europa Law Publishing, 2015)

Warin, C, *Individual Rights Under European Union Law: A Study on the Relation Between Rights, Obligations and Interests in the Case Law of the Court of Justice* (Baden-Baden, Nomos, 2019);

Weatherill, S, 'After *Keck*: Some Thoughts on How to Clarify the Clarification' (1996) 33 *Common Market Law* Review 887

——. 'Justifying Limits to Party Autonomy in the Internal Market: EC Legislation in the Field of Consumer Protection' in S Grundmann, W Kerber and S Weatherill (eds), *Party Autonomy and the Role of Information in the Internal Market* (Berlin, De Gruyter, 2001)

——. 'Free Movement of Goods' (2006) 55 *International & Comparative Law Quarterly* 457

——. 'The Limits of Legislative Harmonization Ten Years after *Tobacco Advertising*: How the Court's Case Law has become a "Drafting Guide"' (2011) 12 *German Law Review* 827

——. 'The Elusive Character of Private Autonomy' in D Leczykiewicz and S Weatherill (eds), *The Involvement of EU Law in Private Law Relationships* (Oxford, Hart Publishing, 2013)

——. 'Use and Abuse of the EU's Charter of Fundamental Rights: on the Improper Veneration of "Freedom of Contract"' (2014) 10 *European Review of Contract Law* 167

——. *The Internal Market as a Legal Concept* (Oxford, Oxford University Press, 2017)

Weiler, JHH, 'Methods of Protection of Fundamental Human Rights in the European Community: Towards a Second and Third Generation of Protection' in A Cassese, A Clapham and JHH Weiler, *European Union: The Human Rights Challenge, Vol II: Human Rights and the European Community: Methods of Protection* (Baden-Baden, Nomos, 1991)

——. 'Epilogue: Towards a Common Law of International Trade' in JHH Weiler (ed), *The EU, the WTO, and the NAFTA: Towards a Common Law of International Trade?* (Oxford, Oxford University Press, 2001)

——. 'Fundamental Rights and Fundamental Boundaries: Common Standards and Conflicting Values in the Protection of Human Rights in the European Legal Space' in R Kastoryano (ed), *An Identity for Europe: the Relevance of Multiculturalism in EU Construction* (New York, Palgrave Macmillan, 2009)

——. '*Van Gend en Loos*: The Individual as Subject and Object and the Dilemma of European Legitimacy' (2014) 12 *International Journal of Constitutional Law* 94

Weiler, JHH and Lockhardt, NJS, '"Taking Rights Seriously" Seriously: The European Court of Justice and its Fundamental Rights Jurisprudence – Part I' (1995) 32 *Common Market Law Review* 51
Wilsher, D, 'Does *Keck* Discrimination Make Any Sense? An Assessment of the Non-discrimination Principle within the European Single Market' (2008) 33 *European Law Review* 3
Witt, A, *The More Economic Approach to EU Antitrust Law* (Oxford, Hart Publishing, 2016)
Wollenschläger, F, 'Article 17(1) – Right to Property' in S Peers, T Harvey, J Kenner and A Ward (eds), *The EU Charter of Fundamental Rights: A Commentary* (Oxford, Hart Publishing, 2014)
——. 'Article 17(2) – Right to Property' in S Peers, T Harvey, J Kenner and A Ward (eds), *The EU Charter of Fundamental Rights: A Commentary* (Oxford, Hart Publishing, 2014)
Wyatt, D, 'Horizontal Effect of Fundamental Freedoms and the Right to Equality after *Viking* and *Mangold*, and the Implications for Community Competence' (2008) 4 *Croatian Yearbook of European Law and Policy* 1
Xenidis, R, 'Transforming EU Equality Law? On Disruptive Narratives and False Dichotomies' (2019) 38 *Yearbook of European Law* 2
Zäch, R, 'Freedom to Compete and the More Economic Approach: Limits Imposed by Law' (2009) 40 *International Review of Intellectual Property and Competition Law* 623

INDEX

www.ingramcontent.com/pod-product-compliance
Ingram Content Group UK Ltd.
Pitfield, Milton Keynes, MK11 3LW, UK
UKHW021543041026
15470UKWH00019B/706

9 781509 920693